FRANK WATERS

Marcia Keegan

FRANK WATERS

FRANK WATERS

A Bibliography
With Relevant Selections From His Correspondence

by TERENCE A. TANNER

Foreword by Frank Waters

MEYERBOOKS
GLENWOOD, ILLINOIS

Copyright © 1983 by Terence A. Tanner

All rights reserved. No part of this book may be reproduced or utilized in any form or by any means, either mechanical or electronic, including xerography, photocopy, recording, or any information storage or retrieval system now known or to be invented, without written permission from the publisher, except by a reviewer wishing to quote brief passages in connection with a review written for inclusion in a newspaper, magazine or broadcast.

ISBN 0-916638-07-3

Special acknowledgment must be made to Mr. Frank Waters for permission to publish his letters; to Mr. Herman Liveright for permission to publish the letter his father wrote to Frank Waters; and to the Collection of American Literature, Beinecke Rare Book and Manuscript Library, Yale University, for permission to publish the letter Frank Waters wrote to Mabel Dodge Luhan on February 14, 1941.

Designed by E. J. Frank

Published by
Meyerbooks
P.O. Box 427
235 West Main Street
Glenwood, Illinois 60425

for Eileen

Contents

Foreword by Frank Waters / ix
Acknowledgements / xiii
Introduction / xv
Chronology / xxv

  A. Books by Frank Waters / 1

AA. Pamphlets by Frank Waters / 233

  B. Contributions by Waters to books by others / 245

BB. Contribution to *Encyclopedia Americana* / 287

  C. Contributions to periodicals / 291

  D. Contributions to *El Crepusculo* / 307

  E. Articles by others containing material by Waters, including interviews / 323

  F. Blurbs / 331

  G. Foreign translations / 335

  H. Selected list of writings about Waters / 339

Index / 346

Foreword

If a foreword to this bibliography may seem offhand like an epitaph to some fifty years of published writings, I refuse to meet the implied demands of a funereal inscription. I'm not yet ready to lay down my pencil with a sigh, and vainly excuse or praise the body of my writings. No writer can pass judgement on his own work.

Nevertheless, this comprehensive bibliography brings me up short for a look back over my shoulder. Terence Tanner for years, with dogged persistence and Sherlock Holmes sleuthing, has unearthed almost everything I've ever written, from my first published piece in my grammar school paper, the *Columbia Sayings and Doings* of October, 1916, to the publication in 1981 of my twenty-first book. What a conglomerate mass of material—articles, essays, forewords and introductions, recorded talks, novelized movie screenplays, government releases, advertising copy, commercial blurbs of all kinds. To me now, most of it seems outdated and worthless. Yet it must have served a purpose, at least my own. A writer lives by his writings, and the poorest of mine helped to carry me through the production of my best.

None of my books, as the bibliography shows, was initially successful. One after another were immediate flops and let go out of print. To Alan Swallow I owe the beginning of their slow re-emergence. A one-man publisher in Denver, Colorado, he alone successfully challenged the custom of large New York publishing houses which advertised a new book with great acclaim, boosted it into a best-seller, then let it go out of print. Swallow believed that if he kept in stock a book he had faith in, it would eventually outsell currently popular titles over a period of years. This he did with a 1942 novel of mine, *The Man Who Killed the Deer*. When the book was dropped from the list of the original New York publisher, he reissued it in a small printing for interested collectors. This led to repeated reprints, new editions, and translations into German, French and Dutch. Since then the book has been constantly in print and is often regarded as a classic of Pueblo Indian life.

Other books of mine have followed the same pattern. *Masked Gods: Navajo and Pueblo Ceremonialism* has been kept in print since its first publication in 1951, and has been issued in a two-volume Japanese translation. *Book of the Hopi* was not advertised by its New York publisher nor reviewed in New York periodicals when it was issued in 1963. It has since been constantly reprinted in hardback and paperback editions, and translated into French, German, and Swedish. So too have other books of mine been reissued long after their first appearance.

Their long life after their initial failure is most gratifying, of course. But their repetitious first flops, with the hard-rock fact they brought in no money, was discouraging. Every writer, whether he admits it or not, hankers after fame and fortune. That I did not attain them was the best thing that ever happened to me. I was compelled to keep following the carrot dangling before my nose by doing still another book.

The reputation I gained of being "the best known unknown writer in America" does not make me uncomfortable. Nor being regarded as solely a "regional writer." Most of my books do reflect aspects of the American Southwest and Mexico, ancient and contemporary. How different is their Indian and Spanish culture and religion from that of the Anglo heritage of the country east of the Missouri. Only now are we beginning to recognize that their values and world views are valid expressions of the universal unity and harmony we all are seeking. Regionalism cannot be divorced and isolated as a part of the encompassing whole. A regional writer, if he fulfills his role, shows how the whole is reflected in each of its parts.

I've never written my books as business ventures. At this late stage they seem stages of my creative development. Their mere writing brought their own rewards.

There's something strange about a book. It reveals, without the writer's knowing it, his motive, personal weaknesses, literary subterfuges, and mechanical contrivances. It tells more than his written words. It seems to me that a book speaks to us from something between the printed lines. If it is honestly written from the heart, with a pure motive, it establishes an indefinable *simpatica* between writer and reader by merely opening a door to what the reader unconsciously knows.

Only rarely does a writer gain such acceptance. But when he does, if only once in a lifetime of prolific work, he is amply rewarded. He can be humbly grateful for having been permitted to speak in a language of the heart understood by many of his unknown and sometimes distant fellowmen.

FRANK WATERS

Acknowledgments

Many people have been instrumental in the compilation of this book. My greatest debt is to Frank Waters himself. He has not only provided answers to my endless questions, but he has been gracious in allowing me almost unlimited access to his records and papers. Without his permission to publish from his correspondence, this book would not exist in its present form. In addition, both he and his wife, Barbara Hayes, have been a constant source of encouragement and have extended to me their friendship and hospitality. Barbara herself has been tireless in providing me with information, and they both read through the letters I included. While they made suggestions concerning the letters included, I was given a free hand and the ultimate responsibility for what is included is my own.

Professor Charles L. Adams, of the Department of English of the University of Nevada, Las Vegas, has been involved with this project almost from the time it formally began. He has been helpful to me far beyond what can be repaid through public thanks.

Other individuals who have been of assistance to me in one way or another are: Robert Anderson, Alan Covici, Joan Daves, Barthold Fles, John D. Gilchriese, Frances Hamill, Diana Huntress, Marcia Kay Keegan, Meredith Little, Paul Lord, Thomas Lyon, John Manchester, John Milton, Anne Nagel, Lee Nash, Father Peter J. Powell, Jack D. Rittenhouse, Elizabeth Swaim, Michio Takayama, and G. Thomas Tanselle.

Donald Ferren and Judy Pentz and the entire staff of the special collections department of the University of New Mexico Library went to great lengths to make my yearly visits both fruitful and pleasant, and were gracious in the face of my endless requests for copying. Other librarians and libraries that deserve thanks are: The Department of Printed Books of the British Library; Peter Hanff, Bancroft Library, University of California at Berkeley; Brooke Whiting, library of the University of California at Los Angeles; Chicago Public Library; Encyclopaedia Britannica Library; Tracy McCallum, Harwood Foundation, University of New Mexico, Taos; Robert Adelsperger, library of the University of Illinois at Chicago; the Library of Congress; the University of Minnesota Library, Minneapolis; Russell Maylone, Northwestern University Library; Orlando Romero, New Mexico State Library; the University of Oklahoma Library; Kenneth E. Duckett, University of Oregon Library; Neda Westlake, University of Pennsylvania Library, Philadelphia; Mary Davis, Penrose Public Library, Colorado Springs; the Skokie Public Library; The Humanities Research Center of the University of Texas; Cameron Hollyer, Toronto Public Library; and David Schoonover, Beinecke Library, Yale University.

I wish also to thank the many publishers who kindly provided me with information, especially Morton Weisman and Donna Ippolito of the Swallow Press, Inc.; others deserving thanks are: Elizabeth Sacksteder, Ballantine Books; Norman Lambert, Cassell Ltd.; Malcolm Ebright, The Center for Land Grant Studies; Eleanor Burton, The Chevron Company; Shelton Stanfill, Colorado State University, Office of Cultural Programs; Cosette Thompson, Context Publications; Crown Publishers; Frank Nipp, Encyclopaedia Britannica; Stephen Roxburgh, Farrar, Straus & Giroux; Carol Sarath, Fenn Galleries, Ltd.; Tom Boardman, Jr., MacDonald Educational Ltd.; The University of Nebraska Press; The University of New Mexico Press; Linda Andrews, The Northland Press; Jim Denton and Shari Schartman, Ohio University Press; Mrs. A. Wiltsher, Penguin Books; Marion M. Meyer, The Pilgrim Press; Patricia Capon, Pocket Books; Robert McCoy, The Rio Grande Press; Mary Hornby, Seaver Books; Rosa Malone, Sierra Club Books; Doris Flowers, Simon & Schuster; Neville Armstrong, Neville Spearman Ltd.; James Clois Smith, Jr., Sunstone Press; James Newcomer, Texas Christian University Press; Hilary Dance, Transworld Publishers Ltd.; and Michele Medinz, The Viking Press. I would also like to thank Geoffrey Fingland of the *Christian Science Monitor* and Antoinnette Elliott of the *Santa Fe New Mexican*.

Introduction

"This writing, as a business, has got me stumped"—so wrote Frank Waters to Burton Rascoe on February 10, 1940. Waters had just published his fifth book, which, like those preceding it, fell upon a largely unreceptive public. In the forty-odd years since he wrote that note to Rascoe, Waters has published over a dozen more books, most of which initially met the same fate as their predecessors. Yet a glance at the current edition of *Books in Print* shows that, with but few exceptions, his books are still in print.

This is not an instance of a forgotten writer newly discovered, rather a writer who has managed to survive on small yet steady sales and a small but ever growing audience. His career has in many respects proved as remarkable as his books. The present book was undertaken, in part, to chronicle his career. Cast in the format of an author bibliography, this book attempts to provide as complete a history of the published writings of Frank Waters as possible.

To achieve this, I have enlarged upon the purely bibliographic details by including a large selection from Waters' correspondence. Since my intention was neither biographical nor critical, I included only those letters which would provide the reader a glimpse of the author's perspective on a particular book as it passed through its various stages of publication—or which told the story of the book's coming into being. For this reason I chose only those letters written prior to publication of the book in question. I was seeking not a backwards retrospective, but a view of the author and the book before they parted company.

Format and Methods

Section A provides a chronological listing of all books written by Frank Waters, including the two novels he co-authored with Houston Branch. Fairly detailed bibliographic information is provided for the earliest printing of each item; somewhat less detailed information is given for later printings. These later printings are listed in chronological order, although subsequent printings within the same edition issued by one publisher have been listed immediately after the first printing by that publisher. (In the case of *The Colorado,* because of the publication history and the time which elapsed between Rinehart & Company's printings, I have listed all printings of that book in chronological order without respect to their publishers.) Only printings in English are listed in this section; foreign printings are listed in Section G. Notice of editions in braille, however, is given in the notes immediately following the description of the earliest printing.

Title pages have been transcribed in quasi-facsimile, using the line as the primary unit of description. Unless otherwise noted, all designations as to typeface and color of printing hold only for the line in which the designation appears. Occasionally, to avoid needless repetition, designations for several consecutive lines have been combined; e.g., "first three lines printed in red." Unless otherwise noted, all type used is roman and is printed in black. Italic type has been transcribed in italic. In most cases the descriptions of title page borders and backgrounds have been separated from the transcription itself and appear immediately beneath the transcription. Certain designations, however, such as "cover title" and "double-page title," appear at the very beginning of the transcription.

Although an effort was made to avoid end-of-line hyphenation in the transcriptions, it proved impossible to avoid it completely. Therefore, to avoid any possible confusion, a double hyphen (=) has been used in all such instances.

Leaf size has been given in inches, with the vertical dimension listed first. In the case of simultaneous publication in both cloth and paperback, the size given is that of the cloth copies; it should be assumed that paperback copies will be slightly smaller. In the collation, unsigned gatherings are enclosed within brackets, and page numbers which do not actually appear on the page are also enclosed within brackets. Gatherings of unsigned books have been assigned arabic numerals. Separately inserted plates or leaves of illustrations are noted just before the pagination.

The contents are listed completely only for the earliest printing, the first printing published in England, and in a few other instances where it seemed of interest. Changes in the contents have been noted for the later printings and usually include a transcription of the copyright page. For later editions, with a few exceptions, only a transcription of the copyright page has been provided, although a notice of all blanks and advertisements is given immediately following the pagination.

Unless otherwise noted, all paper used is wove paper and of an ordinary white or off-white color.

Descriptions of the illustrations vary depending on their importance, but in every case some notice of the illustrations has been provided.

Full descriptions of the bindings have been provided only for the earliest printing, the first printing published in England, and in a few other instances. In all cases the cloth used was that designated by Jacob Blanck, in the first volume of his *Bibliography of American Literature,* as "V" cloth, and so this information has not been repeated throughout the book. Lettering or stamping on the bindings has been transcribed in quasi-facsimile, following the same general rules as for title pages. Lettering or stamping on the spine reads horizontally as the book stands on its bottom edges; spines reading from top to bottom have been designated as "reading vertically." These designations hold for all lettering on a spine until changed by the introduction of a new designation. The nature of vertically lettered spines makes the rendering of differences in type size within a line extremely difficult, and in most cases I have ignored such differences in the transcription. Color designations for the endpapers refer to the paper used. Often the endpapers will be printed on the verso of the front pastedown and the recto of the front free endpaper (verso of the rear free endpaper and recto of the rear pastedown in the case of rear endpapers), and for simplicity I have described such printing as being on the "face" of the endpaper. Unless otherwise noted, all edges are trimmed and unstained. For most later printings no details are given about the bindings other than a statement as to "cloth" or "paperback."

Because they have become accepted as integral parts of the modern book, dust jackets have been described in detail for those books where the binding has also been so described. In the description of the dust jacket I have used the term "printed overall" to mean that those parts (front, spine or rear) so designated are completely printed in the fashion described in such a manner as to disguise the actual color of paper used. The color of the paper used has been provided and the reader should assume that any portion not designated as being "printed overall" appears in the original color of the paper used. Lettering on jackets has been transcribed in quasi-facsimile. In the case of later printings, clothbound books were published in dust jackets, unless otherwise noted.

Publication data have been provided for all printings when known. When publication dates of the earliest printings could not be ascertained with certainty, I have supplied additional information, such as the date the work was listed in the "Weekly Record" of *Publisher's Weekly*. Copyright and deposit information is provided for the earliest printings; deposit dates for English publications refer to the date on which the book was received by the British Library.

A list of reviews is provided for the earliest printings. These listings are not exhaustive and have been provided only to give some slight indication of the book's reception.

Anthologies and other books containing material reprinted from Waters' books are listed immediately following each list of the original printings of the appropriate work. These listings are certainly not exhaustive.

Section AA contains descriptions of all pamphlets and broadsides written by Waters, including unsigned brochures prepared for the Los Alamos Scientific Laboratory and the New Mexico Arts Commission.

Section B contains a chronological listing of Waters' contributions to books and pamphlets written by others, including forewords, introductions, interviews and the like. Only material appearing in a book or pamphlet for the first time is listed here.

Somewhat detailed bibliographic information is provided for these items, although no complete listing of the contents is given. Copyright pages and other pages of special interest, such as colophons, are transcribed; notice of blanks is provided immediately following the pagination. Only the earliest printing of each is described. In those instances where both a trade issue and a limited issue were published, only the trade issue has been transcribed, unless Waters was directly involved with the limited issue. For instance, in the case of *Voices from the Southwest* (B16) all contributors signed the limited issue, and so it has been described.

Section BB provides information regarding Waters' only contribution to an encyclopedia.

Section C lists chronologically all appearances of material by Waters in a periodical, including material reprinted from books or other periodicals. This section does not include interviews with Waters, nor does it include articles by others in which previously unpublished material by Waters is included. Material of this nature has been listed in Section E. Also, this section does not include any of Waters' contributions to *El Crepusculo;* these have been listed in Section D.

Section D contains a complete listing of all editorials and other articles by Waters published in the bilingual newspaper *El Crepusculo,* in Taos, New Mexico.

Section E provides a chronological listing of all interviews with Waters published in periodicals. This section also includes articles written by others which contain previously unpublished material by Waters.

Section F contains a listing of the few blurbs written by Waters which appear on dust jackets or in publishers' announcements.

Section G contains a listing of all foreign translations of Waters' books.

Section H contains a selective listing of the major writings about Frank Waters, both in books and periodicals.

TERMS

EDITION: This word refers to all copies of a given book printed from one setting of type, and includes all subsequent printings made from this standing type, whether such printings were done by offset or from the original plates. With the advent of modern methods of reproduction, this term often covers a long period in a book's life. For instance, Alan Swallow made offset plates from the Rinehart first edition of *The Man Who Killed the Deer,* and hence all of his printings were from this same first edition. The Swallow Press of Chicago continued to use this same edition until 1972, at which time they reset the book. Therefore, the same edition was used by three different publishers for numerous printings of the book.

PRINTING: All copies of a given book printed at the same time, without removing the plates from the press.

ISSUE: An alteration within a single printing, usually affecting the matter of publication and usually accomplished after the date of publication. Often such changes take the form of title page alterations or cancelling of leaves. For instance, if after publication, the publisher altered the remaining sheets by cancelling the title page and substituting a new one, these sheets would then become the second issue of that printing.

STATE: States generally occur when changes have been made during a printing, usually prior to publication. Such changes often take the form of stop-press alterations to correct errors in the text.

Because these two terms—issue and state—are open to some confusion, I have been cautious about their use. In fact, I have not used state at all in the book, and issue has been used only rarely. It should be remembered that both terms refer only to the sheets of a book; any alterations to the binding or dust jackets have no bearing on the status of the sheets and are therefore referred to only as binding variants or states of the binding.

PAPERBACK: This term refers only to the modern paperback book. Pamphlets bound in paper wrappers have been described as bound in wrappers.

PERFECTBOUND: This term designates books in which the folds have been trimmed off and the sheets held together by an application of adhesive along the back edge. Most modern paperback books are perfectbound.

Sources

Although I have used the resources of numerous libraries while preparing this bibliography, I have found only three U. S. institutions which contain significant holdings of Waters' works. The most important institutional collection is in the Waters' archive in the library of the University of New Mexico, Albuquerque, New Mexico. This collection was obtained by the university from Waters himself and contains most of his books in their earliest printing, as well as many of the later printings and editions. The other institutional collections with fairly large holdings are the Library of Congress and the library of the Harwood Memorial Foundation, University of New Mexico, Taos, New Mexico.

I have also relied upon the holdings in a number of private collections. In addition to my own extensive collection, three others were of special help. Besides the books which he sent to the University of New Mexico with his archives, Frank Waters retained an almost complete collection of his works, to which he allowed me access. John D. Gilchriese, of Tucson, Arizona, a collector and long-time friend of Waters, graciously gave me free run of his sizable Waters collection. Professor Charles L. Adams, of the University of Nevada, Las Vegas, not only carefully checked all my entries against his own large holdings, but he kindly sent me many items for my personal examination.

Locations are cited only for those copies used for the descriptions; I have cited the copy in the Waters' archive whenever possible. While two or more citations are usually provided for the earliest printings in Section A, only one citation is listed for most of the secondary printings. Unless the citation notes the presence of a dust jacket, it should be assumed that the copy located lacks the jacket. The most frequently used citations have been assigned the following symbols:

DLC   Library of Congress, Washington, D.C.
NmU   University of New Mexico Library, Albuquerque, New Mexico—the Waters' archive
FW   Private collection of Frank Waters, Taos, New Mexico
TAT   Private collection of Terence A. Tanner

An important, if only implied criterion for selecting the letters included in this work was that the letters had to be extant and accessible. While I made every effort to locate such material, it will be seen from the quantity and quality of the letters included that I had somewhat mixed success. In the case of both *Pumpkin Seed Point* and *Robert Gilruth,* I could locate no letters of interest and so none are included. Waters' first book, *Fever Pitch,* presented a similar problem. However, I was able to locate a letter from Horace Liveright to Waters concerning the book. Given the circumstances, I felt this letter was of sufficient interest to be included.

The most important source for Waters' letters and papers is the archive in the University of New Mexico Library, which contains a large collection of carbon copies Waters made of his own letters. Although Waters retained some material necessary for his continued writings, the university archive consists of almost all the files personally maintained by Waters through 1978. In addition to the extensive amount of correspondence, the collection includes the few daily journals which Waters kept over the years, files relating to his activities on the staff of the Coordinator for Inter-American Affairs and as Information Director for the Los Alamos Scientific Laboratory, an incomplete file of *El Crepusculo,* and typescripts for a number of his books.

The next most important collection is the archives of the Swallow Press, Inc., now in the library of the University of Illinois at Chicago. Consisting of the files and records of the firm from 1967 to 1981, the collection contains a significant number of Waters' letters, as well as typescripts for a number of the books of Waters published by the firm.

Other institutional holdings are:

Arizona Pioneers Historical Society, Tucson, Arizona: a small group of letters concerning the Society's safekeeping of the manuscript "Tombstone Travesty" (later *The Earp Brothers . . .*).

Bancroft Library, University of California at Berkeley: one letter to Joseph Henry Jackson.

Research Library, University of California at Los Angeles: typescript for "The Magic that Persists" and one letter to Willard Houghland, 1947, about the article.

University of Minnesota Library, Minneapolis, Minnesota: seven letters to Frederick Manfred, 1966-67.

University of Oklahoma Library, Norman, Oklahoma: small amount of correspondence with the University of Oklahoma Press, 1947-48, concerning a possible reprint of *The Man Who Killed the Deer.*

University of Oregon Library, Eugene, Oregon: a number of typescripts of unpublished material by Houston Branch and Frank Waters, contained in the Houston Branch papers. This collection is in dead storage.

University of Pennsylvania Library, Philadelphia, Pennsylvania: three short letters to Burton Rascoe, 1940, and one carbon of a letter from Horace Liveright to Waters in 1929.

Penrose Public Library, Colorado Springs, Colorado: typescript for *Midas of the Rockies.*

The Stanford University Libraries, Stanford, California: Two letters to W. Y. Evans-Wentz and an unsigned draft of a letter to George Warrington Bass.

Humanities Research Center, University of Texas, Austin, Texas: 50 letters to Dorothy Brett, three letters to Merle Armitage, 15 letters to Spud Johnson, two letters to J. Frank Dobie, three letters to *Harper's* magazine, and one five page manuscript, untitled, about the Taos Indians.

Beinecke Library, Yale University, New Haven, Connecticut: approximately 200 letters to Mabel Dodge Luhan.

In addition to these institutional holdings, some material, as noted above, is still in the possession of Frank Waters. Also, Waters' notes and materials relating to *The Earp Brothers of Tombstone* are in the private collection of John D. Gilchriese, and the corrected carbon typescript of *Leon Gaspard,* along with two letters to Dora Gaspard, is in my own collection. Professor Charles L. Adams graciously gave me access to his own correspondence with Waters regarding their editing of *Cuchama*.

Unless otherwise noted, my source for the letters was the University of New Mexico Library. Sources for other letters have been designated by symbols, enclosed within brackets, immediately following the date of the letter. These symbols are:

- CtY Beinecke Library, Yale University
- ICIU University of Illinois at Chicago—Swallow Press archives
- PU University of Pennsylvania Library, Philadelphia
- FW Private collection of Frank Waters
- CLA Private collection of Charles L. Adams, Las Vegas, Nevada

In order to avoid confusion between Alan Swallow and the firm which purchased his publishing business after his death, the Swallow Press, Inc., of Chicago, I have consistently referred to the former by either his full name or "Swallow," and to the latter as the "Swallow Press."

Because this bibliography is restricted to published material by Frank Waters, I have not included any information regarding his activity as a staff writer for the Coordinator of Inter-American Affairs during the Second World War. For those interested, however, Waters did save some material in a small file present in his archives at the University of New Mexico. Also, I have not included any information regarding Waters' career as a screen writer. I was unable to unearth any information about the screen plays Waters worked on, and Waters himself kept no records of this work.

As of the present time, Frank Waters is still actively writing. I hope to update this book sometime in the future and welcome any corrections or additions.

TERENCE A. TANNER
Skokie, Illinois
June 26, 1982

Chronology

1902	July 25	Frank Waters born in Colorado Springs, Colorado.
1916	October	Waters' earliest published writing appears in his grade school literary magazine.
1921-1924		Studies engineering at Colorado College, leaves without degree.
1924		Works in Salt Creek Oil Fields, Wyoming.
1925-1936		Works in various capacities for Southern California Telephone Company.
1930	February	*Fever Pitch* published by Horace Liveright.
1931		Travels in Mexico.
1935	June 10	*The Wild Earth's Nobility* published by Liveright Publishing Company.
1936		Begins writing full time.
1937	October	*Midas of the Rockies* published by Covici-Friede.
	November	*Below Grass Roots* published by Liveright Publishing Company.
1940	January	*The Dust Within the Rock* published by Liveright Publishing Company.
1941	February 6	*People of the Valley* published by Farrar & Rinehart.
1942	March	*River Lady*, by Houston Branch and Frank Waters, published by Farrar & Rinehart.

	June 11	*The Man Who Killed the Deer* published by Farrar & Rinehart.
1943-1945		Works as staff writer for the Office of the Coordinator of Inter-American Affairs in Washington.
1946	July	*The Colorado* issued for members of the National Travel Club.
	September 9	*The Colorado* officially published in the Rivers of America Series by Rinehart & Company.
	December 29	Alan Swallow first expresses an interest in reprinting some of Waters' books.
1947	April 10	*Yogi of Cockroach Court* published by Rinehart & Company.
1948	April 23	*Diamond Head,* by Houston Branch and Frank Waters, published by Farrar, Straus.
1949	September-December, 1951	Serves as editor-in-chief of the bilingual weekly newspaper *El Crepusculo,* in Taos.
1950	December 2	*Masked Gods* published by the University of New Mexico Press.
1952-1956		Serves as Information Director for Las Alamos Scientific Laboratory, Las Alamos, New Mexico.
1960	June 16	*The Earp Brothers of Tombstone* published by Clarkson N. Potter, Inc.
1963	October?	*Robert Gilruth* published by Encyclopaedia Brittanica Press.
	December 2	*Book of the Hopi* published by The Viking Press.
1964	October	*Leon Gaspard* published by Northland Press.
1966		Writer in Residence, Colorado State University.
	October 31	*Woman at Otowi Crossing* published by Alan Swallow.
1969	May 1	*Pumpkin Seed Point* published by The Swallow Press, Inc.
1971	June 30	*Pike's Peak* published by The Swallow Press, Inc.

1973	December 28	*To Possess the Land* published by The Swallow Press, Inc.
1975	June 16	*Mexico Mystique* published by The Swallow Press, Inc.
1981	September 1	*Mountain Dialogues* published by The Swallow Press, Inc.
1982	March 1	*Cuchama and Sacred Mountains* by W. Y. Evans-Wentz, edited by Frank Waters and Charles L. Adams, published by The Swallow Press, Inc.

SECTION A

Books by Frank Waters

All of the above within single rules, within a frame of palm-branch ornaments with a small dot at each corner and in the middle of the top, bottom and sides.

7⅜ × 5¼". [1-14⁸ 15⁶]: 118 leaves. Pp. [1-10] 11-83 [84-86] 87-165 [166-168] 169-233 [234-236]. Numbers printed in roman in the center at the foot of the page.

CONTENTS: p. 1, half-title: "FEVER PITCH"; p. 2, blank; p. 3, title; p. 4, copyright notice: "COPYRIGHT | 1930 BY FRANK WATERS | Printed in the United States | of America"; p. 5, dedication: "FOR | *Joseph Dozier*"; p. 6, blank; p. 7, contents; p. 8, blank; p. 9, divisional half-title: "PART ONE | The White House"; p. 10, blank; pp. 11-83, text; p. 84, blank; p. 85, divisional half-title: "PART TWO | The Des= ert"; p. 86, blank; pp. 87-165, text; p. 166, blank; p. 167, divisional half-title: "PART THREE | The White Heart"; p. 168, blank; pp. 169-233, text; pp. 234-236, blank.

BINDING: Orange cloth. Front stamped with two horizontal thick rules in blue, running across the top, approximately 13⁄16" apart; two similar thick rules approximately 1 13⁄16" apart stamped in lower right corner and extending 1 13⁄16" from the fore-edge; one vertical rule stamped along the entire height of the front, approximately 1½" from the fore-edge. A palm tree, stamped in silver, is set within a blue-stamped panel between the two lower rules and to the right of the vertical rule. The title "FEVER PITCH" is stamped in silver and set within a blue-stamped panel between the two upper horizontal rules breaking across the vertical rule. Spine stamped: "[thick blue rule] | [next two lines within a blue stamped panel] [silver] FEVER | [silver] PITCH | [below panel] [thick blue rule] | [silver] Frank | [silver] Waters | [silver] LIVERIGHT | [thick blue rule]". Top edges stained blue; fore and bottom edges untrimmed. Cream-colored endpapers.

DUST JACKET (white paper): Front and spine carry a drawing by Paul Wenck, in red, yellow, and pink, of a man and a woman leading two horses through a desert, with mountains in the background. Signed in red at extreme upper right of front: "WENCK". Lettered on front: "[all in white] FEVER | PITCH | by | FRANK | WATERS". Lettered on spine: "[five lines in white] FEVER | PITCH | by | FRANK | WA= TERS | [publisher's device of a man at a writing desk with the letters 'HL' above him, all in red, within a white oval outlined in red and white] | [two lines in white] HORACE | LIVERIGHT". Rear: Four paragraph blurb for Elliot Paul's *The Amazon,* set between fancy rules, all in red. Front flap: two paragraph blurb for *Fever Pitch* with jacket designer's name, Paul Wenck, at bottom, all in red; rear flap: two paragraph blurb for Peter Freuchen's *Eskimo,* printed in red and black.

Published at $2.50. Exact date of publication and number of copies printed unknown. Copyrighted February 21, 1930; deposited February 24, 1930. Listed in the "Weekly Record" of *Publisher's Weekly* on March 1, 1930.

REVIEWS: *New York Evening Post,* March 15, 1930 (p. 11m); *Outlook,* March 19, 1930 (p. 467); *Boston Transcript,* April 30, 1930 (p. 2); *New York Times Book Review,* June 29, 1930 (p. 6); *Saturday Review of Literature,* July 12, 1930 (p. 1195); *New York Herald Tribune Books,* September 28, 1930 (p. 22).

COPIES: DLC (2 copies); NmU (d.j.; inscribed by Waters to his mother); FW; TAT (4 copies, 2 in d.j.); W. W. Norton Company, New York (Liveright file copy).

A1b Second edition, only printing [1955]

FEVER PITCH | by | Frank Waters | BERKELEY PUBLISHING CORP. | 145 W. 57th Street · New York 19, N. Y.

6⅜ × 4¼". Perfectbound: 64 leaves. Pp. [1-4] 5 [6] 7-47 [48] 49-91 [92] 93-126 [127-128]. Pages 2 and 6 are blank; page 127 carries an advertisement for *Pleasures of the Jazz Age* by William Hodapp; and page 128 carries an advertisement for *S. S. San Pedro* by James Gould Cozzens.

COPYRIGHT PAGE: "[small caps with a capital] COPYRIGHT 1930 [small caps] BY [small caps with a capital] FRANK WATERS | *Published by Arrangement with Liveright Publishing Corp.* | For Joseph Dozier | PRINTED IN THE U. S. A.".

Paperback. Berkeley Books ANC 104. Published at 25¢ in 1955; number of copies printed unknown. Listed in the "Weekly Record" of *Publisher's Weekly* on May 14, 1955.

COPIES: NmU; FW.

NOTE: Although the book had been out of print for many years, Liveright Publishing Company, under the terms of the original contract, maintained rights to the book for the duration of copyright. This edition was brought out much to the surprise of Waters, who opposed the book's republication.

A2 THE WILD EARTH'S NOBILITY

After finishing work on this first volume of his Colorado mining trilogy, Waters sent the manuscript, originally titled "Manitou" to Mr. C. R. Everitt at the Curtis Brown Agency. In a cover letter to Everitt, dated May 5, 1934, Waters wrote:

> Curtis Brown Ltd. through Mr. Rich and Miss Winston has been so splendid in handling my first bit of writing some time ago and encouraging me since, that I am unhesitatingly sending you the manuscript which I have just finished after more than three years work.
> Your office records will show an unsuccessful first novel of mine published in 1930 and another manuscript you returned to me unpublished. I want you to accept these 3 volumes with the assurance that it is the sincerest and best work that I am capable of. The characters, horses, mines, are all from those of my own family, the scenes those of my childhood; the very events have helped to mold my own life. It is the sort of thing a man can attempt but once and I have done it the justice of giving it my best.
> From your standpoint it is, briefly, a three volume narration of a Southern family moving and settling in the Pikes Peak region of Colorado. Its background is the Pikes Peak rush, the Leadville silver strike, and the discovery and development of the Cripple Creek gold camp. To my knowledge it is the only novel that has yet used this territory as its milieu. You may depend upon its authenticity. My grandfather moved to the Pikes Peak region in 1871 when Colorado Springs was laid out as a town. He was the most prominent builder and contractor in town for over forty years. He built the first building of Colorado College which I later attended; the man who married my mother and father became the librarian of the College after retiring from the ministry and his carefully marked files have been available for my use. I have consulted newspaper files back to 1875 and innumerable geological papers on the mines of the district. I have had my own fling at engineering, and knowing the mines in childhood, have lately revisited the Leadville and Cripple Creek camps.
> And yet I would not have you consider "Manitou" merely as a historical novel. It was not written for an episode in the development of the West; the facts are there only because as facts, they could not be wholly ignored. Nor is it expressly a "family novel" such as is now in vogue (though that might help

recommend it to the publishers). It is more an attempt through the lives of three men, each of whom are pivots of action in their respective books, to discover and reveal the approach toward an alignment with their place and time which they, like us, attempted in the degree permitted by their individualistic conception of the meaning of life.

Horace Liveright, Inc. in accepting and naming my first book "Fever Pitch" in June 1929 took an option on the "book rights of the next two full length novels". The firm subsequently turned down one novel and one book of stories and sketches submitted to them. If in your opinion these fulfill the terms of the contract, I would prefer not to submit "Manitou" to these publishers. I understand that Mr. Horace Liveright has died and that his firm is no longer regarded as among the best. After several failures and five years of hard work, three of them on this alone, I am hoping you will consider it worth starting at the top.

Your note of a year ago asking to see my next work was very kind and greatly encouraging. And I am sending you the three volumes of "Manitou" with the hope that you will not be disappointed.

Unfortunately, Everitt returned the manuscript to Waters several weeks later, explaining in a letter, dated May 29, 1934, that the agency could not undertake to offer the book, because it lacked "pace" and failed to hold the reader's attention. After this rejection, Waters apparently went ahead and sent the manuscript to the Liveright Publishing Company on his own initiative. T. R. Smith at Liveright wrote Waters on August 29, 1934, that after a second reading the firm had decided that the book could not be published as it stood. However, Smith outlined some broad revisions which he felt would greatly improve the book, and that if Waters was willing to undertake these revisions, the firm would reconsider the book for possible publication in 1935. Waters responded to Smith's letter on September 8, 1934:

> Your letter regarding MANITOU with your suggestions for revision has been both stimulating and encouraging. Coming on top of a trip down to the Indian country near Shiprock, so familiar and unchanged, it has brought home to me so clearly exactly what I mean the book to be. Some of your criticisms were so correct that I feel I can revise it to suit us both. I am glad to give you my reactions to them.
>
> Manitou is the first of an intended trilogy. The major theme of this first phase is the family's physical struggle to unify themselves with the land. It is brought out by the three key characters: Tom, Boné, and Rogier, each typifying the rude pioneer, the artist, and the prototype of the modern day American with an approach to it by both spiritual divination and science. The basic material for the theme of the second phase—the social struggle between the aristocratic aloofness of the "Old South" and the new democracy engendered by the westward expansion—is also suggested through the inculcation of snobbishness in the children by Mrs. Rogier. With this necessity for laying a secure foundation you can see why I want to take every precaution against this first volume being too inadequate.

However, Book Two is rambling. The very fact that you suggested a substantial reduction in the first and last parts showed me that I had failed to adhere closely enough to my theme. After all it is Bone's story, and the parts you mentioned were the deviations from it. I could not lift it all out bodily, but by rewriting and compressing the necessary parts I am sure it could be cut down about 50 pages to a tight narrative.

Book Three will be the most difficult as it gets back to the broader canvas of the whole family and prepares the groundwork for the social complications to be developed later. Elimination of a third of it (100 pages) will be a real job. I am willing to go through it from first to last and pare it to the barest narrative form consistent with the fulness of theme, eliminating most of the technical mineralogy and geology material.

Altogether I should say the 500 pages of the two books could be reduced to some 400 pages which will be in line with Book One. The main advantage being, of course, a more swift and smoothly flowing narrative adhering closely to its thematic backbone. If you approve of this and there does seem to be a real chance of putting it on your 1935 program, I shall be not only willing to give the time to the revision but will get to work on it immediately with all enthusiasm.

Hearing again the mesmeric sound of an Indian drum at night, and seeing the tumbled adobe walls of that insignificant and lonely post which for so long housed two gentlewomen of courage, bring back so much! It is and will be always "mi tierra"; and this book, sentimentally or otherwise, means a great deal to me. I feel so fortunate in knowing that not yet has any novel attempted to bind between its cover that region—still mine!—between Pikes Peak and the muddy crook of the San Juan.

Waters set to work on the revisions, and on November 5, 1934, sent the revised manuscript off to Smith at Liveright's. On the same day, he sent Smith the following letter:

I am sending to you today the manuscript of MANITOU which has been revised as you suggested on August 29.

The last two books have been reduced considerably. In Book Two, 4 chapters have been eliminated by cutting and compressing the material in the first and last sections.

Book Three has been completely retyped in order to eliminate certain scenes, to rewrite others, and to edit out pages, paragraphs, and sentences wherever possible. In all about 120 pages have been cut out.

This shortens the whole manuscript to a little over 600 pages with Book One and Book Three each 14 chapters of equal length, and a shorter Book Two of 9 chapters.

As you have already approved Book One I am returning it unchanged with the other two.

Smith wrote back to Waters on December 24, 1934, informing him that while he had not yet had a chance to read the revised manuscript other readers had reacted favorably, and he was therefore enclosing a contract for the book.* He asked that Waters accept a small advance, due to financial conditions in the country and to allow them greater latitude in promoting the book. Smith also mentioned that the title "Manitou" had met with resistance in the firm and he asked that Waters think of a better one. Waters responded on January 5, 1935:

> I can't tell you how happy your letter has made me. Manitou has taken all my best efforts for 3 years and your acceptance of it has given me a tremendous lift. I want it to prove so much more successful than my first descriptive tale & justify your confidence & that of Mr. Liveright who was the first to take an interest in what I am trying to do. And I want to achieve your New Year wish—to do better writing than ever before.
> By the time Manitou is published I hope to send you my next book. With the new incentive you have stimulated I am determined to gain your enthusiasm by giving you the best job of mine yet.
> In light of the horribly cheap title given Fever Pitch which has always stuck in my craw, I was not at all receptive to your suggestion to think of a new title for Manitou. Like "Cimarron" which perhaps meant little to the public on its first appearance, "Manitou" seems to express best the theme of the book in one word. Besides a small town at the foot of Ute Pass and a mountain adjacent to Pikes Peak, it has been always the Indian name for the Great Spirit, the place-spirit of the land against which all my characters react in their way. I thought that perhaps a sub-title underneath, as
> MANITOU
A Story of Pikes Peak

---

*No copy of this contract has been located. Under the terms of the contract Waters signed with Liveright on June 11, 1929, Liveright received an option on two books after *Fever Pitch.* For the first book after *Fever Pitch,* the contract outlined an advance of $500.00 against royalties of 12½% on the first 2,500 copies and 15% thereafter; for the second book there was to be an advance of $750.00 against a straight royalty of 15%. Apparently Smith felt, as had Waters, that the two books rejected prior to the submission of "Manitou" voided the terms of the 1929 contract.

From evidence found in Waters' papers the terms of this new contract, apparently signed and dated January 15, 1935, can be determined in rough outline. In a letter to Waters dated April 24, 1935, T. R. Smith enclosed a check for $150.00, "due according to the contract. . . ." No other direct evidence of the advance has been found, but in an entry in his journal on April 21, 1936, Waters noted that he had received a check from Liveright for $50.31, making a total earned by the book to date of $300.31, on sales of 1,200 copies. Certainly this was the first royalty statement received by Waters after publication, and would seem to indicate that he had received an additional advance of $100.00, probably upon publication. This would also suggest a starting royalty of 10%.

The contract also gave Liveright an option on two books to follow "Manitou." Thus, the terms for the two remaining volumes of the Colorado trilogy were covered by this contract of 1935, although with slight modifications which are outlined in the sections dealing with the other books (see: A4 and A5).

would make it instantly intelligible to the reader at first sight. A simple background of the Peak on the cover-jacket might enhance the meaning still more. I have several old pictures of the Peak, the line of covered wagons crawling up the Pass from Manitou, etc I would be glad to send you for suggestions, although this might be intruding on a detail you wish to work out alone.

I have also thought of "The Earth Abides", taken from "One generation passeth away; and another generation cometh; but the earth abideth for ever."

The only other things that have occured to me are:
"Red Earth",
simply the English translation of Colorado from the Spaniards who named the area from its reddish colored earth and fantastic carven cliffs.
"The Long Shadow"
And the first phrase of an old Aztec quotation I copied from a building in Mexico:
"All the Roundness of the Earth"
(is a sepulcher; there is nothing it sustains that in the name of pity it does not conceal and bury.)"

These seem to have a drawback because of The Good Earth, The Earth Turns, etc.

I do hope however you will take another look at Manitou. It is unusual, short, and true. It is not a cheap melodramatic book, and a cheap melodramatic title would be fair neither to the book, the good reader, nor to the reader who wanted a western thriller.

The change you made in relation to the advance is perfectly satisfactory. Every book should prove its worth. Before signing the new contract covering two more books after this, I am taking the liberty of forwarding them to Mr. David Hampton who was recommended to me very highly. I know nothing of the business of publishing and since Mr. Rich has left Curtis Brown I have been at loss to know what is the right thing to do. I am asking Mr. Hampton to get in touch with you at once and as he is in New York I am sure you will approve of his being at hand to discuss anything that comes up. . . .

Smith wrote back to Waters on January 10, 1935, accepting the revisions, but outlining some further cutting and rejecting Waters' suggestions for titles. Smith noted that in the firm they had come up with "Earth of Their Adoption," "The Wild Earth's Nobility," "A Glory from the Earth (from Wordsworth)," "Gold is Where You Find It," and "The Hand of Time." In a follow-up letter on January 24, 1935, Smith informed Waters that they had decided to use "The Wild Earth's Nobility," although he made no mention of the rather cheap sub-title. He further mentioned that they didn't want to use "the dedicatory preface." Smith also told Waters in this letter that he had sent the manuscript off to the compositors and that they were projecting March 25th as the publication date.

On March 30, 1935, Waters wrote to Smith to inform him that he was returning the last batch of galleys with only minor corrections. He wrote further:

... As the preface is being omitted, will you please include the dedication "To Mother." This will not preclude the use of the longer dedicatory essay later if chance makes it possible.

Also, if you think it fitting, you might use the quotation:
Toda la redondez de la tierra es un sepulcro; no hay cosa que sustente, que con titulo de piedad no la esconda y la entierre.
Netzahualcoyotl.

which seems to fit the book exactly. . . .

A2   THE WILD EARTH'S NOBILITY   [1935]

A2   First edition, only printing

[first five lines printed in open face] [small caps] *THE* [caps] WILD EARTH'S | NOBILITY | *BY* | FRANK WATERS | [printed in white script against a thick black rule] Samuel Bernard Schaeffer | [below rule] A NOVEL OF THE OLD WEST

The title page was designed to appear like a poster nailed to a board wall. All the above is printed within a white "poster" panel, which is shaded in gray along the bottom edge, and with a "nail head" outlined in black in both of the upper corners. The entire panel is set against a black background streaked with gray in simulation of wood grain.

$7\tfrac{7}{16}$ × $5\tfrac{1}{4}$". [1-29^8]: 232 leaves. Pp. [i-viii], [1-2] 3-160 [161-162] 163-274 [275-276] 277-454 [455-456]. Numbers printed in roman in headline at outer margin of type page, except for pages 3, 163 and 277, on which the numbers are printed in the center at the foot of the page.

CONTENTS: p. i, half-title: "THE WILD EARTH'S | NOBILITY"; p. ii, "[publisher's device of a man at a writing desk within an oval outlined in black] | LIVERIGHT PUBLISHING CORPORATION | NEW YORK"; p. iii, title; p. iv, copyright notice: "[small caps with a capital] COPYRIGHT, 1935, [small caps] BY [small caps with a capital] FRANK WATERS | *All Rights Reserved* | PRINTED IN THE UNITED STATES OF AMERICA"; p. v, dedication: "[swash capital] *To* | [small caps with a capital] MOTHER"; p. vi, quotation: *"Toda la redondez de la tierra es un sepulcro; no hay | cosa que sustente, que con titulo de piedad no la | esconda y la entierre.* | [small caps with a capital] NETZAHUALCOYOTL"; p. vii, contents; p. viii, blank; p. 1, divisional half-title: "BOOK ONE | SILVER"; p. 2, blank; pp. 3-160, text; p. 161, divisional half-title: "BOOK TWO | GANGUE"; p. 162, blank; pp. 163-274, text; p. 275, divisional half-title: "BOOK THREE | GOLD"; p. 276, blank; pp. 277-454, text; pp. 455-456, blank.

BINDING: Black cloth, lettered on spine only: "[five lines within an orange panel] [small caps] *THE* [caps] WILD | EARTH'S | NOBILITY | *BY* | FRANK WATERS | [below panel, at bottom] [orange] LIVERIGHT". Top edges stained orange; fore and bottom edges untrimmed. Yellow-orange endpapers.

DUST JACKET (white paper): Front and spine printed overall in black streaked with gray to simulate wood grain. Lettered on front exactly as on title page, except that the portion of the "poster" panel above the thick black rule is printed overall in orange with the lettering in white outlined in black; the "nail heads" are also in white outlined in black, with very slight orange shading in the interior. Spine: "[at top within an orange panel, all five lines printed in white outlined in black] [small caps] *THE* [caps] WILD | EARTH'S | NOBILITY | *BY* | FRANK WATERS | [near bottom, within a white panel] LIVERIGHT | [orange panel at bottom]". Rear: "[thick and thin rules] | THE BLACK & GOLD LIBRARY | ARISTOCRATS OF THE BOOK WORLD | [8-line paragraph] | LIST OF TITLES | [11 titles and short comments printed in two columns] | *Ask for Catalog of Complete List at Your Booksellers, or Liveright* | 386 Fourth Avenue, New York | [thick and thin rules]". The front flap carries a three paragraph blurb for this book; the rear flap carries an advertisement for Freud's *A General Introduction to Psychoanalysis* and a blurb about Freud's book by Dr. Smith Ely Jaffe.

Published at $2.50 on June 10, 1935. Number of copies printed unknown. Copyrighted May 14, 1935; deposited May 15, 1935. Originally advertised in *Publisher's Weekly* on January 26, 1935, for publication on March 25, 1935; a later advertisement in *Publisher's Weekly* on May 25, 1935, listed publication as June 10, 1935.

REVIEWS: *Boston Transcript,* June 12, 1935 (p. 2); *New York Times Book Review,* June 23, 1935 (p. 6); *New York Herald Tribune Books,* June 23, 1935 (p. 10); *Saturday Review of Literature,* July 6, 1935 (p. 21); *New Republic,* September 4, 1935 (p. 111).

COPIES: DLC (2 copies); NmU; TAT (4 copies, 2 in d.j.; one advance copy).

NOTE: In order to stir up interest in the work, Liveright sent out 250 advance copies of the book for presentation to the trade and a number of well-known writers. In a letter to Waters dated May 10, 1935, T. R. Smith of Liveright noted that these advance copies would be ready "in a day or two," and Liveright included a notice of these copies in the *Publisher's Weekly* ad on May 25, 1935. Only one copy of the advance issue—consisting of sheets glued into the dust jacket—is known and is in my own collection.

A3   MIDAS OF THE ROCKIES

Sometime after joining up with the David Hampton Agency in 1935, Waters sent on to Hampton the first several chapters of his biography of Winfield Scott Stratton, then titled "Bowl of Gold." Hampton showed the material to Covici-Friede, who expressed a serious interest in the book. On December 4, 1936, Waters sent the first 14,000 words of the manuscript to Covici-Friede and followed this up in May of 1937 with the complete book. Covici-Friede telegrammed him in early June that they had accepted the manuscript for publication.

In a letter dated June 4, 1937, Joel Satz of the Hampton Agency informed Waters that he had worked out a contract with Covici-Friede in which they agreed to an advance of $500.00; $200.00 payable upon signing the contract, $200.00 payable upon delivery of the finished manuscript, and $100.00 payable upon publication. Unfortunately, no copy of this contract has come to light and the royalty rate agreed to is unknown. Satz also informed Waters that Covici-Friede did not like the title "Bowl of Gold" and wanted to use "Midas of the Rockies." Waters responded to Satz on June 6, 1937:

> . . . The Covici terms are quite acceptable and I think you did a swell job in getting them. "Bowl of Gold" seems a better title as it is such a common term throughout the mining world, as exemplified by the Associated Press clipping I once sent you. But if the other seems to Covici more suitable for general appeal I agree to its use. I would suggest:
>
> MIDAS OF THE ROCKIES
> The Story of Winfield Scott Stratton
> or
> MIDAS OF THE ROCKIES
> The Story of Stratton and Cripple Creek
>
> If the first sub-title is used the full name should be insisted upon; he is never referred to any other way.

Enclosed is a final and complete table of contents. The quotations to be used on the title pages of the six chapters may or may not be used. I do not have a blurb, but if required I can pick out within the next ten days a number of colorful incidents which they can use in making one.
  I am having a photostat made of Stratton's signature, and have located a photograph of Myron Stratton which I can have a photographer copy if required. You might let me know if there are any more pictures they would like: for example, a map of the Cripple Creek district, or a photograph of the first little shaft house of the Independence. To get the latter I will have to drive a photographer from Victor up to a remote mine to copy it, but it can be done. Also a 5 by 7 print of the Stratton monument; the blue pictures I simply tore out of a printed report merely to show Covici what it was if required. And you might let me have the dead-line if Strauss doesn't include it in his letter.
  . . . I do have confidence, Joel, and am willing to work. And with this start and your help, I am hoping we strike pay dirt.

A3   MIDAS OF THE ROCKIES   [1937]

A3a   First edition, first printing

MIDAS | OF THE ROCKIES | *The Story of Stratton and Cripple Creek* | BY FRANK WATERS | *New York* COVICI • FRIEDE *Publishers*

8½ × 5⅝". [1-21⁸ 22⁴]: 172 leaves. 6 plates inserted between pages 2/3, 44/45, 90/91, 140/141, 184/185 and 322/323. Pp. [1-12] 13-19 [20-22] 23-60 [61-62] 63-112 [113-114] 115-177 [178-180] 181-233 [234-236] 237-274 [275-276] 277-344. Numbers printed in roman in headline at outer margin of type page, except for pages 13, 23, 63, 115, 181, 237, 277, 331 and 340 on which the numbers are printed in the center at the foot of the page.

CONTENTS: p. 1, half-title: "MIDAS OF THE ROCKIES"; p. 2, *"Also by Frank Waters:* THE WILD EARTH'S NOBILITY"; p. 3, title; p. 4, copyright notice: "[small caps] COPYRIGHT, [caps] 1937, [small caps] BY FRANK WATERS | [five-line notice of reservation of rights, printed in italic] | DESIGNED BY ROBERT JOSEPHY | PRINTED IN THE UNITED STATES OF AMERICA | BY J. J. LIT= TLE AND IVES COMPANY, NEW YORK"; p. 5, dedication: "TO | H. K. ELLINGSON"; p. 6, blank; p. 7, contents; p. 8, blank; p. 9, list of illustrations; p. 10, blank; p. 11, second half-title; p. 12, blank; pp. 13-19, Foreword; p. 20, blank; p. 21, divisional half-title: "PART

18   Section A

ONE: PRAIRIES | *"Our citizens being so prone to rambling and | ex= tending themselves on the frontier will, | through necessity, be con= strained to limit their | extent on the west to the borders of the Mis- | souri and Mississippi, while they leave the | prairies incapable of cultivation to the wander- | ing and uncivilized aborigines of the country."* "; p. 22, blank; pp. 23-60, text; p. 61, divisional half-title: "PART TWO: MOUNTAINS | *"In gold mining, as in art, distance not infre- | quently lends enchantment to the view."* "; p. 62, blank; pp. 63-112, text; p. 113, divisional half-title: "PART THREE: PIKE'S PEAK | *"Hell! The ten= derfeet are taking out gold where | it is, and the miners are looking for it where it | ought to be!"* "; p. 114, blank; pp. 115-177, text; p. 178, blank; p. 179, divisional half-title: "PART FOUR: LONDON | *"O Lord! Keep me from being like some of these | Cripple Creek millionaires, afraid of being | bored by old friends, insolent in feeling toward | those who have not had my luck, and scared to | death lest a dollar go by and I not get it."* "; p. 180, blank; pp. 181-233, text; p. 234, blank; p. 235, divisional half-title: "PART FIVE: CRIPPLE CREEK AGAIN | *"Gold is worth more in the ground than out | of it."* "; p. 236, blank; pp. 237-274, text; p. 275, divisional half-title: "PART SIX: LITTLE LONDON | *" 'Tis not enough to help the feeble up, but to | support him after."* "; p. 276, blank; pp. 277-330, text; pp. 331-339, Afterword; pp. 340-344, Acknowledgments.

Illustrations: A facsimile reproduction of Stratton's receipt for $10,000,000.00 appears on page 220. All other illustrations were reproduced from photographs supplied by the author and were inserted as below:

(facing page)   3:   "WINFIELD SCOTT STRATTON"
                            44:    "CRIPPLE CREEK"
                            90:    "COLORADO SPRINGS IN THE EARLY SEVENTIES"
                          140:    "STRATTON'S INDEPENDENCE AND PORTLAND MINES"
                          184:    "COLORADO SPRINGS TODAY"
                          322:    "THE MYRON STRATTON HOME"

Binding: Blue cloth. Front stamped in gilt with facsimile of Stratton's signature: "W. S Stratton". Spine stamped in gilt: "MIDAS | OF THE | ROCKIES | [fancy rule] | *Frank Waters* | *Covici · Friede*". Top edges stained blue. Tan paper endpapers, with map of the region printed on the face of both front and rear endpapers, printed in brown, and signed in lower right corner: "[script] A. Musick '37".

DUST JACKET (white paper): Front, spine and rear printed overall in orange; the front and spine have a blue band in the center within which appears an illustration of a mountain range with two trees in the foreground. Lettered on front: "[gilt, and printed against a dark blue spectral band] MIDAS | [script] of the Rockies | [white] THE STORY OF STRATTON AND CRIPPLE CREEK | FRANK WA= TERS". Spine: "[gilt, and set against dark blue spectral band] MIDAS | [script] of the | [script] Rockies | [white] WATERS | COVICI-FRIEDE". Rear: plain. Front flap carries a blurb for this book, which is carried over onto the rear flap, which also contains the publisher's imprint at the bottom.

Published at $3.00. Exact date of publication and number of copies printed unknown. Copyrighted October 26, 1937; deposited October 29, 1937. Advertised in *Publisher's Weekly* on July 17, 1937, and again in the issue of September 18, 1937, for publication on October 17, 1937. Listed in the "Weekly Record" of *Publisher's Weekly* on October 23, 1937.

REVIEWS: *New York Herald Tribune Books*, November 14, 1937 (p. 6); *Time*, November 15, 1937 (p. 96); *New York Times Book Review*, January 23, 1938 (p. 18).

COPIES: DLC (2 copies); NmU, FW, TAT (3 copies in d.j.).

NOTE: Although the number of copies printed by Covici-Friede of *Midas* is unknown, Joel Satz told Waters in his letter of June 4, 1937, that Covici-Friede were expecting advance sales of around 2,000 copies. A royalty statement sent to Waters for the period ending June 30, 1938, showed an unearned balance remaining on the book of $161.12, which would indicate that around 1,200 copies had been sold to that time.

Not long after this the firm of Covici-Friede went bankrupt and the rights to *Midas* were sold to the Crown Publishing Company.

NOTE: About the time that Covici-Friede published *Midas*, Mr. H. K. Ellingson, of the Colorado Springs *Gazette*, requested rights to serialize the biography in his newspaper. Covici-Friede turned him down,

20 Section A

feeling that it might have an effect on the book's sales in the Colorado Springs area. After the rights to the book were transferred from Crown to the University of Denver Press, however, permission for serialization was granted to *The Colorado Springs Independent,* a weekly newspaper. The book was serialized in the paper from the week of April 15, 1948 through the week of March 24, 1949.

A3b   First edition, University of Denver Press printing   [1949]

FRANK WATERS | MIDAS | *of the* ROCKIES | STRATTON | CEN= TENNIAL *EDITION* | THE UNIVERSITY OF DENVER PRESS | *1949*

8½ × 5½". [1-22⁸]: 176 leaves; 10 plates inserted. Pp. [1-12] 13-18 [19-22] 23-60 [61-62] 63-112 [113-114] 115-177 [178-180] 181-233 [234-236] 237-274 [275-276] 277-347 [348-352].

Contents: p. 1, half-title; p. 2, "BOOKS by *FRANK WATERS* | [list of 9 titles]"; p. 3, title; p. 4, copyright notice: "COPYRIGHT, 1937, 1949, BY FRANK WATERS | [five-line notice of reservation of rights]"; p. 5, dedication: "The original edition of this book was dedi= cated to H. K. | Ellingson of the *Colorado Springs Gazette,* who insisted | that it be written. | The dedication of this Stratton Centennial Edition must | also bear the name of David P. Strickler, Trustee and | President of the Myron Stratton Home, who for over forty | years has devoted his life to carrying out both the terms | and the spirit of Stratton's will."; p. 6, blank; p. 7, contents; p. 8, blank; p. 9, list of illustrations; p. 10, blank; p. 11, second half-title; p. 12, blank; pp. 13-18, Foreword; p. 19, third half-title; p. 20, blank; pp. 21-330, identical to A3a; pp. 331-341, Afterword; pp. 342-347, Acknowledgments; pp. 348-352, blank.

Illustrations: One illustration which appeared in A3a, "COLORADO SPRINGS TODAY," was deleted for this impression, and a number of others were added:

(facing page)   3:   "[script] W. S. Stratton"
                32: "COLORADO SPRINGS IN THE EARLY SEVENTIES"
                64: "A COLORADO MINING CAMP"
                96: "ORE TRAINS ON UTE PASS"
             128: "COLORADO SPRINGS IN THE EIGHTIES"

160: "THE HIGHEST CAMP IN CRIPPLE CREEK"
192: "CRIPPLE CREEK"
208: "THE ORIGINAL ANTLERS HOTEL"
208: "STRATTON'S INDEPENDENCE AND PORTLAND MINES"
320: "THE MYRON STRATTON HOME"

The facsimile illustration of Stratton's receipt for $10,000,000.00 still appears on page 220.

Another change in the illustrations concerns the frontispiece portrait of Stratton, which in this impression is a somewhat enlarged version of that which appears in A3a, and it contains at the bottom a facsimile of Stratton's autograph rather than his name in type.

Cloth. Published at $3.50 in 1949; number of copies printed unknown. Listed in the Spring Index of *Publisher's Weekly* for publication in January of 1949.

COPIES: TAT (2 copies); NmU (2 sets unbound sheets).

NOTE: Apart from the change in the dedication, the foreword, afterword and acknowledgments were substantially rewritten for this impression. Also, there appear within the text itself four minor changes of facts, all on page 330:

330.6:	$900.	$1,117.
330.11:	1937	1948
330.12:	3,196 years, 7 months and 16 days.	5,252 years, 11 months and 11 days.
330.13:	three thousand	five thousand

NOTE: In at least one bound copy of this impression (TAT), the frontispiece portrait of Stratton has been replaced by a duplicate of the illustration "A COLORADO MINING CAMP" (p. 64). While this may merely be a freak, it should be noted that in the two sets of unbound sheets at NmU all illustrations except for that of Stratton are present with the sheets. It is possible that other copies may appear without the Stratton frontispiece.

NOTE: Alan Swallow first introduced himself to Frank Waters in a letter dated December 29, 1946, in which he inquired about the status of

The Man Who Killed the Deer. In a follow-up letter of February 4, 1947, Swallow not only expressed an interest in republishing *Deer,* but also inquired whether or not there were any other books which might be out of print and which could possibly be included in a series of Waters' reprints. Among the titles then out of print was *Midas of the Rockies,* the rights to which were held by Crown Publishing. Interestingly enough, Swallow told Waters that Crown had written him sometime earlier in an attempt to interest him in bringing out a reprint of the book, but he didn't follow it up, but would then look into the situation.

After Swallow informed Waters that Crown held the rights on *Midas*—they were transfered to Crown on the demise of Covici-Friede—Waters asked his agent, Mrs. Mildred Lyman, of the McIntosh and Otis agency, to inquire of Crown as to the status of the book and to see if it might not be possible to have the rights returned to him. Although at first reluctant, Crown finally released the rights back to Waters in early December of 1947. Waters wrote to Mrs. Lyman on December 10, 1947:

> Good! I am so pleased to learn of the return of the MIDAS rights!
> . . . Stanley Rinehart has just written, saying he is so anxious for me to do another non-fiction book for them that he would pay my expenses to come to New York to discuss any ideas I have. I haven't answered him yet as I don't know whether we are in the clear with him, but neither the trip nor another new book appeals to me now.
> However, if you consider it wise, it might be expedient just now to offer him instead the MIDAS to do as a new book with new photographs and late material, but with no option. If he refuses, we can then submit it to the Swallow Press of Denver to consider doing with William Morrow, or elsewhere. I am still confident that a judicious treatment of it will appeal to the movies here. Will you let me know, so I can answer Stanley Rinehart directly with a sales letter, or leave it up to you to submit elsewhere depending on conditions and your judgment? . . .

Waters went ahead with his decision to offer *Midas* to Rinehart, and on December 19, 1947, he wrote Stanley M. Rinehart about the book:

> I am sorry to have taken so long to answer your letter, but a trip to New York right now seems impossible. However I have been thinking a great deal about a new non-fiction book to follow the COLORADO, and have decided that a reissue of MIDAS OF THE ROCKIES is the best bet.
> This, as you know, is my biography of W. S. Stratton, discoverer of the Cripple Creek gold camp, set against the background of the great boom mining era of the West as covered in "The Outcasts" chapter of THE COLORADO.
> The book was issued in 1937 by Covici-Friede and has long been out of print. It is regarded as the only authentic source material on the subject and has been

widely quoted. As it was written with the full cooperation of the existing $7 million Stratton Estate, still controlling all of Stratton's mines through the Cripple Creek Mining and Development Company for the benefit of the Myron Stratton Home, which cooperation was given me because my grandfather was once Stratton's partner, employer and employee, it is unlikely that any other book will ever be written on the subject.

Last summer when I gave a talk at the Denver Book Fair, the manager of the May Company Book Department there told me that of all my books the MIDAS was most in demand. She has sold 600 copies of THE COLORADO which is 10% of all the trade copies sold since the day of publication. These were sold primarily on her own initiative; whereas the May Company here, like all other department stores, serving six times the population and confronted continually by newspaper headlines about the Colorado River water situation, do not carry the book in stock. For this reason I am inclined to take her judgment that a reissue of MIDAS, if handled properly, would be a good business venture.

There are several other factors pointing to the same conclusion. Since the book has gone out of print one of the greatest deep mining tunnels in the world has been driven into Pike's Peak to drain all mines and open up untouched lower levels, as described in the READERS DIGEST. The legal head of the Stratton estate, visiting me last summer, told me preparations are being made for the largest mining company in the world to work these lower depths. This project is Stratton's dream coming true a half-century after his death. The interest in Stratton himself is increasing as shown by a recent series of articles about him. The Home which he founded has been used as a model by the late English socialist government. With his sound business management and philanthropy, so strange in the time of Tabor's and Walshes' bizarre antics, Stratton's views have pushed forward very well into 1947.

My idea is to reissue the book, not as a mere reprint but as a new revised book similar to HERE THEY DUG THE GOLD by George Willison, Reynal and Hitchock, which is an excellent job on Tabor and Leadville. To do this I think the first chapter and the last chapter should be rewritten to bring it up to date. I have also managed to secure a set of new photographs. You may also have suggestions for other changes.

If you would like to look over the book before forming an opinion, and I hope you do, I will send along a copy to you. In the meantime a Merry Christmas to you and the house.

Rinehart responded with a request to see the book, but three months later informed Waters that they had decided against reissuing the book. Waters then wrote to Swallow on March 22, 1948, that he could have *Midas* to reprint. Swallow first sent a copy of the book to William Morrow in New York, with whom he had a distribution arrangement, to see if they might have any interest. In May, Swallow reported to Waters that Morrow had declined, and that he would now start making plans to do the book himself.

On June 27, 1948, Swallow wrote to Mildred Lyman suggesting that rather than bring out the reprint of *Midas* under the Swallow imprint, that the book be brought out under the imprint of the University of Denver Press, which had started up the previous year and of which Swallow was the editor. Swallow suggested this both because he thought it would be a good book for the press and because it could be brought out quicker under that imprint than his own. Waters agreed to this, and a contract, dated July 9, 1948, was drawn up with the University of Denver Press outlining a royalty schedule of 10% on the first 5,000 copies, 12½% on the next 3,000 copies and 15% thereafter.

A3c   First edition, Alan Swallow printing   [1954]

FRANK WATERS | MIDAS | *of the* ROCKIES | STRATTON | CEN= TENNIAL *EDITION* | THE AMERICAN LIBRARY | *SAGE BOOKS*

Size, collation and pagination identical to A3b. Illustrations identical to A3b.

CONTENTS: Identical with A3b, except that p. 2 now carries a list of 11 books; p. 4, which now carries three additional lines at the bottom: ". . . | Sage Books and The American Library titles are pub- | lished by Alan Swallow, Publisher, 2679 South York | Street, Denver 10, Colo= rado."; and p. 348, which now carries a listing of The American Library titles.

Cloth. Published at $4.00 in 1954; number of copies printed unknown. Listed in the Summer Index of *Publisher's Weekly* on May 29, 1954, for publication on June 7, 1954; however, the September Index of *Publisher's Weekly* for September 4, 1954, lists publication as August 20, 1954.

COPIES: TAT.

NOTE: Waters' contract with Alan Swallow, dated March 27, 1954, outlined royalties of 10% on the first 2,500 copies and 12½% on all copies thereafter.

A3d First edition, first Swallow Press printing [with added introduction by Marshall Sprague] [1972]

MIDAS | OF THE ROCKIES | *The Story of Stratton and Cripple Creek* | BY FRANK WATERS | SAGE BOOKS | [publisher's sagebrush device] | [small caps] THE [caps] SWALLOW PRESS [small caps] INC. | CHICAGO

8½ × 5⁷⁄₁₆". [1-2^{16} 3^{12} (-3^{11,12}) 4-12^{16}]: 186 leaves. Pp. [i-iv], [1-6] 7-11 [12] 13-19 [20-22] 23-32 [32a-32b] 33-60 [61-62] 63-64 [64a-64b] 65-96 [96a-96b] 97-112 [113-114] 115-128 [128a-128b] 129-160 [160a-160b] 161-177 [178-180] 181-192 [192a-192b] 193-208 [208a-208b] 209-233 [234-236] 237-240 [240a-240b] 241-274 [275-276] [276a-276b] 277-320 [320a-320b] 321-347 [348]=368.

CONTENTS: p. i, full-page portrait of Stratton, below which is printed: "WINFIELD SCOTT STRATTON"; pp. ii-iii, double-page map copied from the endpapers of A3a; p. iv, blank; p. 1, half-title; p. 2, *"OTHER BOOKS BY FRANK WATERS* | [list of 11 titles]"; p. 3, title; p. 4, copyright notice: "Copyright © 1937, 1949 by Frank Waters | Introduction copyright © 1972 by Marshall Sprague | All rights re= served | Printed in the United States of America | Third Edition | First Printing | Sage Books are published by | The Swallow Press Incorpo= rated | 1139 South Wabash Avenue | Chicago, Illinois 60605 | This book is printed on 100% recycled paper | *Midas of the Rockies* was first pub= lished by Covici · Friede, | New York, 1937. The Stratton Centennial Edition was | published by the University of Denver Press, Denver, 1949. | The original edition of this book was dedicated to | H. K. Ellingson of the *Colorado Springs Gazette.* | The dedication of the Stratton Centennial Edition | was to David P. Strickler, Trustee and | President of the Myron Stratton Home. | [3 lines of ISBN and Library of Congress catalog data]"; p. 5, contents; p. 6, list of illustrations; pp. 7-11, Introduction by Marshall Sprague; p. 12, blank; pp. 13-19, Foreword; p. 20, blank; pp. 21-330, identical with A3a; pp. 331-341, Afterword; pp. 342-347, Acknowledgments; p. 348, blank.

ILLUSTRATIONS: A number of illustrations were added for this printing. All illustrations are printed on text paper and form integral parts of the gatherings, and so have been given a numbering consistent with the pagination of the book. Normally, each leaf contains two illustrations, but in some cases the verso is blank. These blank pages have been noted below:

p. i, as noted above
pp. ii-iii, as noted above
p. 32a, "Colorado Springs in the early 1870's."
p. 32b, blank
p. 64a, "A Colorado mining camp, Silverton."
p. 64b, "Ore trains on the Ute Pass."
p. 96a, "Pike's Peak (Photo by H. L. Stanley)."
p. 96b, "Colorado Springs in the 1880's."
p. 128a, "Altman, the highest mining camp in Cripple Creek."
p. 128b, blank
p. 160a, "Cripple Creek, with Mt. Pasgah in the background (Courtesy The Denver Public Library | Western Collection. Photo by C. L. McClure."
p. 160b, "Bennett Avenue in Cripple Creek at the height of the boom days."
p. 192a, "Stratton's Independence (center foreground) and Portland (upper right) mines (Courtesy The Denver Public Library Western Collection)."
p. 192b, blank
p. 208a, "The Original Antlers Hotel."
p. 208b, "The second Antlers Hotel (Courtesy Stewart's Commercial Photographers, Colorado Springs)."
p. 220, facsimile of Stratton's receipt, as in A3a
p. 240a, "Cartoonist Steele's view of the struggle over Stratton's bequest | to charity, already a major dispute within two weeks of his | death (from *The Denver Post,* September 28, 1902)."
p. 240b, blank
p. 276a, "The Myron Stratton Home."
p. 276b, "Stratton's room furnishing and clothes, formerly in his quarters at Winfield, now in the | Cripple Creek Museum (Courtesy Stewart's Commercial Photographers, Colorado Springs)."
p. 320a, "Statue of Stratton executed in 1906 by Nellie V. Walker, a | student of Lorado Taft, which was first placed on a bluff in | Stratton Park, then moved to the corners of Nevada and | Pueblo Avenues in Colorado Springs; and now on the grounds | of The Myron Stratton Home."
p. 320b, blank

Published in both cloth and paperback (perfectbound) in May, 1972; cloth copies were published at $6.00 and paper copies at $3.50. 1,000 copies were issued in cloth and 3,998 copies in paper.

COPIES: NmU (cloth); TAT (cloth and paper).

NOTE: Waters' contract with the Swallow Press, dated April 18, 1972, outlined royalties on cloth copies of 10% for the first 3,999 copies, 12½% on the next 3,501 copies, and 15% thereafter; royalties on paper copies were 7½% on the first 4,999 copies and 10% thereafter.

NOTE: The text of the 1937 printing was photo-offset by the Swallow Press for use in this printing. However, the Foreword, Afterword and Acknowledgments were reset for this printing, although using the text of A3b.

A3e   First edition, second Swallow Press printing   [1981]

MIDAS | OF THE ROCKIES | *The Story of Stratton and Cripple Creek* | BY FRANK WATERS | SAGE BOOKS | [publisher's sagebrush device] | SWALLOW PRESS | ATHENS, OHIO · CHICAGO

8⁷⁄₁₆ × 5⅝". Perfectbound: 186 leaves. Pagination identical with A3d.

CONTENTS: Identical with A3d, except for page 2, which carries a listing of 14 titles by Waters, and page 4: "Copyright © 1937, 1949 by Frank Waters | Introduction copyright © 1972 by Marshall Sprague | All rights reserved | Printed in the United States of America | Sage [slash] Swallow Press Books | are published by | Ohio University Press | Athens, Ohio 45701 | Third Edition | First Printing | Reprinted in 1981 by Ohio University Press | *Midas of the Rockies* was first pub= lished by Covici Friede, | New York, 1937. The Stratton Centennial Edition was | published by the University of Denver Press, 1949. | The original edition of this book was dedicated to | H. K. Ellingson of the *Colorado Springs Gazette*. | The dedication of the Stratton Centennial Edition | was to David P. Strickler, Trustee and | President of the Myron Stratton Home. | [two lines ISBN and Library of Congress catalog data]".

Paperback. Published at $9.95 in November, 1981. Number of copies printed unknown.

COPIES: TAT.

A4   BELOW GRASS ROOTS

The manuscript for this work, the second volume in the Pike's Peak trilogy, was completed in April of 1937, and sent by Waters to his agent, David Hampton, for delivery to Liveright. In a letter to Arthur Pell at Liveright on April 22, 1937, Waters wrote:

> I am now glad to be able to answer your letter of almost two months ago by saying that the second book of the Nobility trilogy is finished . . .
>
> There seems to be nothing I can say about it which you cannot ascertain better during your inspection of the ms.
>
> Mechanically it has been cut down to the same length, divided into the corresponding three parts, and carries on the same main and sub-themes laid down in the first book, although it is a complete work in itself.
>
> The outline of the trilogy I have covered in previous letters to Mr. Smith who approved the plan. The Nobility covers the general background of immigration westward to Pike's Peak in 1870; the founding and development of the settlement at its foot into the town of Colorado Springs; the discovery of gold at Cripple Creek and the sudden growth there of the greatest gold camp in the west.
>
> This second book of the trilogy, beginning in 1900, covers the apex of production of the Cripple Creek gold field; the effect of its vast wealth upon Colorado Springs and its transition from a crude pioneering town to a wealthy resort city.
>
> This, as in the first volume, is told through the story of the Rogier family. The second generation is accentuated but not made controlling: to do so would have destroyed the unity of the three books as a whole. For the story is that of the life of one man, the pivot of all action, and the power of whose obsession dominates the lives of all other characters in the book.
>
> The third volume which I have already outlined brings his life to a close—a man who in his own span has lived through three periods of the American West's development: pioneering, transition, and modern. Little London therefore epitomizes the effect of heritage and outside influence on all other such settlements which make up the physical background of our times—and yet is individually portrayed to every fault and virtue to which I have been susceptible throughout my own early twenty years here.

The region has never been exploited "literarily", nor has the human "story" theme to my knowledge ever been attempted. And I am hoping that as the whole plan now unfolds, building upon the recognition of the few critics who saw it for what it is, that its success whatever it is, will justify your faith in the Nobility and overcome its first obviously disappointing reception.

If there are any questions, you will forward them to me? The minor factual material in the Nobility is being used here locally as authentic source material, and I shall be glad to substantiate any material used in this one.

Pell responded on June 2, 1937. In his letter he quoted from a reader's report by T. R. Smith, which underlined the need for the manuscript to be cut, especially in the matter of the mining descriptions. Although Smith recommended against publication as "a great financial risk," Pell accepted the manuscript for publication, saying that he thought it better than *The Wild Earth's Nobility*. He offered Waters an advance of $100.00, with an additional advance of $150.00 to be paid upon completion of the manuscript, which he hoped Waters could revise within the month, for publication in the fall. He also requested that he be allowed to extend their current contract [see p. 11] to include another book after completion of the trilogy.

Waters responded on June 5, 1937:

Thank you for your letter. I have sent word to Hampton's that your plans and a new contract are agreeable to me, and he or Mr. Satz will cooperate with you.

The publication of the trilogy means a great deal to me, and I believe it will justify your faith in it. The statement in the Los Angeles Times review of the Nobility that it "may in time come to be regarded as the best portrayal of that common American phenomenon—the Gold Rush", and Mr. Ellingson's of the Gazette here that it is "one of the finest pioneering novels yet written" express something of the spirit in which I am writing the three books as a unit.

I am attempting to portray the founding and development of a pioneering settlement, with all the factors underlying its growth which today give it the little understood temper of Western America.

And with its background of a gold camp, I want to have in the three volumes every step from its first discovery through the whole process of mining, milling and the effect of its wealth. Not to foist a handbook of mining on the "average intelligent reader" in the guise of fiction, but for once and all to create in authentic fullness a major piece of fiction rooted in the significant milieu of perhaps the greatest gold field in America and one which has never been approached in literature.

Here in Colorado, at least, the first volume has taken hold in the obscure but right way. In Cripple Creek and other libraries I understand the book is being used as a source for authentic material. The Cripple Creek Times-Record refrained from contacting you for permission to serialize it only because of composition costs, and the largest radio station in Denver too considered using it.

Such things of course are not reflected in your sales, but I believe eventually that they will lead to something better than a flashing fancy.

For this reason I do not think it best for the long run to delete all the mining descriptions. Before sending you the manuscript I cut it down from a little over 700 pages to its present 600. However I will be glad to go through it again, tightening up the spots that bother you, paring the narrative wherever possible and cooperating with you fully. . . .

On June 10, 1937, Pell wrote Waters, again stressing the need for cutting the mining descriptions, which, he said, have "burdened three of our readers," and will require more than mere "tightening-up." He requested that Waters prepare a 250 word description of the novel for use as a blurb in their catalogue, and also requested that Waters consider a different title. Waters answered Pell on June 15, 1937:

Thank you for your letter and the extension of the contract which I have signed and returned to Hampton's. I want to assure you that I shall do my very best in cutting the mining descriptions and getting the revisions to you as soon as possible.

Enclosed is the 250 word description, imperfectly expressed but which I hope you can work on.*

I have spent considerable time pondering over titles, but no other seems as peculiarly apt in so many ways as "Below Grass Roots". It seems not only directly expressive of the theme of the book, but consistent with that of "The Wild Earth's Nobility". It is fairly conducive to imagination on the part of the reader, and nothing like it has ever been used before though it is one of the most familiar terms throughout the west. It has designated a period of history, "grass root days"; a type of mining, "grass root bonanzas," and has been used as a "grass root miner", "at the grass roots", "under grass roots" etc. It has been played upon throughout the book, and the three sub-titles derive from it. I am hoping fervently that you agree to retaining it.

A few days later, on June 26, 1937, Waters wrote Pell again:

The carbon copy of Grass Roots is being sent you today, complete and containing all revisions, together with the originals of some twenty rewritten sheets to go in the first copy. The many minor corrections which I have made in ink to save time I hope you will excuse.

In Part One, the first news of Cripple Creek has been rewritten in a lighter, more colorful manner. In Part Three, where most of the mining descriptions occur, the milling process has been greatly simplified, the fire assay has been eliminated entirely, and I have reduced the five-page analysis of the geological theories to the simplest explanation possible to a layman that it is a logical basis

---

*The blurb copy is preserved in carbon at NmU. No copy of the Liveright catalogue has been seen and it is not known whether or not the blurb was used, although it would seem to have been used as the basis for the jacket-blurb.

for Rogier's obsession. The other replacements I hope make for smoother reading.
The very beginning of Part Three I left untouched as it is mostly action and the only description of the mine, as an actual working, in the whole book.
I am hoping that these revisions coincide with your wishes. If not, please be assured of my desire to cooperate with you to the best of my ability.

Pell wrote back to Waters on June 30, 1937, saying that he had received the corrected manuscript and had given it to another reader, and would get back to Waters in a few days. He also told Waters that he had decided to retain the title. On July 6, 1937, Pell sent Waters a copy of the reader's report and asked that Waters once again go over the manuscript "entirely and thoroughly." Waters responded to this reader's report on July 10, 1937:

Your perturbing letter I shall answer as frankly and clearly as I can.
I want to make this last effort to get the book in the best possible shape. You, a publisher, have a necessarily different view of the subject. It is my job as the writer to make my presentation of it coincide with yours, to the end that the result will focus most clearly to the objective reader.
The trouble is not that I cannot see the forest for the trees, or that I am under the egotistical delusion that it could not be changed for the better. It is simply that I do not know what you want.
Mr. Strauss' report I respect and appreciate. Yet it is too self-contradictory and general to be helpful. A book can be short, sharply objective and with a distinctive Spinal column of protruding plot—and thus skeletonized, lack the flesh of life. Or it can be long, wordy, so fat with subjective matter that except to the discerning perspective it is formless. From Mr. Strauss' critical review I am in hopeless confusion over how to "streamline" it (which I understand) without cutting, how to characterize without falling into the short-cut error of caricaturing etc. I feel that all critics, all readers, are unavoidably in the position of a boy who having eaten half a cake pronounces the other half not so satisfying. There is no book written that once read could not be rewritten by each separate reader to suit him better.
In the long "American Tragedy", in the English "Fortunes of Richard Mahoney" and the three volumes of "Jean Cristophe", countless incidents, characters, sub-themes and pages could have been omitted. The stories, as stories, could have been told in a short volume each. And they would have lacked to the long perspective that verisimiltude [sic] and fullness of life which keep them above other tidier tales.
Like theirs, my aim at least has been high: to present for once the West and its period of change divorced from gun-play tradition and historical costuming. Bone's story could be left out as Ona & Jonathan, and other parts could be built up. It is a matter of individual judgment—of dove-tailing each part into the whole; of characterizing by a succession of the seemingly trivial which as in life is transient but enduring; above all, to move the story as swiftly and smoothly as is consistent with the load it is designed to carry.

It is a weakness in any of these things that I hoped Mr. Strauss from his perspective could point out. For if as a whole the thing is sound, then any part erroneously done should stand out and must be corrected.

Otherwise it must be rewritten from start to finish. The handling of each incident must be decided upon again, characterizations built up differently to fit into the whole—and according to a different plan. Obviously this cannot be done now.

Believe me, the book is not formless if you step back a pace. Its "lack of artifice" is a studied answer to those warped, inferior books which pretend to tell effects rather than showing them. And yet it must have many faults.

The book was written twice before sending it to you, of course. It is the best that I could do without some definite idea from you as to how to improve it.

As to how far I will go—any length provided I have an intimation of what is needed. But to stab in the dark is a difficult assignment. It is a long book; as a part of a trilogy it carries forward from the first and foreshadows for the third; the gradual break down of a character like Rogier and the natural absorption of the Cables into the vortex cannot be done in any mere statement; and the style is my natural one for good or bad.

And yet when I receive the manuscript Monday I shall go through it again to look at it as objectively as possible and without overstatement to make it as strong as I can. How much I can do I am not sure. Any further word from you or Mr. Strauss meanwhile I should appreciate. . . .

Pell wrote Waters on July 12, 1937, saying that he had received Waters' thoughtful letter and was asking all readers for another appraisal, with more detailed criticism. On July 28, 1937, Pell sent Waters an eight page condensation of Strauss's reappraisal. Waters responded to this on August 3, 1937:

I have given Mr. Strauss' long criticism considerable study. Instead of certain isolated spots, the book in his opinion requires complete reworking: all characters, scenes, descriptions, on the basis of the general criticism that I have through personal reserve witheld [sic] emotional expression from the characters.

I want to point out, not in argumentative answer but as a justification of my treatment of a set of characters and their setting as an objective novelist, that I attempted to conform my treatment to the subject—the people themselves. In a novel of the Mexican Border, for example, whose characters are violent, spontaneous, uninhibited, my scenes are highly emotional, strongly painted.*
But the Rogiers, aristocratically self-repressed, driven into themselves by false pride and adversity, and more and more betraying in themselves the harsh granite setting above timberline itself—not imagined, for I have lived in those mining camps among their repellent aloofness and taciturnity—required for their treatment a direct reflection of these qualities. For to attain to the utmost

---

*Waters is referring to his novel which was finally published in 1947 as *The Yogi of Cockroach Court*.

unexpressed truth and unity of appeal, the texture of the writing as well as the form must coincide with the substance.

This is the only comment I want to make to Mr. Strauss' report regardless of the many trivial points I could argue. For it is not, of course, a question of arguing, of attempting to uphold one point of view against another. It is a question of making the most good out of a report on which a vast amount of time and thought has been expended, of trying to assimilate the best of a wide experience offered me. It is a good report. I deeply appreciate your time, your work, and I want you to express my thanks to Mr. Strauss.

Now as to how much of it I can follow:

I cannot change my spots and rewrite it completely in a different, more emotional style. Nor can I completely change the organic structure.

But short of a completely rewritten mss. the fuller development of Big Joe, to tie him into the story; the inner struggle of Cable against his atavism to show his frustration and the cause; Ona's fight with her father; and the closer tie-up of Timothy and Prof. Dearson into the theme;—these are excellent points which I think I can do. By cutting down somewhat and replacing with those done in a warmer portrayal, perhaps in a few cases adding a short scene. Plus pointing up the narrative throughout. This reworking seems consistent with the report, short of being entirely rewritten.

I will probably need between two and three weeks if you can let me have that much time. . . .

Pell wrote back to Waters on August 9, 1937, agreeing to most of the suggested changes, but asked to have the corrected manuscript in two weeks at the most, as publication was scheduled for October 6, 1937. The manuscript was sent to the printer on September 3rd, and Waters completed work on the galleys in October. Due to the time problem, page proofs were corrected in the publishing house. On November 3, 1937, Pell wrote that he expected copies of the book in a few days, "which . . . is about record time."

A4 BELOW GRASS ROOTS [1937]

A4   First edition, only printing

BELOW | GRASS | ROOTS | *By* FRANK WATERS | [publisher's device of a man at a writing desk set within a partly shaded semicircle] | *Liveright Publishing Corporation* | NEW YORK

All the above enclosed within a frame of fleuron type ornaments.

7½ × 5⅛". [1-28^8 29^{10} 30-33^8]: 266 leaves. Pp. [i-viii], [1-2] 3-169 [170-172] 173-334 [335-336] 337-523 [524]. Numbers printed in

34 Section A

roman in headline at outer margin of type page, except for pages 3, 173 and 337 on which the numbers are printed in the center at the foot of the page.

Contents: p. i, half-title: "BELOW GRASS ROOTS"; p. ii, blank; p. iii, title; p. iv, copyright notice: "[small caps with a capital] COPYRIGHT, 1937, [small caps] BY [small caps with a capital] FRANK WATERS | [rule] | [three-line notice of reservation of rights] | [small caps with a capital] LIVERIGHT PUBLISHING CORPORATION | PRINTED IN THE UNITED STATES OF AMER= ICA"; p. v, dedication: *"To* | [small caps with a capital] NAOMI"; p. vi, quotation: "The subterranean miner that works in us all, how | can one tell whither leads his shaft by the ever shifting, | muffled sound of his pick? | [small caps with a capital] HERMAN MELVILLE"; p. vii, contents; p. viii, blank; p. 1, divisional half-title: "BOOK ONE | GRANITE"; p. 2, blank; pp. 3-169, text; p. 170, blank; p. 171, divisional half-title: "BOOK TWO | ADOBE"; p. 172, blank; pp. 173-334, text; p. 335, divisional half-title: "BOOK THREE | SYLVANITE"; p. 336, blank; pp. 337-523, text; p. 524, blank.

Binding: Grass-green cloth. Liveright device (as on title) stamped in blind in center of front cover. Spine: "[four lines embossed in cloth color within a gilt stamped panel, within gilt single rules] BELOW | GRASS | ROOTS | WATERS | [stamped in gilt near bottom] LIVERIGHT". Top edges stained green; fore and bottom edges untrimmed. White endpapers.

Dust Jacket (white paper): Front and spine printed overall in brown and with an illustration of a man, from the chest up, in brown, yellow, green and gray. At the top of the front and spine there is a band within which is an illustration of a town in green, yellow, brown and gray. Lettered on front: "[three lines in yellow] BELOW | GRASS | ROOTS | [next two lines in white] *A New Novel By* | FRANK WA= TERS"; Spine: "[three lines in yellow] BELOW | GRASS | ROOTS | [next two lines in white] FRANK WATERS | LIVERIGHT". The rear contains an advertisement, printed in brown, for the "Black and Gold Library," listing 11 titles. The front flap carries a blurb for this book; the rear flap carries a blurb for *The Wild Earth's Nobility*.

Published at $2.50. Exact date of publication and number of copies printed unknown. Copyrighted November 15, 1937; deposited December 18, 1937. Advertised in *Publisher's Weekly* on September 18, 1937, for publication on October 13, 1937. Listed in the "Weekly Record" of *Publisher's Weekly* on November 20, 1937.

REVIEWS: *New York Herald Tribune Books,* November 21, 1937 (p. 10); *New York Times Book Review,* November 28, 1937 (p. 7).

COPIES: DLC (2 copies); NmU (inscribed by Waters on the dedication page: "This, her book. Brother"); TAT (d.j.).

A5 THE DUST WITHIN THE ROCK

Shortly after the publication of *Below Grass Roots,* the second volume of Waters' Pike's Peak trilogy, Arthur Pell of Liveright wrote regarding the book's reception. In his letter of December 15, 1937, Pell told Waters that while the book's sales were disappointing, he had not given up and was anxious to see the final volume of the trilogy. Waters wrote to Pell on December 22, 1937:

. . . I appreciate your having any interest in the third volume.
   This as I see it now, will be the test of the trilogy as a whole. To gather all threads; to maintain its unity despite a change in the pivot of action due to Rogier's insanity; to lend it a meaning beyond the running narrative of a family; to make an end—these are the points which must justify its having been attempted, and I am not minimizing their difficulty or their importance. But with the peak of the Cripple Creek production reached and the beginning of the district's decline, and with the town's historical portion done, there should be no reason for the inclusion of more statistical facts which both your readers and the critics you mentioned objected to. The third volume will depend purely on human reactions, on the outgrowth of character from causes already given, and the narrative skill rendering them upon which in the end every work must depend—beyond and above its secondary informative value as a substantial record of a significant time and place. It is with such an aim in mind, and in such a spirit, that I view the task of completing the last of the trilogy. If there are any other points which you or your staff wish to make at any time, please be assured that I will welcome your frankness as fully as in the past. . . .

On May 5, 1939, Pell wrote Waters acknowledging receipt of the manuscript of the final volume of the trilogy. He wrote Waters again on May 12, 1939, quoting excerpts from two readers' reports on the manuscript, which essentially restated criticisms of the earlier novels. He suggested to Waters that the cutting be done by someone other than Waters, at Liveright's expense. At the end of the letter he asked that Waters extend their contract of January 15, 1935 [see p. 11], but with the addition of another option on a later book; the advance would be $100.00 upon acceptance of the contract and an additional $150.00 when the manuscript for *Dust* was ready for printing.

Waters responded to Pell on May 20, 1939:

> The intent of this letter I hope will not seem as impertinent as it may at first sound; and the enclosed thematic outline of the trilogy may give you a clearer conception of this job to which I have given at least five full years of work—to approximately no end at all.
>
> T. R. Smith's report is dumfounding [sic]. His comments after reading the first volume of the trilogy was one of my greatest encouragements. After reading the second volume he stated that "it is extremely well written" . . . . and that "Someday, this work of Waters will be considered an outstanding piece of Americana." Now he states of all three that "it is interminably overwritten"—a sudden change of opinion that is unaccountable.
>
> Apparently it is based upon a dislike to this third volume for "entering into infinite detail upon mining technique and the people concerned therewith", which is completely erroneous as you know. But what if it did, as the other two which he approved nevertheless? Is mining a taboo literary background? Every other phase of life has been a literary fad, as today we are flooded with fictionalized technicalities of the medical profession and reassured by their authority. Or must we wait until mining comes into fictional favor?
>
> This trilogy is the first major work covering a mining background, and with a thoroughness that will not be duplicated for a long time, and never by a casual popular novelist in the romantic sense. Prospecting, mining, milling: it has been the motivation for the opening of all Western America, and here it is presented as one huge allegory for those who see. Mr. Smith is one who doesn't, and so I have no answer but to ignore his blindness, for I am not concerned with fads in literature nor can I write fast enough to keep up with changing opinion.
>
> Perhaps, I think, it is not a novel in the common accepted form. But it has its validity in its own.
>
> So I can endure the criticisms of its "sprawliness", its "unforced attack", its many minor defects. But for the condemnation, the damning faint praise of certain superficial New York literary "critics" who have never been west of the Alleghenies, are conditioned by current book-forms, literary names and the amount of advertising given their journals, I care nothing—even though they be bell-wethers of a flock blinder than they.
>
> Others besides Smith, students of the West and accredited workers in its medium, have written me calling it a classic of the West. Are they, even in their extravagance, less competent to judge than the mere cursory big-paper reviewers who neither know its material nor the real literary values they prattle of so unknowingly?
>
> Mr. [T. O'Conor] Sloane has perceived and stated exactly one of its aims: "to portray, to study the characters. . . . , to evaluate them in the light of their environment." And that environment is all the vast gangue of new, unknown America whose own continent-culture is just breaking through the soil—and which as yet is seen by so precious and few eyes—but seen.
>
> So that in addition to its narrative vehicle it contains a complete analysis of a

town's growth and temper; a panorama of the West in all its aspects; and a continual play of racial values. These are doubless [sic] the parts which tend at times to slow the speed of the narrative—though this would be minimized if some of them, as the four Winter, Summer etc. passages be set in italics—but they have their place in the three books as one unit, if it be other than a mere narrative of action.

While I have confidence in Mr. Sloane's cutting ability, I think that in all fairness to the whole trilogy of which this is the most important part, I should be given the final option of deciding whether the deletions specified by you would take the teeth out of what I have tried to say behind and above the story narrative itself.

I appreciate your concern that my writing be the best. In return I should like to have you accept these observations likewise for what they may be worth. . . .

. . . having spent five years on this work, I cannot face with equanimity the prospect of giving you still two more books without seeing how the trilogy fares now that it is completed and can be presented as a whole, with the strength of the others behind it. Nor can I see from your standpoint why, after having published three of mine already at no profit and to the extent of some 700 copies each, and with two more in view, you want to string along still further with a dead horse.

I feel a break is due us both, but that it cannot come without a clearer understanding of everything involved. . . .

Pell wrote back on May 26, 1939, agreeing that Waters would have the right to consent to all suggested cuts, and that he wanted the two option books because, while there had been no profit in the earlier books, he still had hopes for his work. On June 22, 1939, Pell sent Waters an eleven page list of suggested cuts for the manuscript. To these suggestions Waters responded on June 27, 1939:

I have gone over Mr. Sloane's suggested cuts. Unlike Mr. Strauss' comments on *Grass Roots,* they are concise, consistent, and reveal a very clear conception of the book as a whole. There is no confusion of his objective and his approach to it: a novel that stands completely alone and self-reliant, a swiftly flowing narrative unimpeded by any observations apart from those deduced from the interplay of the characters and situations themselves, and stripped of all direct references to the two preceding volumes.

That my own approach contradicts his does not imply that either is invalid, but simply that they differ in their long range view.

I still see the trilogy as an unbroken whole, and each discursive passage as relating it to the greater whole of the time and place it tries to interpret.

For this reason I cannot agree with him on some of his suggested deletions. After the first two volumes established and developed the legend of the Kadles, it does not seem consistent to drop it in the third, completely. The disappearance of Tom, the characters of Professor Dearson, the two Zeitlins and old Rawlings—all these require at least a minimized but direct reference to make an end, rather than to leave them dangling in the middle of the trilogy.

Passages on such subjects as mythology were put in to relate consciously the American myth of the West to its time, for the life portrayed in this book is already taking its place as the myth of America. The four passages relating to the four seasons are intended devices to relate the spotlighted setting to the vast Western half of the continent of which it is a part—a lifting of the eyes beyond the geographical boundaries of the book's primary setting.

The aim of it all has been not to present the people and place alone as a bounded unity which only implies its relationship to a greater whole, but to continually present it as an integrated part.

What I would like to do is to reduce such parts as these somewhat, bearing in mind Mr. Sloane's desire for a swift and smooth narrative, but not to eliminate them entirely. His other suggestions can be followed. . . .

A5   THE DUST WITHIN THE ROCK   [1940]

A5   First edition, only printing

[open face] THE DUST | [open face] WITHIN | [open face] THE ROCK | By | FRANK WATERS | [publisher's device of a man sitting at a writing desk, set within a partly shaded semicircle, just below which is a black panel lettered in white: "LIVERIGHT"] | LIVERIGHT PUBLISHING CORPORATION | NEW YORK

All of the above enclosed within intertwined double spiral rules, with asterisk ornaments at each corner.

$7\frac{7}{16}$ × $5\frac{1}{8}$". [1-34^8]: 272 leaves. Pp. [i-x], [1-2] 3-149 [150-152] 153-337 [338-340] 341-534. Numbers printed in roman in headline at outer margin of type page, except for those on pages 3, 153, and 341, on which the numbers are printed in the center at the foot of the page.

CONTENTS: p. i, half-title: "THE DUST WITHIN THE ROCK"; p. ii, blank; p. iii, title; p. iv, copyright notice: "[small caps with a capital] COPYRIGHT, 1940, [small caps] BY [small caps with a capital] FRANK WATERS | [five-line notice of reservation of rights] | PRINTED IN THE UNITED STATES OF AMERICA"; p. v, dedication: "TO THE MEMORY OF | MY FATHER"; p. vi, blank; p. vii, ten-line quotation, printed in italic, credited at bottom: "[small caps with a capital] ORE DRESSING: PRINCIPLES AND PRACTICE"; p. viii: "[two lines within quotation marks] I have graven it within the hills, and my | vengeance upon the dust within the rock."; p. ix, con-

SECTION A

tents; p. x, blank; p. 1, divisional half-title: "BOOK ONE | CONCEN= TRATE"; p. 2, blank; pp. 3-149, text; p. 150, blank; p. 151, divisional half-title: "BOOK TWO | TAILINGS"; p. 152, blank; pp. 153-337, text; p. 338, blank; p. 339, divisional half-title: "BOOK THREE | SILVER"; p. 340, blank; pp. 341-534, text.

BINDING: Blue cloth. Front stamped in gilt at upper right: "[all within a frame of single rule sides and wavy rule at top and bottom] The Dust | Within | the Rock". Spine stamped in gilt: "[three lines within a frame of single rule sides and wavy rule at top and bottom] The Dust | Within | the Rock | [below frame] WATERS | [publisher's device of a man at a writing desk within a partly shaded semi-circle] | LIVERIGHT". Top edges stained purple; fore and bottom edges untrimmed. Cream-colored endpapers.

DUST JACKET (brown paper): Lettered on front: "[orange] The Dust | [thick blue rule] | [orange] Within | [thick blue rule] | [orange] the | [thick blue rule] | [orange] Rock | [thick blue rule] | [two lines within a blue panel outlined at sides with wavy orange rules] [orange] A NEW NOVEL BY | [orange] Frank Waters". Spine: "[three lines within a blue panel outlined at top and bottom with an orange wavy rule] [three lines in orange] The Dust | Within | the Rock | [below panel] [orange] FRANK | [orange] WATERS | [publisher's device as on title page, in blue, with the publisher's name in jacket color within a blue panel]". The rear contains an advertisement for "The Black & Gold Library," listing three titles. The front flap carries a blurb for this book; the rear flap carries a blurb for *Below Grass Roots*.

Published at $2.50. Exact date of publication and number of copies printed unknown. Copyrighted January 19, 1940; deposited February 10, 1940. Although not published until sometime in January of 1940, printing of the book was completed in October, 1939; the author's copies were mailed from New York on October 27, 1939. The book was listed in the "Weekly Record" of *Publisher's Weekly* on January 20, 1940.

REVIEWS: *Saturday Review of Literature*, January 20, 1940 (p. 19); *Boston Transcript*, January 20, 1940 (p. 1); *New York Herald Tribune Books*, January 21, 1940 (p. 4); *New York Times Book Review*, January 28, 1940 (p. 7); *New Republic*, February 5, 1940 (p. 190).

COPIES: DLC (2 copies); NmU (inscribed by Waters to his sister: "Naomi—This last of the Rogiers, of the Kadles and compound gravy, Frank"); TAT (2 copies, one in d.j.); FW.

NOTE: Excerpts from this work were published as "Four Sketches" in *Laughing Horse,* in December, 1939 (see C5).

A6 PEOPLE OF THE VALLEY

In the winter of 1940, Waters travelled to New York with Tony Luhan, carrying with him the manuscript for his recently completed novel "Dam in the Mountains." He brought the manuscript to New York intending to deliver it to Arthur Pell at Liveright, who still held an option on his next two books. Not entirely pleased with his association with Liveright, however, he showed the manuscript to John Farrar, to whom he had been introduced by the novelist Myron Brinig. After he left New York, Waters received a telegram from Farrar on March 9, 1940, informing him that Farrar thought it to be his best book and inquiring how to proceed.

Knowing of Waters' position with Liveright, Farrar & Rinehart undertook negotiations with the Liveright firm for release of their option on Waters' next books. In a letter dated April 8, 1940, Stanley M. Rinehart, Jr. informed Waters that an agreement had been reached with Arthur Pell wherein Liveright would release the two books on option for a payment of $1,000.00. Although not a requirement of the deal, Pell also offered to sell the "plates" for the previous books published by Liveright at $250.00 per set, which offer was turned down by Farrar & Rinehart because they felt the price was too high. In his letter to Waters, Rinehart said that while they very much wanted to publish "Dam," the expense of purchasing the rights from Liveright made it difficult. He suggested, however, that if they could charge off the money against Waters' next two books—$500.00 against "Dam" and $500.00 against a book to follow—they would agree to the terms. In order that Waters might be able to quickly recover the amount charged against him, Rinehart said that the firm would pay a straight royalty on both books of 15%.

Waters agreed to these terms, asking only that in order for him to live, they also allow an additional advance of $250.00. Farrar &

People of the Valley 43

Rinehart agreed to this and a contract incorporating these terms was drawn up.

On May 22, 1940, John Farrar wrote to Waters and enclosed a reader's report on the novel by Stephen Vincent Benét—recommending publication—and informed Waters that he wanted to schedule the novel for publication in January of 1941, in order to have sufficient time for advertising and promotion. He also mentioned that the sales department did not like the title of the book.

Waters responded to Farrar on May 31, 1940:

> January for publication date of the Dam sounds all right—you're the one who knows best. But I can't think of any title more apt to the subject matter and theme. After all, everything—situation, character and underlying allegory, revolves about the dam; and perhaps when your sales department realizes this later they will not only remove their objections, but find it easier to put over.
>
> For the same reason I can't fall in with some of Mr. Benet's criticisms. It is not merely a conflict between two groups of people over a shifting ownership of land made necessary by the advent of a dam. It is a fundamental racial difference between two peoples—one whose life and faith stems directly from the land, despite their thin overlaying topsoil of superficial Christianity. Anyone who knows the Mexican-Indian realizes this is the basis of Mexico's revolutionary and agrarian reforms for the last twenty-five years. And this small isolated valley penetrated by Anglo-cized progress is a Mexico in miniature, a conflict of racial faiths.
>
> To one who does not know Mexican-Indians the "philosophizing" may indeed sound phony; it is not an Anglo concept. But it is an expression of the other, and in this story from their viewpoint it must be taken if it be more than a relating of their then inconsequential surface action.
>
> I am now going over the manuscript again, and will have a few changes. The great length of time covered and the extreme condensation makes necessary the selection of a pivotal incident to focus years of Maria's life. This seeming abruptness of time change is offset by rapid focusing and conciseness; and in the larger rhythm of the whole smooths out better than inconsequential bridging. . . .

On June 21, 1940, Waters wrote again to John Farrar:

> I am sending along the original copy of the Dam, complete with revisions.
>
> The short section P 112-115 is omitted as the only out-of-the-valley scene in the book, which has now an unbroken geographical unity. The necessary material in it has been moved forward to P 151a.
>
> Various pages marked R (replacing) have been rewritten, such as P 211 and P 211a, which intimates the move to another valley, one of Mr. Benet's suggestions.
>
> Some corrections and changes in ink have been made also, which should give you no trouble.
>
> I visualize Maria so clearly that I have drawn a charcoal portrait of her,

although I am no drawer, and am sending along a photograph of it in case you happen to want to use it on the end-papers or otherwise.

Despite the oppressive war news filtering through the pines, the corn comes up boldly through the reddish fields, the trout streams pour full and noisily down the canons, and I am shoe-deep, but with both feet, into a new novel. . . .

Still unhappy about the title, Farrar & Rinehart finally settled upon *People of the Valley,* to which Waters finally agreed.

A6   PEOPLE OF THE VALLEY [1941]

A6a   First edition, first printing

[open face] PEOPLE OF | [open face] THE VALLEY | by | FRANK WATERS | [small caps with a capital] FARRAR & RINE= HART, INC. | NEW YORK [space] TORONTO

8⅛ × 5½". [1-20⁸]: 160 leaves. Pp. [i-vi], [1-2] 3-309 [310-314]. Numbers printed in roman in headline at outer margin of type page, except for pages 3, 25, 46, 69, 103, 132, 176, 208 and 272 on which the numbers are printed in the center at the foot of the page.

CONTENTS: p. i, half-title: "PEOPLE OF THE VALLEY"; p. ii, "[small caps with a capital] BOOKS [small caps] BY [small caps with a capital] FRANK WATERS | [list of 5 titles, including this book]"; p. iii, title; p. iv, copyright notice: "[publisher's device of an 'F' in white and an 'R' in black within a fancy black and white floral oval] | COPYRIGHT, 1941, BY FRANK WATERS | PRINTED IN THE UNITED STATES OF AMERICA | BY J. J. LITTLE AND IVES COMPANY, NEW YORK | ALL RIGHTS RESERVED"; p. v, dedication: "TO THE PEOPLE OF THE BEAUTIFUL BLUE | VALLEY, AND TO THOSE WHO HAVE LOVED IT: | GENTE MUY RETIRADO, MUY CERRADO— | AMIGOS BIEN RECOR= DADO, MUY CARIÑOSA."; p. vi, blank; p. 1, second half-title; p. 2, blank; pp. 3-309, text; pp. 310-314, blank.

BINDING: Oatmeal colored cloth. Lettered on front in red: "[title within blind-stamped single rules] PEOPLE OF THE | VALLEY | [near bottom] FRANK WATERS". Spine lettered in red: "[double

rules] PEOPLE | OF THE | VALLEY | [short rule] | FRANK | WA=
TERS | [double rules] | FARRAR & | RINEHART". Top edges stained
purple; fore and bottom edges untrimmed. Cream-colored endpapers.

DUST JACKET (white paper): Front and spine printed overall with an
illustration of an adobe house in the lower left with a tree in the front
and with three goats in the foreground, set against a mountain range in
the background; in tan, blue, purple, green and white. Illustration
signed on the front in lower right in script: "Syd Browne". Lettered on
front: "[first two lines calligraphic, in purple] People | of the Valley |
[red] FRANK WATERS". Spine: "[first three lines calligraphic, in
green] People | of the | Valley | [red] WATERS | [green] FAR=
RAR & | [green] RINEHART". Rear: "[photograph of the author,
tinted in blue] | [red] FRANK WATERS | [three paragraph notice of
the author, printed in blue] | [double rules in red] | [blue] FAR=
RAR & RINEHART, INC. | [blue] New York [space] Toronto".
Front flap contains a blurb for this book, carried over onto the rear flap,
printed in red and blue; publisher's imprint appears at the bottom of
both the front and rear flaps.

Published at $2.50 on February 6, 1941. Number of copies printed unknown. Copyrighted February 6, 1941; deposited December 23, 1940.

REVIEWS: *Library Journal,* January 15, 1941 (p. 80); *New Yorker,* February 8, 1941 (p. 65); *New York Times Book Review,* February 9, 1941 (p. 6); *New York Herald Tribune Books,* February 9, 1941 (p. 8); *Booklist,* February 15, 1941 (p. 271); *Boston Transcript,* March 15, 1941 (p. 2); *New Republic,* March 17, 1941 (p. 382); *Saturday Review of Literature,* May 17, 1941 (p. 8).

COPIES: DLC (2 copies); NmU (d.j.); FW (d.j.); TAT (d.j.).

NOTE: At least one copy was specially bound in full blue hard-grain morocco, all edges gilt, and with five raised bands on spine. This copy was presented to Waters by the publisher and is currently in the private collection of Frank Waters.

NOTE: This work was published in braille by the New Mexico State Library in 1967. A "Transcription for the Blind" was prepared by the Library of Congress in 1970.

46 SECTION A

NOTE: Although the number of copies printed is unknown, a probable estimate can be made on the basis of certain evidence. The first statement of account issued by Farrar & Rinehart for *People*, dated October 22, 1941, showed total advances to the author of $750.00 plus $22.87 additional charges for editing the manuscript and the author's excess alterations. This statement showed sales of 1,500 regular copies, Canadian sales of 80 copies, other foreign sales of 10 copies and 541 copies distributed free of charge, for a total of 2,135 copies sold or given away. The next statement, dated April 21, 1942, showed regular sales of 49 copies, foreign sales of 2 copies, and 5 copies distributed free of charge. This statement also showed returns of 110 copies. This left an unearned balance against the book of $202.74, with total sales amounting to 2,071 copies, including copies distributed free. On March 30, 1948, Stanley Rinehart reported to Waters that there was an outstanding debit of $47.88 against both *People* and *Deer* (since both books had been negotiated for as a unit). However, at this time there were no copies of either book remaining in stock. *Deer* had been reported as sold out on a statement of April 28, 1947, and against which the $47.88 was charged. By the time *People* had been completely sold out it had recovered for Waters his debit of $772.87; hence it would seem that at least 2,000 copies had been sold at the regular royalty rate. In addition there were reported sales of 92 copies at lower rates and 546 copies given away free. It would seem safe to assume therefore that somewhat more than 2,638 copies were printed, most likely 3,000 copies.

A6b   First edition, Alan Swallow printing   [1962]

[open face] PEOPLE OF | [open face] THE VALLEY | by | FRANK WATERS | [publisher's sagebrush device] | S A G E B O O K S, *Denver*

8 × 5⅜". [1-10^{16}]: 160 leaves. Pagination identical with A6a.

CONTENTS: Identical with A6a, except for p. ii, which is blank; p. iv: "Sage Books are published by | Alan Swallow, 2679 So. York, Denver 10, Colo. | COPYRIGHT, 1941, BY FRANK WATERS | PRINTED IN THE UNITED STATES OF AMERICA"; and p. v, on which the final two lines of the dedication have been altered: " . . . | Gente muy re= mota, muy cerrada— | Amigos bien recordados, muy carinosos.".

Issued simultaneously in both cloth and paperback (perfectbound) in 1962; published at $3.50 for cloth copies and $1.85 for paper copies. Number of copies printed unknown.

COPIES: TAT (2 cloth copies; 1 paper).

NOTE: Waters' contract with Alan Swallow, dated December 29, 1961, outlined royalties of 10% on cloth copies and 7½% on paper copies.

NOTE: From what information is available it is impossible to determine how many printings of *People* Alan Swallow did. Inventory records taken at the end of 1964 show 79 cloth copies and 75 paper copies on hand; records for 1965 show 460 cloth copies and 294 paper copies on hand. However, in reference to the cloth copies there is a note on the 1965 inventory which says "(draw on EB)," which is certainly a reference to Edwards Brothers in Ann Arbor, Michigan, who printed the book for Swallow and were undoubtedly storing copies for him. It would seem that copies stored at Ann Arbor were not listed in Swallow's annual inventories. The inventory taken after Swallow's death in 1966, shows 755 cloth copies and 591 paper copies on hand. Based upon the fragmentary royalty records which I have seen, I think it likely that Swallow did only one printing of this book.

NOTE: A number of changes were made in this printing, mostly reflecting the spelling of Spanish words. These changes were made in a different typeface than that of the rest of the book and are immediately apparent to the eye:

v.2,3:	GENTE MUY RETIRADO, MUY CERRADO— | AMIGOS BIEN RECORDADO, MUY CARIÑOSA.	Gente muy remota, muy cerrada— | Amigos bien recordados, muy carinosos.
3.15:	Cristos	Cristo
4.4:	Rio la	Rio de la
5.5:	las Herreras	los Herreras
16.1:	las Herreras	los Herreras
16.23:	San Gertrudes	Santa Gertrudes
17.14:	San Gertrudes	Santa Gertrudes
17.23:	San Gertrudes	Santa Gertrudes
18.8:	San Gertrudes	Santa Gertrudes
19.26:	San Gertrudes	Santa Gertrudes

48 SECTION A

23.9:	mio	mia
27.4:	Valle de San Gertrudes	Valle de Santa Gertrudes
47.17:	San Ger-	Santa Ger-
54.19:	San Gertrudes	Santa Gertrudes
71.16:	San Gertrudes	Santa Gertrudes
76.5:	San Gertrudes	Santa Gertrudes
77.16:	San Gertrudes	Santa Gertrudes
76.6:	luminarios	luminarias
86.6:	Cristos	Cristo
93.1:	San Gertrudes	Santa Gertrudes
94.6:	de Bautismo	Bautista
108.14:	Quelitas	Quelites
120.4:	Cristos	Cristo
154.16:	San Gertrudes	Santa Gertrudes
167.20:	San Gertrudes	Santa Gertrudes
171.15:	San Gertrudes	Santa Gertrudes
189.4:	compradre!	compadre!
192.2:	chile arribe	chile carribe
211.1:	las	los
225.6:	Mondregon!	Mondragon!
227.3:	Brava, Senora! Brava,	Bravo, Senora! Bravo,
230.1:	San Gertrudes	Santa Gertrudes
230.5:	Cristos	Cristo
255.14:	San Gertrudes	Santa Gertrudes
262.11:	Romeros	Romero
284.23:	Romeros	Romero
285.18:	Romeros	Romero

Two corrections which in light of the above should have been made were not: 187.10 "San Gertrudes", and 210.26 "San Gertrudes".

A6c   First edition, first Swallow Press printing   [1969]

[open face] PEOPLE OF | [open face] THE VALLEY | by | FRANK WATERS | [publisher's sagebrush device] | SAGE BOOKS, *Chicago*

8 × 5⁵⁄₁₆". Perfectbound: 160 leaves. Pagination identical with A6b.

CONTENTS: Identical with A6b, except for page iv: "Sage Books are published by | [small caps] THE [caps] SWALLOW PRESS [small

caps] INC. | 1139 So. Wabash Ave., Chicago, Ill. 60605 | © COPY=
RIGHT, 1941, BY FRANK WATERS | PRINTED IN THE UNITED
STATES OF AMERICA"; and page v, on which the last two lines of
the dedication have been reset, with the "G" in the first word of the
third line printed directly below the "V" in the first word of the second
line.

Paperback. Published at $2.50 in February, 1969. 3,000 copies were printed.

COPIES: NmU; TAT.

NOTE: The opening inventory of the Swallow Press recorded 270 paperbound copies received from the Estate of Alan Swallow. However, Swallow Press royalty records show that 523 copies in paper were sold or given away from August, 1967 to August, 1968; and the inventory taken on July 31, 1968, recorded 399 paperbound copies in stock. Although this data would seem to show that the Swallow Press did a printing of *People* sometime after August, 1967 and before February, 1969, I can find no other evidence of such a printing. Given the fact that Alan Swallow stored copies with his printer in Ann Arbor, it is more likely that these figures represent copies transfered to Chicago after August, 1967.

A6d   First edition, second Swallow Press printing   [1970]

Identical with A6c, except that the dedication on page v has again been reset, this time being completely reset with all four lines in uniform full capitals.

Paperback. Published at $2.50 in September, 1970. 3,116 copies were printed.

COPIES: TAT.

A6e   Second edition, first printing   [1971]

[open face] PEOPLE OF | [open face] THE VALLEY | FRANK WATERS | [publisher's swallow device] | [small caps] THE [caps] SWALLOW PRESS [small caps] INC. | CHICAGO

8½ × 5½". [1¹⁶ 2⁸ 3-7¹⁶]: 104 leaves. Pp. [i-vi], [1-3] 4-17 [18] 19-31 [32] 33-46 [47] 48-68 [69] 70-87 [88] 89-115 [116] 117-136 [137] 138-155 [156] 157-177 [178] 179-201 [202]. Pages vi, 2, and 202 are blank.

COPYRIGHT PAGE: "Copyright © 1941, 1969, by Frank Waters | All rights reserved | Printed in the United States of America | Sage Books are published by | The Swallow Press Incorporated | 1139 South Wabash Avenue | Chicago, Illinois 60605 | This book is printed on 100% recycled paper. | ISBN (clothbound edition) 0-8040-0242-8 | ISBN (pa= perbound edition) 0-8040-0234-6 | Library of Congress Catalog Card Number 78-137435".

Published in both cloth and paperback (perfectbound). Published at $6.00 for cloth copies and $2.50 for paper copies. 3,020 paperback copies were received by the publisher in November, 1971; 1,168 cloth copies were received in January, 1972.

COPIES: TAT (cloth and paper); Swallow Press (cloth).

NOTE: On January 6, 1972, the Swallow Press forwarded copies of this new edition to Waters. However, the cover letter [at NmU] is misdated "1971," and Waters' letter acknowledging receipt of the copies [ICIU] is also misdated "January 13, 1971."

A6f   Second edition, second Swallow Press printing   [1973]

Identical with A6e, except that copies measure 8½ × 5⁷⁄₁₆", and the cover price was changed to $2.95.

Paperback. Published at $2.95 in June, 1973; 3,975 copies were printed.

COPIES: TAT.

A6g   Second edition, third Swallow Press printing   [1976?]

Title page identical with A6e.

8¼ × 5¼". Perfectbound: 104 leaves. Pp. [i-iv], [1-3], 4-17 [18] 19-31 [32] 33-46 [47] 48-68 [69] 70-87 [88] 89-115 [116] 117-136 [137] 138-155 [156] 157-177 [178] 179-201 [202-204]. Pages 2 and 202-204 are blank.

CONTENTS: Identical with A6e, except that the second half-title found in A6e (p. v; verso blank) has been deleted in this printing, and an extra blank leaf appears at the end.

Paperback. Published at $2.95. Date of publication and number of copies printed unknown, although incomplete records of the Swallow Press seem to indicate publication sometime in 1976.

COPIES: TAT.

A6h   Second edition, fourth Swallow Press printing

Title page identical with A6e.

8³⁄₁₆ × 5¼". Perfectbound: 108 leaves. Pagination identical with A6g, except there are four extra blank leaves at the end—pages [205-212].

CONTENTS: Identical with A6g, except for page iv: "Copyright © 1941, 1969, by Frank Waters | All rights reserved | Printed in the United States of America | Sage Books are published by | The Swallow Press Incorporated | 811 West Junior Terrace | Chicago, Illinois 60613 | [three lines ISBN and Library of Congress catalog data, as in A6e]".

Paperback. Date of publication and number of copies printed unknown, but printed after the firm moved to Junior Terrace, late in 1976. No price is printed on the covers.

COPIES: TAT; Swallow Press.

EXCERPTS FROM *People*

A6i   *Santa Fe & Taos: The Writer's Era 1916-1941,* by Marta Weigle and Kyle Fiore. (Santa Fe, Ancient City Press, 1982). Page 84.

A7   RIVER LADY

According to an entry in his journal for March 21, 1941, Waters was approached by David Diamond, literary agent for Houston Branch, who asked if he would be willing to expand Branch's short story "River Lady" into a novel. Diamond told Waters that he had been recommended for the job by John Farrar, of Farrar & Rinehart, who had published *People of the Valley*. Originally Branch had intended for Waters to ghost write the novel for a set fee, but Waters agreed to do the novel only if it was published under both their names and all royalties were split equally. Branch finally agreed to this, and in a letter to Branch on May 22, 1941 [FW], Waters formally outlined their agreement:

> This letter will serve as an agreement between you and me, in regard to my novelizing your original story, "River Lady." Your agent, David Diamond, and my agent, Rosalie Stewart, shall have copies of same.
> My understanding is as follows:
> 1. I agree to novelize your eighty page (approximately) original story now titled "RIVER LADY" and for this work you agree to pay me $1,000.00; payable at the rate of $200.00 per month for five months. The first payment of $200.00 is hereby acknowledged. It is understood that this $1,000.00 is to be considered a definite fee and not an advance royalty, and is to forever remain my property. Failure to pay the $200.00 each month until the $1,000.00 is fully paid will be considered a breach of faith and I, at my election, may terminate the work and this agreement.
> 2. I understand you have signed an agreement with Farrar and Rinehart, publisher, whereby they agree to publish "RIVER LADY" before the end of 1942, and it is hereby understood and agreed by both of us that the royalties derived from the sale of this novel are to be divided equally between us; 50% to you and 50% to me. The work is to be entered for copyright at Washington in both our names, substantially the same as the title page of the novel: "RIVER LADY," by Houston Branch and Frank Waters.

3. In the event of the sale of the novel for serialization in any one of the leading magazines or periodicals, it is understood and agreed that we are to divide the returns equally, 50% to you and 50% to me. David Diamond is to act as agent for the sale of the novel for magazine serialization and he shall receive 10% of the gross amount in the event of sale. However, it is also understood and agreed that David Diamond is not to receive any commission on my royalty through the sale of the novel published by Farrar and Rinehart.

4. If I have to re-write and re-vamp the novel for serialization in the magazines, at their request, before a sale can be consummated, you agree to pay me 25% (¼) of your 50% return on these serial rights. In order to define this: Let us say that I shall not be entitled to any additional payment if it merely entails cutting parts of the novel to fit the serialization requirements, but it is understood that if I have to spend two weeks or more of my time on the creation of new material or developing or building up certain parts of the novel for serialization, I agree to do so, then, and in that event, I am to receive the extra compensation from you for this extra work.

5. I hereby acknowledge that I am acquainted with the fact that you have sold the motion picture rights of "RIVER LADY" to Frank Lloyd and that I shall not participate in any monies derived from that sale. However, you and your agent, David Diamond, agree to use your best efforts to persuade Frank Lloyd to give me screen credit as co-author of the novel.

6. You and David Diamond agree that Farrar and Rinehart will be instructed to change the clause in the existing publication contract already drawn and signed between you and Farrar and Rinehart so that it specifies that all monies due me from the royalties on the sale of the book are to be paid to me direct by Farrar and Rinehart and not as specified in the contract. A copy of that contract is to be given me for my files.

If this is in accordance with your agreement and understanding kindly indicate by signing in the space herein below provided.

A copy of this agreement is in the author's personal files and is signed by all parties named. Although the contract with Farrar and Rinehart was presumably sent to Waters, he was unable to locate a copy in his files, and the terms of the contract are unknown.

Waters recorded in his journal on October 31, 1941, that he had completed work on the manuscript of *River Lady:* "438 pages, about 115,000 words in 4 months. I feel as if a ten-story building had been removed from my shoulders."

A7 RIVER LADY [1942]

A7a First edition, first printing

[script] River Lady | *By HOUSTON BRANCH* | *and* | *FRANK WA=*

54   SECTION A

TERS | [script] Farrar & Rinehart, Inc. | [script] New York [space] Toronto
All of the above within double wavy rules.

8 1/16 × 5 1/2". [1-24⁸]: 192 leaves. Pp. [i-vi], [1-2] 3-162 [163-164] 165-266 [267-268] 269-374 [375-378]. Numbers printed in roman in headline at outer margin of type page, except for pages 3, 165 and 269 on which the numbers are printed in the center at the foot of the page.

CONTENTS: p. i, half-title: "[script] River Lady"; p. ii, blank; p. iii, title; p. iv, copyright notice: "[publisher's device of an 'F' in white and an 'R' in black within a fancy black and white floral oval] | COPY= RIGHT, 1942, BY HOUSTON BRANCH AND FRANK WATERS | PRINTED IN THE UNITED STATES OF AMERICA | BY J. J. LIT= TLE AND IVES COMPANY, NEW YORK | ALL RIGHTS RE= SERVED"; p. v, contents; p. vi, blank; p. 1, divisional half-title: "[all in script] Part One | The Village in the Leaves"; p. 2, blank; pp. 3-162, text; p. 163, divisional half-title: "[all in script] Part Two | The Boat Below"; p. 164, blank; pp. 165-266, text; p. 267, divisional half-title: "[all in script] Part Three | The House on the Hill"; p. 268, blank; pp. 269-374, text; pp. 375-378, blank.

BINDING: Red-brown cloth. Front stamped in gilt: "[double rules] | *River Lady* | [double rules] | HOUSTON BRANCH | *and* FRANK WATERS". Spine stamped in gilt: "[double rules] | *River* | *Lady* | [double rules] | BRANCH | *and* | WATERS | FARRAR & | RINEHART". Top edges stained green; fore and bottom edges untrimmed. Cream-colored endpapers.

DUST JACKET (white paper): Front and spine printed overall with an illustration of a river front scene, with people in the foreground and a riverboat in the background, in red, green, black, brown, orange, white and blue. Lettered on front: *"River Lady* | *By* HOUSTON BRANCH | *and* FRANK WATERS". Spine: *"River* | *Lady* | *by* | BRANCH | *and* | WATERS | [white] FARRAR & | [white] RINEHART". Rear: *"Recent Farrar & Rinehart Successes* | [four works listed, with title and author's name printed in red and with a quotation for each work in black] | [red rule] | FARRAR & RINEHART, Inc. | New York [space] Toronto". Front and rear flap carry a blurb for this work, printed in red and black; publisher's imprint appears on the bottom of both flaps.

NOTE: I have not personally examined a copy of this dust jacket. The description given above is taken from color slides provided me by Mr. Paul Lord, of Northridge, California, owner of the only located copy of the dust jacket.

Published at $2.50. Exact date of publication unknown; number of copies printed unknown, although Waters recorded in his journal that 5,000 copies were printed. Copyrighted March 23, 1942; deposited March 4, 1942. Listed in the "Weekly Record" of *Publisher's Weekly* on March 21, 1942.

REVIEWS: *New York Herald Tribune Books,* March 22, 1942 (p. 10); *New York Times Book Review,* March 22, 1942 (p. 22); *Saturday Review of Literature,* April 11, 1942 (p. 17); *Booklist,* May 1, 1942 (p. 330).

COPIES: DLC (2 copies); NmU; TAT.

NOTE: At least one copy was specially bound in full blue hard-grain morocco, top edges gilt and with five raised bands on spine. This copy was presented to Waters by the publisher, and it can be assumed that Branch was also presented with a copy. Waters' copy is at NmU.

A7b First edition, subsequent Farrar & Rinehart printings [1942?]

At least one other printing of this work has been examined. This copy is identical to the first printing except that the publisher's device has been deleted from the copyright page. Also, in the copy examined, the binding is of a slightly lighter colored cloth, perhaps brick-red or terracotta, and is lettered in black instead of being stamped in gilt; the top edges are unstained.

Although there is no substantial evidence, it may well be that Farrar & Rinehart issued more than two printings. Myron Brinig, a novelist friend of Waters, wrote that John Farrar had told him that three printings were done within a short space of time, totaling 7,000 copies. Waters records in his journal that the book sold 7,000 copies in the first ten days. It is not known to what printing the copy examined can be ascribed, if indeed more than two were issued.

COPIES: TAT.

56 Section A

A7c   First English edition, only printing   [1948]

[open face, fancy] River Lady | By HOUSTON BRANCH and FRANK WATERS | [thick tapered rule] | [publisher's device of a huntress with a bow] | CASSELL | AND COMPANY LTD | LONDON TORONTO MELBOURNE | SYDNEY

7³⁄₁₆ × 4¾". A-I¹⁶ K-L¹⁶ M⁸: 184 leaves. Pp. [1-6] 7-368.

CONTENTS: p. 1, half-title; p. 2, blank; p. 3, title; p. 4, copyright notice: "[three-line notice of conformity with economy standards] | First Pub= lished in Great Britain in 1948 | PRINTED IN GREAT BRITAIN | BY WESTERN PRINTING SERVICES LTD., BRISTOL | F. 847"; p. 5, contents; p. 6, blank; pp. 7-368, text.

BINDING: Orange-tan cloth, lettered on spine only: "[double wavy rules] | RIVER | LADY | [wavy rule] | Houston Branch | and | Frank Waters | [double wavy rules] | CASSELL". White endpapers.

DUST JACKET (white paper): Front and spine printed overall with an illustration of a river front scene with a man and a woman in front of a riverboat, in green, tan, pink, gray, purple and brown, and signed at the top of the front: "[gray swash] barbosa". Lettered on front: "[yellow shaded in red-brown] RIVER LADY | [script] Houston Branch and Frank Waters". Spine: "[first two lines in yellow outlined in red-brown] RIVER | LADY | [all following lines in script] Houston | Branch | and | Frank | Waters | Cassell". Rear: "RIVER LADY | [two-paragraph blurb for the book] | *Houston Branch & Frank Waters*". The front flap carries a listing of ten Cassell novels; the rear flap is blank except at the very bottom: "APT [slash] L97". Pasted onto the front of the dust jacket is a small circular green label, lettered in white: "CAS= SELL CHEAP EDITION 5/-".

Published at 5 shillings in April, 1948; 4,788 copies were printed. Deposited in the British Library on June 2, 1948.

COPIES: NmU (d.j.).

A8 THE MAN WHO KILLED THE DEER

In a letter to Mabel Dodge Luhan, dated February 14, 1941 [CtY], Waters responded to her critique of his recently completed manuscript "The Man Who Killed the Deer."

Your letter re the ms. hit me quite all right. The whole general idea of why you don't like it, I mean, and not the little things I could quibble about.

I think a completely true all-Indian novel will never be written. Not by a white for it would stem, as you say, from his own white psyche. And not by an Indian for the very reason that his own psyche is given to an instinctive, intuitive, non-reasoning and non-evaluating approach, too deeply rooted to emerge into a foreign word-form. His own natural forms exist only as great myth and dance-dramas, ceremonials and sand paintings etc. whose meanings are intelligible to most whites only by translation of their values—and which are gradually becoming less intelligible and lost to the Indians themselves.

So that I feel the truest writing possible of Indian substance is from an outside viewpoint, an honest and direct attempt at translation, rather than the fictional method of working out from within. Even if done by an Indian eventually; for his attempt to render other than the comparatively nonessential outward life, its color, form and smells etc.—his attempt to render the deeper, non-Aryan, pre-Aryan thing, would then be based, as the white's, upon the rational, which is the opposite pole.

Now this, in your sense and mine, is not an Indian novel. To consider it such is to accuse me as a man of sentimentality, and as a writer of real hokum or self-illusions about what I am trying to do.

To write at it in sketch form or essay—coldly; to look at it fictionally through a white participant, as THE WOMAN WHO RODE AWAY [by D. H. Lawrence]; or to project the Indian only as a shadow against a white background, as the SAD INDIAN;—these are the easiest methods. And they are all indirect and depend upon contrast. What this is, is an outside viewpoint with the looker merely eliminated from within the Indian envelope. Which is what confused you. Because the form was so true it left you dissatisfied with the substance.

Now about this substance. I believe, differently from you, that an Indian, like a Fiji Islander and an Eskimo, like people everywhere of all races and conditions, are yet human entities bound by the same simple human ties of human passion. From deep within us all well up old, dark, racial blood-forces. Around us, whether in jungle, mountain or city, exist the same problems of existence and environment. And above us, the same spiritual plane to which we all some day will converge. We are all middle-men, all human, Indian, negro and white. Whatever you say of tribal feeling, there does exist in an Indian the simple emotional ties between man and wife, mother and son, regardless of whether he acknowledges it under the name of love, and despite the fact that the individual feeling is quickly submerged in the tribal. In the Indian this is not the important part of life; it is how this is deepened, enhanced, by the wonderful, unspeakable essence flowing up into it from deep within.

Now this exists, in some measure, in all men. And the problem has forever been how to admit it in a clearer stream, a more unimpeded flow. And so the great religious systems have arisen, age upon age, throughout the world. And as man has striven upward, he has spiritually, as temporally, gone through the same evolutionary changes. The core of Indian esotericism is the belief that he holds, unsullied because unspoken (i.e. not allowed to become dead through crystallization), the dark flower of primeval truth and power. The Lhasas of Thibet believe, likewise, that in their hands they hold alive against time the same spark of the one timeless flame. Nor do they give it up to all to become a dead, crystallized concept. Only to initiates, to initiates who win to it through many reincarnations if necessary. But toward it grope, and have always groped, all men. The Taoist Way, the Buddhistic patterns, remain their shells of endeavor. Now I don't know the Lhasa secret doctrine, nor do I know the Indian belief. But within the Indian form of life, which is as valid as any other, I can suggest briefly the gropings of all men in the groping of Martiniano. For he, like all Indians, is human, fed by the dark irrational flow yet unilluminated for him, and by the need for resolving his faith consistent with the pattern which forms his outward life. The very fact of Peyotism refutes your belief that every Indian, just because he is an Indian, is pure, rich and deep in understanding. If peyote members were, they would have no need for reliance upon a faith that requires an outside stimulus—just as no sect in possession of the awareness of spiritual power within themselves depends upon the paraphanalia [sic] of prayer-wheels and baptismal fonts.

We all break away. We look outward, and inward, and finally see in ourselves the macrocosmic universe, and the world outside as a microcosmic replica of ourselves. And what prompts us, and ever keeps us on the track of self-fulfillment, is that peculiar thing we call conscience which turns us back, or the intuition which illumines the forward step. It might just as well be called a deer.

Now the deer, being a symbol of individual conscience, must also be a mass conscience, because an individual is no more than an evanescent [sic] microcosm in the everlasting macrocosm of all life.So when the individual would break away and be too soon so pure and so rich and so deep and true, the deer also calls him back into that warm flow of impure life of which he is still a part—calls the Indian back to his earthly humaness [sic], to his emotional humaness [sic] as a living man, which he is.

So you see we can't get away from it—that the Indian, pre-Aryan as he is, with all the living wonder the white has lost, is still bound like us to the life of which he is a part—or he wouldn't be here.

We, the white, have gone too far. We have objectified, analyzed and rationalized the wonder and mystery out of life, and the crystallized form of our faith is tumbling on our heads. But the Indian, sunk in contemplation of the wonder and mystery which he cannot or will not reveal in an intelligible translation of meaning, is allowing himself to be destroyed by the same unheeded forces about him. He isn't even perpetuating the wonder in his own bloodstream; his own children are slipping out of his grasp through his failure, not to reveal the secret, but the means whereby they could obtain it for themselves.

This thing of mine, therefore, is not an attempt—a false sentimental one, to word the wordless, but merely to show the groping of one toward it, and away from the wordy meaningless form of the white. He may be Indian, but he is human. And if he fails, it won't be him alone. It will be the whole sheebang—the whole Pueblo culture that will go to pot the same as that of the Plains'. Of what use then the wonder and the mystery of life when it was not strong enough to preserve life? Unless you admit it was a temporal thing whose time is past?

So I think this attempt of mine is justified beyond its faults—which naturally I'd like to reduce. About this conversation business. Was it the very few Indian-in-English things that got your goat—the use of 'she' etc? Or the Indian-to-Indian rendered in good English upon my own premise? Of course it is all a fable! A dead deer reappearing! But was it all just too much to swallow? Or don't you grant me my premise?

Whew! This has grown into a Letter—which I will have to get Naomi [Waters' sister] to type to insure your reading it.

I knew the ms. would be a struggle for you—and that you would make it. My best thanks. And don't withold [sic] any later thought about it if it strikes you.

Apparently, after sending the manuscript to Luhan, Waters undertook some revisions. In his journal, on April 8, 1941, he noted that he had finished the Indian novel, and had "no idea whether it is all stuffy nonsense or fairly good, written piece by piece. . . ." He submitted the manuscript to Farrar & Rinehart in May of 1941, and it was turned over to Stephen Vincent Benét for a reader's report. In his journal on September 11, 1941, Waters noted that Benét's report was highly laudatory, and without a single criticism.

The book was accepted by Farrar & Rinehart under the terms of the contract which was drawn up at the time they published *People of the Valley* [q.v.]. On October 14, 1941, Waters noted in his journal:

Best news ever! Letter from Farrar saying they were 'terribly anxious' to get on with my Indian novel & wanted ok to send it to compositors! I had thought they were going to hold it off till after this *River Lady*. Started in to revise it a little, despite their saying they had not a single criticism.

Finally, on January 9, 1942, Waters noted in his Journal that Farrar & Rinehart had decided to delay the publication of *Deer* to take advantage of the success of *River Lady*.

Interestingly enough, in spite of Mabel Dodge Luhan's dislike of the novel, Waters dedicated the book to her and her Indian husband Tony.

THE MAN
A8 WHO KILLED THE DEER [1942]

A8a   First edition, first printing

THE MAN | WHO KILLED | THE DEER | by | FRANK WATERS | FARRAR & RINEHART, INC. | NEW YORK :: TORONTO
  All of the above within single rules, within wavy rules, within single rules.

8 × 5½". [1-20⁸]: 160 leaves. Pp. [i-vi], [1-3] 4-29 [30] 31-47 [48] 49-72 [73] 74-94 [95] 96-119 [120] 121-141 [142] 143-167 [168] 169-193 [194] 195-217 [218] 219-235 [236] 237-252 [253] 254-269 [270] 271-286 [287] 288-311 [312-314]. Numbers printed in roman in headline at outer margin of type page.

CONTENTS: p. i, half-title: "THE MAN | WHO | KILLED THE DEER"; p. ii, *"Books by Frank Waters* | [list of six titles, including this book]"; p. iii, title; p. iv, copyright notice: "[publisher's device of an 'F' in white and an 'R' in black within a fancy black and white floral oval] | COPYRIGHT, 1942, BY FRANK WATERS | PRINTED IN THE UNITED STATES OF AMERICA | BY THE FERRIS PRINT= ING COMPANY, NEW YORK | ALL RIGHTS RESERVED"; p. v, dedication: "To | Mabel and Tony"; p. vi, blank; p. 1, second half-title; p. 2, blank; pp. 3-311, text; pp. 312-314, blank.

BINDING: Red cloth. Outline of a deer stamped in black on front cover in lower right corner. Spine lettered in black: "[pattern of gilt rules consisting of: thin rule | thick rule | 16 vertical rules closed at top and bottom by thin rules | thick rule | thin rule] | [pattern of two thin rules and one thick rule] | THE | MAN | WHO | KILLED | THE | DEER | [pattern of one thick rule and two thin rules] | WATERS | [pattern of gilt rules as described at top of spine] | [pattern of 12 gilt rules] | [pattern of thin-thick-thin rules] | [pattern of 12 gilt rules] | FARRAR & | RINEHART | [pattern of thin-thick-thin rules] | [pattern of gilt rules as described at top of spine, only somewhat shorter]". Fore-edges untrimmed. Cream colored endpapers.

DUST JACKET (white paper): Front and spine printed overall in red. Lettered on front: "[title in yellow, against an irregular black background of brush strokes, with a white arrow passing through it] THE MAN | WHO KILLED | THE DEER | [three lines to the right of a drawing of a deer in black against an irregular white background] [script] by | [white script] Frank Waters | [white] [script] Author of [roman] PEOPLE OF THE VALLEY". Spine: "[six lines of title in white script] The | Man | Who | Killed | the | Deer | [yellow] WATERS | [two lines of imprint in white script] Farrar & | Rinehart". Rear: "[rule of arrowhead ornaments in red] | [script] Frank Waters | [three paragraphs about the author] | [rule of arrowhead ornaments in red] | FAR= RAR & RINEHART, INC. | New York [space] Toronto". The front flap carries a quote about the book by Stephen Vincent Benét, and a blurb for this book, which is carried over onto the rear flap, printed in red and black; publisher's imprint appears at the bottom of both flaps.

Published at $2.50 on June 11, 1942. Number of copies printed unknown. Copyrighted June 11, 1942; deposited April 7, 1942. Listed in the "Weekly Record" of *Publisher's Weekly* on June 13, 1942.

REVIEWS: *Bookmark*, May, 1942 (p. 17); *Saturday Review of Literature*, June 11, 1942 (p. 9); *New Yorker*, June 13, 1942 (p. 71); *New York Times Book Review*, June 14, 1942 (p. 6); *New York Herald Tribune Books*, June 14, 1942 (p. 10); *Booklist*, July 15, 1942 (p. 443).

COPIES: DLC (2 copies—one rebound); TAT (3 copies in d.j.); Harwood Foundation Library, Taos, New Mexico.

NOTE: A royalty statement dated April 28, 1947, reported *Deer* as out of stock, but with an unearned balance against it of $47.88. Since there is no evidence that any copies of the book were destroyed, it would seem that sales of the book had been in the area of 2,000 copies. Being generous with free copies, we can assume that Rinehart probably printed somewhere in the area of 2,500 copies.

NOTE: This work was published in braille by the New Mexico State Library in 1967.

62 Section A

A8b   First edition, University of Denver Press printing   [1950]

THE MAN | WHO KILLED | THE DEER | by | FRANK WATERS | THE UNIVERSITY OF DENVER PRESS

7¹⁵⁄₁₆ × 5⁷⁄₁₆". Collation and pagination identical with A8a.

CONTENTS: Identical with A8a, except the following: p. ii has a listing of The American Library titles; p. iv: "COPYRIGHT, 1942, BY FRANK WATERS | PRINTED IN THE UNITED STATES OF AMERICA".

Cloth. Published at $2.50 in November, 1950; 1,500 copies were printed. Listed in the "Weekly Record" of *Publisher's Weekly* on November 18, 1950, as published on November 15, 1950.

COPIES: NmU (with author's corrections); TAT.

NOTE: The author's copy at NmU is marked by Waters on the front free endpaper: "Frank Waters | Marked for Corrections", and contains the following changes in ink:

3.10:	serape	sarape
17.30:	Filadelphio	Filadelfio
32.5:	Teodor	Teodoro
48.5:	Campo de Santo	Campo Santo
49.4:	Dia	Día
96.21:	Palemon	Palémon
96.26:	Estefana	Estéfana
96.28:	Batista	Bautista
121.22:	Panchilo	Panchillo
145.21:	flees	fleas
181.1:	Alebardo y Mondregon	Abelardo y Mondregon
181.4:	comodo	cómoda
223.2:	fonetas	onetas
256.25:	lattias	lattillas
258.6:	sabrosas	sabrosos
258.19:	mia	mía
292.10:	Pomosino	Ponoceno
297.3:	Juan de Bautista	Juan Bautista
307.18:	Que	Qúe

These changes do not represent a complete editing of the text, for instance the changes in the names of the characters have been made only once even though they appear more than once in the text.

NOTE: Although Alan Swallow had first approached Waters with the idea of reprinting *Deer* in 1946, he was unable to do one himself due to various financial obligations. It was finally agreed to reissue it through the University of Denver Press, which Swallow headed. Waters' contract with the Press outlined a straight royalty of 7½% on all copies sold; this contract was dated March 9, 1950.

NOTE: On April 17, 1953, Alan Swallow signed a contract with the University of Denver Press in which the Press transferred to Swallow all rights to the book, and in which it was agreed that one-half of the remaining inventory of the book would be purchased by Swallow for $.16 per copy. The remaining copies not purchased by Swallow were sold to a remainder house. On June 23, 1953, Swallow wrote to Waters (letter in the possession of FW) informing him of the transfer of rights and noting that the Press had sold somewhat less than half of the 1,500 copy printing prior to the transfer of rights.

Swallow continued to sell these copies and when his own stock was sold out he purchased all the remaining copies from the remainder house. The last of these copies were sold by Swallow in the summer of 1957.

A8c   First edition, first Alan Swallow printing   [1958]

THE MAN | WHO KILLED | THE DEER | *by* | FRANK WATERS | THE AMERICAN LIBRARY | *SAGE BOOKS*

8 × 5⁷⁄₁₆". Collation and pagination identical with A8a.

CONTENTS: Identical with A8b, with the exception of page iv: "Sage Books are published by | Alan Swallow, 2679 So. York St., Denver 10, Colorado | COPYRIGHT. 1942, BY FRANK WATERS | PRINTED IN THE UNITED STATES OF AMERICA".

Cloth. Published at $2.75 in 1958; number of copies printed unknown. Listed in the "Weekly Record" of *Publisher's Weekly* on July 14, 1958.

64   SECTION A

COPIES: FW.

NOTE: Alan Swallow wrote to Frank Waters on November 7, 1957, informing him that *Deer* had gone out of print during the summer. Now that he had finally sold off all of the remainders from the University of Denver Press printing (A8b), Swallow told Waters that he was considering reprinting the book himself. However, because of the time involved in reprinting the book, the six-months out-of-print limitation would have passed and the rights, under the contract Swallow purchased from Denver, would revert to Waters. Swallow requested that he be allowed to maintain the book on his own list under the existing contract. Waters agreed and Swallow went ahead with the reprinting. He reported to Waters on May 11, 1958, that the sheets were printed and ready for binding and that he hoped the book would be ready by May 30th, if not sooner.

NOTE: Alan Swallow never made any attempt to distinguish between his printings. This 1958 printing can easily be identified by its light blue binding, which is lettered in gilt on the spine only. The dust jacket for this printing was of light blue paper, lettered on the front and spine in gilt, with the rear blank.

A8d   First edition, second Alan Swallow printing, American issue   [1962]

Identical with A8c.

Published in both cloth and paperback (perfectbound) in 1962. Published at $3.00 for cloth copies and $1.85 for paper copies. Number of copies printed is unknown. In a letter to Waters on August 13, 1962, Swallow informed Waters that the sheets were to be shipped from the printer, Edwards Brothers of Ann Arbor, Michigan, on August 24, 1962.

COPIES: Harwood Foundation Library, Taos, New Mexico (cloth); TAT (paper).

NOTE: This printing can be identified by its pastel blue cloth binding, lettered in blue on the spine only. The white paper dust jacket has a deer, in black, and five large arrows, in blue, on the front, and is lettered in black. The paperbound copies were issued in covers identical with the dust jacket.

NOTE: Due to the availability of only fragmentary records, it is impossible to determine how many printings of *Deer* Alan Swallow did after 1962. Certainly the book had begun to sell well and it is entirely likely that Swallow had to reprint the book again to keep up with demand. Frank Waters remembers that Swallow did two more printings, in paperback only, in 1964 and 1965. However, verification of this awaits further evidence.

A8e   First edition, second Alan Swallow printing, English issue   [1962, i.e. 1963]

THE MAN | WHO KILLED | THE DEER | *by* | FRANK WATERS | LONDON 1962 | NEVILLE SPEARMAN LTD

$7^{15}/_{16} \times 5^{3}/_{8}''$. Collation and pagination identical with A8c.

CONTENTS: Identical with A8a, with the exception of page ii, which is blank; and page iv: "© 1942 BY FRANK WATERS | PRINTED IN THE UNITED STATES OF AMERICA | FOR NEVILLE SPEAR= MAN LTD, 112 WHITFIELD ST, W1".

BINDING: Brown paper over boards in imitation of cloth. Lettered on spine only: "[reading vertically] Frank Waters THE MAN WHO KILLED THE DEER Neville Spearman". White endpapers.

DUST JACKET (white paper): Front has a silhouette portrait of an Indian in brown and black, signed in the lower left: "[reading upwards] *Snoaden*". Lettered on front: "[first seven lines in white] THE | MAN | WHO | KILLED | THE | DEER | Frank | Waters". Spine: "[reading vertically] Waters THE MAN WHO KILLED THE DEER Spear= man". Rear blank. The front flap carries a blurb for this book; rear flap carries an advertisement for three other books published by Spearman.

Published at 16 shillings on February 22, 1963; 1,000 copies were printed. Deposited in the British Library on January 23, 1963.

COPIES: NmU (d.j.); TAT.

66   SECTION A

NOTE: The sheets for this English issue were supplied to Spearman by Alan Swallow, who had them printed in Ann Arbor, with a new title page, when he printed his own second printing. The sheets were shipped to England in November of 1962, and bound by Spearman in England. The date of publication is taken from a letter to Waters from his agent Joan Daves; the publisher himself could find no records to indicate the publication date.

NOTE: The terms of the contract between Spearman and Waters for the English publication of *Deer* were outlined in a letter from Joan Daves to Frank Waters on February 14, 1962: There was to be no advance, and with royalties to be 10% on the first 3,500 copies, 12½% on the next 2,500 copies, and 15% thereafter.

A8f   Second [limited, signed] edition, only printing   [1965]

THE MAN | WHO | KILLED | THE DEER | [illustration of a deer in blue appears to the left of the next three lines] *by Frank Waters* | *Illus= trated by Don Perceval* | *Foreword by Lawrence Clark Powell* | NORTH= LAND PRESS · FLAGSTAFF

9 × 6". [1-21⁸]: 168 leaves. Pp. [i-vi] vii-xi [xii], 1-323 [324].

CONTENTS: p. i, limitation notice: "TWELVE HUNDRED AND FIFTY COPIES OF THIS EDITION | WERE PUBLISHED BY THE NORTHLAND PRESS | IN APRIL OF 1965 | [blue] COPY NUM= BER | [short rule on which number appears in ink] | [author's holograph signature]"; p. ii, blank; p. iii, title; p. iv, copyright notice: "COPY= RIGHT 1942 BY FRANK WATERS | This limited edition from Northland Press is produced | through lease of rights from Alan Swal= low, owner of | Sage Books, which publishes the regular cloth and a | Western Sage Paperbooks edition of *The Man Who* | *Killed the Deer.*"; p. v, dedication: "TO MABEL AND TONY"; p. vi, blank; pp. vii-xi, Foreword by Lawrence Clark Powell; p. xii, blank; pp. 1-323, text; p. 324, colophon: "[publisher's device] | *The Man Who Killed the Deer* | was set in Aldus type | and printed on Strathmore Impress. | The book was designed by | Paul Weaver.".

ILLUSTRATIONS: All illustrations in the book are by Don Perceval and are in blue. These illustrations appear on pages: iii, vii, 1, 8, 9, 31, 49,

62, 63, 76, 98, 123, 146, 152, 153, 174, 200, 225, 230, 231, 245, 263, 281 and 298.

BINDING: Blue patterned boards, with designs of Indians and deers in blue, and dark blue cloth. Blue paper label on spine (measuring 2⅝ × 1 3⁄16″), lettered in black: "[double rule] | THE MAN | WHO KILLED | THE DEER | [illustration of deer in blue] | *Frank Waters* | [double rule]". White endpapers.

No dust jacket was issued. Published in a slipcase of blue paper over boards, with printed label on front (measuring 3⅞ × 3 5⁄16″): "[against a blue background outlined by a thick white border] [illustration of a deer in white] | THE MAN WHO KILLED | THE DEER | *by Frank Wa= ters*".

Published at $12.50 in 1965; 1,250 copies printed. Although the limitation notice gives April of 1965 as the time of publication, actual publication must have been somewhat later. Paul Weaver informed Waters, in a letter dated April 28, 1965, that copies were on their way to the binder and he hoped they would be done by May 6th.

COPIES: TAT; Skokie Public Library, Skokie, Illinois.

NOTE: The original agreement drawn up between Paul Weaver of the Northland Press and Alan Swallow, prepared in the form of a letter from Swallow dated August 14, 1964, outlined the following provisions: The Northland Press edition was not to exceed 750 copies; was to be priced at not less than twice the retail price of Swallow's cloth edition; was to carry the accreditation line which appears on the copyright page; and Northland Press was to pay Swallow a royalty of 15% on all copies sold. Weaver agreed to these terms and signed the document on August 18, 1964. However, sometime later Weaver requested of Swallow that he be allowed to enlarge the edition to 1,250 copies, because mounting costs made it impossible for him to recover his investment with only 750 copies. Although he was unhappy over the change, Swallow agreed, in a letter dated February 25, 1965, to increasing the edition to 1,250 copies.

NOTE: Some copies have been noted without a label on the slipcase.

68 Section A

A8g   First edition, first Swallow Press printing   [1968]

THE MAN | WHO KILLED | THE DEER | *by* | FRANK WATERS | [publisher's sagebrush device] | SAGE BOOKS, *Chicago*

8 × 5⅜". Perfectbound: 160 leaves. Pagination identical with A8c.

Contents: Identical with A8c, except for page iv: "Sage Books are published by | The Swallow Press, Inc. | 1139 S. Wabash Ave. | Chicago, Illinois 60605 | COPYRIGHT, 1942, BY FRANK WATERS | PRINTED IN THE UNITED STATES OF AMERICA".

Paperback. Published at $1.85 in 1968; number of copies printed unknown. In a letter to Waters, dated February 13, 1968, Durrett Wagner of the Swallow Press stated that they were "running off a reprinting of *Deer.*" Available records would seem to indicate that the printing was in the area of 2,500 copies.

Copies: TAT.

A8h   First edition, second Swallow Press printing   [1969]

Identical with A8g.

Paperback. Published at $2.50 in January, 1969; 3,177 copies were printed.

Copies: TAT.

Note: The Swallow Press, like Alan Swallow before them, made no effort to distinguish between printings of this book. Although the printing history itself has been derived from inventory and royalty records of the Swallow Press, identification of copies has proved extremely difficult. The above cited copy has been placed within this printing on the basis of advertisements on the rear cover, which list *People of the Valley* at $2.50 for paper copies and $3.50 for cloth copies; *The Woman at Otowi Crossing* at $4.95; *Masked Gods* at $8.50; and *Pumpkin Seed Point* at $6.00. Of course, such evidence is rarely conclusive, and this may be subject to change.

A8i   First edition, third Swallow Press printing   [1969]

Identical with A8g.

Published simultaneously in both cloth and paperback, both perfect-bound, in November, 1969, at $5.00 for cloth copies and $2.50 for paper copies. 3,335 copies were printed, of which 3,000 were issued in paper and 335 copies were cased in cloth.

COPIES: FW (cloth)—no copy of the paperbound has been seen.

NOTE: The only located copy in cloth is in the library of Frank Waters. This copy is perfectbound and cased in dark blue cloth, lettered on the spine only in gilt. The dust jacket on this copy, however, carries the imprint of Alan Swallow on the rear.

A8j   First edition, fourth Swallow Press printing   [1970]

NOT SEEN

Paperback. Published at $2.50 in August, 1970; 5,000 copies were printed.

NOTE: It is probable that the copyright page of this printing carries the added date of the renewal of copyright, 1970. Renewal of the copyright was registered by the Library of Congress on June 30, 1969, and it would seem likely that the Swallow Press would include the renewal date in their printing in 1970.

A8k   First edition, fifth Swallow Press printing   [1971]

THE MAN | WHO KILLED | THE DEER | *by* | FRANK WATERS | SAGE BOOKS | [publisher's sagebrush device] | [small caps] THE [caps] SWALLOW PRESS [small caps] INC. | CHICAGO

8 × 5⅜". [1-10^{16}]: 160 leaves. Pagination identical with A8g.

CONTENTS: Identical with A8g, except for page ii, which is headed: *"OTHER BOOKS BY FRANK WATERS"*, and carries a listing of 11 titles; and page iv: "Copyright © 1942, 1970 Frank Waters | All Rights

Reserved | Printed in the United States of America | Sage Books are published by | The Swallow Press Incorporated | 1139 South Wabash Avenue | Chicago, Illinois 60605 | [small caps] LIBRARY OF CON= GRESS CATALOG CARD NUMBER [caps] 73-149327".

Published simultaneously in cloth and paperback (perfectbound), in January, 1971, at $6.00 for cloth copies and $2.50 for paper copies. 2,037 copies were published in cloth, and 8,108 in paper.

COPIES: TAT (cloth and paper).

A8l   First edition, sixth Swallow Press printing   [1971]

Size, collation (perfectbound) and pagination identical with A8g.

CONTENTS: Identical with A8k, except for page iv: "Copyright 1942, 1970 by Frank Waters | All rights reserved | Printed in the United States of America | Sage Books are published by | The Swallow Press Incorpo= rated | 1139 South Wabash Avenue | Chicago, Illinois 60605 | This book is printed on 100% recycled paper. | [small caps] ISBN (CLOTH= BOUND EDITION) [caps] 0-8040-0193-6 | [small caps] ISBN (PA= PERBOUND EDITION) [caps] 0-8040-0194-4 | [small caps] LIBRARY OF CONGRESS CATALOG CARD NUMBER [caps] 73-149327".

Paperback. Published at $2.50 in December, 1971; 5,101 copies were printed.

COPIES: TAT.

A8m   Third edition, first printing   [1971]

THE MAN | WHO KILLED | THE DEER | • | by | FRANK WATERS | [small caps] PUBLISHED BY [caps] POCKET [publisher's kangaroo device] BOOKS [small caps] NEW YORK

7 × 4$\frac{3}{16}$". Perfectbound: 112 leaves. Pp. [i-vi], 1-217 [218]. Page vi is blank, and page 218 contains a listing of Zane Grey titles published by Pocket Books.

The Man Who Killed the Deer **71**

COPYRIGHT PAGE: "THE MAN WHO KILLED THE DEER | Farrar, Rinehart edition published 1941 [sic] | POCKET BOOK edition pub= lished August, 1971 | [publisher's kangaroo device] [rule] | This POCKET BOOK edition includes every word | contained in the origi= nal, higher-priced edition. It is printed | from brand new plates made from completely reset, clear, easy-to-read | type. POCKET BOOK editions are published by POCKET BOOKS, a division | of Simon & Schuster, Inc., 630 Fifth Avenue, New York, N.Y. 10020. | Trademarks registered in the United States and other countries. | L | [rule] | Stan= dard Book Number: 671-77333-X. | Copyright, 1942, ©, 1970, by Frank Waters. All rights reserved. | This POCKET BOOK edition is published by arrangement with | The Swallow Press, Inc., from whom permission must be obtained | for reproduction of this book in any form. | Printed in the U. S. A.".

Paperback. Published as Pocket Book 77333 at $.95 in August, 1971; 100,000 copies were printed.

COPIES: FW; TAT.

NOTE: The contract between the Swallow Press and Pocket Books, dated August 6, 1970, outlined an advance payment by Pocket Books of $10,000.00 against royalties of 8%.

A8n   Third edition, second Pocket Books printing

NOT SEEN

Paperback. Date of publication and number of copies printed unknown.

A8o   Third edition, third Pocket Books printing   [1972]

Identical with A8m, except for page iv, on which is printed the additional line: ". . . | 3rd printing.........October, 1972 | . . ."; and page 218, which now carries an ad for *The Complete Book of Bicycling*."

Paperback. Published as Pocket Book 77333 at $.95 in October, 1972. Number of copies printed unknown.

72 SECTION A

COPIES: Charles L. Adams, Las Vegas, Nevada.

A8p   Third edition, fourth Pocket Books printing
NOT SEEN

Paperback. Date of publication and number of copies printed unknown.

A8q   Third edition, fifth Pocket Books printing
NOT SEEN

Paperback. Date of publication and number of copies printed unknown.

A8r   Third edition, sixth Pocket Books printing
NOT SEEN

Paperback. Date of publication and number of copies printed unknown.

A8s   Third edition, seventh Pocket Books printing   [1975]

Identical with A8m, except that page ii is blank; page iv now reads: "THE MAN WHO KILLED THE DEER | Farrar, Rinehart edition published 1941 [sic] | POCKET BOOK edition published August, 1971 | 7th printing..................September, 1975 | [publisher's kangaroo device] | L | This POCKET BOOK edition includes every word contained | in the original, higher-priced edition. It is printed from | brand-new plates made from completely reset, clear, easy-to- | read type. POCKET BOOK editions are published by POCKET | BOOKS, a division of Simon & Schuster, Inc., 630 Fifth | Avenue, New York, N. Y. 10020. Trademarks registered | in the United States and other countries. | [rule] | Standard Book Number 671-80330-1. | This POCKET BOOK edition is published by arrangement with The | Swallow Press, Inc. Copyright, 1942, by Frank Waters. Copyright renewed, ©, 1970, by Frank Waters. All rights reserved. This book, or | portions thereof, may not be reproduced by any means without the | permission of: The Swallow Press, Inc., 1139 S. Wabash Ave., | Chicago, Ill. 60605. | Printed in the U. S. A."; and page 218 which is blank.

Paperback. Pocket Book 80330. Published at $1.50 in September, 1975. Number of copies printed unknown.

COPIES: TAT.

NOTE: Although none has been seen, it is entirely possible that there may exist later Pocket Book printings between 1975 and 1981.

A8t   Third edition, eighth Pocket Books printing?   [1981]

THE MAN | WHO KILLED | THE DEER | · | *by* | FRANK WA= TERS | [publisher's device of an arch over which are printed the initials 'WSP'] | WASHINGTON SQUARE PRESS | PUBLISHED BY POCKET BOOKS NEW YORK

7 × 4⅛″. Pagination identical with A8m. Pages ii and vi are blank; page 218 carries a biographical note of the author.

COPYRIGHT PAGE: "[first four lines to the right of four-line high publisher's device as on title] A Washington Square Press Publication of | POCKET BOOKS, a Simon & Schuster division of | GULF & WEST= ERN CORPORATION | 1230 Avenue of the Americas, New York, N. Y. 10020 | Copyright 1942 by Frank Waters | Copyright renewed © 1970 by Frank Waters | Published by arrangement with The Swallow Press, Inc. | All rights reserved, including the right to reproduce | this book or portions thereof in any form whatsoever. | For information address The Swallow Press, Inc., | 1139 S. Wabash Ave., Chicago, Ill. 60605. | ISBN: 0-671-43295-8 | First Pocket Books printing August, 1971 | 15 14 13 12 11 10 | WASHINGTON SQUARE PRESS, WSP and colophon are | trademarks of Simon & Schuster. | Printed in the U.S.A.".

Paperback. Published at $2.50 in September, 1981. Number of copies printed unknown.

74 Section A

Copies: FW; TAT.

Note: The publishers incorrectly listed the address of the Swallow Press on the copyright page; the Press had moved to 811 W. Junior Terrace almost five years earlier.

A8u Fourth edition, first printing [1972]

[open face] THE MAN WHO | [open face] KILLED | [open face] THE DEER | FRANK WATERS | SAGE BOOKS | [publisher's sagebrush device] | [small caps] THE [caps] SWALLOW PRESS [small caps] INC. | CHICAGO

8½ × 5½". Perfectbound: 136 leaves. Pp. [i-vi], [1-3] 4-25 [26] 27-40 [41] 42-61 [62] 63-79 [80] 81-100 [101] 102-119 [120] 121-141 [142] 143-163 [164] 165-184 [185] 186-200 [201] 202-215 [216] 217-230 [231] 232-244 [245] 246-266. Pages vi and 2 are blank.

Copyright Page: "Copyright 1942, 1970 by Frank Waters | All rights reserved | Printed in the United States of America | Sage Books are published by | The Swallow Press Incorporated | 1139 South Wabash Avenue | Chicago, Illinois 60605 | [three lines ISBN and Library of Congress catalog data]".

Paperback. Published at $2.50 in August, 1972. 8,232 copies were printed.

Copies: Swallow Press, Chicago, Illinois; TAT.

Note: Although the ISBN information on the copyright page makes note of a clothbound edition, there was no clothbound issue of this new edition. The number refers to the previous clothbound copies (see A8k) still in print at this time.

A8v Fourth edition, second Swallow Press printing [1974]

Identical to A8u.

Paperback. Published at $3.50 in March, 1974. 8,018 copies were printed.

Copies: TAT.

Excerpts from *Deer*

A8w *The Lively Rhetoric,* edited by Ralph A. Singleton and Alexander Scharbach. (2nd edition: New York, Holt, Rinehart & Winston, 1972). Pages 22-29; 249-257. The first edition of this work contained no selections from Waters.

A8x *Voice from the Bottom: Selections about the American Indian, the Chicano and the Puerto Rican,* edited by Edward Spargo, James A. Giroux and Livia J. Giroux. (Providence, Jamestown Publishing, 1972). Pages 115-119.

A9   THE COLORADO

Waters was first approached to write the work on the Colorado for the Rivers of America Series on May 21, 1942, in a letter from John Farrar. Farrar noted in his letter that they had originally given the book to another writer but that they had rejected his manuscript and had finally decided to find another writer for the book. Waters agreed to undertake the work and a year later, on July 29, 1943, signed a contract with Farrar & Rinehart for the book. This contract outlined an advance of $500.00, as needed, but payable only after work on the manuscript had begun, against royalties of 10% on the first 3,500 copies, 12½% on the next 1,500 copies, and 15% thereafter.

In a letter to Waters dated October 6, 1943, Hervey Allen, who had just assumed general editorship of the Rivers of America Series, inquired of Waters for news of the book and further asked if Waters could provide him with some idea of when the manuscript would be completed. Waters responded to Allen on October 18, 1943:

> It is good to hear that the man who wrote the first page of *The Forest and the Fort* is to take over the editing of the River Books.
>
> I have been writing *The Colorado* for the past twenty years, though the words themselves have yet to be put on paper. Enclosed is my outline for them. A few chapters are done. A great deal of original research material long collected up and down river, in both Spanish and English, is at hand—in heterogenous, apple-box style.
>
> I lack only time. As you know, I am working down here in the Office of Inter-American Affairs a full six days a week. As a rough, safe guess, I would say you could schedule publication of the book a year from now—for the Fall List of 1944.
>
> What I want to stake out—contrary to the Hudson River approach, of being always in sight of the water—is the whole seven-State river basin of the Colorado, as determined at the time of the building of the Boulder dam. This is necessary in light of the fact that this vast arid region, with the control and utilization of the Colorado and its major subsidiaries, will hold the teeming

The Colorado 77

multitudes of our future growth. You will note that a full chapter is allotted to both the Boulder Dam and the All-American Canal, the first projects toward this end. This answers your fear about concentrating too much on the past. It also is necessary, however, in recounting its history, for the Grand Canon was discovered by members of Coronado's expedition up the Rio Grande Valley. In short, I don't want to be limited to the Colorado's river banks.

John also told me once that a previous attempt at this book went overboard into Indian history and romanticism, in case you have struck this snag.

The history of a river can be a pretty dreary thing. And generally, inherently, they all conform to the same pattern.

My aim is to show the life of the Colorado rather than its successive costumes, its meaning above its utility. That it has one makes it one of the great, unique rivers of the world, and is the theme of the book and my reason for wanting to do it. We shall see how close the arrow strikes.

If there are any questions I can answer either now or when you get settled into the saddle, do let me know.

Allen wrote back to Waters on October 25, 1943, saying that he had thought carefully about Waters' outline for the book, and that he felt the material was well organized. His only hesitation, however, was that Waters would have to maintain great care in part II of the book, which treated of the history of the river, so as not to go overboard and detract from the rest of the book. Waters responded to Allen's letter on November 8, 1943:

. . . I am glad you approve of the organization of the material; and that you understood the structure so well is going to make any further suggestions you may have most welcome.

Your point about over-emphasis on Book II is well taken. But by presenting a picture of the country in Book I, I can avoid describing it again historically and concentrate only on the people in Book II; and with proper condensation to avoid the long chronological approach, I think it can whittle down to size.

The big problem, as you know, is not that of weighting equally all parts of the river. It is the blending of all parts, background and people, into a meaningful whole. To create the impression of time and movement without destroying its underlying static unity. Which is one reason why the Grand Canon comes last.

I've got only one suggestion about it as a finished job—and please forgive my butting in on what is a production job. But for my money the one weak point of most of the River Series is their lack of good maps. For this one, I'd like to put in a bid for the best one possible. The territory covered is too large and complex not to have one covering it without crowding or confusion for the reader's easy reference.

I've had trouble with this same problem before. I remember for my "Midas of the Rockies" I finally got hold of a local artist to draw me one to order, and it was reproduced on the inside covers with excellent results. But the time for it is yet a spell off.

78   SECTION A

Although Waters had told Allen to schedule publication for the Fall of 1944, the work was delayed for a number of reasons, not the least of which was Waters' work at the Office for Inter-American Affairs. During the time which Waters was writing the book, arrangements were made with the Russian-born artist Nicolai Fechin, then living in Taos, to illustrate the book. Although Rinehart originally wanted Fechin to do a series of line drawings, they finally agreed to accept charcoal sketches, even though they were afraid they would not reproduce well. When Fechin saw the printed product he was very displeased—and indeed the illustrations are of so poor a quality as to almost detract from the book.

After the manuscript had been turned in to the publisher, the book was scheduled for release in the Spring of 1946—Waters had received galleys in December of 1945 and the book was printed and ready in February of 1946. However, the sales department felt it would be best to delay publication until the fall of the year. In a letter to Waters on April 1, 1946, Stanley Rinehart informed Waters of the decision to delay publication and enclosed an additional advance of $500.00.

After the decision to delay publication was made, Rinehart made arrangements with the National Travel Club for early publication under their imprint for distribution to members of the Club. These copies were printed from the Rinehart plates and announced for release in the July issue of *Travel Magazine*.

Some months after publication by Rinehart & Company, Stanley Rinehart wrote to Waters, in a letter dated April 30, 1947, informing him that they had discovered an error in the original contract for *The Colorado,* drawn in 1943. Instead of royalties of 10% on the first 3,500 copies, 12½% on the next 1,500 copies and 15% thereafter, Rinehart stated that the terms should have been 10% on the first 3,500 copies, 12½% on the next 4,000 copies and 15% thereafter, which terms were standard for all the books in the Rivers Series.

A9   THE COLORADO   [1946]

A9a   First edition, first printing [second published impression]

THE COLORADO | *by* | FRANK WATERS | *Illustrated by* | [small caps with a capital] NICOLAI FECHIN | *Maps by* | [small caps with a

capital] GEORGE ANNAND | RINEHART & COMPANY | INCOR=
PORATED | *New York* [space] *Toronto*
All of the above printed against a background drawing of a Pueblo, in brown, by Nicolai Fechin.

7¹⁵⁄₁₆ × 5⅜". [1-13¹⁶]: 208 leaves; one plate inserted between pp. 164/165. Pp. [i-viii] ix-xii [xiii-xvi], [1-2] 3-15 [16] 17-25 [26-27] 28-33 [34] 35-55 [56] 57-81 [82] 83-103 [104] 105-109 [110-111] 112-131 [132-134] 135-197 [198-199] 200-281 [282-283] 284-292 [293-294] 295-370 [371-372] 373-393 [394] 395-400. Numbers printed in roman in headline at outer margin of type page, except for pages ix, xi, 3, 17, 33, 55, 83, 103, 135, 149, 168, 189, 209, 230, 252, 275, 295, 325, 337, 352, 367, 373, 389, and 395, on which the numbers are printed in the center at the foot of the page.

CONTENTS: p. i, half-title: "THE COLORADO"; p. ii, blank; p. iii, *"Books by Frank Waters* | [list of 6 titles] | *Rivers of America books already published are:* | [list of 29 titles]"; p. iv, series title: "[set against reverse of title page drawing, in brown] THE | RIVERS OF AMERICA | *Edited by* | HERVEY ALLEN *and* CARL CARMER | *As Planned and Started by* | CONSTANCE LINDSAY SKINNER | *Associate Editor* [space] *Art Editor* | JEAN CRAWFORD [space] FAITH BALL | [series device]"; p. v, title; p. vi, copyright notice: "[publisher's device of an 'R' within a circle] | COPYRIGHT, 1946, BY FRANK WATERS | PRINTED IN THE UNITED STATES OF AMERICA | BY J. J. LIT= TLE AND IVES COMPANY, NEW YORK | ALL RIGHTS RE= SERVED"; p. vii, dedication: "TO | CARL, DOC, RALPH AND ED"; p. viii, blank; pp. ix-x, contents; pp. xi-xii, Introduction; p. xiii, blank; pp. xiv-xv, double-page map of the Colorado; p. xvi, blank; p. 1, divisional half-title: "PART ONE | Its Background" p. 2, blank; pp. 3-131, text; p. 132, blank; p. 133, divisional half-title: "PART TWO | Its People"; p. 134, blank; pp. 135-292, text; p. 293, divisional half-title: "PART THREE | Its Future"; p. 294, blank; pp. 295-370, text; p. 371, divisional half title: "PART FOUR | Grand Cañon"; p. 372, blank; pp. 373-388, text; pp. 389-393, Reference Appendix; p. 394, blank; pp. 395-396, Glossary; pp. 397-400, index.

ILLUSTRATIONS: One plate in full color inserted between pages 164/165 from an oil painting by Nicolai Fechin entitled "Indian Ceremonial". All other illustrations are untitled. Double-page illustrations appear on pages 26-27, 110-111, 198-199 and 282-283. Small illustrations within the text appear on pages 38, 48, 93, 159, 172, 218, 266, 312 and 375. The full-page illustrations appearing on the title page and the page facing the title have been noted above.

All maps were drawn by George Annand and with one exception are untitled. This exception is the double-page map on pages xiv-xv, which is titled "The Colorado". The other maps are all full-page and appear on pages 16, 34, 56, 82 and 104.

BINDING: Brick-red cloth. Front: Rivers of America series device stamped in blind in center. Spine stamped in gilt: *"The | Rivers of | America |* [next two lines within a black panel with triple gilt rules at top and bottom] THE | COLORADO | [below panel] FRANK | WATERS | RINEHART". Top edges stained orange. White endpapers.

DUST JACKET (white paper): Front and spine printed with a full-color reproduction of the Fechin oil painting "Indian Ceremonial" in the center, with a gray-green band at the top and a purple band at the bottom. Lettered on front: "[within a wavy white band] RIVERS OF AMERICA | [red script, extending above the white wavy band] The | [red] COLORADO | [white] FRANK WATERS | [within a white wavy band] illustrated by NICOLAI FECHIN". Spine: "THE | COLO= RADO | • | [red] FRANK WATERS | [white] RINEHART & CO.". Rear: "[rule of type ornaments in red] | THE RIVERS OF AMERICA | [list of 28 titles and their authors] | [within parentheses] Other volumes in preparation | [rule of type ornaments in red] | RINEHART & COM= PANY, INC. | Formerly Farrar & Rinehart | New York [space] To= ronto". Front and rear flaps carry a notice of this book, set between a rule of red type ornaments at top and bottom; the publisher's imprint appears on both flaps beneath the lower rule of ornaments.

Published at $3.00 on September 9, 1946; 15,000 copies were printed. Copyrighted September 9, 1946; deposited August 11, 1946.

REVIEWS: *Kirkus Reviews,* July 1, 1946 (p. 318); *San Francisco Chronicle,* August 14, 1946 (p. 14); *Library Journal,* September 1, 1946 (p. 1126); *New York Herald Tribune Weekly Book Review,* September 8, 1946 (p. 5); *Chicago Sun Book Week,* September 8, 1946 (p. 4); *New York Times Book Review,* September 8, 1946 (p. 7); *New Yorker,* September 14, 1946 (p. 110); *Christian Science Monitor,* September 14, 1946 (p. 14); *Saturday Review of Literature,* September 28, 1946 (p. 28); *Booklist,* October 1, 1946 (p. 33).

COPIES: DLC (2 copies); NmU; TAT (6 copies, 5 in d.j.).

NOTE: Although printed in early 1946—galleys were due in December, 1945—this was actually the second published impression: see A9b.

NOTE: At least one copy of this book was specially bound in full red hard-grain morocco and was presented to Waters by the publisher. This copy is currently in the private collection of Frank Waters.

NOTE: *The Colorado* sold almost 10,000 copies in the first several months after its publication, and in March, 1947, Waters was informed that there were plans at Rinehart to do another printing. However, I have found no evidence to indicate that such a printing was done until 1958. The price of the book remained at $3.00 until 1951, when that year's *Books in Print* records that it was raised to $4.00, at which price it remained until 1958. This price increase might be thought to indicate a new printing, but I think it unlikely, unless, of course, the publisher failed to have their device removed from the copyright page, and hence such a printing would be indistinguishable from the first printing. See A9d (note).

After being informed that a new printing was planned, Waters wrote to Jean Crawford at Rinehart, on April 12, 1947, enclosing a list of corrections to be made in the text. These corrections have never been made in any printing of the book, and I have listed them below as a matter of interest:

3.15:	"It is the most sparsely settled area of its size in the"
REV	"It is one of the most sparsely settled areas of its size in the".
38.5:	"their"
REV	"thin"
194.2-3:	"to be a cloud hanging on the horizon. After naming it Pikes Peak and trying to scale it, he proceeded westward across"
REV:	"to be a cloud hanging on the horizon. After trying futilely to scale its steep slopes, he proceeded westward across"
194.22-23:	"Colorado's highest peak whose melting snows drain into the great red river"
REV:	"Long's Peak, once thought to be Colorado's highest

SECTION A

	but now ranked at 14,255 feet as the fourteenth in height"
214.1:	"Jim"
REV:	"Charles"
214.14-15:	"began producing $180,000 a month. Creede, Telluride, Ouray boomed into being, and then Silverton, where Thomas"
REV:	"began producing $180,000 a month. So Creede boomed into being like Silverton, Telluride and Ouray, where Thomas"
278.3:	"impassionless"
REV:	"impassionate"
288.28-34:	"miniatures of trains, complete to detail, high in the Rockies. There's the narrow-gauge lines of D. & R. G.— "Through the Rockies, Not Over Them"—twisting around the peaks and creeping through the gorges; the little narrow-gauge spur running down from San Luis Valley, lately transported bodily to Burma. And for surface trams the U. P., the San Diego and Arizona, the Santa Fe, the crack fliers with the"
REV:	"miniatures of trains running on the first and last narrow-gauge lines in America: the "Galloping Goose" of the Rio Grande Southern and the Rio Grande Western twisting around the peaks of the Colorado Rockies, and the "Chile Line" running down from San Luis Valley. And for surface trams the D. & R. G., the U. P., the San Diego and Arizona, the Santa Fe, the crack fliers with the"
358.1:	"California's"
REV:	"Arizona's"
389.25:	"takes"
REV:	"take"
393.9:	"*Reports, Bulletins, Magazines, etc.*"
REV:	Waters asked that this be set in type other than italic, "as it is a heading for the entries below, which are not books as those above."

GLOSSARY REVISIONS:

Page 395:

    ORIG: "amatrada—a noise-making machine of toothed wood, used by Spanish Colonials of Sangre de Cristo mountains"

The Colorado 83

REV: "amatrada—a small noise-making machine of toothed wood, used by Penitentes during the tinieblas"
ORIG: "aquatcate—a semitropical fruit grown in southwest U. S. and Mexico"
REV: "aguacate—avocado"
ORIG: "Aye de mi!"
REV: "Ay de mi"
ORIG: "bajada—the road or path by which one descends"
REV: "bajada—foothills and lower slopes of mountains or the roads and trails by which one descends them"
ORIG: "cantina—a canteen; a combined saloon and provision store"
REV: "cantina—saloon or bar"
TO BE ADDED: "casino—dance hall or gambling room"
ORIG: "chollo—a halfbreed"
REV: "cholo—half-breed"
ORIG: "chusquatas—alternate name for tortillas used by Indians near Tarascan lake in Mexico"
REV: "chusquatas—tortillas in the dialect of the Tarascan Indians around Lake Patzcuaro, Mexico"
ORIG: "copita—small glass or cup"
REV: "copita—drink of liquor, literally small glass"
TO BE ADDED: "disciplinas—whips of braided yucca fiber used by Penitentes"
TO BE ADDED: "excusado—toilet"
ORIG: "galleta grass—1 inch desert grass in Southwest"
REV: "galleta grass—short desert grass"
ORIG: "guajes—gourds with handles"
REV: "guajes—gourds"
ORIG: "hogan—the Navajo house"
REV: "hogan—Navajo Indian winter dwelling, of wood and adobe, octagonal in shape, with the door always facing east"

Page 396:
ORIG: "loncherias—small, drab cafes in Mexico"
REV: "loncheria—small cafe or sidewalk lunch-counter"

Section A

ORIG: "Laguna Salada—Salty Lagoon"
REV: "Laguna Salada—Salt Lake"

ORIG: "peon—a person bound to service in payment of debt"
REV: "peon—peasant farmer of Mexico, formerly a serf on a hacienda"

ORIG: "piñons—pine trees"
REV: "piñon—low pine of a species bearing nuts called piñones"

ORIG: "pitero—man who plays the flute among Sp. Colonials of Sangre de Cristo mountains"
REV: "pitero—the flute player of the Penitentes"

ORIG: "pito—a reed flute, used by the Sp. Colonials of the Sangre de Cristo mountains"
REV: "pito—a reed flute player of the Penitentes"

TO BE ADDED: "plaza—public square or market place"

TO BE ADDED: "pedregales—desert mosaic of flattened stones"

ORIG: "rurales—police force in Imperial Valley"
REV: "rurales—armed rural police of Mexico"

ORIG: "taco—light lunch with draught of wine"
REV: "taco—Mexican sandwich of meet, cheese, etc. rolled up in a tortilla to resemble a plug, stopper or ramrod, its literal translation"

ORIG: "tequila—Mexican liquor"
REV: "tequila—Mexican liquor distilled from the juice of the tequila agave"

ORIG: "tinieblas—"tiniebla" is Spanish for "darkness;" the last act of the Passion as re-enacted by Brothers Penitent—a moment of silence with everyone kneeling in darkness of their church, followed by tremendous burst of noise symbolizing the resurrection"
REV: "tinieblas—"tiniebla" is Spanish for "darkness;" the last of the Passion as re-enacted by the Penitentes—the period of darkness and silence through which the people wait in the morada, followed by a tremendous burst of noise symbolizing the resurrection"

ORIG: "tortillas—Mexican pancakes, made with Indian corn mashed and baked in a little pan"
REV: "tortillas—Mexican bread of life; pancakes of ground corn

The Colorado   85

     to which lime is added, patted thin and flat between the hands, and cooked over an open fire on a piece of sheet tin"
ORIG: "vega—a flat plain"
REV: "vega—meadow"
TO BE ADDED: "viga—roof beam"
TO BE ADDED: "vapor—steamboat"
TO BE ADDED: "wickiup—brush shelter used by Apaches, Mojaves and other desert Indians"
TO BE ADDED: "Yanqui—Yankee or American"
TO BE ADDED: "yegua parda—buckskin mare"

A9b First edition, second printing [first published impression] [1946]

THE COLORADO | *by* | FRANK WATERS | *Illustrated by* | [small caps with a capital] NICOLAI FECHIN | *Maps by* | [small caps with a capital] GEORGE ANNAND | NATIONAL TRAVEL CLUB

7$^{15}/_{16}$ × 5$^{7}/_{16}$". [1⁸ 2-13¹⁶ 14⁸]: 208 leaves. Pagination identical with A9a. The color plate inserted in A9a was not issued with this impression.

CONTENTS: Identical with A9a, except that the series title and title page do not have the Fechin drawings as background; and p. vi: "[Rinehart device of an 'R' within a circle] | COPYRIGHT, 1946, BY FRANK WATERS | ALL RIGHTS RESERVED | PRINTED IN THE UNITED STATES OF AMERICA | AMERICAN BOOK-STRAT=FORD PRESS, INC., NEW YORK".

ILLUSTRATIONS: Identical with A9a, except, as noted above, there are no illustrations on the series title and title page and the color plate was not issued with this impression.

BINDING: Black cloth. National Travel Club device stamped in gilt in center of front cover, within blind-stamped single rules. Spine lettered in gilt: "[fancy rule] | [thin-thick-thin rules] | THE | COLORADO | [thin-thick-thin rules] | FRANK | WATERS | [publisher's device of a sailing vessel on the ocean, within a circle] | N·T·C | [fancy rule]". Cream colored endpapers.

86   Section A

Dust Jacket: Not seen.

Published in July, 1946. Price unknown. 1,493 copies were printed. A full-page review and advertisement appeared in the July, 1946 issue of *Travel Magazine* (p. 31).

Copies: University of South Florida, Tampa, Florida; TAT.

Note: In a letter to Frank Waters on July 29, 1946, Adelaide A. Sherer, Managing Editor for Rinehart & Company, informed him that arrangements had been made in April, 1946, for a special edition of *The Colorado* to be issued by the National Travel Club. She informed him in that letter that the Club printed from Rinehart's plates a total of 1,493 copies, and paid a royalty of $.391 per copy plus a plate rental of $.009 per copy.

A9c   Second edition, only printing   [1947]

1236 AN ARMED SERVICES EDITION PUBLISHED BY AR= RANGEMENT WITH | RINEHART & COMPANY, INC., NEW YORK | [rule] | [script] The Colorado | BY | FRANK WATERS | *MAPS BY* | GEORGE ANNAND | [publisher's device of an eagle within an oval outlined in black, white and black, with the words "ARMED SERVICES EDITION" within] | EDITIONS FOR THE ARMED SERVICES, INC. | A NON-PROFIT ORGANIZATION ESTABLISHED BY | THE COUNCIL ON BOOKS IN WARTIME, NEW YORK

6⅜ × 4". Perfectbound: 192 leaves. Pp. [1-6] 7-8 [9-10] 11-22 [23] 24-84 [85] 86-131 [132-134] 135-283 [284] 285-363 [364] 365-379 [380] 381-384. Pages 6 and 10 are blank.

Copyright Page: "TO | CARL, DOC, RALPH AND ED | [small caps with a capital] COPYRIGHT, 1946, [small caps] BY [small caps with a capital] FRANK WATERS | *All rights reserved* | MANUFACTURED IN THE UNITED STATES OF AMERICA".

Maps: The maps by George Annand which appeared in A9a were also used in this edition; the double-page map appears on pages 4-5, two full-page maps appear on pages 23 and 85; and three text maps appear on pages 39, 59, and 106. The illustrations by Nicolai Fechin were not used in this edition.

Paperback. Published price unknown. Date of publication and number of copies printed unknown. In a letter to Waters on April 11, 1947, Stanley M. Rinehart reported that the Armed Service Edition was just in. In the letter, Rinehart informed Waters that the usual run of these editions was around 20,000 copies.

COPIES: NmU.

A9d   First edition, third (second Rinehart) printing   [1958]

Title identical with A9a, except there is no Fechin drawing as background.

$7^{31}/_{32} \times 5^{3}/_{8}''$. Collation and pagination identical with A9a. The color plate inserted in A9a is not present in this printing.

CONTENTS: Identical with A9a, except for the following pages: p. ii: "*Rivers of America Books* | [series device] | [list of 23 titles, the first being *The Alleghany* and the last being *Lower Mississippi*]"; p. iii, contains a list of 29 more titles in the series, the first listed on that page being *The Mackenzie* and the last being *Songs of the Rivers of America;* p. iv: the background drawing by Fechin has been deleted; and p. vi: "COPYRIGHT, 1946, BY FRANK WATERS | ALL RIGHTS RE= SERVED | PRINTED IN THE UNITED STATES OF AMERICA".

Cloth. Published at $4.50, sometime in 1958? Number of copies printed unknown.

COPIES: TAT.

NOTE: The only indication for the date of this printing comes from the *Cumulative Book Index* for 1957-58, which records a clothbound edition of the book, published at $4.50. *Books in Print* for 1958 records the price of the book as $4.50, while in the *Publisher's Trade List Annual* for 1957 the price is still listed as $4.00.

   The list of titles in the Rivers series on pages ii and iii does not include a listing of *The Merrimac*, which title is listed in *Books in Print* for

1958 as "in preparation" and which is listed in *Books in Print* for 1959 as having been published in 1958. Also, a number of titles listed on pages ii and iii were not published until 1956, which certainly places this printing after that date at the earliest.

One other bit of evidence for the date of this printing is to be found on the dust jacket. Although it is dangerous to build a case on "transferable" evidence, I think it not unreasonable in this instance. On the dust jacket of my personal copy, which is the only one I have been able to locate, the price has been clipped off, but the word "Second" is still visible at the top of the front flap. Assuming that Rinehart was indicating this to be the second printing (although they might well have incorrectly used the word edition), it can be determined that this jacket was not printed substantially in advance of the book it is on, because *The Merrimac* is listed among the titles in the series on the rear of the jacket.

A9e   First edition, fourth (third Rinehart) printing   [1959]

Title page identical with A9d.

$8 \times 5^{11}\!/_{32}''$. Perfectbound: 208 leaves. Pagination identical with A9a; the Fechin color plate inserted in A9a is not present in this printing.

CONTENTS: Identical with A9d, except for page ii, which now carries a listing of 24 titles, the last being *The Mackenzie;* and page iii, to which *The Merrimac* has been added as the first listed title on the page, making a total of 29 titles.

Paperback. Published at $1.95 sometime in 1959; number of copies printed unknown. Listed in the "Weekly Record" of *Publisher's Weekly* on December 28, 1959.

COPIES: FW; TAT.

NOTE: This paperback printing is listed in the *Cumulative Book Index* for 1959, and first appears in *Books in Print* in the 1959 volume. In a letter to his agent Marie Rodell on September 28, 1959, Waters mentioned that Rinehart had brought out "a new paperback edition this summer."

The Merrimac, which had been added to the listing of the series in this printing, was published sometime in 1958; it is listed in the 1958

Books in Print as "in preparation", and appears in the 1959 *Books in Print* with a 1958 publication date.

NOTE: Although the number of copies printed is unknown, the publisher reported to Waters in 1966 that 1,300 copies remained in stock.

A9f   First edition, fifth printing—augmented   [1974]

The | *COLORADO* | [acorn and floral ornament] | *by FRANK WATERS* | *illustrated by NICOLAI FECHIN* | *maps by GEORGE ANNAND* | *HOLT, RINEHART AND WINSTON* | New York Chicago San Fran= cisco

8 × 5⅜". Perfectbound: 214 leaves. Pp. [i-vi] vii-xxii [xxiii-xxvi], [1-2] 3-400 [401-402]. Pagination of pages 3 to 400 identical with A9a.

CONTENTS: p. i, half-title: *"The | COLORADO"*; p. ii, "[Rivers of America Series device] | RIVERS OF AMERICA | *edited by Carl Carmer* | *as planned and started by* | *Constance Lindsay Skinner* | *asso= ciate editor Jean Crawford"*; p. iii, title; p. iv, copyright notice: "Copyright, 1946, by Frank Waters | Preface to the 1974 edition copyright © 1974 by Frank Waters | All rights reserved, including the right to reproduce | this book or portions thereof in any form. | Pub= lished simultaneously in Canada by Holt, Rinehart | and Winston of Canada, Limited. | Library of Congress Catalog Card Number: 73-10984 | ISBN: 0-03-089389-5 | Printed in the United States of America: 054"; p. v, "TO | CARL, DOC, RALPH AND ED"; p. vi, blank; pp. vii-viii, contents; pp. ix-xx, "Preface to the 1974 Edition", signed at the end of page xx, "FRANK WATERS | *Taos, New Mexico* | *September, 1973"*; pp. xxi-xxii, Introduction; p. xxiii, blank; pp. xxiv-xxv, double-page map of the Colorado basin; p. xxvi, blank; pp. 1-400, identical with A9a: pp. 401-402, blank.

ILLUSTRATIONS AND MAPS: Identical with A9a, except that the double-page map by George Annand appears on pages xxiv-xxv in this printing; and the inserted color plate by Fechin found in A9a was not issued with this printing.

Paperback. Published at $4.95 in 1974; number of copies printed unknown. Deposited in Library of Congress July 25, 1974.

90 Section A

Copies: DLC (rebound); NmU; FW; Skokie Public Library, Skokie, Illinois.

Note: Although this printing contains none of the corrections requested by Waters in 1947 (see A9a), it does contain one change which was specifically requested by Waters at the time of this printing:

255.27-30: "At the time of the massacre, the chiefs White Antelope | and War Bonnet, were away—talking peace and appease- | ment, although there is no record of their carrying umbrel= las. | What happened when they heard? "Peace in our time"?"

1974: "At the time of the massacre, the old chief White Ante- | lope was standing in front of his lodge with folded arms, | calmly singing his death song. He was murdered by the cav- | alry who mutilated him horribly."

Note: The new preface written for this printing was supposedly printed first in the *New York Times* on January 5, 1973, under the title "Colorado Fever", but see the note to C69.

Excerpts from *The Colorado*

A9g *The Place No One Knew: Glen Canyon,* by Eliot Porter. (San Francisco, Sierra Club Books, 1963). Pages 24, 25, 156.

A9h *Time and the River Flowing: Grand Canyon,* by Francois Leydet. (San Francisco, Sierra Club Books, 1964). Pages 20, 111.

A9i *Colorado: A Literary Chronicle,* edited by W. Storrs Lee. (New York, Funk & Wagnalls, 1970). Pages 447-452.

A9j *Grand Canyon of the Living Colorado,* by Roderick Nash. (San Francisco/New York, Sierra Club/Ballantine Books, 1970). Page 98.

A10   THE YOGI OF COCKROACH COURT

Waters wrote the first version of this novel in 1927 and submitted the manuscript—then titled "Barby"—to Liveright, some time after publication of *Fever Pitch,* in 1930. Liveright rejected the manuscript, and Waters submitted it to various other New York publishers, including Farrar & Rinehart, who turned it down in 1936. Nearly twenty years later, however, Rinehart & Company did accept for publication a revised version of the novel.

In a letter to John Selby of Rinehart on June 27, 1946 [misdated 1947 in the carbon at NmU], Waters wrote:

> Your letter about the Cockroach Court ms. has made me feel very good indeed.
> I don't like those newspaper stories toward the end either. The problem was how to deviate, for once, from the personal point of view of the four participating characters in order to show the distorted perspective of them by the outside world. There were only two ways to do it. Straight narration from the omnipotent author's point of view. Or dragging in an outside character to present it. Both were bad; no matter how thin you cut it, it would still be exposition.
> Hence I came to the conclusion that taking the bull by the horns would be best—sacrificing smoother technique for immediate effect by condensing the whole thing boldly, absolutely objectively, in two pages, immediately following the old man's analogy between local and world-wide events. With your present word of caution now, it might be well to insert a sentence linking these newspaper stories to his repugnance of them as given on p. 11. But do let me have any further thoughts you have about it.
> The contract I'll let you arrange according to your own better judgment. The only suggestion I have is that it might best be for only this book, without the usual option on the "next book". The reason is that my next books are not wholly mine. One is a large art album of Nicolai Fechin's paintings and drawings, for which I have done some comments and his biography. [This work was

never published, but see C22.] He is handling the publishing of it himself. I am also contracting to develop a story with a collaborator for Paramount, being paid by them on a flat basis. This novelized version—like *River Lady* of some years ago—will probably be published under a joint arrangement between Paramount and Farrar and Straus. [The book was published as *Diamond Head* by Frank Waters and Houston Branch—see A11.]

Due to John Farrar's pulling out of your own house, with evident complications you know better than I, I don't want to get into an unethical position even in good faith.

Also Hervey Allen suggested that my own next book be a re-doing of Lewis and Clark's original diary, which might have to be handled on a different basis than an original novel. However, if you want to add an option on "another" book in general terms to cover this possibility it will be O.K. Anyway you will know what is reasonable.

The main thing is that we can go ahead with this on the heels of *The Colorado*.

Selby responded to Waters on July 8, 1946, saying that even with the situation as outlined he hoped to be able to include a "next" book in the contract if possible. He informed Waters that he would have the contract drawn up to include an advance of $1000.00 against royalties starting at 10% for the first 3,500 copies, 12½% on the next 1,500 copies and 15% thereafter, with half the advance payable upon signing the contract and the balance due on publication. He also remarked that he thought the idea of fixing up the newspaper business a good one, and that it could probably be as Waters had suggested. He asked that Waters send the sentence suggested earlier to him and it would be inserted in the manuscript.

Waters responded to Selby on July 13, 1946:

I'm a little surprised that you aren't continuing a straight 15% royalty these days. However, I think that if you'd eliminate entirely the 10% gradation, and make it 12½% on the first 5,000 copies and 15% thereafter it would be in line for writers you have had some time and on which you are not making a first plunge in the dark.

As I mentioned, there is no reason why you can't include an option on another book to be arranged for later, in these general terms, as we don't know what it will be yet—Hervey Allen's suggested Lewis and Clark journal, your Dam book, or an original novel of my own. . . .

Stanley Rinehart answered this letter himself in order to settle the matter of the royalties. In his letter to Waters of July 22, 1946, he said that the firm could not agree to Waters' request for royalties starting at 12½%, but would be willing to make the royalties 10% on the first 3,500 copies and 15% thereafter. Waters agreed to these terms, and a contract, dated August 6, 1946, was drawn up.

In a letter to John Selby on August 16, 1946, Waters reflected upon *Yogi:*

This contract for THE YOGI winds up for me many years of work on four closely related books. Two of them you have published and have been flat failures. Two are yet to come out; and as we both want them to do much better, I am taking the liberty of pointing out some of the things which correlate all four in the hope it will be of some value to you for promotion purposes.

THE COLORADO presents a factual, overall picture of the region embraced by all four. As you know, it is divided into three general topographical areas—the mountain, plateau and desert, with their various racial types.

PEOPLE OF THE VALLEY, THE MAN WHO KILLED THE DEER and THE YOGI OF COCKROACH COURT comprise what I have always regarded as a Dark-Skin or "Colorado Maduro" Trilogy of these indigenous types.

PEOPLE OF THE VALLEY was laid in the mountain area, portrayed the rural Spanish-Americans (Mexicans), and used as a religious background the cult of the Penitentes which although little known is still today of strong political importance.

THE MAN WHO KILLED THE DEER was laid in the plateau region, and was of course about Pueblo Indians with the primary theme their religious ceremonialism which permeates all the details of their daily life.

THE YOGI OF COCKROACH COURT, which ends the trilogy and prompts this view, is quite as original and off the beaten track. It is laid in the desert region, and is about the conglomerate cross-breed underworld of the whole area—the part Mexican, part Indian, part white, mestizos, criollos and coyotes. There is not a white Anglo of importance in it. In background and characters, it is of a piece with the others.

I have never been able to account for the complete failure of the first two, particularly in view of their excellent critical reviews. Perhaps the first came out before so many Government agencies, States and writers became seriously concerned with this racial minority.

On THE DEER we ourselves missed the boat completely by presenting it as an innocuous idyllic, Indian "love-story" which it wasn't. Now, for perhaps the first time in literature, the public has become greatly interested in our "Vanishing Americans". This is natural and inevitable; it stems from the current vogue in extreme sectionalism, nationalism, Americanism, which is making the Rivers of America Series such a success. The value of Indian books, next to mere readability, is judged by their ethnological content—i.e. accurate portrayal and sound interpretation of their customs, ceremonialism, dance and art forms, which alone differentiates them from the white. The success of a dozen later books of less intrinsic merit bear this out, as well as the constant requests I am receiving for THE DEER. For this reason I am hoping that if THE COLORADO and THE YOGI meet with any success, you will seriously consider reissuing THE DEER.

What sets THE YOGI apart, and may give it a sales impetus the others did not have, is its more general substance. It is at once a universal and realistic "love-story", and yet for the first time I'm aware of it presents in novel form the Eastern yogic ideology opposed to Western sociology and psychological

94   SECTION A

method, that Aldous Huxley, Arthur Koestler, Isherwood and Van Druten have been plugging so successfully in essay form, to say nothing of the learned treatises of Mumford Jones and F. S. C. Northrop.

Its paradox is that it is at once a "Western" yarn and a novel of strictly modern ideas, both of which may have a different reading public to appeal to. The only way I reconcile this, in my own mind at least, is that this novel, like the others, seems concerned with basic patterns of religious thought as well as with sociological surface action. This, for any writer, seems as valid an approach as any other—though the first two didn't prove it.

At any rate, the main thing I'm trying to get over is that there has been a consistent theme and premise running through all these books. They have not been hit and miss, mere photographs of local scenes. And for you to hit upon it, as a publisher, might be of some value in avoiding another dud. . . .

Unfortunately, the work did not sell any better than either *Deer* or *People*. An interesting sidelight to the fate of YOGI involved Rinehart's attempt to market the book in England. Adelaide Sherer, managing editor at Rinehart, reported to Waters on May 1, 1947, that their London agent reported to them that Peter Davies Ltd. had turned down the novel as "unsavoury" because of the lesbianism of the main female character, and the agent further doubted whether any reputable English firm would touch the book.

THE YOGI OF
A10   COCKROACH COURT   [1947]

A10a   First edition, first printing

[small caps] THE Yogi of | Cockroach Court | By FRANK WATERS | RINEHART & COMPANY, INC. | 19 New York 47
                                                                              Toronto

8⅛ × 5½". [1⁸ 2-9¹⁶ 10⁸]: 144 leaves. Pp. [i-vi], [1-2] 3-263 [264] 265-275 [276] 277 [278-282]. Numbers printed in roman in headline at outer margin of type page, except for pages 3, 18, 43, 60, 80, 101, 124, 143, 163, 190, 218, 240 and 265, on which the numbers are printed in the center at the foot of the page.

CONTENTS: p. i, half-title: "The Yogi of Cockroach Court"; p. ii, "Books by Frank Waters | [list of 8 titles]"; p. iii, title; p. iv, copyright notice: "The line quoted from *Hindustan* on p. 65 is reprinted | by per=

The Yogi of Cockroach Court 95

mission of The Forster Music Publisher, Inc. | Copyright, 1918 and 1946 by FORSTER MUSIC PUB- | LISHER, INC., Chicago, Ill. | [publisher's device of an 'R' within a circle] | COPYRIGHT, 1947, BY FRANK WATERS | PRINTED IN THE UNITED STATES OF AMERICA | BY J. J. LITTLE AND IVES COMPANY, NEW YORK | ALL RIGHTS RESERVED"; p. v, quotation: "Nos infaman y nos menoscaban, porque somos plebeyos. | Solo nosotros que lo hemos sentidos sabemos lo que | son penas, lo que son congojas, como es notorio! | *Hexotziquense";* p. vi, blank; p. 1, second half-title; p. 2, blank; pp. 3-17, Prologue; pp. 18-263, text; p. 264, blank; pp. 265-275, Epilogue; p. 276, blank; p. 277, Acknowledgments; pp. 278-282, blank.

BINDING: Red paper over boards in imitation of cloth. Stamped on spine only in gilt: "[reading vertically] *The* YOGI *of* COCKROACH | COURT [wavy rule] *Frank Waters* | [horizontally] *Rinehart"*. Top edges stained yellow; fore and bottom edges untrimmed. White endpapers.

DUST JACKET (white paper): Front and spine printed overall in purple. The front contains a small illustration of two wooden buildings and a barren tree, in yellow and white. Lettered on front: "[white] THE [triangle ornament] YOGI [triangle ornament] OF | [following lines in yellow] *Cockroach* | *Court* | *by* FRANK WATERS". Spine: "[reading vertically] [white] *The* YOGI *of* [yellow] COCKROACH | [yellow] COURT *by Frank Waters* [small version of illustration on front] | [horizontally] [yellow] *Rinehart"*. Rear lettered all in purple: "[thick-thin rules] [photograph of the author] | [five line notice of the author] | [thick-thin rules] | RINEHART & COMPANY, INC. | 232 Madison Avenue [space] New York 16, N.Y.". The front flap carries a blurb for this book, which is carried over onto the rear flap, all printed in purple; the front flap also contains a notice that the jacket was designed by Alan Haemer, and both flaps contain the publisher's imprint at the bottom.

Published at $2.75 on April 10, 1947. Number of copies printed unknown. Copyrighted April 10, 1947; deposited February 22, 1947.

REVIEWS: *Kirkus Reviews,* February 15, 1947 (p. 110); *San Francisco Chronicle,* April 10, 1947 (p. 14); *New York Times Book Review,* April 13, 1947 (p. 12); *New York Herald Tribune Weekly Book Review,* April

96   SECTION A

27, 1947 (16); *Saturday Review of Literature,* May 24, 1947 (p. 12); *Chicago Sun Book Week,* June 8, 1947 (p. 2).

COPIES: DLC (2 copies); NmU; TAT (5 copies, 3 in d.j.).

NOTE: At least one copy of this printing was specially bound in full blue hard-grain morocco, with five raised bands on the spine. This copy was presented to Waters by the publisher and is currently in the private collection of Frank Waters.

A10b   First edition, first Swallow Press printing   [1972]

[small caps] THE Yogi of | Cockroach Court | FRANK WATERS | SAGE BOOKS | [publisher's sagebrush device] | [small caps] THE [caps] SWALLOW PRESS [small caps] INC. | CHICAGO

8¼ × 5¹⁵⁄₃₂″. Perfectbound: 144 leaves. Pagination identical with A10a.

CONTENTS: Identical with A10a, except for page ii: "BOOKS BY FRANK WATERS | [list of 12 titles]"; and page iv: "Copyright © 1947 by Frank Waters | All rights reserved | Printed in the United States of America | Sage Paperback 1972 | Sage Books are published by | The Swallow Press Incorporated | 1139 South Wabash Avenue | Chicago, Illinois 60605 | This book is printed on recycled paper | ISBN 0-8040-0613-X | LIBRARY OF CONGRESS CARD CATALOG NUMBER 72-91922 | *The Yogi of Cockroach Court* was first published by | Rinehart & Company, Inc., New York, 1947 | The line quoted from *Hindustan* on page 65 is reprinted by | permission of The Forster Music Publisher, Inc. | Copyright 1918 and 1946 by Forster Music Publisher, Inc., Chicago".

Paperback. Published at $2.75 in November, 1972; 3,492 copies were printed.

COPIES: FW; TAT.

NOTE: The quotation which appears on page v has been reset in this printing. In A10a the three lines of text are justified along the right margin, whereas in this printing the lines are not justified.

NOTE: Frank Waters' contract with the Swallow Press for this paperback reprinting was dated April 18, 1972, and outlined royalties of 7½% on the first 4,999 copies, and 10% thereafter. The contract also outlined a royalty schedule for a clothbound issue (10% on the first 3,999 copies, 12½% on the next 3,501 copies, and 15% thereafter), but no clothbound copies were issued.

A10c First edition, second Swallow Press printing

Identical with A10b, except that copies measure 8½ × 5¹⁵⁄₃₂″. While the copyright page still gives the publisher's address as 1139 South Wabash, the address given on the rear wrapper is 811 W. Junior Terrace.

Paperback. Published at $3.50. Date of publication and number of copies printed unknown.

COPIES: TAT.

NOTE: Although no precise date can be fixed for this printing, it must have been accomplished after the move to 811 W. Junior Terrace in 1976. According to existing royalty records, the inventory on hand at the close of 1975 was 432 copies (of A10b), and sales for the two previous years had averaged between 400 and 500 copies. This would seem to indicate further that this printing was accomplished sometime in 1976 or early 1977.

A11 DIAMOND HEAD

Houston Branch, with whom Waters had collaborated on *River Lady* [see A7], first proposed the idea for this book in a letter to Waters on March 2, 1946. In this letter, Branch told Waters that he had worked up a story in the hopes of getting John Wayne at Republic to star in the film. When Wayne got married, Branch submitted the story to Paramount. Paramount rejected it, but showed it to Cecile B. DeMille, who expressed interest. In order to make the film more appealing to DeMille, Branch wished to enlarge his idea into a novel, and proposed that he and Waters do the novelization after he finished working up an outline for DeMille.

Arrangements were made through Branch's agent, David Diamond, and on April 17, 1946, Diamond wrote to Waters that he had worked out a deal with Farrar and Straus to publish the novel. The highlights of the proposed contract included a guaranteed first printing of 25,000 copies, with an advance of $2000.00 (half to be paid on signing and the balance upon delivery of the manuscript) against royalties of 12½% on the first 5,000 copies and 15% thereafter. Publication was tentatively scheduled for September of 1947.

Branch sent the manuscript as he had worked it up—roughly 300 pages—to Waters in June of 1946, and Waters began work on his novelization. On August 27, 1946, Branch wrote to Waters that DeMille had decided against doing the picture, but that Dave Diamond thought it could still be sold to a studio after the novel was published.

Sometime in the Spring of 1947 the manuscript was sent to Farrar and Straus, who sent it to an independent reader. This reader's report was sent to Waters, who responded to John Farrar on July 14, 1947:

> I returned from a short stint of reading manuscripts at Denver to find your reader's report on our own manuscript. I sent it on to Branch and have his comments to add to my own.

I think the report good for the most part, and that most of the minor changes can be made without difficulty.

However, the report poses on the first page a major problem that worries us both; that is, that the book as a piece of historical fiction is weakened by the fictional parts which were added to make it popular romantic fiction. Last March in California, Branch and I solved this same contention by deciding that rather than produce a straight historical narrative of undoubted historical value but of limited appeal, we should slant it toward wide appeal by making it romantic fiction based on historical truth. The movie people interested in it confirmed this decision; like the general public, they are more interested in story than in history. Hence our last revisions were made to integrate these two viewpoints.

During the three months you have had the ms., we have been hoping that your report on it would accept this premise and measure our success with it. As it is, it is a little confusing. We are wondering if it represents the opinion of the Mr. Beecroft you mentioned, as regards the possible reaction of book clubs, which would be most important; if it coincides with your own editorial viewpoint; or whether it is simply the opinion of a disinterested reader. Also we are still anxious to receive your suggested alternate titles so that the one chosen may be embodied in the manuscript if necessary. . . .

Farrar responded to this letter on July 21, 1947. In his letter he informed Waters he also wanted a romantic novel, but that he thought it necessary to make the novel as believable as possible, not from the standpoint of the historical events upon which it was based, but rather such that the novel would achieve its own reality within its setting. Farrar also mentioned that he liked "Victory Spring" for a title, but thought that "Diamond Head" would probably be best.

Waters undertook to revise the manuscript in light of Farrar's suggestions, and returned it to John Farrar with a cover letter dated August 29, 1947:

Here is the revised DIAMOND HEAD under its new title: some 80 revised pages to replace those in your original copy; and also my complete second copy with a few minor corrections in ink as well.

We have made practically every change suggested by Peggy Jones. Added some sub-sections to strengthen the motives and characters of Old Macy, Abigail and Selida, which should clear up the mother business and the marriage. Rewritten the last chapter. Embodied the title DIAMOND HEAD in the text as the code-word for the secret mission, like the "operation-" in the last war. And I have tried to clean up the writing in the last half of the narrative.

The only change we didn't make was to eliminate Kirby's return to his native love. Kirby was purposely built sentimental and romantic as a foil to Richards' rational and practical nature. This seems wholly reasonable. The South was full of such young men. And after the Civil War, in the vast westward expansion, the world was over-run by men like him seeking new homes, new outlets, to recoup their losses and prestige. It is quite conceivable that one of them settled in Roa Pua to start a trading company. And his human weaknesses don't detract from his important participation in the venture. Unless no hero in these days can have an Achilles heel.

If you'll buy that, I think we have a pretty tight narrative in all respects and I hope you all agree. . . .

In a letter sent over both their signatures on March 9, 1948, Branch and Waters described their method of collaboration to Louise Dreifus, Managing Editor of *Writer's Digest:*

Miss Ely of Farrar, Straus and Company, has sent us the galleys of your interesting article about collaboration, and we are glad to add some comments on our own.

Neither of us believe in collaboration, and yet we have successfully collaborated on two novels: RIVER LADY, published by Farrar and Rinehart and now being produced as a Technicolor motion picture by Universal-International, and DIAMOND HEAD to be published April 15th by Farrar, Straus and Company.

One of us has written nearly one hundred original stories for the movies. The other has written six novels and two non-fiction books. Both of us are stubbornly set and highly individualistic in our manner of working. One develops an idea by means of story structure, plot; the other by character. One strives for pace; the other for fullness. One aims at effect by the accurate detail achieved by competent research; the other by the impressionistic mood. And to add to these differences we live a thousand miles apart. Thus, to sit down and work together from scratch would be impossible; we would never finish the first page.

But it is precisely these great differences between us which have enabled us to work apart on the same thing, for we have a profound respect for each other's capacities and methods and have learned to use them to compliment [sic] our own.

Once agreed on an idea—the time, setting and general theme for a book, we meet and discuss it thoroughly. One of us develops the plot structure and sets the pace in a brief outline, alone and without hindrance in California.

Weeks or months later the other, in New Mexico, begins to expand this outline in full narrative form. He develops the main characters, creates minor ones, builds in subsidiary incidents. He has complete freedom to work in his own way, guided by the salient scenes already set as guideposts. He knows where he is going, the effect to be achieved; but it is up to him to find his own way.

During this year or more of writing, the California partner is just as busy. He supplies all calls for authentic research material; receives each chapter as it is finished and makes suggestions to enhance its effect; and is ready to make a thousand-mile jaunt at frequent intervals to discuss the various stages of progress.

Our current DIAMOND HEAD is a good example of the immense effort required. The story of the little-known Confederate raider, the SHENAN-

DOAH, laid in the time of the Civil War, and against such diverse backgrounds as Richmond, the whaling port of New Bedford, cosmopolitan London, the tropical island of Roa Pua, Hawaii under the old monarchy, and the Arctic, it required over forty books for research, the investigation of old archives and visits to a dozen museums throughout the United States. To do all this research, as well as the writing, would have required of one man at least five years work. And he probably would have been bogged down by the sheer abundance of this material. But getting together in the fall, and again next summer in a little log cabin high on Lobo Mountain in northern New Mexico, we were able to steer our course through 58,000 miles of sea, through every ocean in the world, and to circumnavigate the globe—interrupted only by the cry of coyotes behind the fringe of pines.

The book was finished in March after two years work and brought to California. Here came the real test of collaboration—a complete agreement on the manuscript, page by page, with all necessary revisions, ommissions [sic] and additions. And again, months later, after receiving suggestions from the publisher for more changes.

But the creative work had been done; we were no longer writers. We were, or tried to be, purely objective readers with the single desire to eliminate every incident, descriptive paragraph and phrase that did not hold attention and contribute to the flow and effect of the whole.

At such a time the publisher, if he is the right publisher, enters into the collaboration. In our case Mr. John Farrar was indeed an apt collaborator. One of the finest editors in the country, he has had wide experience with work and writers of every kind. Moreover he had published our RIVER LADY, knew our work. We had no hesitation in adopting his suggestions for minor changes.

By the time we received galley proofs, then, we had no doubt that we had produced a book that neither one of us could have produced separately. Indeed, it seemed not ours at all. Rather a complete narrative that stood confidently on its own feet. A happy collaboration between a subject three-quarters of a century in the past; two writers in California and New Mexico, a thousand miles apart; and an editor in New York, two thousand miles farther away. A collaboration which to prove itself completely successful, must require the last and final collaborator of all—the readers, few or great, to whose enjoyment all our combined work has appealed.

A11 DIAMOND HEAD [1948]

A11a First edition, first printing

Diamond Head | B Y | HOUSTON BRANCH and FRANK WATERS | [rule] | [five-point star] | FARRAR, STRAUS AND COMPANY | *1948*
 All the above within single rules.

7^{15}⁄$_{16}$ × 5⅜". [1-12^{16}]: 192 leaves. Pp. [I-II], [i-iv] v-vii [viii], [1-3] 4-57 [58] 59-114 [115] 116-177 [178] 179-221 [222] 223-287 [288] 289-371 [372-374]. Numbers printed in italic in headline at outer margin of type page, except for page v which is numbered in roman in the center at the foot of the page.

CONTENTS: p. I, half-title: "Diamond Head | [short rule] | [five-point star]"; p. II, *"Also by Houston Branch and Frank Waters:* RIVER LADY"; p. i, title; p. ii, copyright notice: *"Copyright, 1948, by Hous= ton Branch and Frank Waters* | [2-line notice of reservation of rights, in italic] | [publisher's device of a calligraphic 'f' and 's'] | *Manufactured in the U.S.A. by H. Wolff, New York | Designed by Stefan Salter"*; p. iii, contents; p. iv, blank; pp. v-vii, "Author's Note," signed at end: "H. B. and F. W."; p. viii, blank; p. 1, second half-title; p. 2, blank; pp. 3-371, text; pp. 372-374, blank.

BINDING: Gray cloth. Lettered on spine only in blue: "BRANCH and | WATERS | [five-point star in red] | Diamond | Head | [five-point star in red] | FARRAR | STRAUS". White endpapers.

DUST JACKET: The dust jacket has been noted in two variants, both printed on white paper. The order given below is arbitrary; no priority is known.

A. Front and spine printed overall with an illustration of a man and a woman with Diamond Head in the background, in green, blue, yellow, red, brown, tan, purple and black; signed in the extreme lower left "[purple script] Barojá [?]". Lettered on front: "[fancy type, white shaded in purple] DIAMOND | [next two lines in yellow with swash capitals] *Houston Branch and | Frank Waters* | [fancy type, white shaded in purple] HEAD [yellow italic with swash capitals] authors of "River Lady" ". Spine lettered in white: "[first three lines with swash capitals] *Branch | and | Waters* | [reading vertically] [fancy type, shaded in blue] DIAMOND HEAD | [horizontally] [two lines with swash capitals] Farrar | Straus". Rear: "THE STORY OF THE *Shenandoah* | [three paragraph blurb] | FARRAR, STRAUS AND CO. | 53 E. 34th St., New York 16, N.Y.". The front flap contains a blurb for this book which is carried over onto the rear flap.

B. Identical with the above, except that the title on the spine is shaded in yellow, and the other lines on the spine are printed in yellow.

Published at $3.50 on April 23, 1948; 25,000 copies were printed. Copyrighted April 23, 1948; deposited April 21, 1948.

REVIEWS: *Kirkus Reviews*, February 15, 1948 (p. 95); *Library Journal*, April 15, 1948 (p. 651); *New York Times Book Review*, May 2, 1948 (p. 7); *New York Herald Tribune Weekly Book Review*, November 14, 1948 (p. 38).

COPIES: DLC (2 copies); NmU; FW; TAT (3 copies, one of each variant of the jacket and one copy without jacket).

A11b   First edition, only English printing   [1950]

[all within single rules] Diamond Head | BY | HOUSTON BRANCH and FRANK WATERS | [rule] | [five-point star] | LONDON [star ornament] NEW YORK | T. V. BOARDMAN & COMPANY LIMITED | 14 COCKSPUR STREET, LONDON S.W.1 | *1950*

7½ × 5³⁄₁₆". [A⁸] B-H⁸ J-U⁸ W-Z⁸: 192 leaves; the final leaf, Z8, which is blank, has been used as the rear pastedown. Pagination identical with A11a.

CONTENTS: Identical with A11a, except for page ii: *"First published in Great Britain 1950 | Copyright throughout the British Empire Market | (except Canada)* | PRINTED AND BOUND IN GREAT BRITAIN | BY THE HOLLEN STREET PRESS LTD. LONDON W. 1.".

BINDING: Mauve cloth, stamped in silver on spine only: "DIAMOND | HEAD | HOUSTON | BRANCH | and | FRANK | WATERS | Boardman". White endpapers at front; Z8 used as rear pastedown.

DUST JACKET (white paper): Front carries an illustration of a man and a woman with a ship in a harbor in the background, in blue, pink, black, white, brown and gray, and is signed at the lower right: "[script] Sington". Lettered on front: "[first two lines in black shaded in pink] DIAMOND | HEAD | [all the following lines in script] Houston | Branch | Frank Waters". The spine carries a slightly different illustration of the same man and woman, and is lettered: "[first two lines in pink] DIAMOND | HEAD | [script] Houston | [script] Branch | [irregular rule] | [script] Frank | [script] Waters | [pink] BOARDMAN". The

104   SECTION A

rear carries advertisements in red and black for A. B. Guthrie's *The Way West* and Elleston Trevor's *Chorus of Echoes*. Front and rear flaps carry a blurb for this book in red and black.

Published at 10s, 6d on July 27, 1950. In a letter to the compiler, dated June 27, 1980, Mr. Tom Boardman, Jr., wrote: "in those days we were printing between 2,500 and 3,500 copies of novels." Deposited in the British Library on August 25, 1950.

COPIES: NmU.

NOTE: The contract drawn up between Boardman and Farrar, Straus on July 18, 1949, outlined an advance payment upon printing of £75 against royalties of 10% on the first 2,500 copies, 15% on the second 2,500 copies, and 20% thereafter.

A11c   Second edition, only printing   [1951?]

This edition was retitled *Secret Affair,* and published as Reader's Choice Book #32, by the St. John Publishing Company of New York. No copy has been seen.

NOTE: The contract between the St. John Publishing Company and Farrar, Straus was originally signed on December 14, 1949, and called for an advance of $500.00 against royalties of ¼¢ on the first 25,000 copies and ½¢ thereafter. Dave Diamond objected to the royalty schedule, and a new contract, dated December 19, 1950, was drawn up with royalty rates set at 1¢ for the first 150,000 copies and 1½¢ thereafter, and with an additional advance of $250.00. According to this contract, publication was scheduled for early in 1951. It would seem that the book was not terribly successful, and the rights were returned to Farrar, Straus in March, 1952.

NOTE: The correspondence in the files of Farrar, Straus & Giroux refers to this as an "All-picture edition".

A11d   Third edition, only printing?   [1954?]

Diamond | Head | by | Houston Branch | and Frank Waters | Authors of: | RIVER LADY | A DELL BOOK

6⅓ × 4¼". Perfectbound: 192 leaves. Pp. [1-7] 8-9 [10-11] 12-65 [66-67] 68-124 [125] 126-188 [189] 190-232 [233] 234-299 [300-301] 302-384. Pages 2, 6, 10, 66 and 300 are blank.

COPYRIGHT PAGE: "Published by | DELL PUBLISHING COMPANY, INC. | 261 Fifth Avenue | New York 16, New York | Copyright, MCMXLVIII, | by Houston Branch and Frank Waters. | All rights re= served. | Reprinted by arrangement with | Farrar, Straus and Young, Inc., | New York, N. Y. | Designed and produced by | Western Printing & Lithographing Company | Cover painting by George Garland | Printed in U. S. A.".

Paperbound. Dell book D127. Published at $.35. Exact date of publication and number of copies printed unknown.

COPIES: NmU; TAT (2 copies).

NOTE: According to notes in the files of Farrar, Straus & Giroux, the contract with Dell was dated July 25, 1952, and a further letter of agreement regarding the royalty was dated March 11, 1953. Rights were returned to Farrar, Straus on November 28, 1955.

NOTE: Dell may have issued more than one printing of this book, but I have failed to find any evidence of this.

A12   MASKED GODS

In a letter to Frank Waters, dated July 30, 1947, Charles Allen, then editor of the University of New Mexico Press, wrote and asked Waters if he would be interested in doing a book for the Press on the Navaho Country, along the lines of his *Colorado*. After visiting with Waters in Taos, Allen again wrote on October 3, 1947, saying that the publications committee at the Press had considered the idea of the Navaho book and that they were enthusiastic about it and requested Allen to do all he could to encourage Waters to write the book.

Waters responded to Allen on October 20, 1947:

> I am beginning, between-times here, to organize my material for a book on the Hopis and Navajos. Your letter, though, poses several questions.
>
> Had your Committee agreed to reprint THE MAN WHO KILLED THE DEER, I would have agreed to your standard 10% royalty rate. Not only because as a regional writer I'd like to play ball with a regional publishing house, but because there is a definite demand for the DEER which could best be measured and exploited to both our interests by a house majoring in such subjects of primary interest in the Southwest. On a strictly commercial basis, however, it perhaps ought to be submitted on the same royalty basis that it would command from the New York houses publishing my other books, such as Rinehart & Co. which published THE COLORADO, or Farrar and Straus who are publishing my next book.
>
> There is also the question of whether you would attempt to reach the national market, such as THE COLORADO reached, or whether you would depend solely upon your local outlets. If you regard the book as being of primary regional interest it would naturally fall into the same category as the DEER, for which you believe there is not enough demand to justify reprinting despite the fact that it has already proved itself, whereas this one has yet to be critically sold as it were.
>
> Also your title THE NAVAJO COUNTRY bothers me. The "country" series of regional books being issued by Duell, Sloane and Pearce—PINON COUNTRY, DESERT COUNTRY etc.—would seem to claim it. And rather than a casual, informative book on the area, I want to make it a definitive, interpretative book on Indians. . . .

Allen responded to Waters on October 24, 1947, assuring him that the Press would attempt to reach a national market for the book, and that it was agreed that he should receive his standard royalty rate. Also, Allen informed Waters that he had chosen the title only by way of illustrating the subject of the book, and that Waters could choose any title he saw fit. Allen wrote again on December 1, 1947, asking if Waters could possibly do something for the *New Mexico Quarterly Review,* of which Allen had just been made acting editor. Waters responded on December 3, 1947:

> I have been postponing answering your last letter about the Navajo book from day to day under the press of a dozen impending and conflicting projects. Rinehart is insisting I come to New York to discuss doing a non-fiction book before making any other commitments. A French writer vacationing in Taos has telephoned, urging me to edit his book for Doubleday. I have a tentative date at M G M to discuss doing a story for them which I must prepare for. A previous story I novelized for Universal-International is now under production and I have been trying to secure rights for a cheap reprint edition. On top of all this galley proofs of a new novel are coming in from Farrar, Straus, New York [*Diamond Head*]. All this is most upsetting and unproductive, and I have been waiting till things clear up.
>
> However I suppose that is the usual situation with a double-job editor like yourself. I will write you definitely later about the Navajo book, but can assure you now I am planning to do it. Regarding the piece for the QUARTERLY REVIEW, I will do my best to get something to you by Christmas.
>
> It will be non-fiction. Something on the order of the leading article I did for last Summer's New Mexico Issue of the SOUTHWESTERN REVIEW. It was reprinted in the editorial pages of the SANTA FE NEW MEXICAN together with some critical letters about it, and a second article answering them, from July 29 to August 5, inclusive. It will not carry on the controversy, but will recapitulate some of the views. Does that sound OK?

Allen agreed to Waters' idea for the article, and also later agreed to have the article be incorporated as a chapter in the Navajo book, on which Waters had begun work early in 1948. Shortly after publication of the article, as "The Crucible of Conflict" in the Fall, 1948 issue of the *New Mexico Quarterly Review,* Waters wrote to Allen, in a letter dated September 24, 1948, apprising him of developments in the work:

> Many thanks for mailing me some copies of the Fall QUARTERLY REVIEW and a check for the article.
>
> I spent considerable time this summer travelling through the remote parts of the Navajo reservation, making field trips with an ethnologist, a doctor and a nurse, and also with some missionaries. Added to all the research stuff I have, this gives me a lot of fresh material to work. I shall probably remain here [Los

Angeles] to do it, as our little Taos house is not fit for winter living, and I have some odd jobs to finish here.

I am attaching for your information a detailed working outline, complete to sub-titles, of the first part of the book. This has been completed—about 225 pages—and comprises a brief history of the Navajos, Apaches, Hopis and Pueblos up to the present.

I am now working on Part Two which is told from the Indian point of view—their cosmography, legends and myths, an interpretation of their dances, ceremonialism and symbology.

Part Three, very short, will be an attempt to reconcile this with the meanings of our own religion, science and sociological trends along the line indicated by my current article.

As you can see, it is a much longer book, and a more definitive one, than first contemplated—and a much bigger job. It is really tough going, a process of boiling down and distillation all along. And it's going to take me another good year to finish it. I hope it will be worth it. At least there will be no other one as ambitious in scope or intent. . . .

On November 22, 1948, Waters wrote to Fred E. Harvey, director of the University Press, asking that the Press once again consider the possibility of reprinting *The Man Who Killed the Deer*. He mentioned to Harvey that full rights to the novel had been returned to him, and that it might do nicely as a follow-up to the current *New Mexico Quarterly Review* article. Having had no response from Harvey, he wrote to him again on January 28, 1949:

I am wondering if you received my letter of November 22, 1948. If you did not, or if it happened to be mislaid in your files before you could answer it, I will be glad to send you a copy.

The present Navajo and Pueblo book is growing into one much more intensive and important than I realized at the start. In it I am trying to synthesize the ceremonialism of the Navajos with that of the different Pueblo groups; to parallel this with the meanings explicit in the Eastern philosophy of Buddhism and Taoism; and to reconcile these in turn with the tenets of Western science as expressed in the biological Radiobiogenesis Theory, the geological Nebular Theory, the Atomic Theory as postulated by Einstein, and modern psychology. Along with a complete history of the region and the interjection of personal anecdotes in a lighter vein, my aim is to present all this in a clear, readable style appealing to the average reader, as was *The Colorado*. Nevertheless the treatment is requiring such a vast amount of original and expensive research that it seems to be the sort of a job usually accomplished under a Foundation grant of some kind. I am wondering if there is one available to the University under which this book might qualify with your approval.

If I recall correctly, research for John Collier's book on the *Indians of the Americas* was done with the help of The Viking Fund of New York, and Frank Dobie is now doing a book on the history of the mustang under a grant from the Rockefeller Foundation, as was done the Navajo ceremonial *Where The Two Came to Their Father* by Maude Oakes.

Any information you can give me about this will be appreciated. I am eager to conclude my research here in California where there is available information; to make another extensive field trip similar to last year's; and to proceed with the collection of photographs and paintings, and the preparation of drawings and sketches for illustrations. The book should be ready for inclusion on your list for next year.

Sometime after sending this letter to Harvey, Waters received a letter, dated February 15, 1949, from Joaquin Ortega, editor of *The New Mexico Quarterly Review,* informing him that the International Literary Pool of Unesco had requested permission to reprint "The Crucible of Conflict," and Ortega wished to know if Waters had any objections to this. Waters responded on February 18, 1949:

Thanks for your enthusiastic letter. You have my permission—and blessings!—to submit The Crucible of Conflict to UNESCO's International Literary Pool for republication. [I have found no evidence that it was reprinted.] Just so long as I still retain book publication rights, for it is the key motif of the book I'm doing.
Right now I'm deep into it—400 pages deep. A complete historical outline of the whole area. Followed by an outline of Navajo and Pueblo ceremonials, some thirty of them: synthesizing these, drawing their parallels in the Eastern philosophy of Tibetan Buddhism and Chinese Taoism; and then reconciling them in turn with the tenets of Western Science as expressed in the biological Radiobiogenesis Theory, the geological Nebular Theory and the Atomic Theory as postulated by Einstein . . .
It will be necessary for me to make another extended field trip as I did last summer. . . .

Fred Harvey of the University Press finally responded to Waters' letter of January 28th on February 23, 1949. In this letter Harvey stated that he could well understand Waters' need for a research grant and suggested a number of possible foundations, as well as offering to bring the possibility before the Publications Committee at the Press. He also brought up the question of *The Man Who Killed the Deer,* which he told Waters he was hoping to be able to include in a new series of Southwestern classics, subject to Publications Committee approval. In a follow-up letter of March 22, 1949, Harvey wrote Waters that the Publications Committee had again turned down *Deer,* and furthermore took the attitude that they should not get involved in a research grant for a non-faculty member.

On March 12, 1949, Waters sent a short note to Joaquin Ortega at the *New Mexico Quarterly Review* enclosing a copy of a letter he had received from the United Indian Traders Association, which responded favorably to Waters' article on "Navajo Trading Posts," which had appeared in the Winter, 1948 issue of the Review. This article, like "The Crucible of Conflict," formed a portion of the Navajo book he was preparing for the University Press. In answering Waters' note on April 2, 1949, Ortega recounted to Waters the excellent reception both articles had received and asked if there wasn't yet another article which might be culled from the work-in-progress, specifically something dealing with modern missions to the Indians. Waters tentatively accepted this offer on April 29, 1949:

> . . . I have gone into all the modern Missions in considerable detail—their history, their secular school function, and the relationship of the various religious creeds to that of Indian ceremonialism. A lot of this is straight-from-the-shoulder; a little too much for such a conservative organ as I take you to be.
> But I could give you a pleasant descriptive excerpt of around 15-18 pages covering:
> 1. A personal account of the founding of the first Protestant Navajo Mission in the late 1890's and the San Juan flood which swept it away in 1911. (My two old maid aunts participated.)
> 2. The founding of the Presbyterian Mission at Ganado (using its abandoned equipment), together with the up-to-date story of Dr. Salsbury, its famous Sagebrush Surgeon.
> 3. A resume of the largest Catholic Mission, St. Michaels, and Father Berard Haile, the famous Navajo scholar who opened it in 1901.
>
> I've got the religious tie-ins between Navajo ceremonialism and Catholicism, Protestantism, the Presbyterian, the Mormons and Christian Science for later use if you want them.
> Also a chapter on Toynbee's A STUDY OF HISTORY vs. the Grand Canon; another on the Sun Temple of Mesa Verde vs. the atomic reactor at Los Alamos, which might interest you later.
> It's all just a question of what your new editorial policy is. . . .

On May 21, 1949, Waters again wrote to Fred Harvey at the University Press, bringing him up-to-date on the progress of the manuscript:

> My work on the Pueblo and Navajo book suggested by you will soon be finished. I am enclosing a TABLE OF CONTENTS complete with chapter and section headings. There is not much to say about it except that I believe it is the most comprehensive book yet written on the area. There is no aspect of the subject not thoroughly covered from both the White and Indian viewpoints.
> Part One consists of an historical outline, from our point of view, of the Navajos and Pueblos within a frame of reference which includes the Spanish conquest of Mexico and the Anglo conquest of the United States.
> Part Two, a mytho-religious history from the Indian viewpoint, is an interpretative analysis of Indian ceremonialism. It synthesizes the meanings of Navajo sings, Rio Grande Pueblo dances, Zuni katchinas and Hopi ritualism with the ceremonialism of the Aztecs and Toltecs. Compares them with the meanings explicit in the Eastern philosophies of Buddhism and Taoism. And

reconciles them in turn with the religious, biological, atomic, psychological and geological tenets of the West.

Part Three recapitulates the effect of this predominant ceremonialism upon the secular life and character of the Indians, and our relationship to them.

The book will run about 600 typed pages when finally condensed. This is slightly longer than my previous THE COLORADO; and like it, it has been written for the general reader in a clear narrative style, dramatized whenever possible and lightened with personal anecdotes. It is a better book and should do as well as THE COLORADO with a total of 50,000 copies in all its three editions. In the Southwest particularly it should be a stock item for many years. Some excerpts from it, as you know, have already appeared in the NEW MEXICO QUARTERLY REVIEW, SOUTHWEST REVIEW and the YALE REVIEW.

This letter is to inquire if you now wish to confirm your acceptance of it with a formal contract, or to indicate the terms under which you would like to handle it as previously stated by Mr. Allen. These would include your estimate of the size of the first printing, the approximate time of publication, and whether illustrations are desired. The latter point would of course be necessary as I would have to make arrangements for the loan or reproduction of valuable paintings, photographs etc. not easily obtainable.

Fred Harvey responded to this letter on June 9, 1949, after having conferred with the Publications Committee. He informed Waters that while the Committee was much impressed with the description and outline and he had no doubt it would be accepted, it was policy to formally accept works only after submission of manuscripts. He also inquired of Waters what his usual royalty rate was, so that they might come to some arrangement on this matter. Waters wrote back on June 27, 1949:

The completed manuscript is being sent to you under separate cover.

In going over it for the first time since it has been put together, I find some minor revisions necessary. Others probably will be indicated when I ask the United Indian Traders Association, the National Congress of American Indians, Father Berard Haile and other authorities in various fields to look over certain chapters. Meanwhile Dr. Allen undoubtedly will have suggestions for still more. Nevertheless, I believe you will find it a fairly clean text to start on, and I will welcome your own comments.

As I remember my understanding with Dr. Allen, we agreed that a straight 10% royalty rate would apply if the Committee passed on the reprinting of the MAN WHO KILLED THE DEER; otherwise a royalty rate approximating those applying on my previous books with other firms. He later confirmed this tentative agreement after the Committee decided against reissuing the DEER.

As examples of these previous royalty rates, my contract on THE COLORADO provided for 10% on the first 3,500 copies, 12½% on the next 1,500, and 15% over 5,000, with $1000 in advance to help cover research expenses.

My last contract with Rinehart and Company raised this to 10% for the first 3,500 copies and 15% thereafter, with a $1,000 advance.

My last book was contracted to Farrar, Straus and Company on the basis of 12½% to 5,000 and 15% over, with $1,000 advance.

With these as a guide I'm sure an arrangement can be reached in line with your own policy, the size of the printing you anticipate etc. Cassel of London and the Libraire Hachette in France have brought out editions of two of my books, and should be interested in considering foreign reprint rights to this one.

Dr. Allen wrote me a brief note before leaving for Stanford, inquiring about illustrations. I am writing him that I will make tentative arrangements to borrow for reproduction some of the best material available. These include old Navajo and Pueblo water colors from the private collection of Miss M. E. J. Colter, interior decorator and designer for all of the Fred Harvey houses; the series of oil paintings on Pueblo dances which Miss Dorothy Brett of Taos is now doing; a collection of photographs from the Santa Fe and Fred Harvey systems; and various items from the Southwest Museum and other collectors. As the plan of the whole book is based upon the katchina, which is also the letterhead symbol for the Press, I have also suggested the use of katchina reproductions for all three parts of the book. From all this material he should be able to select whatever seems appropriate after his perusal of the text and will be permitted by the budget allowed. . . .

Harvey wrote to Waters on July 1, 1949, that he had received the manuscript, then titled "The Four Corners Country", and was eager to read it. He also informed Waters that Charles Allen had left the Press some time earlier and that he, Harvey, would go over the question of the illustrations after he read the manuscript, although he feared that the budget would restrict the use of illustrations considerably.

While waiting to hear further from Harvey, Waters spent some time working on the article on Indian Missions for the *New Mexico Quarterly Review*. Joaquin Ortega accepted the article for publication in August of 1949, and the piece appeared in the Spring, 1950 issue of the *Review*.

On August 8, 1949, Harvey wrote again to Waters about the manuscript, informing him that the Publications Committee had not yet had a chance to meet and that no decision had been made concerning publication. Finally, on December 7, 1949, E. B. Mann, acting director of the Press, wrote Waters a short note informing him that the Publications Committee had turned down the manuscript. Waters wrote back to Mann on December 15, 1949:

My thanks to you personally for replying so promptly after our conversation.

I must insist, however, after spending over two years' work on a book solicited by your Press, on concrete and specific reasons for its rejection by your Publications Committee.

In checking through my files of our correspondence, which you also have on record, I find that on July 30, 1947 your Editor wrote me for an appointment to discuss my writing a book for the Press on the Navajo country similar to THE COLORADO.

Our verbal agreement as to the title, scope, substance and royalty rate was later confirmed by his letters dated October 3 and October 24, after further substantiation by both the Director and the Publications Committee which "requested me (the Editor) to do everything in my power to encourage you to write this book."

One year later, on September 22, 1948, the Director wrote asking when he might expect the manuscript, as he had to schedule publication about a year in advance. My reply of September 24 promised it in one more year (this fall). It also included a detailed outline of the work already done, which your Editor approved.

As a further check on the material and style, several excerpts from the manuscript were published in the NEW MEXICO QUARTERLY REVIEW, and its Editor's enthusiastic approval are also on file together with letters from the United Traders Association and a request from UNESCO for reprint rights. And as late as February 23, 1949, the Director of the Press expressed himself as "very glad that you are doing such an extensive book on the Navajo and Pueblo", although he could not secure a research grant in order to facilitate my research in California.

On June 9, 1949 the Director again wrote, saying that if I would send the manuscript he would endeavor to "close the matter of a contract as soon as possible". He then acknowledged receipt of the ms. on July 1st.—which was the last time I heard from the Press until he and you called on me here, in October. Even at this late time you both still expressed a desire to publish the book, as originally agreed upon.

In view of this original solicitation, and complete confirmation of all details during its two-year preparation by Editor, Director and Publications Committee, the latter's present and abrupt rejection I cannot accept without a definite reason. Hence I must insist upon a concrete and concise statement as to its unsatisfactoriness—its subject matter and scope (consistently approved), its factual accuracy (fully documented), its reading appeal (as shown by its published excerpts and correspondence regarding them), or some of its new, unorthodox views of a yet unknown subject which may not be in line with the academic viewpoints of some of the University's approving staff (which excerpts have not been discussed with me editorially, as is customary).

As a professional writer, I do not take assignments for two years' full-time work either gullibly, hastily or lightly. I know from the experience of twelve published books when a competent job has been done. From my own editorial experience, both in Washington D.C. and as the present editor of our small, historic newspaper here, I also know that, as a prelude to publication, editorial cooperation must be extended to bring certain passages into line with the publishers' house policy. No book, even from a competent writer, is ever rendered perfect; none are wholly condemned.

A prompt direct statement from the Committee which urged all power be brought to bear upon me to do this book, as to whether their present peremptory action is prompted by specific reasons embodied in the manuscript, or influenced by causes without, will be appreciated.

114   SECTION A

Waters sent copies of the above letter to both Charles Allen, former Editor at the Press, and Joaquin Ortega. In response to Waters' letter, Ortega made a visit to Taos to discuss with Waters possible ways to remedy the situation. Some time after his return to Albuquerque, Ortega met with E. B. Mann and others at the Press. In a letter to Waters on January 14, 1950, Ortega related to Waters that the Press had agreed to a second look at the manuscript. Not only would Ortega himself read the manuscript, but it was agreed that two more readers would go over it, one a "technical" and the other a "general" reader. It was further agreed that after this was finished Waters would be supplied with a complete report embodying the reactions of all the readers. Waters replied to Ortega on January 17, 1950:

> This is to thank you for your trip up here and your personal interest in this peculiar case, and to acknowledge your letter . . .
> Since talking to you I have received and opened the returned MS. It was sent via Railway Express, which does not come to Taos, necessitating a delay in sending to Raton for it by truck delivery. The first volume was badly scrawled with a red grease-pencil, impossible to erase. Other pages, evidently in worse shape, had been retyped. But in the retyping, most of the page numbers had been omitted, together with many words and lines of the text. The second and third volumes were untouched, possibly indicating that they had not been read. Also the revised pages requested by Mr. Harvey and Mr. Mann had been returned with my letter of transmittal.
> This is not pertinent here, save for the fact that it will take until your suggested date of January 25th to clear up the MS or obtain a carbon copy from my California files.
> My natural feeling about the matter, after reading these marginal notes, is that due to the opposition of the Publications Committee and the psychological result of the Vernon Young article ["Frank Waters: Problems of the Regional Imperative," New Mexico Quarterly Review, Autumn, 1949], the book would not be accepted for publication even though passed upon by new readers. I am glad to hear you do not feel the same way. Hence I am quite willing to resubmit the complete three volumes for a chapter by chapter report, as you suggest, to give us something concrete to work on towards a satisfactory solution. . . .

Waters resubmitted the manuscript in early February, and, after waiting almost two and one-half months, finally received the decision in a letter from Mann dated April 18, 1950. In his letter Mann informed Waters that the Publications Committee had accepted the manuscript for publication provided that Waters was willing to edit and revise those portions of the manuscript most heavily criticized by the readers. A further proviso was that the published book was to include a foreword by a noted anthropologist stating the anthropological objections to the work and which would further point up the fact that the book was written in an attempt to interpret the Navajo life in a manner transcending the purely scientific viewpoint. Mann stated that a typed copy of all reader's reports would be sent to Waters as soon as possible, and that he thought it best for the two of them to get together and personally discuss how to proceed with the work.

After meeting with Waters, Mann wrote again on May 10, 1950, to tell Waters that Dr. Paul Walter, one of the readers whose report Waters had found to be in sympathy with his own views, had agreed to help in the editing and revising of the manuscript. Mann also enclosed a contract with the letter. The contract outlined a royalty rate of 10% on the first 5,000 copies, 12½% on the next 3,000 copies and 15% thereafter, but did not contain any provision for an advance. After Waters objected to this, Mann wrote on May 18, 1950, that the general policy of the Press was to make no advance payments, but that he would take up this matter with the Publications Committee. He reported back to Waters on June 2, 1950, that the Publications Committee had approved an advance payment of $500.00 against royalties payable upon receipt of the manuscript. In the same letter Mann also suggested two alternate titles for the book: "Masked Gods" and "Navajo Heartland."

Waters responded to this letter on June 7, 1950:

. . . I am sending Dr. Walter Part I of the Ms. today, and will have the revised Part II for him very shortly. Some 40 pages in each have been rewritten and retyped, in addition to the routine editing. On this basis, you may count on having the entire job completed by July 15th anyway.

Now as to titles.

I don't like NAVAHO HEARTLAND. It carries the connotation of the famous "heartland" concept originated by the Englishman McKinder, adopted by the German Nazis for their geopolitical drive for Lebensraum and now has been taken over by Russia itself which they conceived as the "heartland" of the world. This agricultural, economic and political connotation is wholly European in origin, non-religious, and of course wholly irreconcilable with the ideology of the Navahos and Pueblos. I have used the phrase casually several times in the text, but with a far different meaning which is explicit in its use. But for a title, no.

However, you have my O.K. for MASKED GODS provided, as in CORONADO, you use a subtitle as you suggested:
MASKED GODS
Navaho and Pueblo Ceremonialism
or
MASKED GODS
The Meaning of Navaho
and Pueblo Ceremonialism
I prefer the latter, but would be content with the former.

I'll write Dr. Walter direct about the revised Ms. I'm sending.
Many thanks and let me be of any assistance I can at any time.

On the same day, Waters wrote to Paul Walter:

I am sending you to-day Part One for your final approval and editing. About 40 pages have been rewritten and retyped, as well as minor editing of the rest, and the pages have been renumbered in consecutive order.

In almost all cases I have made an attempt to meet the detailed criticisms in the various readers' reports. The biggest improvements have been in bringing more into focus the parallels of modern psychology. This will be of great aid in clearing up the objectionable feature in Part Three later—i.e. the overemphasis on the Buddhistic parallels.

Merely to be consistent I have used the spelling "Navaho" instead of "Navajo", and "Spanish-American" instead of "Hispano" for Mexican residents of this area since the American occupation. The inconsequential choice, I think, should be left to you and the Press' house-custom. Also what foreign words, Aztec, Spanish, Navaho, Pueblo etc. should be italicized, capitalized [sic] etc.

All such matters I leave to your own judgment. Please feel free to edit the text as you see fit. I fortunately have a third copy here, so for any questions or further necessary revisions you may simply refer to the page and paragraph in a letter.

I have nearly finished revising Part Two, which should be ready for you soon. . . .

Waters was informed in a letter dated June 9, 1950, that the matter of the anthropologist who would write the foreword to the book was now taken care of, Dr. Clyde Kluckhohn of Harvard having agreed to read the manuscript and write the foreword. Mann also mentioned that the Press wanted to schedule the book for release in November if that seemed possible.

Waters wrote again to Paul Walter on June 19, 1950:

Part Two goes back to you today, with practically all your markings in copy intact and your suggestions followed.

The exceptions are:

About 30 rewritten pages rearranging the context somewhat to make deletions and point up the text.

The retention of two quotes, as I have written to the publishers for permission to use the brief excerpts. If it does not come, I'll rewrite them with reference to the author.

I also retained the two paragraphs on P. 249 and 256 which give a personal, immediate "frame" to the objective and abtruse [sic] discussion of the Chinese dualities (cut down somewhat). And also the 1½ page digression on Mrs. Elsie Clews Parsons during the Snake Dance, on P. 436-437. I did this only after discussion with two successful novelists here. They agreed, particularly on the

Parsons digression, that it was sound technique to break the tediousness of description and the tension of a long build-up just before a climax, in order that the reader might come to it fresh and relaxed.

These are mere tricks to obtain and insure reader interest. But I am trying to use every device to get over the serious themes of the whole.

Indeed, the whole problem of construction on this book has been changes of pace, the mixture of the personal with the impersonal, to make an otherwise dull treatment interesting to the non-technical reader.

However, if you feel they are utterly out of place here, do edit them out.

I am now starting in on Part Three which requires much rewriting, revision and deletion. For this reason I'd suggest you not waste too much time working the present copy. Your comments as to what passages to take out entirely, and what chapters to cut down to mere sub-chapters or paragraphs, would be helpful. . . .

All the revisions on Part Three were completed within the scheduled time and the complete manuscript, including Kluckhohn's favorable foreword, went to the printer in September. Although publication was originally scheduled for early in November, it was pushed back to November 15th due to a delay at the printer's. The delay was even longer than anticipated and final publication was not until December of 1950.

A12   MASKED GODS   [1950]

A12a   First edition, first printing, first issue

MASKED GODS | [brown] . . . . NAVAHO | AND PUEBLO | [brown] CEREMONIALISM | FRANK WATERS | THE UNIVER= SITY OF NEW MEXICO PRESS
   Title and author's name set to the right of a drawing adapted from a Navaho sand painting, printed in black and brown.

$9^{11}/_{16} \times 6^{5}/_{8}$". [1-13^{16} 14^{12}]: 220 leaves. Pp. [1-6] 7-8 [9-10] 11-13 [14-16] 17-161 [162-164] 165-336 [337-338] 339-438 [439-440]. Numbers printed in italic at the foot of the page at outer margin of the type page.

CONTENTS: p. 1, half-title: "[partially open face] MASKED GODS"; p. 2, blank; p. 3, title; p. 4, copyright notice: *"Copyright 1950 by the | University of New Mexico Press, Albuquerque, New Mexico | All rights reserved"*; p. 5, dedication: "TO JANEY"; p. 6, blank; pp. 7-8, Foreword by Clyde Kluckhohn; p. 9, contents; p. 10, illustration from a

118 SECTION A

Hopi pottery design in brown; pp. 11-13, Introduction; p. 14, blank; p. 15, full-page illustration from an Acoma pottery design in brown and white, with divisional half-title printed in the lower right corner: "[all within a white panel] [script] Part One: The Masks | *To refuse to perceive the unique face of man | under the masks that cover it, is no longer a | sign of force but rather of senility.* . . . | ELIE FAURE"; p. 16, contents for part one; pp. 17-161, text; p. 162, blank; p. 163, full-page illustration identical with p. 15, with divisional half-title printed in upper left corner: "[all within a white panel] [script] Part Two: The Gods | *The modeler of gods, at bottom, is the | spiritual universe has= tening unceasingly | in pursuit of its center of gravity.* . . . | ELIE FAURE"; p. 164, contents of part two; pp. 165-336, text; p. 337, full-page illustration identical with that on p. 15, with divisional half-title printed in lower right corner: "[all within a white panel] [script] Part Three: | [script] Man-Mask and God | *For What is man but the root and the flower, | the image and the substance of the universe itself?* . . . | MASKED GODS"; p. 338, contents of part three; pp. 339-438, text; p. 439, colophon: "*MASKED GODS was designed and decorated | by Ralph Douglass, Professor of Art at The | University of New Mexico. The jacket design is | based on the Hopi helmet mask worn by Kipok | Kachina, the four feathers symbolizing the Four | Directions. The case stamping is from a Hopi pot- | tery design. The end sheets are from an Ácoma | pottery design symbolizing clouds and rain. The | title page drawing is adapted from a Navaho | sand-painting. The drawing on page 10 is from | a Hopi pottery design; that on page 161 is from | a Santo Domingo pottery design; that on page | 336 is from a Zuñi pottery design; and that on | page 438 is a personified rainbow figure from a | Navaho sand-painting. The decorations for the | chapter initials are from similar Navaho, Pueblo, | and other Indian sources.* | [new paragraph] *The book is set in 11 point Caledonia on 13 point | body; side heads in 14 point Caledonia italic; fo- | lios and running heads in 8 point Caledonia italic. | Typographical design by The University of New | Mexico Press. Printing and binding by Ameri- | can Book-Knickerbocker Press, Inc., New York.*"; p. 440, blank.

ILLUSTRATIONS: All illustrations in the book were adapted from Indian designs by Ralph Douglass, and appear on pages: 3, 10, 15, 161, 163, 336, 337 and 438.

BINDING: Oatmeal colored cloth. Front and rear with Hopi pottery design at top in gold. Stamped on spine: "[thick gold rule] | [partially open face] MASKED | [partially open face] GODS | [series of three connected squares, ascending left to right] | [script] Waters | [seven gold rules] | [thick gold rule] | [at bottom] THE UNIVERSITY | OF NEW MEXICO | P R E S S". White paper, endpapers printed on the face of front and rear in brown with an Acoma pottery design.

DUST JACKET (light purple paper): Front and spine printed with an illustration of a Hopi Kachina mask in blue, purple, black and jacket color, against a black background. Beneath the mask there is a 3" high band in jacket color within which are a series of six purple rules at the top, one thick purple rule in the middle, and three purple rules near the bottom. Lettered on front: "[script—in jacket color] Frank Waters | [within the jacket-color band beneath the six purple rules] [partially open face] MASKED | [beneath thick purple rule] [partially open face] GODS [tree branch design in purple and blue] | [at bottom, against a black background] [script—in purple] Navaho and Pueblo Cere≠ monialism". Spine lettered in script: [purple] Masked | [purple] Gods | [small triangle design in purple] | [blue] Frank | [blue] Waters". Rear with black and white photograph of the author at top right: "[on line with bottom edge of photograph] [script] Frank Waters | [two paragraphs about the author and three quotations about the book by Stephen Vincent Benét, Joseph Henry Jackson and Clyde Kluckhohn, all printed in purple] | THE UNIVERSITY OF NEW MEXICO PRESS | ALBUQUERQUE". Front and rear flap carry a notice of this book, printed in purple.

Published at $6.50 on December 11, 1950; 4,645 copies were printed. Copyrighted December 11, 1950; deposited December 27, 1950.

REVIEWS: *San Francisco Chronicle*, January 14, 1951 (p. 8); *New York Times Book Review*, August 12, 1951 (p. 7); *New York Herald Tribune Weekly Book Review*, September 2, 1951 (p. 9).

COPIES: DLC (2 copies—one rebound); NmU; FW; TAT (4 copies, 3 in d.j.).

NOTE: In 1952, the University of New Mexico Press lowered the price of the book to $5.00. All copies remaining in stock had the price changed by a rubber stamp on the front flap of the dust jacket.

NOTE: In some copies of the first printing there was inserted a slip of blue paper, measuring 2½ × 5½":
"Mr. La Farge has requested the editors to state that his | attitude towards traders on the Navaho reservation is not | hostile, but is much the same as Mr. Waters' own. (Page 94). | He has also requested the editors to state that Drekoff | recommendations on traders' mark ups and a levy on their | gross volume were not included in the Krug report, and not | only were not supported by La Farge but were opposed by | him. (Page 153).—*Editors.*".

This slip was inserted by the press in response to a threatened law suit by Oliver La Farge. In a letter dated February 28, 1951, Frank Andrews, attorney for La Farge, wrote to the University of New Mexico Press stating La Farge's objections to several references to him in the text of *Masked Gods*. Andrews suggested in his letter that litigation could be avoided if the press recall all copies of the book in the hands of distributors and retail outlets, secure a retraction from Waters, and omit the objectionable passages from all future printings.

After learning of La Farge's objections, Waters supplied Mann with a detailed list of the sources for his statements about La Farge, and armed with this information Mann was apparently able to convince La Farge that any lawsuit would prove fruitless, if not beneficial to the sales of *Masked Gods*. In a conciliatory gesture, the University of New Mexico Press offered to print up a statement of La Farge's objections.

Although no records exist as to the number of slips that were printed, the Press informed me that they were placed into "about half the edition." At present I know of only two copies of the book containing the La Farge disclaimer—both in my own collection.

Interestingly enough, La Farge's position in this matter did not stop him from reviewing the book for the *New York Herald Tribune* on September 2, 1951.

NOTE: Portions of this work originally appeared in three articles published in the *New Mexico Quarterly Review:* "Crucible of Conflict," Autumn, 1948 (see C12); "Navajo Trading Posts," Winter, 1948 (see C13); and "The Navajo Missions," Spring, 1950 (see C16).

A12b   First edition, first printing, second issue   [1964]

Identical with A12a, except for the presence of an inserted leaf between pages 4 and 5, which reads:

"Unique, Limited, Signed Edition | THE original edition of *Masked Gods* had been out of | print for two years when Sage Books arranged to publish a second | edition. After the Sage edition had been on the mar= ket for a year | and a half, it was discovered that, through an error at the original | bindery, three hundred copies of the first University of New Mexico | Press edition were still in existence. This edition has been prized | because it contains color printing and an introduction which were | not possible to use in the less expensive second edition by Sage Books. | Therefore, it seemed a special opportunity to offer the admir= ers | of Frank Waters' great book—indeed a unique edition—these copies | of the first edition, signed by the author and numbered. | SAGE BOOKS | Alan Swallow, Publisher | *Of this edition, signed by the au= thor, this is number* [number stamped in blue] | [Author's signature]".

The paper on which this notice is printed is a yellowish laid paper, with chain lines measuring 21 mm. apart.

Published at $6.50 in late May or early June, 1964. Although the limitation noted in the inserted notice is 300 copies, only 294 copies were actually discovered and so issued.

NOTE: In a letter dated October 1, 1963, Roland Dickey of the University of New Mexico Press sent Waters the surprising news that 294 copies of the original printing of *Masked Gods* had just been discovered at the American Book-Stratford Press in New York, copies apparently lost in the handling 13 years before. Dickey suggested to Waters that the Press would undertake to sell these copies, giving Waters the same royalty as before, or that because of a possible conflict with Alan Swallow, who now owned the rights to the book, they would sell the copies to Swallow.

After Alan Swallow heard the news of the discovered copies, he wrote to Dickey on October 17, 1963, telling Dickey that while he could understand how such a thing happened, he was not pleased about it. In response to Dickey's suggestion that the Press undertake to market the copies, Swallow warned him that he would consider such action damaging to his own rights in the book, and in violation of his contract with Waters. To Dickey's alternate suggestion that Swallow purchase the books from the Press, Swallow agreed to do so only at the price per copy of his own impression: $1.566 per copy; and with the purchase date to be mutually agreed upon for some time in the future. The University of New Mexico Press agreed to these terms.

Upon settling with New Mexico, Swallow arranged with Waters to have the 294 copies issued in a limited signed edition, with inserts to be prepared by the University of New Mexico Press. 350 inserts were mailed to Waters for signing in May of 1964. Waters then shipped the inserts to Swallow, who had them inserted in the extra copies.

According to a royalty statement for the period ending June 30, 1965, Swallow found a ready market for these copies, the last 14 of which were reported sold in this statement.

A12c   First edition, Alan Swallow printing   [1962]

MASKED GODS | [gray] .... NAVAHO | AND PUEBLO | [gray] CEREMONIALISM | FRANK WATERS | [publisher's sagebrush device] | SAGE BOOKS, *Denver*
> The title and author's name are set to the right of a drawing adapted from a Navaho sand painting, as in A12a, but the drawing in this printing is printed in gray and black.

9¾ × 6¾". [1-26^8 27^4 28^8]: 220 leaves. Pp. [1-10] 11-13 [14-16] 17-161 [162-164] 165-336 [337-338] 339-438 [439-440].

CONTENTS: p. 1, half-title; p. 2, blank; p. 3, title; p. 4, copyright notice: *"Copyright 1950 by Frank Waters | Second edition | Illustrations and calligraphy are by Ralph Douglass | Sage Books are published by | Alan Swallow, 2679 South York Street, Denver 10, Colorado"*; p. 5, dedication; p. 6, blank; p. 7, contents; p. 8, drawing from a Hopi pottery design (identical with that on p. 10 of A12a); p. 9, repeat of title page, without publisher's device or imprint; p. 10, blank; pp. 11-438, identical with A12a; p. 439, identical with A12a, except that the second paragraph has been deleted; p. 440, blank.

ILLUSTRATIONS: Identical with A12a, except for pages 8 and 10 as noted above. All illustrations are printed in black in this printing.

Cloth. Published at $5.75 in 1962; number of copies printed unknown. Swallow originally intended publication for September, 1962, but in a letter to Waters on October 10, 1962, he noted that copies were just then being bound. Evidence would seem to indicate that 4,000 copies were printed (see note below).

COPIES: TAT.

NOTE: The text of this printing is identical with A12a, except that Clyde Kluckhohn's introduction was not reprinted. Although at the time of Swallow's reprinting, the rights for the book had reverted back to Waters, the rights for the introduction were still held by the University of New Mexico Press and they refused to release the rights for Swallow's printing.

NOTE: Waters' contract with Alan Swallow, dated May 15, 1962, outlined royalties of 10% on the first 4,000 copies, 12½% on the next 3,500 copies, and 15% thereafter.

NOTE: Although incomplete, what information has become available allows one to make an estimate of the number of copies printed by Alan Swallow. An inventory at the close of 1964 recorded only 2,000 unbound copies stored in Boulder; the inventory for 1965 records 671 bound copies on hand and 1,000 unbound sheets in Boulder. The inventory record taken at the time of Swallow's death in 1966 recorded 467 bound copies on hand, with no reference to any unbound copies. A royalty statement issued by the Estate of Alan Swallow for the period ending July 31, 1967 showed sales of 334 copies; and the opening inventory of the Swallow Press of Chicago on August 1, 1967 recorded 165 copies transferred from the estate. However, royalty records of the Swallow Press show that in the period from August 1, 1967 to July 31, 1968, 244 copies of *Masked Gods* had been sold, which would seem to indicate that the unbound copies were discovered at some point and delivered to the Swallow Press. At the time the Swallow Press reprinted the work themselves, in August, 1969, they also began paying Waters at the rate of 12½% on copies sold. Since by the terms of the contract, as noted above, this rate was to begin after 4,000 copies had been sold, it is perhaps safe to assume that Alan Swallow printed 4,000 copies in 1962, binding 2,000 immediately and storing the rest awaiting demand.

A12d   First edition, first Swallow Press printing   [1969]

MASKED GODS | [gray] . . . . NAVAHO | AND PUEBLO | [gray] CEREMONIALISM | FRANK WATERS | SAGE BOOKS | [pub-

lisher's sagebrush device] | [small caps] THE [caps] SWALLOW PRESS [small caps] INC. | CHICAGO
Title and author's name printed to the right of drawing as in A12c.

9$^{11}/_{16}$ × 6¾". Collation and pagination identical with A12c.

CONTENTS: Identical with A12c, except for page 4: *"Copyright 1950 by Frank Waters | Second edition | Illustrations and calligraphy are by Ralph Douglass | Sage Books are published by | Swallow Press, 1139 South Wabash Avenue, Chicago, Illinois 60605"*.

Cloth. Published at $8.50 in August, 1969. 2,000 copies were printed.

COPIES: TAT.

A12e First edition, second Swallow Press printing [1973]

Title page identical with A12d

9 × 6". [1-2^{16} 3^4 4^8 5-15^{16}]: 220 leaves. Pp. [1-8] 9-13 [14-16] 17-161 [162-164] 165-336 [337-338] 339-438 [439-440]. Pages, 6, 14, and 164 are blank.

CONTENTS: p. 1, half-title; p. 2, "BOOKS BY FRANK WATERS | [list of 12 titles]"; p. 3, title; p. 4, copyright notice: "Copyright © 1950 by Frank Waters | All rights reserved | Printed in the United States of America | Second Edition | Published by | The Swallow Press In= corporated | 1139 S. Wabash Avenue | Chicago, Illinois 60605 | Illustra= tions and calligraphy by Ralph Douglass | [3 lines ISBN and Library of Congress catalogue data]"; p. 5, dedication; p. 6, blank; p. 7, contents; p. 8, drawing from a Hopi pottery design; pp. 9-10, Foreword by Clyde Kluckhohn; pp. 11-439, identical with A12d; p. 440, "SAGE PAPER= BACK SERIES | [list of 18 titles]".

Published in both cloth (issued without dust jacket) and paperback (perfectbound) in 1973. Published at $10.00 for cloth copies and $4.95 for paper copies. 3,520 copies in paper were received by the publisher in April, 1973; 1,553 cloth copies were received in July, 1973.

COPIES: NmU (paper); TAT (cloth and paper).

NOTE: Clyde Kluckhohn's foreword was reinserted into this printing.

A12f   First edition, third Swallow Press printing   [1977?]

Title identical with A12e

8^{31}⁄$_{32}$ × 6". Perfectbound: 220 leaves. Pagination identical with A12e.

CONTENTS: Identical with A12e, except for page 4, on which the publisher's address is given as " . . . |811 West Junior Terrace | Chicago, Illinois 60613 | . . .".

Paperback. Published at $4.95. Date of publication unknown, but presumably issued after the move to Junior Terrace, possibly in 1977. Number of copies printed unknown.

COPIES: TAT.

NOTE: Although the copyright page reflects the fact of the move to Junior Terrace, the publisher's address listed on the rear cover incorrectly shows 1139 S. Wabash.

A12g   Second edition, first printing   [1970]

[fancy] MASKED GODS | NAVAHO AND PUEBLO CEREMO= NIALISM | [fancy] FRANK WATERS | BALLANTINE BOOKS • NEW YORK | An [next word in sans-serif type with swash 'x'] Intext Publisher

7 × 4⅛". Perfectbound: 240 leaves. Pp. [i-vi] vii-xii [xiii-xiv] xv-xviii, [1-2] 31-158 [159-160] 161-347 [348-350] 351-459 [460-462]. Pages vi, 2, 160, 348, 350 and 460 are blank. Page 461 carries a note about the author, and page 462 carries an advertisement for R. D. Laing's *The Politics of Experience*.

COPYRIGHT PAGE: "Copyright 1950 by Frank Waters. | This edition published by arrangement with | The Swallow Press, Inc. | First Print= ing: February, 1970 | Cover photo: New Mexico | Department of Development | Design: Jim Driver | Printed in the United States of America | BALLANTINE BOOKS, INC. | 101 Fifth Avenue, New

York, N. Y. 10003 | Illustrations and calligraphy are by Ralph Doug=
lass".

ILLUSTRATIONS: A number of the illustrations from the first edition
were used in this edition in reduced format. They appear on pages xiv,
1, 159, 349 and 459.

Paperback. Ballantine Walden Edition 345·01873·7·165. Published at
$1.65 in February, 1970. 49,885 copies were printed.

COPIES: TAT.

NOTE: The foreword by Clyde Kluckhohn was included in this edition,
and appears on pages xi-xii.

A12h   Second edition, second Ballantine printing   [1973]

Identical with A12g, except that page iv has been reset: "Illustrations
and calligraphy are by Ralph Douglass | Copyright 1950 by Frank Wa=
ters | All rights reserved. | SBN 345-01873-7-165 | This edition published
by arrangement with | The Swallow Press, Inc. | First Printing: Feb=
ruary, 1970 | Second Printing: January, 1973 | Printed in the United
States of America | BALLANTINE BOOKS, INC. | 101 Fifth Avenue,
New York, N.Y. 10003"; and page 462 now carries an ad for Waters'
Book of the Hopi.

Paperback. Ballantine Walden Edition 345·01873·7·165. Published at
$1.65 in January, 1973. According to the publisher, approximately
90,000 copies were printed.

COPIES: TAT.

A12i   Second edition, third Ballantine printing

NOT SEEN

Paperback. Date of publication and number of copies printed unknown.

A12j   Second edition, fourth Ballantine printing   [1975]

The title page is identical with A12g except that the final line has been deleted.

CONTENTS: Identical with A12g except that page ii is blank; page iv now reads: "Copyright 1950 by Frank Waters. | All rights reserved. | This edition published by arrangement with | The Swallow Press, Inc. | First Printing: February, 1970 | Fourth Printing: September, 1975 | Printed in the United States of America | BALLANTINE BOOKS | A Division of Random House, Inc. | 201 East 50th Street, New York, N.Y. 10022 | Illustrations and calligraphy are by Ralph Douglass" and page 462 carries an ad for *Book of the Hopi* (as in A12h).

Paperback. Ballantine/ Nonfiction 24838. Published at $1.95 in September, 1975. According to the publisher, 25,000 copies were printed.

COPIES: TAT.

NOTE: In a letter to me dated January 9, 1981, the publisher reported only two printings of *Masked Gods:* December, 1972 (90,000 copies) and September, 1975 (25,000 copies). Given the inaccurate information, it may well be that other printings exist, although no copies from printings after 1975 have been located.

EXCERPTS FROM *Masked Gods*

A12k   *The Southwest in Life and Literature: A Pageant in Seven Parts,* edited by C. L. Sonnichsen. (New York, Devin-Adair, 1962). Pages 217-236.

A12l   *The Shadow Within,* edited by Richard L. Cherry, Robert J. Conley and Bernard A. Hirsch. (Boston, Houghton Mifflin, 1973). Pages 435-445.

A12m   *The American Landscape: A Critical Anthology of Prose and Poetry,* edited by Jack Conron. (New York, Oxford University Press, 1973). Pages 453-458.

A12n   *The Essay: Structure and Purpose,* edited by Richard L. Cherry, Robert J. Conley, and Bernard A. Hirsch. (Boston, Houghton Mifflin, 1975). Pages 113-114.

A13   THE EARP BROTHERS OF TOMBSTONE

Although the first draft of *The Earp Brothers of Tombstone*—then titled "Tombstone Travesty"—was written in the 1930's, Waters was then unable to find a publisher interested in the book. He later used the work for a chapter in *The Colorado* and then deposited the manuscript with the Arizona Pioneers Historical Society. In the late 1950's, Waters again considered publication of the work and sounded out the possibility with a number of people. On May 21, 1959, Clarkson Potter, then just beginning his own publishing firm, wrote to Waters, saying that Tom Hopkins at Doubleday had spoken with him about the Earp manuscript and that he might possibly be interested in the book.

Waters responded to Potter on May 25, 1959:

> On my way back home here I stopped in to see Tom Hopkins who sang praises of you as editor of Dial Press and a man thoroughly familiar with Western Americana. I had intended to write you about a book which will be ready in about a month, but the news you were in the process of starting your own publishing house deterred me. I appreciate your writing me, and will lay it on the line—the only way I can.
>
> The book is the autobiography of Mrs. Virgil Earp told in her own vernacular as she related it to me some twenty years ago, thus presenting for the first time a warm, eye-witness, woman's account of the celebrated affairs at Tombstone.
>
> Interposed with this narrative, and substantiating it with documentary research, is a complete exposé of the Wyatt Earp fiction current today. As the true facts are so astounding, every statement has been verified by record, attributed to dependable sources, and footnoted to give it undeniable authenticity.
>
> For obvious reasons the book was not published in 1936, but upon the deaths of Mrs. Virgil Earp and the third Mrs. Wyatt Earp, was donated to the Arizona Pioneers' Historical Society at Tucson as a piece of Western Americana in which somebody someday might be interested. However in my book, *The Colorado,* Rivers of America Series, published in 1946, I gave a short resumé under

a sub-chapter "The Outlaws" which roused a storm of controversy. The book ms. has since been kept in a locked file at the Society, and I am now bringing it up to date with a number of new, shocking materials which I have unearthed and which have not yet come to light.

The Wyatt Earp craze is now reaching its peak. Houghton Mifflin's spurious biography of Wyatt by Stuart N. Lake has sold a half-million copies since 1931. The Wyatt Earp national TV series has an estimated audience of 37 million, and it will not move into the Tombstone setting until September. Its producers and sponsors are flooding the country with Wyatt Earp vests, tin badges, toy pistols. Tombstone is undergoing a big boom in real estate, preparing for a movie company's footage this Fall. The recent biographies of Bat Masterson and Doc Holliday are also in preparation for additional TV series—both adhering to the same, fictional, outworn theme. Dodge City has renamed Front Street as Wyatt Earp Avenue . . . The time is psychologically ripe for this book to make a big splash indeed.

The new material I unearthed just this March. It has not yet come to light, and in my need to establish copyright or prior right to it, I prepared a short article and sent it to a New York agent to place with a magazine. Unfortunately, I then discovered the agency had handled the Bat Masterson book and TV series, and I have been unable to obtain any answers to my continuous letters about it. The recent *LIFE* series, of course, feature the Western background and illustrate the book's timeliness.

For all these reasons I would like to try to find a publisher for the book familiar with this extraordinary tale of the West; who realizes that it at last—after eighty years—ends the most controversial subject in Arizona; who is willing to put his neck out in exposing America's favorite two-gun marshal; and whose house is capable of advertising and distributing it as widely as it deserves.

This is a tall order for a new publishing house, likely as necessary to make a conservative start in life. It may also be the opportunity it needs. In any event, I will be glad to hear from you frankly. This is a story that stands by itself, but it needs someone to handle it who realizes it is a hot potato and is not afraid to give it the works. . . .

Potter's response was positive and Waters sent him a copy of the manuscript to read. On August 3, 1959, Potter wrote to Waters that he had read through the manuscript and definitely wanted to publish the book, but only if Waters would agree to stick to the story of the Earps, deleting references to the "myth" created by Stuart Lake and other previous writers on the Earps.

Because of his uncertainty about Potter's newly begun firm, Waters also sent a copy of the manuscript to his literary agents Marie Rodell and Joan Daves, Inc. In a letter to Waters dated September 8, 1959, Marie Rodell wrote that she had finished the manuscript, and in her letter she outlined her reactions to the book. In addition to criticism which mirrored that of Potter, she also thought that greater detail concerning the latter part of Allie Earp's life would be helpful. Because John Farrar at Farrar, Straus was considering another of Waters' books [*The Woman at Otowi Crossing*], she told Waters that she thought it best to also show him the Earp ms., and assuming Waters' concurrence would send it over to Farrar.

Waters wrote back to Mrs. Rodell on September 9, 1959:

. . . The original typed copy of the Earp manuscript was sent to you by separate mail this morning. Duplicates can be made from it probably easier than from the carbon copy you have. I am glad indeed that you are offering it in the first serial, TV and feature film fields without delay . . . Whether it is wise to send it over to John Farrar before he gives a decision on the Otowi novel I don't know, but I shall trust to your judgment.

In any event, let's wait for his reactions before going into your suggestions for changes. As the ms. is now, there is not a specific reference to Lake in the whole body of the narrative; they have all been changed to references only to "fiction". My feeling is that these are necessary, even if set in italics as you suggest, for the reason that this book is not presenting a new and unfamiliar story. It is settling once and for all the most controversial and familiar story of the Southwest, upon whose fictional concept has been built a bibliography of at least a thousand published items, some nine full-feature films, radio programs, and the current weekly TV series which has been running four years and is witnessed by thirty-seven million people. Throughout the West at least there is a huge reading public brought up from childhood on these allegedly authentic incidents with whose every date and detail they are familiar. To avoid referring to this body of fiction, and to present this book only as another item in the vast Earp-Tombstone bibliography, would deprive us of a major sales appeal which could be made on the basis of its final authoritative version, as well as on the intensely human, warm and womanly narrative. This alone justifies the thorough documentation of twenty years of research. Such an appeal, I'm inclined to believe, is one that no TV or motion picture company can afford to ignore; the book knocks out of focus the stock Earp story, and offers a completely new and irrefutable viewpoint upon which another series of Western Americana can be built in any media.

The skimpiness of Allie's last years is intentional. There just wasn't anything dramatic or interesting in them. I'm rather glad there wasn't, for Tombstone was the high climax of the book as of their lives and everything later would be an anticlimax that can't be prolonged.

However I like your bringing up these points so forthrightly in anticipation of a publisher's reaction. In answer to a note from Clarkson Potter, I have written him that Mrs. Daves has left for a month in Europe. By that time Farrar will have reached some decision, and you and Mrs. Daves can pick up from there. . . .

Marie Rodell wrote to Waters again on September 22, 1959, telling him that Farrar, Straus had informed her that while they were definitely interested in the Earp book, they were concerned about possible legal action by Stuart Lake, and therefore wished to give the manuscript a legal reading, thus delaying a definite decision. Waters responded to Mrs. Rodell on September 28, 1959:

... I did deal with Lake's threatened suit in the Introduction to the Earp book. Ground for the suit was this statement in my *The Colorado,* Rivers of America Series: *"Wyatt Earp, Frontier Marshall,* his purported autobiography dictated to Stuart N. Lake . . . is not an autobiography at all. It is the most assiduously concocted blood-and-thunder piece of fiction ever written about the West". . . . I refused to make a public retraction. Lake's attorneys went to Tucson, got my original Earp ms. out of the closed files of the Arizona Pioneers Historical Society, and dropped the suit. *The Colorado* has gone into several printings, including a new paper-back edition this summer, and the statement still holds. There is no such statement in the present Earp ms.; the facts speak for themselves. I would welcome a suit. It would be supported by the Arizona Pioneers Historical Society which concurs in my views; also the State Archives. It would blow the whole top off many things I have not written, and create so much publicity the book would be a sensation. Hence there will not be a suit. Lake's last two suits—one against Twentieth-Century-Fox—were thrown out of court, his allegations were so patently silly. The Farrar Straus attitude is frightened and over-cautious for no reason. I have no objections to a legal reading, but I would hope it would not run into weeks of quibbling about unwarranted trivialities. And by that time they should have made a decision on the Otowi ms. also.

Potter wrote me again, saying he would also like to consider the novel. This can be kept on ice, I think, until Farrar's review of both books. . . .

Waters wrote to Joan Daves on October 9, 1959:

Mr. Clarkson Potter wired me yesterday, asking me to telephone him. I talked to him early this morning. He said he was most confused after talking to you, but wanted it understood that he was enthusiastic about the Earp ms. and would also like a chance to consider the Otowi ms.

There was little I could do save lay the cards on the table that I was leaving to you the placing of both books; that you did not know yet whether John Farrar was interested in either or both; and hence you were undecided whether to split the books between two publishers or to try and find one publisher for both. I suggested that it would be easier for you to include him in your decision if he would get an appointment with you and frankly outline his financial backing, his distribution set-up, what advertising budget he could allow, and what kind of a job he could do. An interview with him, if you can spare the time, might clear up his standing for all of us.

If he is running a marginal operation, he should not be considered at all. But if he is starting a promising house with good backing, his persistence and enthusiasm on this matter might be an indication he will follow through, and warrant consideration in case of a rejection by Farrar and the necessity for spending months in later submissions. I would then not be averse to making a deal with him for either book. A prompt April release of the Earp book, even with his fewer sales, might insure a better chance for a TV or movie sale than a publication delayed until the market is glutted with Tombstone material; and a prompt contract for the Otowi book would also insure its German release before Christian Wegner is cooled off by a still longer delay. Both of these books may be regarded as somewhat off-beat by conservative and cautious publishers like John Farrar, and they both have an element of timeliness.

However I am quite content to rely on your own judgment. Handle the matter any way you choose. . . .

Not long after this, Waters was informed by his agents that John Farrar's reaction to the Earp book was somewhat mixed, and that he felt that substantial changes would be required before he would wish to publish the book. Mrs. Rodell and Mrs. Daves agreed with Farrar, feeling that greater dramatic impact could be achieved from the human interest standpoint of Allie's narrative. Waters responded to this appraisal on November 9, 1959, in a letter to Joan Daves:

. . . I agree completely with your and Mrs. Rodell's objective appraisal of the Earp ms. To thoroughly exploit its dramatic possibilities and reach the largest potential market, there should be eliminated from the book all controversial matter and much of the historical background, relying wholly on Allie's own first-hand narrative with its human interest. This now, however, would require a complete re-casting of the entire ms. It would also require a new and difficult (and perhaps impossible) job of research into Allie's later years during which, as I mentioned to Mrs. Rodell, nothing of dramatic interest happened, and which would at best seem anti-climaxical to the Tombstone period. This would mean a long postponement, tied up as I am with this Hopi project and as I hope to be with the Otowi revisions, and might not then be worth the long delay.

Hence after some heart-searching, I have decided that perhaps our best bet is to notify Clarkson Potter that he can put the book on his Spring list, and I will make all possible revisions along Mrs. Rodell's suggestions, within its present framework, to give Allie more play. This will allow Potter to take advantage of its Americana values, which will be of permanent interest to that market, and yet give it more general reading interest as a trade book. I hope that you can then offer it, either the revised ms. or the galleys, to the women's magazines who themselves can editorially delete all but Allie's own narrative, as they would have to do anyway for length.

I will do these revisions during the two weeks I am here [in Los Angeles] and send you the revised pages for both copies of the ms. If this is agreeable to you, please feel free—both yourselves and Mr. Potter—to edit out any material that still interferes too much, so that we will have the best presentation possible. A new trade title—something like *Five Brothers and a Wife* or *The Woman in the Gang*—might also help. . . .

A little over a week later, on November 18, 1959, Waters wrote to Clarkson Potter:

I have asked Mrs. Daves to turn over to you the Earp book for release, ending a controversy of sorts that has kept you waiting far too long. For your extreme patience I have a great admiration and many thanks.

The delay and controversy were unavoidable, as I agree with Mrs. Daves that in order to exploit the book's maximum sales possibilities it should be completely rewritten to eliminate almost all of the controversial and factual research material, relying solely on Allie's first-hand narrative. This would give her a story quite suitable for women's magazines and for a trade book of general interest, with a maximum return to both of us. I have finally decided against this for several reasons, one of which is that I feel the research material should at long last be made public as it will be of permanent interest in the field of Americana. She agreed that as you know this field so well, the book should be turned over to you.

I am sending her, however, some 30-40 revised pages. The changes are not drastic, but they move the story along more smoothly and with more emphasis upon Allie. Every allusion to Lake has been omitted; fictional versions of unimportant controversial incidents have been deleted; the rambling Dodge City interlude has been condensed into a sub-chapter interposed in Allie's narrative. I have also suggested a trade title of more catchy and general interest—*SPADE FLUSH*—with the basis for it given on P. 23 and several follow-up references placed throughout the narrative. In all, I think you will find the ms. in good shape to settle once and for all this controversial subject in the field of Western Americana, and to appeal also to the general reader as a warm and human narrative. Please do not hesitate to write me direct regarding any other revisions you would like made, beyond your own editing....

On November 21, 1959, Joan Daves wrote to Waters that she had made arrangements with Potter to handle the book and they had agreed upon the terms: An advance of $1,000.00 against royalties of 10% on the first 5,000 copies, 12½% on the next 5,000 copies, and 15% thereafter. Potter wrote to Waters on November 23, 1959, enthusiastically agreeing to the changes which Waters had outlined. In his letter however, he strongly objected to the title *Spade Flush* because of connotation about blacks. Wishing to avoid catchy titles, and wanting a title which would indicate the contents, Potter suggested: *The Fighting Earps of Tombstone, The Earp Family in Tombstone, The Earp Story,* or *Wyatt Earp and His Brothers in Tombstone*.

Waters wrote to Joan Daves on November 27, 1959:

Thank you for your letter of November 21st. The terms for the Earp book agreed upon by you and Clarkson Potter are quite agreeable to me also, and you can send over to him right away the ms. and the revised pages. I received a letter from him and talked with him by telephone this morning. He wants to announce it next week in order to get it on the Spring list, and for this he needed agreement on a title immediately. *Spade Flush* he did not like at all, as it carried connotations of Negroes in modern slang. Hence we both agreed on a

134 SECTION A

straightforward factual title: *The Earp Gang of Tombstone: The Story of Mrs. Virgil Earp*. This is the first time the Earps have ever publicly been called a gang; the title is arresting, and it is backed up by the research material. We both feel that the title is good and that the book should do all right. There were fifteen thousand people for the Tombstone fracas last month; Lake's book is just out in a new paperback edition with new extravagant claims; the Bat Masterson and also the Doc Holliday TV series are catching on; and the Wyatt Earp TV series is now at the Tombstone setting. So with all this, the book should be arresting if it is well presented. No changes in the revised pages, by the way, will have to be made on account of the new title. . . .

Sometime during production of the book, the title was changed slightly to its present form.

A13   # THE EARP BROTHERS OF TOMBSTONE   [1960]

A13a   First edition, first printing

THE | STORY | OF | MRS. | VIRGIL EARP | THE EARP BROTH= ERS | OF TOMBSTONE | by | FRANK | WATERS | [publisher's device of a sea-creature within an oval] *Clarkson N. Potter, Inc.* [slash] *Publisher* | NEW YORK

$8^{3}/_{16} \times 5^{1}/_{2}$". [1-8^{16}]: 128 leaves. pp. [i-viii], [1-2] 3-10 [11-12] 13-46 [47-48] 49-77 [78-80] 81-123 [124-126] 127-176 [177-178] 179-219 [220-222] 223-237 [238-240] 241-247 [248]. Numbers printed in roman in headline at outer margin of type page, except for pages 3, 13, 49, 81, 127, 179, and 223, on which the numbers are printed at the bottom at the outer margin of the type page.

CONTENTS: p. i, half-title: "THE EARP BROTHERS | OF TOMB= STONE"; p. ii, "by | FRANK WATERS | [11 titles listed]"; p. iii, title; p. iv, copyright notice: *"Library of Congress Card Catalog Number: 60-8927* | Copyright© 1960 by Frank Waters | *All Rights Reserved* | DESIGNED BY HARVEY SATENSTEIN | MANUFACTURED IN THE UNITED STATES OF AMERICA BY | BOOK CRAFTSMEN ASSOCIATES, INC., NEW YORK | *First Edition"*; p. v, dedication: "To Aunt Allie and those old- | timers of Arizona whom I have | let tell their tale as they | would have it told, this their | book is respectfully dedicated."; p. vi, blank; p. vii, contents; p. viii, eight-line quotation, unsigned; p. 1, divisional half-title: "Introduction | THE ANATOMY OF A WESTERN LEGEND"; p. 2, blank; pp. 3-10, Introduction; p. 11, divisional half-title: "Part One | MISSOURI RIVER CROSS= INGS— | THE BEGINNING OF THE TRAIL"; p. 12, blank; pp. 13-46, text; p. 47, divisional half-title: "Part Two | THE SANTA FE TRAIL | AND MORE CROSSINGS WEST"; p. 48, blank, pp. 49-77, text; p. 78, blank; p. 79, divisional half-title: "Part Three | TOMB= STONE—THE END OF THE TRAIL"; p. 80, blank; pp. 81-123, text; p. 124, blank; p. 125, divisional half-title: "Part Four | THE O. K. CORRAL— | A TRAVESTY ON THE TRAIL"; p. 126, blank; pp. 127-176, text; p. 177, divisional half-title: "Part Five | BOOT HILL— SOME MARKERS | OF THE TRAIL"; p. 178, blank; pp. 179-219, text; p. 220, blank; p. 221, divisional half-title: "Part Six | TOMB= STONE OBITUARY"; p. 222, blank; pp. 223-231, text; p. 232, blank; p. 233, divisional half-title: "Part seven | ACKNOWLEDGMENTS"; p. 234, blank; pp. 235-237, text; p. 238, blank; p. 239, divisional half-title: "Part Eight | CITATIONS AND COM= MENTS"; p. 240, blank; pp. 241-247, text; p. 248, blank.

PAPER: Printed on laid paper, with chain lines measuring 21 mm. apart.

BINDING: White cloth with brown speckles. Lettered on spine only in brown: "[reading vertically] The EARP BROTHERS of TOMB= STONE | FRANK WATERS | [horizontally] [publisher's device as on title] | *Clarkson N. | Potter"*. White paper endpapers, printed on the face of both the front and rear endpapers with a map, in brown, of "COCHISE COUNTY, A. T. | IN THE 1880'S", with an inset map of Tombstone.

DUST JACKET (white paper): Outline sketch in orange of three Earp brothers on front. Lettered on front: "The first complete and | authentic account of Wyatt, | Morgan, Virgil, James | and Warren Earp, | in Tombstone, Arizona | in the 1880's, | based on the | recollections of | Mrs. Virgil Earp. | [next four lines printed in brown] THE | EARP | BROTHERS | OF TOMBSTONE | [orange] THE STORY OF MRS. VIRGIL EARP | BY FRANK WATERS". Spine printed overall in brown and lettered in orange: "[reading vertically] THE EARP BROTHERS | OF TOMBSTONE | FRANK WATERS |[horizontally] [publisher's device as on title]| *Clarkson N. | Potter, Inc."*. Rear printed overall in orange and lettered in black: "FRANK WATERS | [black

136   SECTION A

and white photograph of the author] | [fifteen line biography of the author]". The front flap carries a blurb for this book, which is carried over onto the rear flap, which also carries a notice that the jacket was designed by Christopher Simon; all printed in black and orange.

Published at $5.00. Exact date of publication and number of copies printed unknown. Copyrighted June 16, 1960; deposited July 8, 1960. A set of advance galley proofs, in the possession of Mr. John Gilchriese, Tucson, Arizona, has a review slip pasted on the front giving the date of publication as June 16, 1960. Although the publisher would not release production figures for this book, Clarkson N. Potter, in a letter to Waters on March 16, 1960, noted that current orders were running over 30,000 copies, with more coming in every day.

REVIEWS: *Kirkus Reviews,* May 1, 1960 (p. 375); *Library Journal,* June 1, 1960 (p. 2168); *Chicago Sunday Tribune Book World,* July 24, 1960 (p. 2); *Time,* August 1, 1960 (p. 71); *San Francisco Chronicle,* September 4, 1960 (p. 21); *Booklist,* November 1, 1960 (p. 142).

COPIES: DLC (2 copies); NmU (d.j.); FW (d.j.); TAT (4 copies in d.j.).

NOTE: At least one copy was bound in full brown hard-grain morocco and presented to Waters by the publisher. This copy, with an inscription from Clarkson N. Potter, is currently in the library at the University of New Mexico.

A13b   First edition, first English printing   [1962]

The Earp Brothers | of Tombstone | the story of Mrs. Virgil Earp | Frank Waters | Neville Spearman Ltd

8½ × 5⁷⁄₁₆". [1-8¹⁶]: 128 leaves. Pagination identical with A14a.

CONTENTS: Identical with A14a, except for page ii which is blank, and pave iv: "© Frank Waters 1962 | published by Neville Spearman Ltd | 112 Whitfield St, London W1 | printed in Great Britain by | D. R. Hill= man & Sons, Ltd, Frome Somerset".

BINDING: Noted in two variants; no priority known:

A. White paper over boards in imitation of cloth. Lettered on spine only in gilt: "[reading vertically] Frank Waters THE EARP BROTH=ERS OF TOMBSTONE Neville Spearman". White endpapers.

B. Black paper over boards in imitation of cloth. Lettered on spine only, as above, but in red. White endpapers.

DUST JACKET (white paper): Front and spine printed overall in orange and black and with the figure of a gunfighter outlined in black. Lettered on front in white: "THE | EARP | BROTHERS | OF TOMBSTONE | by Frank Waters | The first complete and | authentic account of Wyatt | Morgan, Virgil, James | and Warren Earp, | in Tombstone, Arizona | in the 1880's, | based on the | recollections of Mrs. Virgil Earp | Neville Spearman". Lettered on spine in white: "[reading vertically] Neville Spearman [space] Frank Waters [space] THE EARP BROTHERS OF TOMBSTONE". Rear blank. The front flap carries a blurb for this book, printed in orange and black; the rear flap carries an ad for Glenn Clairmonte's *Calamity Jane,* printed in orange and black.

Published at 21 shillings in 1962; number of copies printed unknown. Deposited in the British Library on July 16, 1962. In a letter to me on June 3, 1980, Neville Armstrong of Spearman Ltd. wrote that he thought the press run to be around 3,000 copies.

COPIES: TAT (3 copies white binding, d.j.; one copy black binding, d.j.).

NOTE: Two of the copies in my collection, both in the white binding, have the first line of the copyright page inked over. Considering the fact that the line should have recorded the copyright date as 1960, rather than 1962, this may represent the publisher's attempt to somewhat crudely correct the error. However, it is impossible to make any judgment as to the exact nature of these copies.

A13c   First edition, second English (Spearman) printing?

NOT SEEN

In his letter to me of June 3, 1980, the publisher wrote: "I think that we did go back for a 2nd impression of probably 1500."

138   SECTION A

A13d   First English edition, only printing   [1963]

[first three lines outlined in white and black] THE EARP | BROTHERS | OF TOMBSTONE | BY FRANK WATERS | [publisher's device consisting of the head of a dog with a book in its mouth, in white, and set within a black square panel] | TRANSWORLD PUBLISHERS | LONDON

7$\frac{1}{16}$ × 4$\frac{3}{8}$″. Perfectbound: 128 leaves. Pp. [1-10] 11-18 [19-20] 21-87 [88] 89-233 [234] 235-247 [248] 249-255 [256]. Pages 2, 6, 8, 10, 20, 88, 234 and 248 are blank. Page 256 carries an ad for other Corgi books.

COPYRIGHT PAGE: "THE EARP BROTHERS | OF TOMBSTONE | A CORGI BOOK | Originally published in Great Britain | by Neville Spearman Ltd. | PRINTING HISTORY | Spearman Edition published 1962 | Corgi Edition published 1963 | © Frank Waters 1962 | [5 lines regarding conditions of sale and reservation of rights] | Corgi Books are published by Transworld Publishers Ltd. | Park Royal Road, London N.W. 10. | Made and printed in Great Britain by | Hunt, Barnard & Co., Ltd., Aylesbury, Bucks.".

Paperbound. Corgi Books GW 1331. Published at 3s. 6d. in June, 1963. Deposited in the British Library on June 13, 1963. Number of copies printed unknown.

COPIES: NmU.

NOTE: The number of leaves in this printing, which is the same as that of the first edition, should not obscure the fact that this is a new edition and not another printing within the first edition.

A13e   First edition, first Bramhall House printing   [1966]

THE | STORY | OF | MRS. | VIRGIL EARP | THE EARP BROTH= ERS | OF TOMBSTONE | by | FRANK | WATERS | *Bramhall House* | NEW YORK

8 × 5$\frac{5}{16}$″. Perfectbound: 128 leaves. Pagination identical with A14a.

CONTENTS: Identical with A14a, except for page iv: "Copyright © MCMLX by Frank Waters | *Library of Congress Card Catalog Number:*

60-8927 | All Rights Reserved | DESIGNED BY HARVEY SATEN=
STEIN | MANUFACTURED IN THE UNITED STATES OF AMER=
ICA | *This edition published by Bramhall House,* | *a division of Clarkson
N. Potter, Inc.* | (A)".

Published in paper over boards in imitation of cloth (with plain white endpapers), at $1.98, in July, 1966. The number of copies printed is unknown; a royalty statement, dated March 24, 1967, reported 2,875 copies sold during the period of July 1, 1966 to December 31, 1966.

COPIES: TAT.

A13f First edition, second Bramhall House printing

Identical with A14e, except that the letter "B" appears within parentheses in the final line of the copyright page.

Published in paper over boards in imitation of cloth, at $1.98. Date of publication and number of copies printed unknown.

COPIES: TAT.

A13g First edition, first University of Nebraska Press printing [1976]

THE | STORY | OF | MRS. | VIRGIL EARP | THE EARP BROTH=
ERS | OF TOMBSTONE | by | FRANK | WATERS | [publisher's bison device with lettering below: 'A | BISON | BOOK'] | *University of Ne=
braska Press* | LINCOLN *and* LONDON

8 × 5⁵⁄₁₆'. [1-8¹⁶]: 128 leaves. Pagination identical with A14a.

CONTENTS: Identical with A14a, except that p. ii is blank; p. iv: "Copyright © 1960 by Frank Waters | All rights reserved | Manufac=
tured in the United States of America | First Bison Book printing: 1976 | Most recent printing indicated by first digit below | 1 2 3 4 5 6 7 8 9 10 | Bison Book edition reproduced from the 1960 edition published by Clark- | son N. Potter, Inc. by arrangement with the author. | Library of Congress Cataloging in Publication Data | [11 lines]"; p. 80 now carries

the map of Cochise County, which served as the endpaper for A14a; and p. 126 carries the map of Tombstone, which appeared as an inset on the endpapers of A14a.

Published simultaneously in cloth (without dust jacket) and paperback (perfectbound) as Bison Book 618 in May, 1976. Published at $10.95 for cloth copies and $3.75 for paper copies. 322 copies were issued in cloth and 4,060 copies in paper.

COPIES: NmU (cloth); TAT (paper).

A13h   First edition, second University of Nebraska Press printing   [1979]

Identical with A14g, except that the sixth line on the copyright page deletes the numeral "1" from the series of numerals.

Paperback. Bison Book 618. Published at $3.75 in November, 1979; 2,600 copies were printed.

COPIES: TAT.

A14   ROBERT GILRUTH   [1963]
A14   First edition, only printing

Britannica Bookshelf-Great Lives | Engineering Space Exploration | ROBERT GILRUTH | *by Frank Waters* | *Photographs courtesy of the* | *National Aeronautics and Space Administration.* | *Illustrations by Phil Vessels from NASA drawings.* | ENCYCLOPAEDIA BRITANNICA PRESS, INC. | *Chicago, Illinois*

$8\frac{3}{16} \times 5\frac{1}{2}''$. [1-6^{16}]: 96 leaves. Pp. [1-6] 7-152 [153] 154-159 [160] 161-182 [183] 184-191 [192]. Numbers printed in italic and enclosed within brackets in the center at the foot of the page.

CONTENTS: p. 1, half-title: "Engineering Space Exploration | ROBERT GILRUTH"; p. 2, blank; p. 3, title; p. 4, copyright notice: "[five lines printed in italic and roman acknowledging sources of quotations] | *COPYRIGHT © 1963 by ENCYCLOPAEDIA BRITANNICA PRESS* | *LIBRARY OF CONGRESS CATALOG NUMBER: 63-13515* | [three lines in italic concerning reservation of rights under international copyright conventions]"; p. 5, contents; p. 6, blank; pp. 7-152, text; p. 153, blank; pp. 154-159, text; p. 160, blank; pp. 161-182, text; p. 183, blank; pp. 184-191, text; p. 192, blank.

ILLUSTRATIONS: All illustrations are from photographs, except for two drawings by Phil Vessels, which are printed in red and black. Except where noted they are small photographs set within the text; pages: 12, 15 (full-page), 58 (drawing), 66 (full-page), 69, 92, 94, 127 (full-page), 144, 146 (full-page), 148 (full-page) and 175 (full-page drawing).

BINDING: Issued simultaneously in both a regular trade binding and a library binding:

142   SECTION A

TRADE BINDING: Red paper over boards, peculiarly textured in imitation of the porous quality of sheep. Front stamped in gilt with a pattern of five irregular open-face five-point stars, with a horizontal rule running from the hinge into the pattern of the stars. Spine stamped in gilt: "[reading vertically] Robert Gilruth [one irregular open-face five-point star] [rule, perpendicular to the lettering] [two irregular open-face five-point stars] *Waters* [two irregular open-face five-point stars] *En=cyclopaedia | Britannica | Press"*. Rear stamped in gilt with three irregular open-face five-point stars, with a horizontal rule running from the hinge into the pattern of stars. Gray-blue endpapers.

LIBRARY BINDING: Blue cloth, lettered on spine only in gilt: "[rule] | [series of seven dots] | [next four lines within a pink panel outlined at top and bottom in gilt] *Robert | Gilruth* | [three solid five-point stars] | *Waters* | [beneath panel] [series of seven dots] | [rule] | ENCYCLO= PAEDIA | BRITANNICA | PRESS". White paper endpapers printed overall on the face of the front and rear endpapers in brown, and with various illustrations of a paintbrush, globe, feather, type punch and tennis racket, in white and blue. Issued in this binding without dust jacket.

DUST JACKET (white paper): Lower two thirds of front and spine printed with a large photograph of the moon with stars in the background; a space vehicle in blue, black and white, is superimposed on the moon photograph near the lower right corner of the front; and a small black and white photograph of Gilruth appears at the top left of the front, breaking into the margin of the moon photograph. Lettered on front: "BY FRANK WATERS | Engineering space exploration | [blue] Robert | [blue] Gilruth". Spine: "[reading vertically upwards] [three lines in white near foot of spine] *Encyclopaedia | Britannica | Press* [in center, in white] ENGINEERING SPACE EXPLORATION [near top, in brown] Robert Gilruth". Rear: "[inset black and white photograph of Waters, set to the left of the first two lines] Frank | Wa= ters | [brown rule] | [three paragraph notice of the author] | [blue rule] | [at right immediately beneath rule] 61072". The front flap is printed in black and blue, mostly in italic, with a biographical notice of Gilruth, which is carried over onto the rear flap, at the bottom of which appear three lines in roman identifying the illustrator and acknowledging sources for cover illustrations. Issued with trade binding only.

Published at $2.95 for the trade binding and $2.36 for the library binding. Exact date of publication unknown; 25,000 copies were probably printed. Copyrighted July 8, 1963; deposited October 31, 1963. Listed in the "Weekly Record" of *Publisher's Weekly* on November 4, 1963.

REVIEWS: *Christian Science Monitor,* November 14, 1963 (p. 10B); *Library Journal,* January 15, 1964 (p. 412).

COPIES: DLC (2 copies in trade binding); Chicago Public Library (2 copies in library binding); Encyclopaedia Britannica, Inc., Chicago, Illinois (trade binding, d.j.); TAT (trade binding, d.j.).

NOTE: Waters received an advance of $2,500.00 against a small royalty, the nature of which I have been unable to learn. The work was originally intended to be a biography of Robert Gilruth, but Waters, after interviewing Gilruth, could not find sufficient material and the project was changed to a history of Project Mercury, focusing on Gilruth.

The book was published as one of a series of works for a monthly juvenile book club sponsored by the Encyclopaedia Britannica Press. In a phone interview, Mr. Frank Nipp, formerly an editor with Encyclopaedia Britannica Press and still employed by Encyclopaedia Britannica, informed me that the usual press runs for titles in this series was 25,000 copies.

A15 BOOK OF THE HOPI

After learning that the Charles Ulrick and Josephine Bay Foundation of New York was considering a major study of the Hopi Indians, and might possibly be interested in his collaboration, Waters wrote to Frederick H. Howell, vice-president of the Foundation, on June 2, 1959:

> White Bear has just written me from Phoenix, Arizona, suggesting that I write you directly for information concerning the Charles Ulrick and Josephine Bay Foundation's desire to obtain someone to work into book form the Hopi historical material which he is collecting on a tape recorder.
>
> He would like for me to do the writing, as you know, and I am interested in learning the nature of the material, the scope of the project, and any other information concerning it, the Foundation, and your needs.
>
> I have done considerable work along similar lines including the two following books which you may consult for reference: *The Man Who Killed the Deer* . . . [and] *Masked Gods: Navajo and Pueblo Ceremonialism* . . .
>
> Before committing myself to another piece of work along similar lines, I would want to know that it would comprise more than a few myths and legends of a light and "popular" nature; that the basic information is sound and authentic, justifying the work I would put in on it to make it stand up under the same long and close scrutiny of the two books mentioned above. I have not been able to meet with White Bear to discuss this yet, but from the high moral tone of his letter and the deep sincerity with which he assures me it is the voice of his people which must be put down, I feel confident that the material will come from the heart of a people who must be heard.
>
> We too have a great need for such a book as I believe this may well be. For several years the Navajos, recognizing that their old Singers were dying without being able to hand down their knowledge to young men in the Service as GI's, have been passing on their religious and cultural heritage to the whites for preservation. These include the many Ways so scholarly transcribed by Father Berard Haile with the express permission of the Navajo Tribal Council; also such individual ceremonies as the Way "Where the Two Came to Their Father", recorded, transcribed and published under the auspices of the Bollingen Foundation.
>
> The Hopi history and ceremonialism is perhaps the most complex and pro-

found of any tribal group on the continent. The katchina concept alone has defied professional "classifiers" for years on end. If White Bear and the Hopi elders are now willing to "give" something of their history and its underlying significance, it will be a deeply significant gift of immense value to future generations. If done right, with depth and scope, it will be comparable to the *Popul Vuh* of the Quiche Mayas—the oldest book in America, corresponding to the Christian Bible. It would of course be a work in which I would feel privileged to participate, and I will be happy to learn what you have in mind.

Howell responded on June 9, 1959, by saying that if White Bear and Waters felt it possible to work together on the project, that the foundation would be amenable to underwriting the work, and that all the parties should get together to discuss ways of getting the project started. Howell wrote again on July 16, 1959, suggesting that both Waters and White Bear come to New York to discuss the project.

Waters responded to Howell's suggestion on July 22, 1959:

Thank you for your letter of July 16th suggesting that I come to New York to discuss the Hopi History project. I will be glad to do so. The next time I go to Santa Fe I will make a tentative plane reservation for Monday, August 24th. If this date does not prove to be convenient for you, it can be changed to fit in with your schedule.

I also believe this exploratory conference is necessary. As a result of my talk in Gallup with White Bear, he and I are in full agreement as to the general scope and nature of the projected book. It is my impression from listening to one of his long tape recordings, however, that not too much of the actual, needed material has been collected and tape recorded. The bulk of it still remains to be researched, verified, and transcribed. My main concern is that the material be authenticated and corroborated by accounts from a number of Hopi elders in order to insure that the book is not solely White Bear's own personal views, but a corroborated account with tribal permission for public release. White Bear assures me he can obtain this supplemental information from some twelve other responsible spokesmen. . . .

In order that we may all be in agreement as to the content and organization of the book, and have a predetermined plan for collecting the material, I will prepare and bring to New York with me a tentative working outline. This can be modified by your own views of what is necessary, and then reviewed with White Bear for final assurance that he and his other spokesmen can cover the ground indicated. This in no wise indicates a lack of faith in White Bear's knowledge and ability to secure all the material needed. It is simply a precaution justified by the great scope and complexity of Hopi ceremonialism and the traditional, obdurate Hopi secrecy about it.

With the project more thoroughly outlined, we will all then be in a better position to discuss the ways and means of accomplishing it. . . .

The text of Waters' outline mentioned in the above letter is as follows:

SECTION A

OUTLINE FOR HANDLING WHITE BEAR'S HOPI MATERIAL
by
Frank Waters

The following brief outline is proposed as a working plan for building into book form the original and research material to be collected, recorded, and also illustrated with water-color and line drawings, by Kacha Honawah (White Bear); written by myself (Frank Waters) with additional background commentary; and published under the auspices of the Charles Ulrick and Josephine Bay Foundation, Inc.

The Book: Nature and Scope

The book will present, from the Hopi point of view, the complete and ritually esoteric history of the Hopi tribe from Creation to the present time. It is a world-view of life, deeply religious in nature, which has been preserved unchanged from antiquity. Containing material that has never been made available to professional historians and anthropologists, the book will be an authenticated record of wide cultural and ethnic import. More significantly, it will be a timely contribution from perhaps the oldest indigenous inhabitants of America to a humanity at large now suffering an era of world unrest and moral confusion. The word "Hopi" itself means "peace", and Hopi ceremonialism has been immemorially preoccupied with maintaining harmony in the universe. This message of peace, this concern with helping to preserve the inherent harmony of the universal constituents of all life, is a challenging affirmation of faith by a dwindling tribe of Indians facing possible extinction. They reaffirm for all of us everywhere the basic tenets of man's imperishable belief in the fullness and richness of life granted him by the power of his creative forces.

This book is not intended to serve as a professional paper—neither a social or psychological study, nor an anthropological report. It is an exposition of the Hopi Way by Hopi elders given here to the world for the first time. It will be written simply and clearly, adhering as much as possible to the Hopi idiom; a narrative text acceptable at face value to all alike, ethnologists, anthropologists, historians, religious people of all faiths, and with as wide appeal as possible to the general reading public in any country in which it may be published.

Collection and Preparation of Material

White Bear is a Hopi. He speaks for his people with knowledge handed down to him through generations. His own personal knowledge will be supplemented by verbal accounts from some twelve of his ceremonial Fathers, clan members, and responsible tribal Elders which he will record in the Hopi language on a tape recorder. The recordings will provide a permanent record in the Hopi language of the original source material, attesting that the material is not solely White Bear's own personal views, but a collaborative account given with express permission for public release in this form. White Bear will provide Frank Waters with a literal translation into English of these recordings, interpretations of rituals and ceremonies, and answers to questions as they arise.

From this rough material Frank Waters will write the book in finished form. He is already familiar with the general pattern of Pueblo ceremonialism and has published two books on the subject: *Masked Gods: Pueblo and Navajo Ceremonialism,* and *The Man Who Killed the Deer,* a novel on Pueblo ceremonialism. In writing the book, he will work closely with White Bear on the Reservation and elsewhere to insure complete unity in handling the material.

It is normally assumed that universal truths are not the exclusive property of any one race, nation, creed or sect; any mytho-religious system with the universal scope of Hopi ceremonialism is paralleled in many essentials by other great systems throughout the world. These parallels with Christianity and other world religions, with religious philosophies of the East such as Tibetan Buddhism and the Vedantic system of India, and with the formal modern sciences of the West—as psychology, atomic physics and geology—will be pointed out by means of a commentary. Such comparisons will aid in the understanding of the basic meaning of the Hopi Way, expressed in its own unique and indigenous idiom.

Conversely, they will provide for this book a framework of reference universal in extent—limited not to the milieu of a small tribe isolated on three remote desert mesas, but embracing all segments of mankind with their inherent faith in the one divine creative power that guides their common destiny.

Following is the tentative structure of the book and the salient points to be covered:

PART ONE: HOPI CREATION MYTH

An overall narrative outline of the Hopi cosmogenesis and cosmography; the creation of mankind; the three underworlds and the successive Emergences from each; the function and responsibility of man imposed upon him by the Creator; the laws to which he must adhere in order to achieve his appointed task; the Hopi conception of time; the relationship of the individual to the universal whole as a microcosmic replica of the macrocosm; the Hopi conception of world harmony.

PART TWO: HOPI HISTORY

A detailed narrative review of Hopi history from the Emergence to the present fourth world to the present time. This includes the history of the people's first Emergence on the continent of America in prehistoric times; the migrations; the genesis of corn, a botanical mystery; the founding of Oraibi—the oldest, continually inhabited town in the United States; division into clans and their designated responsibilities; founding of seven Hopi pueblos on the three Hopi mesas; significance of the location; relationships of the Hopi to the surrounding tribes—the ancient cliff-dwellers on Mesa Verde, the prehistoric occupants of Pueblo Bonito and Chetro Ketl, the Navajos, Utes and Apaches, the Aztecs from Mexico, and the derivative modern pueblos of Zuni, Acoma, and the Rio Grande; and finally with the gradually encroaching Spanish and Anglo settlers whose coming was foretold and whose races were symbolized by the directional colors of the sacred corn.

PART THREE: HOPI CEREMONIALISM

An interpretative explanation of the rituals, ceremonies, kiva observances, dances, songs and prayers comprising the major Hopi ceremonials such as the Powamu, Niman Katchina, Soyal, the Flute and the Snake-Antelope ceremonials, the Marau, Lakon and Oazol. Stress will be laid not on the ethnological details common to reportorial accounts as found in Smithsonian Reports, but on the underlying meaning of the ceremonials as traditional techniques for helping to maintain universal harmony through the evocation of the creative power for the good of all. The functions of the priests, clans, and all participants will be delineated; the katchina concept and its purpose; the power that Hopi ceremonialism exerts upon all other pueblos; its borrowing by the Navajos for inclusion in their sacred Ways; and comparison with Aztec and Maya beliefs and rituals.

PART FOUR: SECULAR VS. CEREMONIAL POWER
This section implicitly poses the primary problem confronting the whole world today—the conflict between ruthless temporal and morally religious forces for the domination of mankind.

The Hopi reference frame will include: the encroachment of modern civilization upon the traditional Hopi way of life, politically, economically, and ideologically; exodus of people to Moencopi; abandonment of Oraibi; government control and restrictions; impending loss of land to the Navajo tribe; attrition of handicrafts, customs and habits due to materialistic stresses; breaking down of ceremonialism. Also the efforts to combat it: peaceful resistance to Spanish domination; resistance to American domination by aloofness and secretiveness; obdurate clinging to ceremonial beliefs by the elders; continuance of dances despite government threats, missionary protests, and public outcry; continued acceptance of the religious over the economic values of the present; appeal to the United Nations for peaceful settlement of world problems the Hopi way; release of the material in this book for the first time. Significance of the exploration of outer space by rockets, satellites and missiles, and of the rapid development of psychology and psychiatry, as portending a new symbolic Emergence to the fifth world through the evolutionary development of the human mind—confirming, at the end of the book, the initial premise that man is a microcosmic replica of the macrocosmic universe and that his evolutionary journey up through the symbolic underworlds has been made within himself.

Late in August of that year Waters, White Bear and Howell met in New York and discussed the project in detail. A "Memorandum of understanding" was drawn up by Waters after his return to Taos, which outlined the outcome of this meeting. This memorandum was dated September 1, 1959, and sent by Waters to Howell in the form of a letter, headed at the top: "MEMORANDUM OF UNDERSTANDING | Between | Charles Ulrick and Josephine Bay Foundation, Inc. | And | Frank Waters and White Bear:"

In compliance with your request, I am giving below my understanding of the conclusions reached during our discussion with you regarding the White Bear project:

It is my understanding that the Charles Ulrick and Josephine Bay Foundation, Inc. has approved the "Hopi history" project proposed by you and White Bear, and the method of procedure and the general outline of the finished book which I submitted to you.

The Foundation has expressed its willingness to contribute $350 per month to

White Bear to enable him to move back to Oraibi, Arizona and obtain tape recordings of the necessary source material. The Foundation will also grant to me $100 per week during the time I am writing the text. It is understood that I have waived any salary; the grant will cover only incurred expenses while doing research in Los Angeles, travelling back and forth to the Hopi Reservation from Los Angeles and my home in Taos, New Mexico, secretarial and stenographic expense, and other project-connected expenses.

These grants will be made for an initial period of twelve months, with the understanding that they may be extended in whole or in part up to a total period of twenty-four months, at which time the manuscript will be in finished form to submit for publication. The Foundation reserves the right to terminate its sponsorship of the project at the end of three months, or at any time thereafter, if the material does not come up to anticipation or warrant continuance of the project. I reserve the same right to abandon the project. It is recognized that the source material constitutes, according to Hopi concept, ritual tribal property held inviolate for many generations. The entire project is based upon committments [sic] made to White Bear by many clan chiefs and other Hopi elders that now, in this form, the material may be publicly released. Their giving of the material in tape form, constituting a permanent record, also constitutes their permission for release. If however their full collaborative cooperation is withheld later, neither White Bear nor myself will be held accountable for the expenses incurred to that time, nor will be expected to produce the material. This is a recognized risk justified by the unprecedented nature of the project.

I do not guarantee that the book when finished will be published. I will, however, make every effort to place it with a publishing house capable of giving it national distribution. If placed as have been all of my published books, the publisher will assume full costs of production and distribution, and the resulting author's royalties will be divided equally between White Bear and myself.

In the event it is decided that the book should be amply illustrated with color plates, black-and-white drawings, maps, and photographs by White Bear, a publisher may require that the high costs of color reproduction be partially borne by the Foundation; or that the retail price of the book be advanced to cover the costs, which will of course lower the size of the printing. My own feeling is that it is too early to decide on the format of the book. It will have to be written and discussed with prospective publishers before deciding on any publishing procedure. In the event the Foundation may wish it, I will be glad to turn over these problems for discussion with the agency which handles the placement of my other books, when the time comes.

On the same day on which he sent Howell the "Memorandum," Waters also sent a copy of the agreement to Carl Dentzel at the Southwest Museum, along with the following letter:

Dear Carl:
I have just returned home from New York after several days of discussion with the directors of the Charles Ulrick and Josephine Bay Foundation, Inc., and White Bear, a Hopi from Oraibi, regarding a project which will also be of

interest to you as the director of the Southwest Museum. Enclosed is a description of the project.

The Foundation approved the project as described. It has expressed its willingness to grant White Bear financial assistance to the extent of $350 per month for an initial period of twelve months, which may be extended as necessary, for the purpose of recording the source material. It will also defray my travel, research and miscellaneous expenses while I am writing the text to the extent of $100 a week for the same period; I have waived any salary, I feel so strongly the necessity for giving the Hopi people this opportunity to voice their message at long last.

The charter of the Foundation, however, expressly prohibits financial grants to individuals, but not to institutions. I have suggested, accordingly, that in line with the Southwest Museum's long record of preserving and promoting interest in the cultural heritage of the Southwest, that you might be willing to serve as an intermediary. Your assistance would comprise no more than accepting a financial grant from the Foundation specifically earmarked solely for this project, and mailing a check each to White Bear and myself monthly during the period. Such assistance, which I hope would require a minimum of bookkeeping, would permit the Foundation and ourselves to get the project under way immediately and without any legal difficulties.

In order to save time, I am sending a copy of this letter to Mr. Howell and I would appreciate it very much if you would write your reactions to this proposal directly to him. . . .

On September 21, 1959, Carl Dentzel wrote to Waters that the Museum had approved the outline of assistance for the project. On the same day, the Foundation forwarded its first check to the Museum in amount of $2,350.00, for the first three months. Under the terms of the agreement between the Museum and the Foundation additional funds would be supplied afterwards, with the aggregate not to exceed $15,000.00. Following the required signing of pertinent documents, Waters wrote to Dentzel on October 26, 1959:

I'm glad to hear that White Bear is at Oraibi and beginning work . . .

You may put me on your records as beginning work on November 1st. If the weather holds, I shall fly down with a friend here (Brice Sewell, the trader) for a three-day trip to the Casa Grande ruins near Chihuahua. These newly excavated ruins may prove to be an archeological link between the Hopis and the Aztecs, confirming the oral tradition I hope to get from White Bear and his informants, and I want to get their set-up and feeling. I shall then go on to Oraibi to spend some time with White Bear on my way to Los Angeles . . .

I would appreciate it if you would classify all funds paid me as reimbursed expenses rather than salary payments, in accordance with the Memorandum of Understanding. If they are reported as salary payments I would have to include them for Income Tax purposes. I would also have to report them to the Writers' Guild, of which I am a member. This would lead to difficulties; for my registered salary is far in excess of this amount, and this non-contractual work at a lesser sum would clearly be considered a violation. However, as our research work on this project is clearly outside the scope of work covered by the Guild, and is not a gainful occupation, their correct reportage as merely expense amounts will avoid all misunderstanding. . . .

After starting to work on the project, Waters wrote to Howell on November 9, 1959, from Los Angeles, giving the first of his many informal reports:

> I have delayed answering your letter of October 27 as I left Taos the day after it arrived for Oraibi. The little two-room house White Bear is fixing up for me to live in was not yet ready; there was no room to be had at the school as the place was besieged with bed-bugs; so I came on here to stock up on research before returning in two weeks for the beginning of the yearly round of ceremonials.
> While I was there I met several of our informants, laid out a working plan, and discussed several touchy points. White Bear already has made several long tapes—not yet translated into English—and done a lot of ground work. I am impressed more than ever by the deep sincerity of the people we are working with, and by the depth of the information to be obtained. There is no doubt as to the importance of the project and that we are off to a good start. It will be slow going at first, but the scope is so large I am not eager to rush matters.
> The Ranking book [John Ranking, *Historical Researches on the Conquest of Peru, Mexico, Bogota, Natchez and Talomeco, in the 13th Century.* . . . London, 1827] you mentioned is indeed pertinent. It strikes at the heart of our study—and at the one unsolved mystery of America. For this reason I would like you to hold off sending it to me (if I cannot get it through the Southwest Museum) for a couple of months or more. And I would like to hold off discussing its premise with you right now also. It is too involved to do justice to in a letter. The myth of the Seven Cities established by the Portuguese is substantiated historically by letters to the King of Portugal in the 14th century, and by Cabot to the King of England, although popular legend transferred them to newly discovered America later. Also the Mongolian invasion with elephants in the 13th century seems too late to be substantiated by fact. However I'm not negative about this. Myth is invariably right, although a few dates and references may be in error. In fact, there is a current Pueblo legend of an invasion of small yellow men long ago. So let me hold off with a clear mind until I get the Hopi story of their migrations to this continent and I can check all archeological and historical references, including the Ranking book. There are some inscriptions on the cliffs around Oraibi, I understand, that tie in with this subject and which we will investigate and photograph. I also will fly down with a trader friend of mine to see the newly excavated ruins at Casa Grande, Chihuahua some time this winter. These undoubtedly connect the Hopi and the Aztec peoples, and will substantiate the material which White Bear is now beginning to tape.
> It is stimulating to me that you are doing some reading along our line, and I hope you continue to give me anything pertinent which you run into. If we can all pin down the prehistoric "history" of the Hopi and the routes of their migrations, it will solve a mystery that no ethnologist has dared to guess at pub-

licly and will offer a new basis for the study of Aztec and Inca civilization. So shoot along all the information you pick up. . . .

On January 4, 1960, Waters sent to Howell his evaluation of the project at the end of its first three months:

This letter, copy of which is being sent to Mr. Carl S. Dentzel, comprises my evaluation of the material submitted to me in accordance with our *Memorandum of Understanding* of September 1, 1959, and my joint report to the Foundation and the Southwest Museum of the first three months progress on the Hopi project.

1. *Material Recorded and Translated*

Ten tapes of source material have been recorded and translated into approximately 118 typed pages. Slightly more than half of this relates to the first two ceremonials just concluded, answers specific questions, and is excellent—specific, original, and of quality high enough to use directly in the text. The remainder consists of scattered remarks on many subjects, is not cohesive, and is too generalized for text usage although it will be useful for background reference.

In order to gather material at a quicker rate and on a more orderly basis that will enable me to work on the text as soon as possible, a suggested schedule of work was drawn up on December 9 and agreed to by White Bear and myself . . . This will have to be adhered to in general outline if the work is accomplished in the time allotted for it.

2. *Observational and Historical Research*

Since my arrival here on November 22, White Bear has been orienting me fully to important sites, deciphering petroglyphs, introducing me to informants, and supplying additional information for my notes. We have seen the first two ceremonies of the year. All this, combined with the taped records, has given me complete notes ready for final writing on the full symbolism and meaning of the Wuwuchim and Soyal ceremonies. This is new material, not contained in ethnological nor popular literature, with all the depth and scope we hopefully anticipated.

A small start has been made on historical research which will be continued, according to our schedule, when I return to the Southwest Museum's excellent library in Los Angeles.

3. *Hopi Cooperation*

The premise of a preponderant number of Hopi clan and kiva chiefs willing and eager to give out necessary information, as stated in my first *Outline for Handling White Bear's Hopi Material* and as further understood during our meeting in New York, has not been substantiated by fact. Many important clan leaders in Hotevilla, proposed as the primary source of our information, were found to be ignorant and suspicious of the project, and reluctant to talk.

Accordingly, a four-hour meeting of eight of them was called on December 10, at which the purpose of the Foundation and the project was fully explained with the functions of the Southwest Museum, White Bear and myself. At its conclusion the members agreed to advise us of their decision.

A second meeting, following talk misinterpreting our explanation despite the fact it was recorded on tape, was held on December 17 to include members not present at the first meeting. Full explanation was again given with the assurance that informant elders would be given the book to review for accuracy before publication. David Monongva, included on our list of willing informants, then formally declared that he was unwilling to talk or cooperate with the project. The meeting was adjourned with the notice we would be informed of the decision of the others.

On December 22 we were so informed that all elders had decided not to talk nor to cooperate with us.

This stand is surprising in view of the assurances previously given White Bear; especially so as Dan Kochongva, religious leader of all kivas and head of all Traditionalists, has to date been our chief informant and staunchest supporter. But behind it looms an inter-tribal political rivalry now shaping that has been precipitated by this project itself; which will undoubtedly result in a Hopi split as disastrous as the historic Oraibi-Hotevilla split of 1906; and which will affect the course of Hopi life.

Without going into its devious ramifications, I will mention only that the long-delayed Navaho-Hopi boundary dispute has now been set for a court hearing in April. Hopi boundaries will be claimed by the location of ancient shrines. In preparation for this, three men are jockeying for leadership; Dan Kochongva, ceremonial leader and our supporter; David Monongva, who has turned against him and us; and James Ponguaguama, holder of one of the sacred tablets, who has just returned here after living for two years in Santa Domingo. The latter two face two alternatives. By allying themselves with the Tribal Council (regarded by Traditionalists as a puppet government of the Indian Bureau for administering temporal affairs), they will have to relinquish religious authority to Kochongva who will then supply us all information needed. Or they must usurp him as religious leader, leaving him deserted by his associates at the age of eighty, in which case, again, he will tell me everything in order to preserve it against the breakdown of all ceremonialism. Hence he is sitting it out with Hopi patience. I cannot predict how long this deadlock will continue without indulging in wishful thinking.

Our own best course of action has been to take a stand against letting ourselves be placed in a wrong light. I have sent out word that while I will answer any questions from others, I will answer no more questions nor attend any more meetings attended by those who have given us their own decision. Also that I have withdrawn the offer to present the book to informants for review, thus holding ourselves free to report all the above facts as they occur. Meanwhile White Bear is contacting the other informants given on his original list, and trying to obtain other informants in the villages on Second and First Mesa, not affected by this impending split on Third Mesa. This will give us the representative viewpoints required for most of the material in the book.

In short, this rather negative state of Hopi affairs can be made to work to our advantage. It gives us material for the contemporary last part of the book at this crucial time when we are witnessing the last full Hopi moon and a cultural erasure. And it emphasizes as nothing else the importance of getting a full record of this wonderful ceremonialism now before it passes forever. No other successful attempt can ever be made. This of course is the primary purpose of the project.

4. *Conclusion*

Despite a rather slow start and the present state of Hopi affairs, I feel we have satisfactorily broken ice. The material is here we hoped for, but it will not come with the ease anticipated. The continued prerequisite of the project remains what it was: to tape and translate needed material of quality high enough to be used in the text, and systematically enough to enable the book to be written within the time allotted for it.

I unhesitantly recommend that the project be continued for another three months with the following suggestions:

a) That if at the end of this time, April, 1960, all satisfactory material is not taped and translated for *Part One: The Creation Myth* and for the Powamuya ceremony, a re-evaluation be made of the project and the need for a complete revision of our procedure.

b) There exists a question as to the disposal of the taped records. According to my understanding in New York, the Foundation reserved the right to place the tapes with a custodian like the Southwest Museum where they would be preserved as a permanent record readily available for reference in case of any question as to the authenticity of the book when published. I believe that White Bear has a different understanding, feeling that the tapes are his personal property and should remain in his possession. Accordingly, I suggest that he and the Foundation clear up this question without delay.

c) When the custodian for the tapes is decided upon, I suggest that the tapes be sent to him bi-monthly, at the same time the translations are sent to me, in order to avoid possible loss or misplacement.

d) Another evaluation report will normally be in order at the end of three months, and we will keep you informed of developments.

In conclusion I want to assure the Foundation and the Museum that White Bear and myself are more enthusiastic about the project than ever before, and that the developments met here accentuate beyond all doubt the importance of recording now, in the brief time they are still available, the deeply profound truths and meanings of Hopi ceremonialism and history.

Howell reported back to Waters in a letter dated January 7, 1960, informing him that the Foundation had carefully considered his report and recommendations and had agreed to continue the project. Howell further reported that the Foundation and White Bear had agreed that the tapes should be sent to the Southwest Museum, which would then make a copy of the tapes to be returned to White Bear for his personal use.

By April of 1960 the project had proceeded along the lines suggested in Waters' report of January, and the project was continued. On May 8, 1960, Waters again informally reported recent developments in a letter to Howell:

... The Hopi problem is acute, with so many ramifications in the fields of local and national politics, economics, sociology, and psychology, that it is going to take a concerted and major effort to solve it. For this reason I believe our book is going to be of more help and importance than any of us envisioned. It should serve as a basic statement, omitting no facet of the interwoven mesh, for the longer I work on it I see how closely the traditional and progressive elements are intertwined. Only when it is all put down, from scratch, can one see the problem whole. And we are progressing slowly but well indeed. I have completed the major winter ceremonies, and by fall I expect to cover all the ceremonies. At present I am working on the Creation Myth while White Bear is gathering material for the migrations of the clans. By next winter, with all this religious and traditional material under our belt, we should be ready to tackle current developments with all their ramifications. Our timing is fortunately right. The old Chief died two weeks ago. The Hopi-Navajo court hearing is postponed. And we are slowly gaining access to new friends and information. ...

On January 6, 1961, Waters wrote to Carl Dentzel at the Southwest Museum, giving him an informal report on the first full year's progress:

... Concluding the first year of work, we have completed research on all the ceremonies in the annual cycle. My text will be finished and ready for publication by June 1st, including a number of sketches by White Bear and a glossary of all Hopi words used which we have spelled out phonetically and which I want to submit to an etymologist for proper spelling. This material will comprise a volume of more than 200 pages containing facts and interpretations never before released. The Foundation should know that this ceremonialism has been done first because it is the core of all Hopi life; without first understanding this, the rest of the material to follow would be comparatively meaningless. It is most fortunate indeed that we gathered this material during the past year; for this year there are so many deviations in the ceremonies from the traditional pattern that we could not now nor in the future obtain it. The Foundation has, accordingly, enabled us to make a most valuable contribution by securing this information before the final dissolution of these great annual cycles of ceremonies.

There still remains another volume to be done, which I have mapped out and for which White Bear is now collecting material. It will comprise the complete Creation Myth; the legends and routes of migrations by the various clans; reproductions and readings of pictographs and petroglyphs to substantiate the legends; and a complete history from the Hopi viewpoint of the tribe in historical times up to the present political, economic and social period of transition. At a later time we should discuss the possibilities of doing this second volume under the auspices of the Foundation and your own direction. I want here only to point out a couple of instances that illustrate its importance.

This summer wide public release was given the finding of a small stone image, said to be a kachina, by Dr. Martin of the University of Chicago. Subsequent University of Chicago publications show that nothing at all is known about this image. We ourselves visited the excavation site two times, located pictographs drawn near the site, and talked with many of our informants about it. As a result, we have positively identified the image (which is not a kachina as alleged) by name and function, the clan to which it belonged, why it was left in the excavated ruin, the ancient name of the ruin, and all the legends pertaining to it. This instance should remove any doubt that our present project is making as important a contribution as that made by the professional archeological and anthropological staffs of one of the great universities known for its work in this field. It also illustrates my premise that Southwest archeology is comparatively meaningless unless it is illumined by the light of living legend still preserved by the descendants of the prehistoric builders.

Two important court hearings were held this fall: the long-delayed land dispute between the Hopi and Navajo tribes, and the Hopi suit against the Government, a preliminary hearing of which was held before a U. S. Land Commissioner at Grand Canon. Attempts were made to prove Hopi land occupation by the location of ancient shrines. Several very old Hopi elders were put on the stand as witnesses. Their memories were faulty. The Navajo Tribal Council lawyer cast some aspersion on Hopi religious beliefs. As a result of the ensuing squabble, the hearing was dismissed and postponed until next April at Washington D. C.

We attended the hearings, and at Grand Canon tape-recorded the witnesses' testimony to play back later to groups of Hopis. It was quite obvious that the needed material—the basic material needed by the presiding Land Commissioner, and both the Hopi and Navajo legal counsellors—was exactly the information that we on this project are gathering and arranging in proper form for general use of all people and agencies dealing with these tribes. In many instances we could have immediately supplied the answers to questions that remained unanswered. It is also quite obvious that the all-embracing, authentic record being provided by our Hopi project is badly needed in many quarters, and will long stand as a basic report. Every attempt should be made to complete it. I doubt very much that it could be done in the future by anyone else if White Bear, his informants and myself are disbanded and the internal Hopi rupture continues to spread dissension among the people.

Mr. Fred Howell is satisfied with the progress we are making so I have not made these observations to him as the context of a yearly report. Please feel free to discuss them with him in person if you happen to go to New York, or to send him a copy of this letter if and whenever you feel it necessary. White Bear and myself still welcome, of course, your valuable advice and suggestions as we proceed.

Although Dentzel did not forward Waters' report directly to Howell, he did, on January 19, 1961, incorporate much of it in a letter to Howell. Howell wrote back on January 22, 1961, that the Foundation had approved the extension of the project through the balance of the year. He also reported that the Foundation felt that the results of the project should be consolidated and published in only one volume, rather than a series of volumes. Several months later, on May 4, 1961, Waters sent another report to Dentzel:

In compliance with your request, I am sending this brief report to bring you up to date on the Hopi project.

The following three sections will be completed by October 1st at the end of our two-year period:

PART ONE
THE MYTHS: CREATION OF THE FOUR WORLDS
PART TWO
THE LEGENDS: MIGRATIONS OF THE CLANS
PART THREE
THE MYSTERY PLAYS: THE CEREMONIAL CYCLE

These three parts will comprise about 375 pages of text including small black-and-white drawings to illustrate symbols, pictographs and petroglyphs, and ceremonial objects mentioned in the text. To these should be added, if possible, several full-page color illustrations of prominent kachinas, an altar and its sandpainting, and a kiva mural.

Despite the continuous difficulties encountered, detailed to you in my report of last January, the originality, richness and fullness of this material exceeds the high hope I had at the beginning of the project. I believe you will find it a book whose scope and authenticity on the subject has not been equalled, and one which can never be duplicated in the future due to the swift deterioration of Hopi culture. The Foundation should feel justly proud of having made it possible.

The major part of the above three sections has been completed in draft form. There still remains some rewriting and the addition of some new material; a glossary of some 1,000 Hopi words spelled phonetically which will be put in consistent order by an etymologist; and the drawings, now in quick pencil sketches, which I am having White Bear put in finished form for reproduction; and finally an editing and re-typing of the complete manuscript . . .

There remains to be done

PART FOUR
THE HISTORY: THE LOST WHITE BROTHER

which is the historical period beginning with the arrival of the Spaniards, and which will include the Pueblo Revolt of 1680, the murder of the Spanish priests at Oraibi, the destruction of Awatovi, the coming of the Americans, and the economic, social, and political aspects of Hopi life to the present time.

There is no doubt that this will be the only all-inclusive book on the Hopis to be written, and that it will serve as a source book for government, ethnological, and other workers, as well as for the general public, for years to come. For this reason Part Four should be done to complete its full scope, if the Foundation sees fit to extend its sponsorship. I would be quite willing to complete it . . . However, I would undertake it only on a salary basis to be determined by you and the Foundation. I have never regarded this project as a lucrative venture. But two years of very difficult work on the present financial basis, all of it required for travel and other incurred project expenses, is about as far as I can go.

Sometime later in the summer, Dentzel broached to Howell the subject of the manuscript's eventual publication, suggesting at first the possibility that publication might be undertaken by the Bollingen Foundation. After Howell responded that he felt it would be best if publication were to remain under the sponsorship of the Bay Foundation rather than bringing in another party, Dentzel suggested that the Foundation underwrite the costs of publication, the book to be released under the imprint of the Southwest Museum. After receiving word from Howell about these developments, Waters wrote to Howell on August 22, 1961:

> Thank you very much for your letter of August 15 and enclosures. Your answer to Carl Dentzel's letter is in tone with my own feelings.
> I do not want to minimize or retard in any way Carl's encouraging interest and unflagging help, but I feel it would be unwise to release the book through a small Pacific Coast publisher or printer. Such firms are excellent printers and turn out beautifully designed books, mostly on contract to individuals and organizations for a specific number of copies for their specific uses. They do not have national distribution facilities for releasing copies through retail outlets to the general public; promotional facilities for advertising in trade media and the general press; nor for placing review copies and insuring competent reviews. They do not have, as do most large Eastern publishers of trade books, representatives or connections with foreign publishers who might be interested in preparing translated editions. More importantly, they do not keep the book in print; their responsibility is usually limited to one specific printing. Hence the release of the book by such a printer might, at the outset, greatly limit its field of distribution to educational and scientific centers, and professional readers . . . In which case the distribution would be somewhat guided by the Southwest Museum, and the book might have to be edited to insure that its views would not offend the orthodox academic view.
> The Bollingen Foundation is outstanding for its release of books of this type. Because this is their special field, they send out researchers, writers and artists to the field, print and release the finished book, carrying through the project from beginning to end. I doubt that they would be inclined to publish a book conceived by and prepared under the auspices of another Foundation, to whom the major credit for its presentation would be properly due. Conversely, I would not think it good policy for the Charles Ulrick and Josephine Bay Foundation to enlist the aid of another Foundation unless this is necessary. I concur heartily in your feeling that the Foundation should carry the whole thing through if possible.
> I propose that the book when ready be submitted to a leading New York publisher with full facilities for designing, art work, printing, promotion, national distribution, and connections with reviewers and foreign publishers, together with a tentative Foundation offer to subsidize the cost of printing, all other costs to be normally borne by the publishing house. This is a normal procedure for books of this type. When the book is approved for publication and an estimate of the cost is made, you can then present concretely the matter to your Board of Directors.
> My New York literary agent, to whom I entrust the handling of all my own books, fortunately stayed here with me for a few days before he returned to New York. He did not read the book, but I discussed the matter with him and

he concurred in the views stated above. He would be glad to handle the placement of the book, submitting it, drawing up the contract, and investigating with the publisher any foreign sales possibilities. His fee is simply the customary 10% agent's commission on author's royalties, so his desire to obtain the widest distribution possible would coincide with ours.

Hence he would in effect be acting as the Foundation's representative, relieving you (as he does me) of all direct negotiations with the publisher. This would not preclude presenting Carl's suggestions for format and museum distribution, nor my own for working up White Bear's drawings, nor your own suggestions for the book's overall presentation.

This is a rather blunt expression of my suggestions for procedure which I would have preferred to bring out in a friendly meeting with you and Carl in New York. I have only mentioned it here lest things develop too fast and far on the Pacific Coast. . . . I do not want to tread on anybody's toes, and am preparing a long Introduction to the book acknowledging the aid of all who made the book possible. Furthermore I think it might be gracious if you directed that a certain number of copies be set aside for Carl to send to the directors and friends of the Southwest Museum as a token of the Foundation's appreciation of his aid.

Unfortunately my agent will not be in New York when Carl and I arrive in October. He is leaving for his annual trip to Europe and the Book Fair early in October and will not return until November 1st. If, however, you would like to discuss the handling of books with him, as an objective agent who makes this his business, feel free to telephone him and ask him to call at your office for a chat . . .

I am now laboriously correcting the spelling of some 600 Hopi words in the ms. worked out by Mr. Hughes of Columbia University with White Bear two weeks ago, and still patiently waiting for some more material I requested of Bear. This will not come in, in time for the complete ms. to be retyped before we come to New York. However, I will bring a complete but unrevised copy so you can see exactly what has been accomplished. . . .

After completing the preliminary draft of the manuscript, Waters sent copies off to both Howell and Dentzel. Dentzel acknowledged receipt of the manuscript, which he praised in highly laudatory terms, in a letter to Waters on September 29, 1961. Howell acknowledged receipt of the manuscript on October 5, 1961, and in that letter informed Waters that Carl Dentzel was planning to come to New York to place the manuscript himself, apparently unaware of the plans to have Waters' agent undertake the placement. Waters replied to Howell's letter on October 9, 1961:

I'm afraid Carl Dentzel hasn't kept you as fully informed as I supposed. He is arriving in Santa Fe on Wednesday to act as a chairman of the section of the Western History Conference to be held October 12-14. The next day, October 15, we will fly to New York together and call you the first thing Monday morning. I will see him in Santa Fe and confirm these plans. If anything has thrown him off schedule, I will wire you.

The ms. you have comprises the first three parts of the book as proposed, and represents what we have accomplished in the two years allotted us for the project, up November 1st. It has not been completely finished . . . Despite the difficulties, we have unearthed far more material than I ever hoped for; and it is so dove-tailed in every detail, despite the extraordinary complexity of the subject, I am satisfied it is correct. As a result I believe that in the two-year period we have come up with a 400-page book that offers for the first time a full and concise handling of a most complex subject that no one has ever cracked before, and which should stand as a basic source book for years. Considering all factors involved, I firmly feel an extra good job has been done, and I am hoping that before we meet in New York you will have had time to read all the ms. and weigh it for yourself.

Part Four, the last part, remains to be done. It comprises the whole historical period from the arrival of the Spaniards up to the present time, with all the pending land suits. White Bear has sent me some material for it, and is presumably gathering more. However, this part will require more pure historical research on my part than material collected by him, by the very nature of the material. To treat it fully as the three previous parts, I would estimate that it would take me about six months from November 1st if the Foundation wished to extend the project. If the Foundation does not want to extend it beyond January 1st, I can cover the material quickly and incompletely in summary form. Or the project can be terminated on November 1st, as originally planned, with the present and already full 400 pages. To determine this, I think you should have time to review all that has been covered, and I would be quite willing to postpone our trip to New York if Carl Dentzel is also willing, as I also wish his evaluation of it.

Only three copies of the typescript are available. You have one, Carl Dentzel has one, and I am still making revisions and minor additions in my file copy as late material comes in from White Bear. For this reason he has not been given a copy to go through. I have written him that I will bring a copy for him to go through when I go to the Hopi country this fall . . .

I have not engaged an agent, Bart Fles, to handle the placement of the book. He handles all my other books, is quite competent, and I believe we could all benefit from his help. I have not heard from Carl Dentzel of his own plans or suggestions for publication. But when I see him this week we will discuss all suggestions and possibilities to be presented to you for decision. Fles wrote me that you had talked together, and I'm glad you could get his views as he is leaving for Europe the 14th and cannot be there when we arrive.

My own feelings about the book are the same as when we started, if not better. It is valuable indeed to have obtained from an Indian tribe, for the first time, their complete story of their origin, life, and religion. To my knowledge it has not been achieved before. But with the unrest and resentment against the imposition of our rational materiality spreading throughout all Middle and South America, whose heritage is also Indian, this psychological revelation of Indian thought and religious belief, wholly indigenous and antipathic to our own, makes it very significant indeed. It raises the book to a psychic level far above the political, economic and cultural levels on which this nation as a whole meets other nations and peoples. I am rewriting the Introduction to include this feeling, and if Part Four is to be done it also will develop it more fully. For this reason I would like, myself, to see that publication offers it the maximum possibility of distribution. However, we can discuss all these ramifications when we meet next Monday, and I'm looking forward with great pleasure to seeing all of you again. . . .

After Howell met with Waters and Dentzel in New York, the Foundation agreed to provide Waters with funds for a ten week period, beginning January 1, 1962, in which to complete work on Part Four. The Foundation also agreed to the suggestion that it underwrite the costs of publication when the manuscript had been placed with a New York publisher.

On March 5, 1962, Waters wrote Howell about the status of the manuscript:

I'm now on the last leg of Part Four and should finish it in about three weeks. Meanwhile retyping of the rewritten first three parts is coming along. Would you like me to send you each part as it is finished, or wait and send you the complete ms.?

Your letter to Henriette Mertz about her *Pale Ink* I liked very much. Its terse and concise statement of our own aims hit the nail right on the head. I am wondering if you would not think it appropriate for you to develop this thinking in a short Foreword in the book to precede my own lengthy Introduction. A Foreword is always written by someone other than the author. No one is more suitable than yourself who conceived this project, instigated it, and directed it; and who knows, better than anyone else, its hopeful aim and implications—the reasons why the Foundation, with its far vaster interests, saw fit to support it so wholeheartedly . . .

Now about publishing. Contractual arrangements for publishing, in accordance with the Foundation's charter, must be made by the Southwest Museum. Dentzel during his last visit here a month ago was utterly opposed to my interposing an agent—Barthold Fles—to place the book. He felt, perhaps rightly, that he himself had better taste and judgment as to how the format should be. And he insisted that he had the time and willingness to contact and discuss its publication with prospective publishing houses.

For my part, as I have discussed it with you and him, I am opposed to letting the book come out under the auspices of the Southwest Museum—either being published by the Southwest Museum itself, or by a small printer in Los Angeles under contract to the Museum.

Hence we agreed that Dentzel should be permitted to discuss publication with a number of publishing houses in New York, Los Angeles or elsewhere who would submit bids on an impartial basis, allowing us to choose the best offer. If this is agreeable to you, I would like for the offers to be looked at by us jointly—yourself, Dentzel and myself—so that we could agree on the best.

I see no field of disagreement between any of us, including the publisher selected, in wanting the widest distribution of the best printed book we can

162   SECTION A

manage. But I think our basic premise should be kept firmly in mind by all of us—that this, essentially, is the Foundation's project which should be carried through to its primary satisfaction. . . .

After receiving word from Howell, in March of 1962, that he would be pleased to write a foreword for the book, Waters wrote again to Howell on March 22, 1962:

Good! I'm delighted that you will do the Foreword! There will be no second thoughts.
I'm sending off the last chapters today to be typed. The complete ms. will be typed, bound, and a copy sent to you and to Carl Dentzel about April 15. When you receive it, and read through the last part and my expanded Introduction, you can then write the Foreword to be included before a publisher is selected.
This completes the ms. within the time agreed upon and for which funds were made available. Between now and publication, however, there is a great deal of sporadic work to be done. I must take the completed Part Four to White Bear in either Phoenix or Oraibi and go over it with him, then make the necessary revisions. Some revisions may be necessary after you go over it also. Last revisions and corrections must then be made on the galley proofs run off by the publisher. More important, I want to keep in continuous touch with Carl during the process of receiving bids from publishers, making the final selection, and determining the format of the book, the reproduction of the drawings, and the cut lines for the photographs. Carl assures me that he has the time, as well as the strong desire, to initiate all contacts with prospective publishers without interposing an agent. But he is a busy man, unfamiliar with New York publishers, and I feel a responsibility to the Foundation to help see the project through to a successful conclusion rather than turning it completely over to him. So rest assured I will continue to give my best support. . . .

After delivering the completed manuscript to both Howell and Dentzel, there arose some confusion concerning the nature of the book and its publication. Waters addressed himself to these problems in a letter he wrote to Carl Dentzel on July 9, 1962:

Fred Howell, White Bear and I, after our telephone conversation with you last week, were quite concerned and felt perhaps you and your staff were confused about the basic premise of the Hopi book.
If the Foundation had desired a formal, scientific study of the Hopis, it would have entered into an arrangement with an institution like Harvard University, the Universtiy of Chicago, or a large museum to send out a large staff from its departments of ethnology, sociology and political science to make such a study.
This was not the wish of the Foundation. The purpose of the project, as conceived, instigated, and directed by Fred Howell for the directors of the Foundation, was to offer in narrative form for the general public the mytho-religious history of the Hopis which underlies their secular life in all aspects. It was hoped that this would provide a background for the first time which would

be helpful to the Hopis and to white agencies in dealing with them during their present plight. White Bear was selected to obtain Hopi spokesmen to make tape recordings of all source material used in order to insure authenticity and multiple viewpoints. I was given a free hand to arrange and write the material in readable form, with full liberty to interpret aspects not familiar to readers within our usual frame of reference. At my suggestion the Southwest Museum was asked to administer the funds provided by the Foundation and to keep in its files for permanent record the original tape recordings. It was never intended from the start that the book be re-edited in the mold of a scientific study for the primary benefit of academic institutions. All this was clearly set forth in a Memorandum to the Foundation before its directors authorized the project.

The book is now finished. Fred is satisfied that it adheres to this basic premise, and so states in his Foreword. White Bear has approved the ms. in detail. He finds that it adheres to the original taped material given him by 30 Hopi spokesmen, embracing nearly 30 Hopi clans, and that it expresses the traditional Hopi viewpoint, the basic ground of tribal belief. Within the limits under which I have worked—limits of traditional Hopi secrecy, inter-tribal splits, and personal difficulties of which you are aware—I myself feel that I have amply fulfilled my obligation to the Foundation and to the Hopis. Whatever the book's minor faults, it has, for the first time, opened up the whole field of Hopi mythology, clan legend, and ceremonialism in a body of text and drawings that is inter-related and integrated in every respect. It has achieved what no scientific study could begin to approach, for it has been written from the inside out, on the instinctive, intuitive level of the Hopis, and not from the outside, rational and statistical method followed by scientific observers. All this is clearly explained, and reiterated time and again, in the Introduction to the book. There is no doubt as to what the book is based on, and what it must stand on.

Whether the mythic and symbolic view of life of the Hopis is approved by the rational, scientific view of academicians is of little consequence to our own objective. For it is our ignorance and discounting of such a viewpoint that has characterized our national and state governments, orthodox churches, and ethnological institutions throughout all their dealings with the Hopis. And as Fred points out in his Foreword, it is an attitude that is being seriously questioned throughout the world today. Your own objections to it I can understand, as a precedent has already been set.

Ten years ago the University of New Mexico contracted with me to write *Masked Gods,* and during its writing published chapter after chapter in its *New Mexico Quarterly*. Upon its completion, however, the University Press refused to publish it on the grounds that the heads of the departments of ethnology, anthropology, and archaeology objected to its deviation from their orthodox views. Upon my threat of suit for breach of contract, the book was then submitted to the foremost man in the field, a strict academician, for advice and decision. He was Clyde Kluckhohn, head of the Department of Anthropology, Harvard University. He recommended that the book be published as it was, without editing; wrote the Foreword himself; and in it recommended the book even to professional readers on the basis that it approached the subject at the mythic and symbolic levels that lie beneath the surface of ethnological documentation—his own field. It was a broad viewpoint without bias for a man in

164 SECTION A

his position, and I have always been happy that the book's warm and long acceptance has amply justified his recommendation.

Hence I see no point in your desire to re-edit the book in order to make it palatable to academic institutions at the expense of its own inherent premise. Nor did I see fit to point out in detail the countless errors, untruths and misbeliefs about the Hopis consistently perpetuated in innumerable scientific treatises by scholars reputed to be authorities. But as Fred suggested, we would welcome from you a short Preface, like that of Clyde Kluckhohn in *Masked Gods,* which would confirm your great interest and invaluable help in the book's long preparation, and yet disclaim any responsibility for the views in it with which you and your staff do not agree.

Our immediate problem now, since the book was finished two months ago, is to place it with a publisher for general release as expeditiously as possible. To tread water until Fall, when you hope to go to New York, seems a waste of valuable time that could be used to open negotiations with several publishers who might be contracted with when you arrive, instead of waiting another few months and then undergoing a lead time of at least six months before publication. There are many reasons from a Foundation viewpoint why a release next Spring is desirable. One of these is that the Hopis' land suits against the national government and the Navajos are pending; there is a disastrous split between Traditional and Tribal Council factions; and other economic and political troubles whose source is not understood. The prompt appearance of the book, whatever minor controversy it causes, will set before all factions and outside agencies the whole texture of traditional Hopi belief and provide a basis to work from that has never been available before.

We are hoping that you accept this letter in the spirit in which it is written, and that we can all rely on your continued interest and help in offering suggestions how we can best hurry the book along toward publication.

Waters sent a copy of this letter to both White Bear and to Howell. Howell replied in a letter on July 19, 1962, that the Foundation felt that the letter to Dentzel outlined their position exactly, and that he felt sure it would have favorable results. In a follow-up letter on August 7, 1962, Howell wrote that he had not received any response from Dentzel and that soon it would be necessary to proceed without him, and that he, Howell, looked to Waters for a plan of procedure. Waters responded on August 10, 1962:

. . . Carl has not replied to my letter of July 9. I am glad you have resolved to break this curious deadlock, and will proceed accordingly.

Barthold Fles is due here any day. If he believes he can handle the book to all our best interests, I will turn the ms. over to him with our specified requirements and the names of the three best publishing houses to contact when he returns to New York. Any one of these which is willing to meet the requirements, after reviewing the ms., can then draw up a draft contract for your and my approval. Carl can then be asked to sign it for us and give to the publisher his suggestions for format. I anticipate he will be glad to do so. Otherwise I shall find another non-profit institution to act on our behalf.

In the event Fles does not welcome the opportunity to act as our agent, there is another larger agency in New York which successfully handled my last book here and in England and which will be happy to handle it.

I foresee no problems in placing the book, and I will be glad to go to New York to discuss it with the agent, the publisher, and yourself when the contract is ready to be drawn. The big problem now is to begin negotiations and allow a publisher time to review the book and put in his bid, without wasting time, in order to get it on the Spring list.

A long associate of the late Dr. Carl Jung, living in Zeurich [sic], came up to see me for a brief visit last week. I discussed with her the premise of the book. She believes, as we do, that its mytho-religious viewpoint provides a depth psychology which will prove its greatest value. When she returns to Switzerland she will help us to place it for foreign translation. . . .

Finally, on August 27, 1962, Howell and Dentzel discussed the book by telephone, and shortly thereafter Dentzel forwarded to Howell two reviews of the manuscript written by "his anthropologists." These rather supercilious reviews scathingly denounced the book, attacking the very premise under which it was written. Concluding that the manuscript was at best "unscientific," they stipulated that the Southwest Museum should completely disassociate itself from the work and that all references to the Museum and its staff be removed from the text. Howell wrote to Waters on August 29, 1962, outlining his conversation with Dentzel and enclosing copies of the reviews. Howell suggested that as Dentzel had disassociated the Museum from the project, that Waters seek the assistance of another institution to carry through on the publication aspect. Waters responded on September 4, 1962:

Your letter has given me deep admiration for your judgment and forthrightness, and respect for your unstinted loyalty, and I'm most grateful. Your feelings are not misplaced.

I'm not too upset over these vitriolic reviews . . . they are pitched to such a low level. What we are confronted with here is the old frigid attitude of entrenched academicians against newly revealed truths at variance with narrow, orthodox belief . . .

I am writing this instead of telephoning you so you will have it on record in case any question comes up from Mr. Neal or other Directors of the Foundation.

In going over the detailed criticism I find that they attack the basic premise of the book; that every fact in it was given me by our Hopi informants as recorded on tape . . . Every fact—from the Creation through the Migrations and into the Ceremonials—is repeated time and again, tying into an integrated whole. What we have is a great synthesis of ancient tradition given life and utterance for the first time. Whether it conforms to orthodox, limited views of outsiders is of no consequence. For this is the Hopi view, constituting a mytho-religious, a depth psychology different from our own . . .

Hence to revise the ms. as these curators suggest—stating the name of every informant for every quote, etc.—would not only transpose the book from a free-flowing narrative into a dull, academic text-book. It would descend into an argumentative treatise on anthropological homegrounds. The book must be offered on its own premise, simply, positively. Any attacks on it will only create minor controversy which will arouse more public interest in it.

Yet as you say, this attempt to discredit is a blessing in disguise. Following your suggestion I will go through the ms. carefully and take every advantage of the critical comments. Revised pages will be sent you. I will write White Bear to collect photographs, and would appreciate your writing him to do the same. All this will take some time and I appreciate your offer of reimbursement on any basis you wish. I am about to start in on another project, but will postpone its deadline in order to carry this Hopi project through to a successful conclusion.

Barthold Fles was here two weeks. He reviewed the ms. carefully and has taken it to New York with him. He will offer it to a publisher we agreed upon before he leaves for a three-week trip to Europe on September 20. A contract for publishing should be drawn in draft form by the time he gets back. I can then go to New York to review it with you, and will have another non-profit institution willing to sign it on your behalf. I have just written Fles to telephone you in case anything comes up or to advise you. Please feel free yourself to telephone him at any time. . . .

I am not at all discouraged at these comments. After many years I've found that the bigger a thing is, the more trouble it meets initially. Only mediocrity has an easy path—and a short life. . . .

After having taken the manuscript from Waters in Taos, Barthold Fles showed the manuscript to the Viking Press. Viking was interested in publishing the book, but they were somewhat concerned about the Dentzel reviews. Viking accordingly commissioned John Collier, Sr., former United States Commissioner of Indian Affairs, to write a report on the book. Collier wrote Fles on October 25, 1962, that he had finished reading the manuscript, and had shown a copy of his report to Waters, who agreed to all corrections of factual inaccuracies peripheral to the thesis of the book. Collier's comprehensive report—over which he had spent five days' work—was in general highly laudatory, and found the essence of the book to be an important and permanent record of Hopi life, which in its scope and fullness went beyond anything done before. Interestingly enough, Collier even had high praise for the historical sections, including the treatment of recent Hopi history, in which Waters in part attacked Collier's own role as Commissioner of Indian Affairs. Collier's recommendation to publish the book was accepted by Viking and they agreed to undertake publication, with the understanding that $10,000.00 would be provided by the Charles Ulrick and Josephine Bay Foundation to cover the printing and production costs.

Waters then approached the Helene Wurlitzer Foundation, of Taos, to act as intermediary for the Bay Foundation; to accept the $10,000.00 from the Bay Foundation and turn it over to Viking. On the conditions that the book was okayed by the Hopis themselves, and that the relationship between the two foundations be clearly stated to the Viking Press, the Wurlitzer Foundation agreed to act for the Bay Foundation. These terms were met, and the Wurlitzer Foundation formally accepted the arrangements on February 28, 1963.

The formal contract issued by Viking, dated February 1, 1963, outlined an advance to Waters of $2,500.00 against royalties of 10% on the first 5,000 copies, 12½% on the next 2,500 copies, and 15% on all copies thereafter. Furthermore, all royalties were to be divided between Waters and the Bay Foundation (as reimbursement for their advance against production costs) on the following basis: Royalties on the first 2,500 copies were to be paid to Frank Waters; royalties on the second 2,500 copies were to be divided equally between Waters and the Foundation; on the third 2,500 copies the royalties were to be divided on a 60/40 basis between Waters and the Foundation; on all copies sold thereafter the royalties were to be divided such that 5/6ths went to Waters and 1/6th to the Foundation, up to the original amount of $10,000.00. As for all of Waters' royalties, it had been agreed by both Waters and White Bear (outlined in a letter sent to Fles and signed by both men on November 20, 1962 [FW]) that all royalties remitted to Fles by the Viking Press were to be divided on a 60/40 basis between Waters and White Bear, less, of course, Fles's agent fee. Under the terms of the Viking contract, Fles retained sole rights for the sale of foreign rights, and all royalty payments under foreign rights were paid only to Waters.

A15 BOOK OF THE HOPI [1963]

A15a First edition, first printing

[entire title page printed against a gold background] BOOK OF THE | [fancy] HOPI | [drawing from mound pottery skunk painting, in red, orange, white, yellow, tan and black] | BY FRANK WATERS | *Draw=*

168 Section A

ings and source material recorded by | OSWALD WHITE BEAR FREDERICKS | NEW YORK: THE VIKING PRESS

9¾ × 6¹³⁄₁₆″. [1⁸ 2-12¹⁶]: 184 leaves. 3 gatherings of four leaves each of photographic illustrations sewn in between pages 94/95, 190/191 and 286/287. Pp. [I-VI] VII-XVII [XVIII], [1-2] 3-27 [28-30] 31-122 [123-124] 125-247 [248-250] 251-337 [338-340] 341-347 [348-350]. Numbers printed in roman in headlines at outer margin of type page, except for pages 3, 12, 17, 21, 23, 31, 37, 47, 54, 59, 67, 72, 87, 90, 97, 103, 109, 113, 125, 137, 154, 165, 174, 189, 198, 210, 218, 231, 239, 251, 258, 270, 278, 286, 293, 301, 307, 314, 322, 329, 341 and 342, on which the numbers are printed in the center at the foot of the page.

CONTENTS: p. I, half-title: "BOOK OF THE HOPI | There is no such thing as a little country. | The greatness of a people is no more deter- | mined by their number than the greatness of | a man is determined by his height. | —Victor Hugo"; p. II, illustration against gold background, printed in blue, white, orange, brown, gray and black; lettered near bottom: "[at far right] OPPOSITE: FIGURE 43. POTTERY MOUND | [at far left] FIGURE 55. MALE-FEMALE PÁHO [at far right] SKUNK PAINTING"; p. III, title; p. IV, copyright notice: *"Copyright © 1963 by Frank Waters. All rights reserved. | First pub⸗ lished in 1963 by The Viking Press, Inc., 625 Madison Avenue,* New York 22, N. Y. | *Published simultaneously in Canada by The Macmillan Company of Canada Limited | Library of Congress catalog card number: 63-19606* | M B G | *Set in Baskerville, Electra, Bernhard Modern and Post Roman types | Printed in the United States of America"*; p. V, Foreword by Frederick H. Howell; p. VI, illustration printed against a gold background in green, black, white and orange; lettered at bottom: "[at left] FIGURE 36. EAGLE CLAN LEADER [at right] OPPOSITE: FIGURE 61. CORN MURAL"; pp. VII-VIII, contents; pp. IX-X, list of photographs; pp. XI-XIV, Introduction; pp. XV-XVII, *"A note about the compilation of the book:"*; p. XVIII, blank, p. 1, divisional half-title: "PART ONE | THE MYTHS: | Creation of the Four Worlds"; p. 2, blank; pp. 3-27, text; p. 28, blank; p. 29, divisional half-title: "PART TWO | THE LEGENDS: | Migrations of the Clans"; p. 30, four line drawings; pp. 31-122, text; p. 123, divisional half-title: "PART THREE | THE | MYSTERY PLAYS: | The Ceremonial Cycle"; p. 124, blank; pp. 124-247, text; p. 248, blank; p. 249, divisional half-title: "PART FOUR | THE HISTORY: | The Lost White Brother"; p. 250, blank; pp. 251-337, text; p. 338, blank; p. 339, divisional half-title: "KEY TO HOPI PRONUNCIATION | GLOSSARY OF HOPI WORDS"; p. 340, blank; pp. 341-347, text; pp. 348-350, blank.

ILLUSTRATIONS: 3 gatherings of 4 leaves each of photographic illustrations bound in as noted above, and listed on pages IX-X. Small black and white illustrations and line drawings appear on pages 23, 30, 32, 33, 38, 39, 40, 41, 44, 45, 47, 50, 51, 52, 54, 56, 59, 60, 62, 63, 64, 65, 66, 74, 75, 76, 77, 78, 79, 80-81 (double-page), 82, 83, 84, 88, 90, 91, 93, 94, 101, 103, 104, 105, 106, 107, 108, 109, 113, 114, 127, 130, 133, 140, 151, 166, 189, 260, 261, 262 and 263. Full color illustrations, all printed against gold backgrounds, appear on pages:

p. II: "MALE-FEMALE PAHO" as described above.
p. III: "POTTERY MOUND SKUNK PAINTING" as described above.
p. VI: "EAGLE CLAN LEADER" as described above.
p. VII: "CORN MURAL" printed at top of page in blue, yellow, red, white, black, brown and gray.
p. X: "EAGLE CLAN SYMBOLS" printed at bottom of page in blue, yellow, white, orange, green, black and red-brown.
p. XI: "RELIGIOUS LEADER, AWATOVI" printed at top of page in gray, brown, white, yellow and red.
p. XIV: "QUALETAQA" printed at bottom of page in yellow, black, brown, white, red and blue.
p. XV: "TWO HORN MONGKO" printed at top of page in blue, white, black, yellow and brown.

BINDING: Red cloth sides and yellow cloth spine. Front has an illustration of the Second Bear Clan Tablet (from p. 32) stamped in blind in the center. Spine lettered in blue: "BOOK | OF | THE | HOPI | [phoenix ornament] | WATERS | [Spider Clan symbol from p. 39] | FRED=ERICKS | [Parrot Clan symbol from p. 54] | THE | VIKING | PRESS". Top edges stained orange. White paper endpapers, printed overall on face in gold, and with an illustration of "Naloonangmomwit" from pp. 80-81, printed in black, gray, green, brown and white, and lettered at bottom right: *"Figure 36."*.

DUST JACKET (white paper): Front and spine printed overall in gold. Lettered on front: "[all within a large yellow panel outlined in orange] BOOK OF THE | [fancy] HOPI | [drawing from pottery mound skunk painting in red, yellow, white, tan, orange and black] | BY FRANK WATERS | *Drawings and source material recorded by* | OSWALD

WHITE BEAR FREDERICKS | The first revelation of the Hopis' his= torical and religious world-view of life | . . . voluntarily made for pos= terity by Hopi elders. . . interpreting the hither- | to unknown meanings and functions of their year-long ceremonial cycle.". Spine: "BOOK | OF THE | [fancy] HOPI | [detail from larger illustration on front in red, tan, black, yellow and white] | FRANK | WATERS | [ornament] | Oswald | White Bear | Fredericks | THE | VIKING | PRESS". Rear: [all against a yellow background] [illustration of "Eagle Clan symbols from page X, printed in blue, white, black, brown, yellow, green, tan and red-brown] | *Book of the Hopi* reveals for the first time: | [6 paragraphs printed in roman about the book] | [paragraph about the illustrations printed in two columns] | THE VIKING PRESS·PUBLISHERS · NEW YORK". Front and rear flaps printed against yellow backgrounds with a blurb for this book; a quotation from John Collier, Sr. appears within a white panel on the front flap.

Published at $10.00 on December 2, 1963; 4,000 copies were printed. Copyrighted December 2, 1963; deposited December 23, 1963.

REVIEWS: *Library Journal,* December 15, 1963 (p. 4782); *Atlantic Monthly,* January, 1964 (p. 120); *American Anthropologist,* October, 1964 (p. 1189); *Natural History,* October, 1964 (p. 13).

COPIES: DLC (2 copies—one rebound); FW (d.j.); TAT (d.j.).

NOTE: At least one copy was specially bound in half brown morocco and marbled boards. This copy was presented to Waters by the publisher and is currently in his private collection.

A15b   First edition, first printing, Book Find Club issue ?

NOT SEEN

According to the records of the Viking Press, at the time the first printing of this work was in the press an additional 1,000 copies were printed for distribution by the Book Find Club.

Although such copies may well be indistinguishable from the regular Viking copies, they might possibly have been bound in a binding of lesser quality, as is often the case with book club copies. Although there is no evidence to show it was distributed by the Book Find Club, there is in my own collection a copy of the first printing in such a binding. This binding is identical to that of A15a, except that the cloth used for the spine is of a lesser quality, being of a much smaller wove pattern and more yellow in color. The front end papers of this copy are identical with those of A15a, but the rear endpapers are of plain light green paper with green fibers. Also, the top edges are stained blue (as are later Viking printings).

That this copy may not represent the Book Find Club copies is supported by the fact that the final gathering of photographic illustrations inserted after page 286 is defective; there are no illustrations on the verso of the first leaf, the recto of the second leaf, the verso of the third leaf and the recto of the fourth leaf. The records of the Viking Press proved unilluminating in regards to this copy, and it may well be a freak, without bibliographical significance.

A15c   First edition, second Viking Printing   [1964]

Identical with A15a, except for the presence of the additional line on the copyright page: *"Second Printing June 1964"*.

Cloth, with top edges stained blue. Published at $10.00 in June, 1964. 2,500 copies were printed.

COPIES: TAT.

A15d   First edition, third Viking printing   [1967]

NOT SEEN

Cloth. Published sometime in 1967; 2,000 copies were printed.

A15e   First edition, fourth Viking printing   [1969]

NOT SEEN

Cloth. Published sometime in 1969; 2,000 copies were printed.

172   SECTION A

A15f   First edition, fifth Viking printing   [1971]

Identical with A15a, except for the presence of an additional line on the copyright page: *"Fifth Printing August 1971"*.

Cloth. Published at $12.50 in August, 1971. 4,000 copies were printed.

COPIES: FW.

NOTE: In this printing the binding is slightly different from the bindings for A15a and A15b. The sides are of red paper over boards and have no stamping. The spine is of a cheaper cloth and the stamping on the spine is different: "[reading vertically] BOOK OF THE HOPI WATERS FREDERICKS | [horizontally] VIKING".

A15g   First edition, sixth Viking printing [first Viking Compass printing] [1972]

Title page identical with A15a, except printed against a white background, and the large design is printed in black and gray.

7½ × 5". Perfectbound: 180 leaves; 12 leaves of photographic illustrations, printed on text paper, inserted. Pp. [I-V] VI-XIV [1-2] 3-27 [28-30] 31-122 [123-124] 125-247 [248-250] 251-337 [338] 339-345 [346]. Pages 2, 28, 124, 248, 250, 338 and 346 are blank.

CONTENTS: p. I, half-title; p. II, "BOOKS BY FRANK WATERS | [list of 9 titles]"; p. III, title; p. IV, copyright page: *"Copyright 1963 by Frank Waters | All rights reserved | First published in 1963 | Viking Com= pass Edition | issued in 1972 by The Viking Press, Inc. | 625 Madison Avenue, New York, N. Y. 10022 | Distributed in Canada by | The Mac= millan Company of Canada Limited | SBN 670-18024-6 (hardbound) | 670-00365-4 (paperbound) | Library of Congress catalog card number: 63-19606 | Printed in U. S. A."*; p. V, Foreword by Frederick Howell; p. VI, list of illustrations; pp. VII-VIII, contents; pp. IX-XI, Introduction; pp. XII-XIV, note on the compilation of the book; pp. 1-337, identical with A15a; p. 338, blank; p. 339, Key to Hopi pronunciation; pp. 340-345, glossary; p. 346, blank.

Book of the Hopi 173

Paperback. Viking Compass Edition C365. Published at $3.25 in September, 1972. 5,000 copies were printed.

COPIES: NmU; FW.

NOTE: Although this printing does contain the photographic illustrations found in A15a, none of the colored text drawings was used, which accounts for the difference in the preliminary pagination.

NOTE: Frank Waters has another copy of the above in his library measuring 7¾ × 5⅟16″.

A15h First edition, seventh Viking printing (second Viking Compass printing) [1973]

NOT SEEN

Paperback. Published in October, 1973. 2,500 copies were printed.

A15i First edition, eighth Viking printing (third Viking Compass printing) [1975]

NOT SEEN

Paperback. Published in July, 1975. 2,500 copies were printed.

A15j Second edition, first printing [1969]

[first three lines in fancy type] BOOK | OF THE | HOPI | BY | FRANK WATERS | Drawings and source material recorded by | OSWALD WHITE BEAR FREDERICKS | BALLANTINE BOOKS · NEW YORK

7 × 4⅛″. Perfectbound: 224 leaves; 16 leaves of photographic illustrations inserted between pages 200/201. Pp. [i-vi] vii-viii [ix] x-xxiii [xxiv], [1-2] 3-34 [35-36] 37-149 [150-152] 153-304 [305-306] 307-412 [413-414] 415-423 [424]. Page ii carries a listing of four other books published by Ballantine, and page 424 carries an advertisement for Eliot

Porter's *In Wildness is the Preservation of the World*. Pages xxiv, 2, 150, 152, 306 and 414 are blank.

COPYRIGHT PAGE: "Copyright © 1963 by Frank Waters | All rights reserved. | Library of Congress Catalog Card Number: 63-19606 | This edition published by arrangement with | The Viking Press, Inc. | First printing: September, 1969 | Printed in the United States of America | BALLANTINE BOOKS, INC. | 101 Fifth Avenue, New York, New York 10003".

Paperback. Ballantine Walden Edition 01717. Published at $1.25 in September, 1969. Number of copies printed unknown.

COPIES: TAT.

NOTE: The photographic illustrations in this edition are the same as those in A15a, except that because of the smaller leaf size a number of the illustrations which had appeared on a single side of the leaf in A15a were separated in this edition, and they appear by themselves, thus increasing the number of inserted leaves.

NOTE: In response to an inquiry, Ballantine Books informed me that their records showed that they first printed *Book of the Hopi* in September, 1972, in a press run of 160,000 copies; again in July, 1974, in a press run of 50,000 copies; and finally in July, 1978, in a press run of 55,000 copies. That their records should exclude their actual first printing, as described above, is curious. Even more curious is the fact that four other printings have been seen. These, identified as the "fourth," "tenth," "eleventh," and "twelfth" printings, are described below. Other printings which have not been seen, but which on the basis of the evidence of the noted printings would seem to have been published, are also listed below.

A15k   Second edition, second Ballantine printing [1970]
NOT SEEN

Paperback. Date of publication listed in record on the copyright page of the fourth printing as September, 1970; number of copies printed unknown (see A15j; note).

A15l   Second edition, third Ballantine printing [1971]

NOT SEEN

Paperback. Date of publication listed in record on the copyright page of the fourth printing as March, 1971; number of copies printed unknown (see A15j, note).

A15m   Second edition, fourth Ballantine printing [1971]

Title page identical with A15j, except that an additional line appears at the very bottom: ". . . | An [next word in sans-serif type with swash 'x'] Intext Publisher".

Size, collation and pagination identical with A15j.

Contents identical with A15j, except for page iv: "Copyright © 1963 by Frank Waters | All rights reserved. | Library of Congress Catalog Card Number: 63-19606 | This edition published by arrangement with | The Viking Press, Inc. | First Printing: September, 1969 | Second Printing: September, 1970 | Third Printing: March, 1971 | Fourth Printing: August, 1971 | Printed in the United States of America | BALLANTINE BOOKS, INC. | 101 Fifth Avenue, New York, New York 10003 | An [next word as on title page] Intext Publisher".

Paperback. Ballantine Walden Edition 01717. Published at $1.25 in August, 1971. Number of copies printed unknown.

COPIES: Charles L. Adams, Las Vegas, Nevada.

A15n   Second edition, fifth Ballantine printing

NOT SEEN

Paperback. Date of publication and number of copies printed unknown.

A15o   Second edition, sixth Ballantine printing

NOT SEEN

176   SECTION A

Paperback. Date of publication and number of copies printed unknown.

A15p   Second edition, seventh Ballantine printing

NOT SEEN

Paperback. Date of publication and number of copies printed unknown.

A15q   Second edition, eighth Ballantine printing

NOT SEEN

Paperback. Date of publication and number of copies printed unknown.

A15r   Second edition, ninth Ballantine printing

NOT SEEN

Paperback. Date of publication and number of copies printed unknown.

A15s   Second edition, tenth Ballantine printing [1976]

Title page identical with A15j.

Contents identical with A15j except that page ii is blank; page iv now reads: "Copyright © 1963 by Frank Waters | All rights reserved. Pub= lished in the United States by Ballantine | Books, a division of Random House, Inc., New York, and simul- | taneously in Canada by Ballantine Books of Canada, Ltd., | Toronto, Canada. | Library of Congress Catalog Card Number: 63-19606 | ISBN 0-345-24317-X-195 | This edi= tion published by arrangement with The Viking Press, | Inc. | Manu= factured in the United States of America | First Ballantine Books Edi= tion: September, 1969 | Tenth Printing: April, 1976"; and page 424 which now carries an ad for *Seven Arrows* by Hyemeyohsts Storm.

Paperback. Published as Ballantine / Nonfiction 24317 at $1.95 in July, 1976. Number of copies printed unknown.

COPIES: TAT.

NOTE: The final line added to the title page of the fourth printing, "An Intext Publisher", does not appear on the title page of this printing.

A15t Second edition, eleventh Ballantine printing [1977]

Identical with A15s, except for changes on page iv: ". . . | ISBN: 0-345-27573-X | . . . | First Ballantine Books Edition: September 1969 | Eleventh Printing: December 1977"; and for page 424 which now carries an ad for the "MS Read-a-Thon."

Paperback. Ballantine / Nonfiction 27573. Published at $2.50 in December, 1977. Number of copies printed unknown.

COPIES: TAT.

A15u Second edition, twelfth Ballantine printing [1978]

Identical with A15t, except that the final line on page iv now reads: "Twelfth Printing: August 1978"; and page 424 carries an ad for eight new books from Ballantine.

Paperback. Ballantine / Nonfiction 27573. Published at $2.50 in August, 1978. 55,000 copies were probably printed (see note to A15j).

COPIES: TAT.

A15v First edition, first Penguin Books printing [1977]

Title page identical with A15g, except imprint reads: ". . . | PENGUIN BOOKS".

$7^{11}/_{16} \times 5^{1}/_{16}''$. Perfectbound. Collation and pagination identical with A15g. Illustrations identical with A15g.

178 Section A

Contents: Identical with A15g, except that p. I carries a note about the author; P. II carries the Victor Hugo quotation noted in A15a; and p. IV: "Penguin Books Ltd, Harmondsworth, Middlesex, England | Penguin Books, 625 Madison Avenue, New York, New York 10022, U. S. A. | [3 lines of addresses for Penguin Books in Australia, Canada, and New Zealand] | First published in the United States of America by The Viking Press 1963 | Viking Compass Edition published 1972 | Re⸗ printed 1973, 1975 | Published in Penguin Books 1977 | Copyright © Frank Waters, 1963 | All rights reserved | LIBRARY OF CONGRESS CATALOGING IN PUBLICATION DATA | [7 lines of data] | Printed in the United States of America by | The Murray Printing Company, Westford, Massachusetts | Set in Linotype Baskerville | [9 lines regarding conditions of sale]".

Paperback. Published at $3.95 in June, 1977. 5,000 copies were printed.

Copies: FW; Charles L. Adams, Las Vegas, Nevada.

A15w   First edition, second Penguin printing [1978]

NOT SEEN

Paperback. Published in June, 1978. 5,000 copies were printed.

A15x   First edition, third Penguin printing [1979]

Identical with A15v, except for the addition of a line on the copyright page: ". . . | Reprinted 1978, 1979 | . . .".

Paperback. Published at $3.95 in August, 1979. 10,000 copies were printed.

Copies: Charles L. Adams, Las Vegas, Nevada.

A16 LEON GASPARD

In a letter to Paul Weaver of the Northland Press, dated November 19, 1963, Waters outlined the plan for publication of the book:

> John Gilchriese, Field Historian of the University of Arizona, has recommended your press most highly and I believe has spoken to you about a project we have in mind.
> You probably know of the paintings of Leon Gaspard. He is one of the painters who came out of Russia to dazzle the West after the turn of the century, and which included Anisfield, Bakst, Remisoff and Roerich. He paints in an Asiatic color key with a brilliant palette, and his work has spanned sixty years and four continents. He has collectors in both America and Europe who think it is time to bring out a book on him and his work. I am helping to initiate it, after writing his biography.
> The text is now finished. It comprises 14 short chapters containing a total of about 35,000 words, and covering his entire career—his boyhood in Mother Russia, his art student days in Paris at the turn of the century, his travels in China, Mongolia, Tibet, North Africa, and the American Southwest, and his life in Taos. The aim has been a narrative as colorful as his life and paintings, enlivened by his inimitable stories and deepened by his interpretive comments on art.
> We are now ready to meet the problems of publication.
> All of us desire a dignified, monograph-sized book, about 8½ × 11 inches, with an excellent type-case and good paper, illustrated with 14 full-page, full-color reproductions of his best paintings—one for each chapter. Reproductions should probably be done by the four-color plate process, rather than by cheaper processes like off-set which would not do justice to his brilliant color key. Full size transparencies will be made by a man who will photograph the paintings selected in the galleries of various collectors, and will be furnished the printer. Offhand, I would say an initial printing of 2,500 copies would be required. The press selected should have a distribution set-up and be able to fill mail orders. We anticipate being able to subsidize the total expense. Mr. Gaspard is now about eighty years old, so we would like to produce the book as a tribute to a living man rather than to delay too long.
> If this project is in your line and interests you, we would appreciate receiving

from you a preliminary estimate of the cost, including reproductions of the paintings, printing, and binding, and a sample of a color reproduction such as you would recommend for our use.

My own last book, *Book of the Hopi*, published by the Viking Press in New York, is due out December 2. It is a beautiful job containing some exquisite color reproductions of ancient kiva murals. For this book, however, we are inclined toward a smaller press due to the comparatively small printing.

Weaver was interested and his proposal was accepted and the manuscript was placed with Northland Press. In an agreement drawn up between Weaver and Gaspard in January of 1964 [copy in possession of Frank Waters], Weaver agreed to print a trade edition of 2,000 copies and a limited edition of 500 copies. It was also agreed that Gaspard's subsidy to Northland Press of $6,000.00—on Weaver's insistence—was to be treated as a loan, payable at 6% interest at regular periods. The agreement also called for Northland to issue a special portfolio containing a set of the 14 color reproductions suitable for framing. These portfolios were to be sold with the understanding that a royalty of 15% was to be paid to Gaspard and 5% to Waters. For some reason—no doubt due in part to Gaspard's untimely death—these portfolios were never issued.

In the separate contract which Waters signed with Northland Press on January 17, 1964, it was stipulated that Waters was to receive a royalty of 10% on all copies sold of the first printing, and 12% on all subsequent printings.

A16   LEON GASPARD   [1964]

A16a   First edition, only printing, trade issue

LEON GASPARD | *by Frank Waters* | [publisher's device, in gold, of an evergreen branch beneath which is a rule, beneath which are the initials 'NP'; all within an oblate square] | *Northland Press* | *Flagstaff, Arizona* | *Mcmlxiv* [Facsimile signature of Leon Gaspard, in gold, set along the inner margin, reading upwards]

12 × 8¾". [1-7^8 8^6]: 62 leaves. Pp. [i-viii], 1-5 [6] 7-11 [12] 13-19 [20] 21-24 [25] 26-27 [28] 29-32 [33] 34-37 [38] 39-41 [42] 43-45 [46] 47-52 [53] 54-55 [56] 57-63 [64] 65-69 [70] 71-79 [80] 81-84 [85] 86-87 [88] 89-97 [98] 99-101 [102] 103-105 [106] 107-109 [110] 111-112 [113] 114 [115-116].

Numbers printed in swash in the outer margins, just below the third line of type, except for pages 1, 7, 13, 21, 29, 39, 47, 57, 65, 71, 81, 89, 99 and 107, on which the numbers are printed in roman at the bottom of the page at the outer margin of the type page.

CONTENTS: p. i, half-title: "LEON GASPARD"; p. ii, blank; p. iii, title; p. iv, copyright notice: *"Copyright 1964 | by | Frank Waters |* Li= brary of Congress Catalog No. 64-20419 | PRINTED IN THE UNITED STATES OF AMERICA"; pp. v-vi, contents and list of illustrations; p. vii, note concerning Gaspard's help with the book and his approval of the finished manuscript; p. viii, illustration [see below]; pp. 1-114, text; p. 115, blank; p. 116, colophon: "[publisher's device] | This book, set in the Aldus type of Herman [sic] Zapf, | has been printed on Teton Text paper at Northland Press, | Flagstaff, Arizona and bound at the | Ros= well Bindery of Phoenix. It was designed by | Paul Weaver in collab= oration with John Anderson.".

ILLUSTRATIONS: All the illustrations in the book are full page and with one exception reproductions of Gaspard paintings. Unless otherwise stated, the illustrations are printed in color:
- p. viii: "TAOS PUEBLO FIRE DANCE—Christmas Eve"
- p. 6: "CATHEDRAL OF ST. BASIL—Moscow"
- p. 12: "TWILIGHT IN MONTPARNASSE, PARIS"
- p. 20: "BRIDAL GATHERING IN SIBERIA"
- p. 25: *"On the Seine in 1899"* (black and white)
- p. 28: "CLAUDIA"
- p. 33: *"A Russian Patriarch"* (black and white)
- p. 38: "TWINING CANYON"
- p. 42: *"Early Russian sketch"* (black and white)
- p. 46: "OLD MOSCOW"
- p. 53: *"Self portrait in Vitebsk"* (black and white)
- p. 56: "PROCESSION OF THE LAST LIVING BUDDHA IN OUTER MONGOLIA"
- p. 64: "WINTER IN PEKING"
- p. 70 "NAVAJO WOMEN"
- p. 80: "PRINCESS NIRGIDMA OF TARGUT, MONGOLIA"
- p. 85: *"A French type"* (black and white)
- p. 88: "BUFFALO DANCE AT ZUNI"
- p. 98: "TAOS INDIAN GIRL"
- p. 102: *"A Reclining figure"* (black and white)
- p. 106: "CORN DANCE AT SANTO DOMINGO"

SECTION A

p. 110: *"Gaspard's last sketch"* (black and white)
p. 113: *"Leon Gaspard"* (black and white photograph)

BINDING: Charcoal cloth. Gaspard's facsimile signature stamped in gilt, reading upwards, near outer edge of front cover. Spine stamped in gilt: "[reading vertically] LEON GASPARD [author's name in smaller type face] *Frank Waters*". Slate gray endpapers.

DUST JACKET (white paper): Front lettered in gold as on front cover, with additional line in black in center: "LEON GASPARD". Spine lettered as binding, in black. Rear: blank. Front flap carries a blurb for this book; the rear flap a note about the author, beneath which appears the publisher's device and imprint.

Published at $14.50 in October, 1964 (exact date unknown); 2,000 copies were printed. Copyrighted December 3, 1964; deposited January 4, 1965.

COPIES: DLC (2 copies); NmU (d.j.); TAT (2 copies, d.j.).

A16b   First edition, only printing, limited, signed issue

Issued simultaneously with A16a was a limited signed issue of 500 copies. This issue is identical with A16a, except that it measures 12⅜ × 9¼", and that p. i carries a limitation notice rather than the half-title:

"This edition, specially bound | and signed by the author, | is limited to | 500 copies, | of which this is | number _____ | [author's signature]"

Although the limitation notice mentions that this issue is specially bound, the binding is identical with that of A16a. However, this limited edition was published without a dust jacket, but was issued in a plain slip case of the same cloth as the binding.

COPIES: TAT.

A16c   Second edition, only printing, trade issue [1981]

LEON GASPARD | by Frank Waters | with a Foreword by Forrest Fenn | Fenn Galleries, Ltd., Santa Fe [slash] Northland Press, Flagstaff

11³¹⁄₃₂ × 9″. [1-8⁸ 9⁶ 10⁸]: 78 leaves. Pp. [i-vi] vii-xi [xii], [1] 2-7 [8] 9-15 [16] 17-23 [24] 25-35 [36] 37-45 [46] 47-51 [52] 53-61 [62] 63-69 [70] 71-75 [76] 77-89 [90] 91-97 [98] 99-113 [114] 115-119 [120] 121-124 [125] 126-129 [130] 131-133 [134-135] 136-140 [141] 142 [143] 144.

CONTENTS: pp. i-ii, blank; p. iii, half-title: "[facsimile autograph of Leon Gaspard] | LEON GASPARD"; p. iv, blank; p. v, title; p. vi, copyright notice: "Copyright © 1981 by Frank Waters | All Rights Reserved | Revised Edition | First Edition 1964 | ISBN 0-87358-299-3 Cloth Edition | ISBN 0-87358-300-0 Limited Edition | Library of Congress Catalog Card Number 81-84089 | Composed and Printed in the United States of America"; p. vii, contents; pp. viii-ix, list of illustrations; p. x, black and white photograph of Gaspard, captioned *"In French Air Force uniform, World War I";* p. xi, Foreword by Forrest Fenn, dated July 25, 1981; p. xii, blank; pp. 1-129, text; p. 130, blank; p. 131, black and white illustration of Gaspard's "LAST SKETCH"; p. 132, two-line note regarding Waters' Afterthought; p. 133, Afterthought by Frank Waters, dated August, 1981; p. 134, blank; p. 135, divisional half-title: *"The Art of Leon Gaspard";* pp. 136-140, list of illustrations from Gaspard's paintings, with credits; p. 141, divisional half-title: *"Photographs by Leon Gaspard";* p. 142, list of photographs taken by Gaspard reproduced in the book, and with credits for other photographs; p. 143, blank; p. 144, colophon: *"Designed by Tom Knights | With end paper design by Pam Smith | Text and display composed in phototype Optima | Printed on Optimum Gloss | At the Press in the Pines |* [Northland Press device] *| Northland Press | Bound by Roswell Bookbinding | Phoenix".*

ILLUSTRATIONS: The number of illustrations was greatly increased for this edition, and includes, besides Gaspard's paintings, a number of photographs taken by him. Unless otherwise noted, all illustrations of Gaspard paintings are in color; the Gaspard photographs are tinted in blue. Titles of paintings are taken from the captions. Both full-page illustrations and smaller illustrations appearing on a page without any text have been designated as full-page.
 p. x: photograph of Gaspard, as described above.
 p. 2: photograph of chest built and decorated by Gaspard
 p. 3: "BORIS GODUNOV" (full-page)
 p. 4: photograph of detail of chest shown on p. 2
 p. 5: "OLD MOSCOW"
 p. 6: Gaspard photo "The Marketplace"
 p. 7: "PEASANT WOMAN IN MARKET" (full-page)

Section A

- p. 8: Gaspard photo "Woman with Basket"
- p. 9: "LITTLE RUSSIAN MARKET"
- p. 10: "ON THE DVINA RIVER"
- p. 11: "THE MUSICIANS"
- p. 12: Gaspard photo "At Work on the Ice"
- p. 13: Gaspard photo "Smiling Ice Cutter"
- p. 13: "CUTTING ICE"
- p. 15: "RUSSIA-1915" (full-page)
- p. 17: "A FRENCH TYPE" (full-page)
- p. 21: "LITTLE MITTENS IN PARIS"
- p. 25: "RUSSIA-1920"
- p. 27: "VIATKA, SIBERIA—1939" (full-page)
- p. 29: "A SIBERIAN BAND" (full-page)
- p. 30: Gaspard photo "Patriarch's Quiet Moment"
- p. 30: Gaspard photo "A Meeting of Generations"
- p. 31: "A RUSSIAN PATRIARCH" (full-page)
- p. 33: "GIRL OF MOSCOW" (full-page)
- p. 35: "RUSSIA" (full-page)
- p. 37: "RUSSIAN PEASANTS IN THE SNOW" (full-page)
- p. 39: "TAOS PUEBLO"
- p. 43: "TWINING CANYON" (full-page)
- p. 47: "LES ARTISTES INCONNU" (full-page)
- p. 53: "KOCHANTEZEO MONGOLIAN WOMAN"
- p. 57: "PROCESSION OF THE LAST LIVING BUDDHA IN OUTER MONGOLIA"
- p. 59: Gaspard photo "A Pleasant Roadside Interlude"
- p. 61: "PRINCE IGOR" (full-page)
- p. 63: "PAMIR—1923"
- p. 65: "BABRIKA"
- p. 71: "CANTON—1926" (full-page)
- p. 73: "WINTER IN SUCHOW"
- p. 77: "TAOS INDIAN GIRL"
- p. 79: "GIRL OF TAOS" (full-page)
- p. 81: "INDIAN CHIEFS" (full-page)
- p. 85: "INDIAN WITH RED HEADBAND" (full-page)
- p. 87: "VISITING APACHE" (full-page)
- p. 89: "PUEBLO INDIAN BABY" (full-page)
- p. 91: "PRINCESS NIRGIDMA OF TARGUT, MONGOLIA" (full-page)
- p. 95: "BABRIKA" (full-page)
- p. 97: "MARKET DAY" (full-page)

p. 99: "CLAUDIA" (full-page)
p. 103: "TWO RUSSIAN GIRLS" (full-page)
p. 105: "THE BRIDGE PESQUASHEK" (full-page)
p. 107: "KUCHANTZE, MONGOLIAN PRINCESS" (full-page)
p. 109: "KING SOLOMON" (full-page)
p. 110: photograph of Gaspard holding a self-portrait
p. 111: "SELF-PORTRAIT" (full-page)
p. 112: "NOULA KARAVAS"
p. 113: "RUSSIAN IN WINTER COAT" (full-page)
p. 115: "SAN GERONIMO DAYS"
p. 118: photograph of Leon and Dora Gaspard
p. 121: "BUFFALO DANCE AT ZUNI PUEBLO" (full-page)
p. 123: "DORA IN THE CZAR'S WEDDING CHAPEL" (full-page)
p. 125: "TAOS PUEBLO FIRE DANCE—CHRISTMAS EVE" (full-page)
p. 127: "SANTO DOMINGO CORN DANCE" (full-page)
p. 131: "LAST SKETCH" (full-page; black and white)

PAPER: Optimum Gloss.

BINDING: Blue cloth, with full-color reproduction of Gaspard's painting "Old Moscow" pasted on the front cover. Stamped on spine in gilt: "[reading vertically] FRANK WATERS [facsimile autograph of Leon Gaspard] NORTHLAND PRESS [slash] FENN". Blue laid-paper endpapers, with chain lines measuring 23 mm. apart.

DUST JACKET (white glossy paper): Front contains a facsimile signature of Leon Gaspard, in gilt, beneath which is a large color reproduction of Gaspard's painting "Old Moscow". Lettered on spine as on binding, but in black. Lettered on rear at bottom: "[small caps] ISBN 0-87358-299-3 [caps] NORTHLAND PRESS [slash] FENN". Front flap carries a blurb for this book, carried over to the rear flap, which also contains a notice of the limited edition of the Northland Press publication *Nicolai Fechin,* by Mary N. Balcomb; the Northland Press imprint and device appear at the bottom.

Published at $60.00 in October, 1981; 4,000 copies printed.

COPIES: TAT.

NOTE: The endpapers designed by Pam Smith were issued only with the limited signed issue.

A16d   Second edition, only printing, limited, signed, issue

Identical with A16c, except for an inserted limitation leaf between the front free end paper and page i; also, page i contains the half-title in this issue, and a full-page color photograph of Leon Gaspard appears on page iii.

LIMITATION NOTICE: (printed on a very fine translucent paper): "THIS SPECIALLY BOUND AND SLIPCASED | EDITION OF | LEON GASPARD | IS LIMITED TO 150 | INDIVIDUALLY NUMBERED AND | SIGNED VOLUMES | YOUR EDITION NUMBER IS | [number in ink below which is Waters' signature]"

BINDING: Dark blue cloth. Stamped on front in gilt with Gaspard's facsimile signature "gaspard" reading downward. Spine stamped in gilt: "[reading vertically] FRANK WATERS [Gaspard's facsimile signature] NORTHLAND PRESS [slash] FENN". White paper endpapers, with marbled design on face of both front and rear endpapers, in purple, blue and white.

SLIPCASE: Dark blue cloth, as on book. On the front near the opening is pasted a full-color detail from Gaspard's self-portrait (page 111 in the book), within a thick gilt-stamped oval. No dust jacket was issued.

Published at $200.00 in December, 1981.

COPIES: TAT.

NOTE: In their Spring, 1976, catalogue, the Northland Press announced that *Gaspard* was to go into a second printing. In a letter to Jim Howard, editor at Northland Press, dated September 7, 1976, Waters brought up this second printing:

   I notice your current catalogue . . . lists a reprint of *Leon Gaspard* for fall issuance. As I mentioned during our visit last April, I'm most agreeable to this provided that you substitute some good paintings for the extremely poor ones reproduced in the first edition, and include necessary revisions in the text. Not knowing when or how soon you're scheduling the reprint, I thought we might discuss these changes while we have time available.

As Paul [Weaver] remembers, Dora [Gaspard] would not permit him to take back major Gaspard paintings for reproduction, foisting on him several extremely poor ones instead. These notably include the painting of "Navajo Women" on page 70 which in build, posture and facial construction do not look like Navajo women by any stretch of the imagination—and for good reason, as Martha Reed, an Anglo dress designer here posed for both figures. Two other poor ones are the painting on page 12 and the sketch on page 103, both of Dora. And the "Last Sketch" on page 111 is of course an outright copy of the painting on page 106. Substitution of these by some of the really fine Asiatic paintings reproduced in the Maxwell Galleries brochure should be made. This should cause little expense as the color separations are not doubt available.

Included with this letter are the revisions to be made in the text. They are deletions of non-essential personal data about Dora. The book is of course about Gaspard; and this triviata is decidedly out of place, particularly in light of what has happened since.

Enclosed also is a new foreword, to precede the present Introduction, which seems appropriate and necessary to bring the subject up to date. . . .

On October 4, 1976, the Northland Press responded to Waters' letter, informing him that advance orders for the second printing totalled only 70 copies, and that therefore they had decided against reissuing the book.

On September 4, 1980, Forrest Fenn, of Fenn Galleries in Santa Fe, wrote Waters regarding his own desire to bring out a new edition of *Leon Gaspard,* with an increased number of illustrations. Fenn suggested that Waters be paid a royalty of 10% of the gross. Waters agreed, and on December 23, 1980 [FW], wrote Fenn, enclosing revisions:

I'm delighted you're going ahead with the Gaspard book so promptly.

Enclosed are the revisions you wanted right away. I've kept them to a minimum to avoid causing trouble for the compositor. I wish you would look them over carefully, question any of them, or suggest changes or additions. Especially the Postscript to be added as Page 115.

It seems to me that something should be added here to bridge the time since Gaspard's death. But so many things have happened, all negative and unpleasant, I'm not sure this somewhat bare statement is enough. . . .

EXCERPTS FROM *Leon Gaspard*

A16e *Leon Gaspard 1882-1964.* Exhibition catalogue published by Maxwell Galleries Ltd., San Francisco, n.d. [1967.] Pages 7, 10, 14, and 23.

A16f *Leon Gaspard*. Exhibition catalogue published by Arrowsmith-Fenn Galleries Ltd., Santa Fe, New Mexico, n.d. [1974.] Pages [2-3].

A17 THE WOMAN AT OTOWI CROSSING

On August 22, 1957, Waters sent the manuscript of his novel *The Woman at Otowi Crossing* to Harper & Brothers for their consideration. During the time which Harper had been inquiring about the book, Waters was also asked by Little, Brown if they might be able to see the manuscript. Shortly after sending the manuscript to Harper's, Waters wrote to John A. S. Cushman at Little, Brown, on August 31, 1957:

... I have promised Mr. Bessie of Harpers a look at the manuscript, without making a formal submission as I don't know whether it has any basis of appeal to his house. I don't know that it would appeal particularly to you, as it is an off-beat book.
   It is a modern novel which shows the birth of the Atomic Age (the secret city of Los Alamos, the Alamogordo bomb, nuclear tests in Nevada, and thermonuclear tests in the Pacific) against the background of the American West with all of its Western Americana that it now displaces (the baby railroads, ghost mining towns, primitive Spanish villages, and vast Indian reservations flooded with uranium miners). This birthplace of a new technological civilization is also the birthplace of the first civilization in America. Hence with all the modern atomic doings are contrasted the ruins of its oldest cities, the great Navajo and Pueblo ceremonials, and all the values of the ancient past... A salute to the Atomic Age and a nostalgic farewell to the American West as we have all known it.
   The novel will be long—500-600 pages, a peculiar contrast of modern scientific rationalism and ancient Indian mysticism, and told through the viewpoints of four characters. With its vast scope, real significance, and timed for this International Geophysical Year, I feel that it will appeal to a large public indeed if real enthusiasm is expended on its publication. That is one trouble I have had in the past ... slow starts, no interest, then a dogged slow persistence in print. So you can see why, in an effort to correct this, I would like to find for this book not merely a publisher, but the right publisher. ...

190   SECTION A

Finally, after almost two months, Waters received word from Harper & Brothers that they had decided against publishing the novel. On October 21, 1957, Waters again wrote to Cushman at Little, Brown:

> My novel is finally finished, and I am sending it to you this week by regular mail. I hope that it justifies your continued courtesy and long patience with me.
>
> Mr. Bessie of Harper & Brothers has returned, at my request, the draft sent him several weeks ago after continuing to hold it without comment. I am sorry about this misunderstanding, but at least the book goes to you in the clear.
>
> I also recently sent the spare carbon to Mrs. Ann Harris, a story editor of Whitney Pictures, Inc., Los Angeles, who so kindly wrote to you about me last Spring. The only person who has yet read and reported on the book, she has just written me enthusiastically about it. She believes that it is ready now to submit to certain studios to cover for picture possibilities. For a woman with her experience and reputation, this is practical enthusiasm indeed. I see nothing wrong with her talking to certain key people about it, or letting them review the manuscript while you too are reading it. Yet I have the feeling that if you accept the book for your list, you might prefer to decide the timing and manner of presentation. As in the case of Harper's, I want to avoid any breach of ethics. In any event, will you let me know if I should ask Mrs. Harris to hold off until you make your own decision on the book?
>
> I am going to let the book speak for itself without my superfluous comment. I only want to say that as I acted as the Information officer for the Los Alamos Scientific Laboratory and also served in Nevada during the early test series, you need not question the security aspect of the background information about these phases of the book. It is all unclassified or declassified, although much of it has never been used in fiction.

Unfortunately, in December of 1957, Little, Brown also rejected the manuscript. Mr. Cushman informed Waters that they felt the book was contrived, the conflicts too black and white, and the ending sentimental rather than symbolic. Waters next approached Harcourt, Brace and Company in a letter dated March 22, 1958:

> I am now completing five years work on a rather unusual novel. Enclosed is a reference list of some of my previously published books, most of them in the field of Western Americana. You will note that several of them have been slow starters at best, only to be re-issued repeatedly and to become recognized as among the best on their subjects. For this reason I would like to find a publisher receptive to the general idea of this novel before sending it out.
>
> The story revolves around an obscure and solitary woman who runs a lunch room at a remote river crossing in northern New Mexico. The immediate vicinity is at once the birthplace of the oldest civilization in America and the newest—the technological space-rocket civilization introduced by the Atomic Age. In no other area in the world are juxtaposed so closely the Indian drum and the atom smasher, all the values of the prehistoric past and the impending future.

Through the experiences of a young atomic physicist is developed for the first time in fiction the establishment of top-secret Project Y on Los Alamos Mesa directly above the Crossing; the development and testing of the first A-bombs in New Mexico and Nevada, and of the first H-bomb in the Marshall Islands of the Pacific.

This scientific background is counterpointed through the eyes of a young woman anthropologist with the archeological and anthropological background of the past: the ruins of the prehistoric cliff-cities nearby, the contemporary Indian pueblo whose people descended from the primitive cliff-dwellers, and their own traditional dances, myth-dramas and secret ceremonials.

A third satellite character is a newspaper man who is preoccupied with the journalistic present. Through his nostalgic reporting, we watch the current transition of the West—the passing of the last "baby" railroads, the ghost mining towns coming to life with the uranium boom, the modernization of primitive little Spanish villages, the industrialization of scenic resorts, all the Western Americana that we of our generation have known and loved. In this deceptively simple framework is outlined in human terms the whole life span of fabulous America.

Within this revolving wheel of past, present and future, as it were, stands the Woman at Otowi Crossing. In the light of a mystical experience which she undergoes, she gradually sees these characters and happenings in one perspective. The meaning of this strange experience is interpreted for her by her old gardener and dishwasher, a Cacique in the Indian pueblo across river, solely in terms of his own indigenous ceremonialism—both because such mysticism is an inherent trait among Pueblo Indians and a dominating feature of their life, and also to avoid all reference to wordy and controversial viewpoints outside the scope of the novel's wholly American milieu.

These four principal characters with their emotional relationships, contradictory interests, and personal conflicts provide, as they must, a strong story with constant changes of pace, scene, viewpoint and action.

I don't want to sound extravagantly enthusiastic after being confronted with its difficult problems for so long. It is a "serious" novel and 550 pages long. Yet I believe that this novel should appeal to a large and diverse reading public, especially as it is timed for this International Geophysical Year which has seen the first rocket satellites launched into orbit with all their implications. . . .

Harcourt, Brace responded to this letter with a request to see the manuscript, which Waters sent on April 8, 1958. On May 5, 1958, they informed Waters that they were rejecting the manuscript; they felt that the reportorial aspects of the novel did not blend well with the purely fictional aspects, and that the characterizations were insufficient to carry off a novel of such scope.

After receiving this rejection, Waters then wrote on May 9, 1958, to Mrs. Mary Abbot of the McIntosh and Otis Agency, with which he had had an earlier association:

Section A

You may remember clearing the rights of one of my previously published books for me several years ago [*Midas of the Rockies*]. It has now been re-issued twice. In any case I am enclosing a reference list of my published books to give you background material about me.

After six years work, I now have something new to offer and I need an agent. I will outline briefly what I have, and I wish you would advise me frankly if you believe your agency is the one to handle my particular output to both of our advantages, or if you would recommend another for any reason...

The Woman at Otowi Crossing ... is a long novel of 550 pages, a major effort on which I have spent five years. Enclosed is a short resume of it*. Last fall I sent the first rough draft of it to Mr. Bessie of Harper's. After re-working it this Winter, I sent the ms. to Harcourt, Brace and Company. Enclosed are copies of their letters. What strikes me is that in spite of their rejections they offered no specific objections nor indicated any revisions could be made to suit them. They confirm my considered judgement that the book is essentially sound, and if placed in the right hands minor revisions can be done to make it a major piece of fiction. It is an unusual book with great scope, and with five years spent on it after doing some ten serious books, it has unusual possibilities if carried through. I am now writing Mr. Wickenden at Harcourt, Brace to send the ms. to you direct, instead of returning it to me. I wish you would give me your opinion of it before sending it out.

John Farrar is an old friend of mine; he has published several of my books. So has Stanley Rinehart, as you will notice on my reference list of published books. Yet for some reason, I did not feel that either of their houses was the one for this, though it might be wise to take advantage of my previous connections with them. Not every publisher will like this book. But one will like it very much. Just who, I don't know ... I have not kept up with publishers lately, and rely on your judgement.

The first draft was also read by a friend of mine, Mrs. Anne Harris, former Story Editor of C. V. Whitney Pictures, Inc. Hollywood, with whom I had a year's writing contract. She is enthusiastic about its great picture possibilities and wanted to offer it. She was formerly the Story Editor for David Selznick, before going to Whitney's, and is now with the Writer's Guild of America, West, Inc. With her intimate working knowledge of studios, agents, and material, her judgement seems reliable. The book, however, should not be offered until its publication is assured and galleys are run off. At this time, I would like some arrangement made for her to work with you or your representative there in handling it, if possible.

All this, however, is of minor importance to finding the right publisher for it. You will note that a good many of my books are still currently in print, or have been re-issued time and again during the past ten years, and have been accepted as authoritative source books in their field of Western Americana. These two new ones are just as sound and much more timely. The long Otowi book is a tremendously ambitious project; a book that will demand great effort, and which will eventually justify it. I am quite willing to expend all the time and

---

*This resume is essentially a word-for-word duplication of the March 22, 1958 letter sent to Harcourt, Brace.

effort necessary on it. But I also think it may take more of your own effort than perhaps you wish to afford. Hence I am writing you fully and frankly; and after looking over the ms. being forwarded to you, I hope you will believe it worth your effort.

Mrs. Abbot's response to the manuscript was negative; she felt it to be too contrived and therefore did not feel she could undertake to successfully place it with a publisher. She suggested to Waters that he send the manuscript to Miss Patricia Schartle, an ex-editor newly associated with the Constance Smith Agency in New York. Waters sent the manuscript to Miss Schartle in January of 1959; her response was favorable, but after failing to place the book with Norton, Dutton and Coward-McCann the manuscript was again returned to Waters. In June of that year, Waters sent the manuscript to Joan Daves at the Marie Rodell Agency, who was also very receptive to the book. She attempted to place the book with John Farrar and later with McGraw-Hill, both of whom rejected it.

After the manuscript was returned to him in December of 1960, Waters undertook to revise the manuscript. On April 4, 1961, Waters wrote to Barthold Fles:

> I'm sending off to you today the ms. of my novel *The Woman at Otowi Crossing*.
> I have spent about eight years on it, off and on. The ms. has been offered several times in its many stages. The rejections on the whole were justified. It was an enormous work containing, in part, the whole inside story of the development of Los Alamos. During this last revision I have coldly and objectively cut it down from 700 pages to 540, eliminating all passages of technical material and paring all incidents to make it a tight and fast narrative with many changes of pace. Despite its vast scope, everything in it is closely interlocked. This is my 14th book and it is soundly conceived, constructed and written.
> One of the very early versions was sent to Mrs. Maria Honheit of Christian Wegner Verlag in Hamburg, Germany. . . . Herr Wegner wanted to publish the book, but only after it first appeared here in this country. I have no doubt that Editions Albin Michel in Paris, now translating my *Deer,* would also take it after publication here.
> Now as to placing it at last. Will you please take your time and read it all through carefully before deciding to handle it? Then if you do, please let me know two or three publishers you feel might want it. I have not yet been able to secure a list of those who saw the early versions, but I'm sure I would recognize their names if you select any of the same ones—which we should avoid.
> Personally I would like to have it submitted first to Knopf, as I mentioned to you, as I believe they will recognize it as Western Americana of a new and high order. Rather than just mailing it over there for a kid reader to thumb through, a talk with the editor regarding it and my background would reassure him he's not getting a quick, off-beat book.

194 SECTION A

But your own judgment as how to handle it I rely on. I feel you can place it if you have no reservations about it.

After unsuccessful efforts to place the book with Alfred A. Knopf, Little, Brown (a re-submission), and Viking, Fles wrote to Waters on November 22, 1961, that Doubleday was somewhat interested. However, they thought the book to be in reality two books, but that if Waters was willing to substantial revision, they would consider publishing the novel. Waters responded to Fles on November 26, 1961:

Doubleday is the only one which has shown enough interest in the Otowi book to offer suggestions for revisions which would make it acceptable to them, so we owe it to them and ourselves to take advantage of Ken McCormick's offer. Tell him I will appreciate them and consider them most seriously.

In making them, I wish he would keep in mind that I haven't gone off half-cocked, lost all perspective, and crammed the book with everything I could think of. It is the story of four people whose lives are so closely intertwined that I have developed them from four points of view, hoping that by these often contradictory viewpoints I could develop the characters more fully and bring light to bear from many directions on the main theme of atomic development. If the result is confusing, the job has not been done. But to recast the book from one single point of view might, I am afraid, pare down its great scope and significance to an insignificant narrative. So I am greatly interested in his comments and will certainly not hesitate to make revisions if we can preserve, in principle, the values inherent in the book....

After receiving further word from Doubleday, Waters again wrote Fles, on January 3, 1962 (carbon at NmU misdated 1961):

Your letter of last November 22 stated that Ken McCormick felt the novel was really two novels and that he would send suggestions for revision.

Margaret Cousins' letter of December 21, however, does not indicate which one of the two embodied novels Doubleday thinks most pertinent. Nor does she give any specific suggestions for revision. She merely states that three of the four principal characters are not convincing—mainly, I gather, because of the use of their own viewpoints and the "furniture", abortion, cancer, work details etc, used to characterize them. Hence there just isn't any idea expressed with which I can agree or disagree, save that the book is not satisfactory.

While I don't expect a complete analysis, or a blueprint of how it should be written, and I appreciate her desire to be helpful, this review is disappointing considering the many months Doubleday have held it and their interest in the general idea.

Without any guiding principles for revision, any specific goal to shoot at, I think any committment or agreement is out of the question, as we have no common premise to start from. It is merely up to me to rewrite the book so it will be satisfactory. If this is done, it should be as satisfactory to Doubleday as to any other publisher or vice versa.

So send back the ms. and I will undertake to rewrite it as soon as I can get to it, simply bearing in mind that it is too cluttered and that the many changes of viewpoints cause confusion. . . .

Waters set to work on the revision of the novel and in November of 1962 sent the revised manuscript to Fles. Unfortunately, Doubleday rejected the new version, as did Holt, Rinehart & Winston, and William Morrow. Finally, Waters turned the manuscript over to Alan Swallow. After Alan Swallow unsuccessfully attempted to interest other publishers in the book, Waters finally decided to turn the manuscript over to Swallow for publication under his imprint. In a letter to Swallow, dated April 7, 1966, Waters reflected on some of the problems he had with the work:

. . . I'm glad Haydn's [an editor at Harcourt, Brace] letter about the Woman didn't disturb you. His comments put me right back where I started: the extremely long first version which contained all the internal stuff he wanted. It didn't work in 750 pages and wouldn't have worked in 1,000. The inner development of four complicated characters with their inner relationships to each other slowed down the pace to what Ortega y Gassett said of Proust's *Remembrance of Things Past,* "a paralytic novel". The only natural alternative seemed to be to restrict it to the Woman's point of view permitting this inner development—which I next tried. What just as naturally resulted was an exposition of the psychic development of what most people would regard as an abnormal character—one certainly they would not accept in fictional terms, making a novel that completely disregarded all its inherently dramatic values. My third version tried to straddle the fence between dramatic extrovert action and introverted character development. I introduced a first-person narrator to explain each of the characters step by step, a scheme to have your cake and eat it too. Finally I realized you just can't fake anything, successful as it might first appear. You have to accept your own premise. We all live two lives, separated by the psychical Iron Curtain that makes us all schizophrenic, but they meet and blend in our daily actions as plain people. So I at last did the natural thing: let the Woman epitomize one pole of our dual nature, counterpointing the extroverted scientific process of nuclear fission, and throwing her into perspective against the other characters. The problem remained to develop these other characters without building up innumerable incidents and action that would detract and detour from the main line of the story. This I solved by introducing contradictory views of other participants to give the effect of a series of mirrors reflecting different aspects of the same image. This not only helped to round out the main characters, but permitted me to contract the time element within the confines of the story instead of expanding it far beyond. For example, we see what kind of woman Emily became years afterward due to the effect of the casual incidents in which we saw her participate as a young girl. This may offhand at first appear to be a structural fault, a rupture in the chronological time sequence. Yet it adheres to the basic premise of the Woman that every cause contains the effect, that both the past and the future are embodied in every moment of time. At any rate, after years of work on a book whose scope and depth and time element posed a real problem, the whole thing finally clarified in this treatment. I couldn't add or subtract anything more that wouldn't distort the whole web. Whatever its faults, it had jelled for me.

It still has faults, but it does reflect the original conception; and I would rather it be criticized for oversimplification than hailed as a literary exposition of current values that have no real significance. What I would hope for is that the novel will go down easily, like a sugar pill, so that its implicit meanings will dissolve and begin to work. In other words, that the book will not be immediately exhausted but take hold of the imagination.

Now I don't have any idea how you might present it to stimulate initial interest. A New York publisher like Trident, I gather, would exploit it for its exciting atomic background, get a good sale, then drop it. The main advantage in your publishing it, as most of my books curiously have a delayed reaction, is that you can keep it in print long enough for its values, whatever they may prove to be, to assert themselves. So handle it in any manner you wish. Every tub has to stand on its own bottom, but no one ever knows just what is its own center of gravity.

The contract Waters signed with Swallow, dated May 5, 1966, outlined royalties of 10% on the first 4,000 copies, 12½% on the next 3,500 copies, and 15% thereafter. There was no advance paid.

A17 THE WOMAN AT OTOWI CROSSING [1966]

A17a First edition, first printing, first binding

The Woman | at Otowi Crossing | *a novel by* | FRANK WATERS | Alan Swallow, *Denver*

8½ × 5½". [1-19^8]: 152 leaves. Pp. [1-10] 11-80 [81-82] 83-138 [139-140] 141-208 [209-210] 211-300 [301-304]. Numbers printed in roman in the center at the foot of the page.

CONTENTS: p. 1, half-title: "The Woman | at Otowi Crossing"; p. 2, "OTHER BOOKS BY FRANK WATERS | [list of 14 titles]"; p. 3, title, p. 4, copyright notice: "©1966 by Frank Waters. | Library of Congress Catalog Card Number: 66-25961 | FIRST EDITION | FIRST PRINTING"; p. 5, dedication: "TO NAOMI | This last of the many versions she has | struggled through with me for so long."; p. 6, "NOTE | [10 lines concerning the woman on whose life the novel is loosely based] | F.W."; p. 7, Prologue (printed largely in italic); p. 8, blank; p. 9, divisional half-title: "THE WOMAN AT OTOWI CROSSING | Part One"; p. 10, blank; pp. 11-80, text; p. 81, divisional half-title: "THE WOMAN AT OTOWI CROSSING | Part Two"; p. 82, blank; pp. 83-138, text; p. 139, divisional half-title: "THE WOMAN AT OTOWI CROSSING | Part Three"; p. 140, blank; pp. 141-208, text; p. 209, divisional half-title: "THE WOMAN AT OTOWI CROSSING | Part Four"; p. 210, blank; pp. 211-297, text; pp. 298-300, Epilogue; pp. 301-304, blank.

BINDING: Gray cloth, speckled with white. Stamped on spine in gilt: "[reading vertically] [small caps] FRANK WATERS [caps] THE WOMAN | AT OTOWI CROSSING [small caps] SWALLOW". White endpapers.

DUST JACKET (white paper): Front: "[series of three sketches of mushrooms in black, against a series of horizontal bands in yellow, pink, red and yellow] | THE WOMAN | AT OTOWI CROSSING | [series of four sketches of arrowheads in black, against a series of horizontal bands in yellow, red, pink and yellow] | FRANK WATERS". Spine: "FRANK | WATERS | [reading vertically] [red] THE WOMAN | [red] AT OTOWI CROSSING | [horizontally] SWALLOW". The rear contains a black and white photograph of the author, set to the left of a paragraph notice of his life and works; all of this is set above a paragraph from the publisher, signed at the bottom "Alan Swallow". The front flap is printed in red and black with a blurb for this book, which is carried over onto the rear flap, which also contains a credit at the bottom: "Cover design by Helen Strong".

Published at $4.95 on October 29, 1966. Approximately 2,000 copies were printed, of which approximately 1,500 copies were issued in the above described binding, and the balance bound up in 1970 (see A17b). Copyrighted October 14, 1966; deposited October 24, 1966.

REVIEWS: *Colorado Springs Gazette Telegraph,* November 11, 1966 (p. G-8).

COPIES: DLC (2 copies); NmU (d.j.); FW (d.j.); TAT (2 copies in d.j.).

NOTE: Alan Swallow died on Thanksgiving Day, 1966, about one month after the publication of *Woman*. His estate reopened the publishing business in February, 1967, and continued operations until August, 1967, at which time the business was sold, renamed the Swallow Press, Inc., and removed to Chicago.

Available records indicate that Alan Swallow printed approximately 2,000 copies of *Woman*. Of this number, about 1,500 copies were bound prior to August, 1967, at which time the estate paid Waters royalties on a total sale of 1,074 copies, and transferred 445 copies to the new owners in Chicago. In addition, at least 542 unbound copies were transferred to Chicago some time after August, 1967, and later bound up by the Swallow Press in their own binding (see A17b).

In a letter dated February 4, 1967, Waters wrote to Martin Miller, attorney for the Swallow estate: "I am delighted you are reprinting the Otowi novel immediately to keep up with the demand. . . ." Although there is no evidence to indicate that Swallow's estate did reprint the book—and given the circumstances it seems highly improbable—there is some reason to believe that the estate did bind up additional copies between February and August, 1967. An inventory taken at the time of Alan Swallow's death recorded only 282 bound copies of *Woman* in stock, even though, as indicated above, the estate transferred 445 bound copies to Chicago some months later. It seems probable that when the estate foresaw that existing bound stock would not keep up with demand that they ordered some, but not all, of the remaining copies bound up. Waters' letter to Miller could then be read as the author's misinterpreting the fact of binding with a new printing, or, what is more likely, that the information he was provided was ambiguous or misleading.

Thus, if the figures are accurate, it would appear likely that of the 2,000 copies printed, Alan Swallow immediately bound only half, storing the balance awaiting demand. After his death, his estate found it necessary to bind an additional 500 or so copies. At the time the business was sold in August, 1967, there remained on hand 445 bound copies and 542 unbound copies which were transferred to the new owners.

NOTE: This work was published in braille by the Johanna Bureau for the Blind and Visually Handicapped, Chicago, Illinois, in 1972.

A17b   First edition, first printing, second (Swallow Press) binding [1970]

In 1970, after the Swallow Press had sold off the remaining bound copies of the first printing of *Woman,* they bound up for sale the unbound sheets of A17a transferred from the estate of Alan Swallow. These copies are identical with A17a, except for the bindings and dust jackets, as described below:

BINDING: Pastel blue-gray cloth, lettered on spine only: "[reading vertically] [small caps] WATERS [caps] THE WOMAN | AT OTOWI CROSSING | [horizontally] SAGE | [publisher's swallow device] | SWALLOW". White endpapers.

DUST JACKET: Identical with A17a, except for the imprint at the foot of the spine: "SAGE | [publisher's swallow device] | SWALLOW", and the rear, which contains on the bottom half, instead of the note from Alan Swallow, a listing of books headed: "*other Sage Books by Frank Waters*", and lists four books, including Pumpkin Seed Point (at $6.00). The price listed on the front flap is $6.00.

These copies were issued at $6.00 in September, 1970; 542 copies of the sheets of A17a were issued in this binding and dust jacket.

COPIES: TAT (2 copies, d.j.).

A17c   First edition, first Swallow Press printing   [1970]

The Woman | at Otowi Crossing | *a novel by* | FRANK WATERS | SAGE BOOKS | [publisher's sagebrush device] | [small caps] THE [caps] SWALLOW PRESS [small caps] INC. | CHICAGO

Size, collation and pagination identical with A17a.

CONTENTS: Identical with A17a, except for page 2, which has been reset with the heading in italic and listing 11 titles, the last of which is *Pike's Peak*; and page 4: "Copyright © 1966 by Frank Waters | All rights reserved | Printed in the United States of America | First Edition | *Second Printing 1970* | Sage Books are published by | The Swallow Press Incorporated | 1139 South Wabash Avenue | Chicago, Illinois 60605 | LIBRARY OF CONGRESS CATALOG NUMBER 66-25961".

Cloth (identical with A17b). Published at $6.00 in October, 1970; 1,570 copies were printed.

SECTION A

COPIES: TAT; Swallow Press.

A17d   First edition, second Swallow Press printing   [1981]

The Woman | at Otowi Crossing | *a novel by* | FRANK WATERS | SAGE BOOKS | [publisher's sagebrush device] | SWALLOW PRESS | ATHENS, OHIO · CHICAGO

8½ × 5½". Perfectbound: 152 leaves. Pagination identical with A17a.

CONTENTS: Identical with A17a, except for page 2, which carries a listing of 14 titles by Waters; and page 4: "Copyright © 1966 by Frank Waters | All rights reserved | Printed in the United States of America | First Edition | *Second Printing 1970* | *Reprinted in 1981 by* | *Ohio Uni= versity Press* | Sage [slash] Swallow Press Books | are published by | Ohio University Press | Athens, Ohio 45701 | LIBRARY OF CON= GRESS CATALOG NUMBER 66-25961 | ISBN 0-8040-0415-3".

Paperback. Published at $8.95 in June, 1981; number of copies printed unknown.

COPIES: TAT.

A18 PUMPKIN SEED POINT

After his experience in attempting to place *Woman at Otowi Crossing* with a New York publisher, it would seem that Waters chose to give Alan Swallow the first reading of *Pumpkin Seed Point*. Sometime after receiving the manuscript in February, 1966, Swallow accepted the book for publication. The contract, dated May 6, 1966, outlined royalties of 10% on the first 4,000 copies, 12½% on the next 3,000 copies, and 15% on all copies sold thereafter. As in the case of *Woman,* Swallow paid no advance on the royalties.

In an undated letter to Waters, Swallow reported that he was planning on issuing *Woman* in September of 1966, and that this would be followed by *Pumpkin Seed Point* in late November or early December. Due to difficulties encountered in typesetting *Woman* and Waters' revising of the manuscript, *Pumpkin* still remained in manuscript at the time of Swallow's death on Thanksgiving Day, 1966.

In May of 1967, May Swallow told Waters that the Estate of Alan Swallow was going ahead with the book, and that design work had already been started by a designer in Albuquerque, and that a portion of the work had already been typeset.* However, it would seem that the printing of the book was not scheduled to begin until after the transfer of the firm to the Swallow Press, Inc., of Chicago. Although they apparently went ahead and typeset the book sometime in the early part of 1968, difficulties were encountered with the designer in Albuquerque. Although the book was advertised by the Swallow Press for publication in 1968, the difficulties continued and the book was continually delayed. Finally, the Swallow Press undertook to have their own design work done on the book, and it was finally published in May of 1969.

*Conversation recounted by Waters in a letter to Marvin Miller, attorney for the Estate, on July 22, 1967.

A18   PUMPKIN SEED POINT   [1969]

A18a   First edition, first printing

PUMPKIN SEED POINT | [directly beneath title] by FRANK WA=
TERS | [publisher's sagebrush device] | SAGE BOOKS, CHICAGO

9 × 5^{15}⁄$_{16}$″. [1-6^{16}]: 96 leaves. Double-page map inserted before the first gathering. Pp. [i-x] xi-xiii [xiv], 1-175 [176-178]. Numbers printed in roman at the foot of the page at the outer margin of the type page.

CONTENTS: p. i, half-title: "PUMPKIN SEED POINT"; p. ii, blank; p. iii, title; p. iv, copyright notice: "Copyright © 1969 by Frank Waters | All rights reserved | Printed in the United States of America | Sage Books are published by The Swallow Press Incorporated | 1139 South Wabash Avenue Chicago, Illinois 60605 | LIBRARY OF CONGRESS CATALOG NUMBER 76-75741 | Acknowledgments | [four paragraphs of acknowledgments and permissions] | Map on inside cover by L. Matis | [two lines of credits for illustrations] | Cover and Book Design by L. Miller and V. Seper [slash] Chicago"; p. v, blank; p. vi, blank; p. vii, dedication: "[at upper right] for SUSIE"; p. viii, blank; p. ix, contents; p. x, blank; pp. xi-xiii, Foreword; p. xiv, blank; pp. 1-173, text; pp. 174-175, Glossary; pp. 176-178, blank.

ILLUSTRATIONS: The illustrations in this book are in the form of small designs which appear at the head of each chapter. They were designed by Alfred Young and L. Miller, and appear on pages: 1, 14, 26, 43, 55, 63, 74, 86, 100, 111, 127, 140, 157 and 168. The double-page map inserted before the half-title depicts the "Four Corners Country" (but is untitled) and was drawn by L. Matis.

BINDING: Brown cloth. Lettered on spine only in brown: "[reading vertically] WATERS PUMPKIN SEED POINT [publisher's swallow device] SWALLOW". Yellow endpapers.

DUST JACKET (white paper): The front contains a large silhouette of an Indian's head in brown. Lettered on front in brown: "PUMPKIN | SEED | POINT | FRANK WATERS". Lettered on spine in dark brown: "[reading vertically] WATERS PUMPKIN SEED POINT [publisher's swallow device] SWALLOW". Rear: "[design from page 74 in dark brown] | [dark brown] OTHER SAGE BOOKS BY

FRANK WATERS | [notice of four books with titles printed in dark brown and blurbs in light brown[| [publisher's swallow device, in dark brown, set to the left of the following two lines, which are printed in dark brown] [small caps] THE [caps] SWALLOW PRESS [small caps] INC. | 1139 S. WABASH AVENUE CHICAGO, ILLINOIS 60605 | [reading vertically upwards along hinge and printed in dark brown] Cover and Book Design by L. Miller and V. Seper [slash] Chicago". The front flap carries a blurb for this book, printed in dark brown and light brown; the rear flap contains a photograph of the author and a biographical notice printed in dark brown and light brown.

Published at $6.00 on May 1, 1969; 4,000 copies were printed. Copyrighted May 1, 1969; deposited June 16, 1969.

REVIEWS: *Publisher's Weekly,* February 3, 1969 (p. 61); *Library Journal,* April 1, 1969 (p. 1512).

COPIES: DLC (2 copies); NmU (d.j.); TAT (2 copies, d.j.).

NOTE: Chapter 6 was originally delivered as a talk at the Fourth Annual Arizona Historical Convention in March, 1963, and published as "Two Views of Nature: White and Indian", in the May, 1964 issue of *South Dakota Review* (see C34). Chapters 9 and 10 were originally published as *Mysticism and Witchcraft* in 1966 (see AA6).

NOTE: The double-page map, according to the note on the copyright page, was apparently intended to be used as the front endpapers. Although only inserted into these copies of the first printing, the map was used as the endpapers in the second printing (see A18b).

A18b   First edition, second Swallow Press printing   [1971]

PUMPKIN SEED POINT | [centered on the page] by FRANK WA⸗ TERS | SAGE BOOKS | [publisher's sagebrush device] | [small caps] THE [caps] SWALLOW PRESS [small caps] INC. | CHICAGO

Size, collation and pagination identical with A18a. The double-page map inserted in A18a has instead been used as the endpapers in this printing.

204   Section A

CONTENTS: Identical with A18a, except for page ii: *"OTHER BOOKS BY FRANK WATERS* | [list of 11 titles]"; and page iv: "Copyright © 1969 by Frank Waters | All rights reserved | Printed in the United States of America | Sage Books are published | by The Swallow Press Incorpo= rated | 1139 South Wabash Avenue | Chicago, Illinois 60605 | Second Printing 1970 | [balance of page identical with A18a]".

Cloth. Published at $6.00 in April, 1971; 2,080 copies were printed.

COPIES: TAT.

A18c   First edition, third Swallow Press printing   [1973]

Pumpkin Seed Point | Being Within the Hopi | FRANK WATERS | SAGE BOOKS | [publisher's sagebrush device] | [small caps] THE [caps] SWALLOW PRESS [small caps] INC. | CHICAGO

8¼ × 5¼". Perfectbound: 96 leaves. Pagination identical with A18a.

CONTENTS: p. i, half-title: "Pumpkin Seed Point | Being Within the Hopi"; p. ii, identical with A18a; p. iii, title; p. iv, copyright notice: "Copyright © 1969 by Frank Waters | All rights reserved | Printed in the United States of America | Third Printing, 1973 | Sage Books are published | by The Swallow Press Incorporated | 1139 South Wabash Avenue | Chicago, Illinois 60605 | [small caps] ISBN [caps] 0-8040-0635-0 (Paper) | [small caps] LIBRARY OF CONGRESS CATALOG NUMBER [caps] 76-75741 | Acknowledgments | [four paragraphs identical with A18a] | [three lines identical with final three lines of A18a, omitting credit for map]"; p. v, dedication: "[centered on page] *for SUSIE*; pp. vi-vii, double-page map identical with that in A18a; p. viii, blank; p. ix, contents; p. x, blank; pp. xi-xiii, Foreword; p. xiv, blank; pp. 1-175, identical with A18a; p. 176, "SAGE PAPERBACK SERIES | [list of 18 titles]"; pp. 177-178, blank.

Paperback. Published at $2.50 in April, 1973; 5,112 copies were printed.

COPIES: TAT.

A18d   First edition, fourth Swallow Press printing   [1981]

Pumpkin Seed Point | Being Within the Hopi | Frank Waters | SAGE BOOKS | [publisher's sagebrush device] | SWALLOW PRESS | ATHENS, OHIO · CHICAGO

8½ × 5⅜". Perfectbound: 96 leaves. Pagination identical with A18c.

CONTENTS: Identical with A18c, except that page ii now lists 14 titles, the change in the title page as noted above, and page iv: "[first three lines identical with A18c] | Reprinted in 1981 by Ohio University Press | Sage [slash] Swallow Press Books | are published by | Ohio University Press | Athens, Ohio 45701 | [balance of page identical with A18c]". Page 176 is blank in this printing.

Paperback. Published at $5.95 in September, 1981; number of copies printed unknown.

COPIES: TAT.

EXCERPTS FROM *Pumpkin Seed Point*

A18e   *Toward Composition: Readings for Freshman English, University of Minnesota,* edited by members of the Freshman English Staff. (Dubuque, Iowa, Kendall/Hunt Publishing Co., 1970). Pages 404-411.

A19   PIKE'S PEAK

Anticipating that there might be some difficulty in finding a publisher willing to publish his long manuscript revision of his Colorado mining trilogy, Waters prepared a history and outline of the manuscript after he completed work on the book in early 1969.

PIKE'S PEAK
By
Frank Waters

    This memorandum outlines the background of a novel entitled *Pike's Peak* which was published many years ago in separate volumes as a Colorado mining trilogy, and is now condensed into a one-volume narrative.

Publishing History

    The original trilogy, my first novels, had for their milieu the greatest gold camp in America—Cripple Creek, Colorado on the slope of Pike's Peak. The period covered was roughly from 1870 to 1930, during which three generations of one family were fictionally developed.

    The novels were published by Liveright Publishing Corporation, New York, under the titles: *The Wild Earth's Nobility,* 1935; *Below Grass Roots* 1937; and *Dust Within the Rock,* 1940. All had the faults of a writer's first work. They were far too long, diffuse, and repetitious, the trilogy comprising a total of 1511 pages, about 476,000 words. The books soon went out of print, aided by the death of Horace Liveright and the virtual collapse of his publishing house.

    Nevertheless the trilogy has been used as a subject for Masters' dissertations at the University of Denver and University of South Dakota. A recent article, "Character and Landscape: Frank Waters' Colorado Trilogy" by William T. Pilkington of Southwest Texas State College, published in the Fall 1967 issue of Western American Literature, is enclosed. Thomas Lyon of Utah State University is covering the trilogy at some length in his forthcoming book for Twayne Publishers' U. S. Authors Series. Martin Bucco of Colorado State University in his recent Southwest Writers' Series booklet asserts it is "America's greatest mining saga". And John R. Milton, editor of the *South Dakota Review* has stated it will be regarded as an "American classic".

    This developing critical interest after so many years indicates, I believe, the popular interest this book would arouse if reissued now in a shorter, more read-

able form. Accordingly I have rewritten the trilogy, condensing it to 270,000 words or to some 800 printed pages.
Historical Background
Pike's Peak is the best known mountain in the United States. Since 1859, when the Pike's Peak Rush began with thousands of covered wagons crossing the Great Plains with the slogan "Pike's Peak or Bust" emblazoned on their canvas, it has been a beacon for a century of gold-seekers, settlers, invalids, and tourists. No gold then was discovered near Pike's Peak. But at its feet grew up Colorado Springs, financed with English capital, largely settled by English colonists, and so British in manner and tone it became known as "Little London"—a European-style spa in the midst of the crude American West.

During the fabulous reign of Colorado silver, prospectors passed by Pike's Peak on their way to the silver strikes at Leadville, Aspen, and the boom camps in the Saguache, Sangre de Cristo, and San Juan mountains. Then, as late as 1890, an obscure carpenter, Winfield Scott Stratton, discovered gold along Cripple Creek, on the slopes of Pike's Peak—only twenty miles west and a mile straight up from the lobby of the fashionable Antlers Hotel. Within ten years his mine, the Independence, was sold for $10,000,000 and has produced $28,000,000. The adjoining mine, the Portland, produced more than $60,000,000. By the turn of the century Cripple Creek's 475 mines were leading the world in the production of gold. From an area of only six square miles the district produced $450,000,000 worth of gold—as much as both the Mother Lode of California with only $270,000,000 and the Klondike with a mere $186,000,000.
Structure and Theme of Novel
It is a curious fact that despite our interest in all phases of Western Americana there has not yet been a major work of fiction with a mining background. This novel divides itself naturally into three parts which successively develop all stages of the mining industry: the discovery of surface indications of gold, development of underground workings to mine the ore, and the milling processes by which it is refined. Yet this book is no more a handbook of mining in fictional guise than it is a mere historical novel. Its validity depends upon its progressive development of human depth in theme and characters.

The principal character is Joseph Rogier who crosses the plains by wagon train to the new settlement at the foot of Pike's Peak. Becoming a successful contractor and builder, he helps to build up the town into the Saratoga of the West, and rears a large family. For years he scoffs at the rich silver strikes being made everywhere. But with the discovery of gold on Pike's Peak, he succumbs to gold-fever. Into the shafts of mine after mine he sinks his prosperous business, all his property, his stable of harness horses; he ruins the lives of his family. He finally dies as an old white-headed man vainly attempting to dig a tunnel into the base of Pike's Peak from his back garden in town, six miles away.

He does not find gold. Yet this is not, emphatically, a down-beat novel. Rogier's search for what he thought was gold is the hard-rock allegory of man's indomitable search for the nameless and formless truth within his own granite depths.

Pike's Peak is psychologically a modern novel whose universal theme is expressed for the first time in fiction in mining terms.

208 SECTION A

He enclosed the memorandum in a letter to his agent, Joan Daves, on June 2, 1969:

> Here is a major selling job I hope you will take on. The enclosed memorandum will give you the background and details.
>
> If you decide to make the effort, I strongly urge you, busy as you are, not to take the long time to read the mss. Simply take my word that the exhaustive reworking of the original version is a good job.
>
> The selection of a publisher to whom to submit it is the big problem. This is a ms. of nearly 1,000 pages and it is about the West. Any publisher in the country when queried will answer he is eager to see the ms. Why not? A look costs nothing—just in case!—though it may take months, even though the house is not interested in Western material, and does not want such a long and expensive job of production.
>
> This was the case with Farrar, Straus, and Giroux, the only people who have seen it. . . . Farrar had published several books of mine years ago, most apologetically, and remaindered them as quickly as possible—all of which have been picked up by other publishers who have kept them in print for more than twenty years. The firm kept this ms. only three weeks fortunately . . . the ms. should never have been submitted or accepted. . . .
>
> The status of other publishers I don't know. But I would hope that with this background material, and your knowledge of publishers, you could talk with several, and submit only to one which is not traditionally opposed to anything Western, nor initially frightened by 1,000 pages to the extent that, before reading a page, would assume it could be cut to a tidy story of 300 pages.
>
> Certainly there is a publisher for this book. All of my books have been slow starters, but they last. This should count to a publisher if you can find him.
>
> Use the enclosed memorandum verbally or by rewriting it, in any way you choose, and let me know if you wish the ms. sent you. . . .

On June 5, 1969, Waters followed up this letter with another to Joan Daves:

> On Monday, shortly after mailing you the material on *Pike's Peak,* I left for Sedona. In Albuquerque I stopped for a luncheon talk with John Jenkin of the Swallow Press, Chicago, which has just published my *Pumpkin Seed Point,* a hold-over ms. of the late Alan Swallow. Jenkin had just read the Martin Bucco pamphlet reference to the Colorado mining trilogy, and queried me about it. I told him the book had been done and would be placed in your hands; that I thought it too big a project for his Swallow Press.
>
> Jenkin telephoned the editor, Durrell [i.e. Durrett] Wagner, that evening, and today I received a long letter from Wagner. He is prepared to meet all competition for the book as regards advance, royalties, advertising, and general handling.
>
> Alan Swallow of Denver re-issued four of my books after the original publishers had dropped them, and successfully kept them in print for years . . . Upon his sudden death this new firm organized in Chicago under his name bought all the stock and titles, including my unpublished ms. *Pumpkin Seed*

Point, and is continuing to keep all my titles in print with growing sales. . . . It seems natural they want to keep my new books on their list.

Despite my previous trouble [over delays in *Pumpkin Seed Point*], there would be some advantages to letting them have *Pike's Peak*. They already have five of my titles in print; and while initial sales might be lower, they would probably keep it in print with the others, one book helping to sell the others.

This, however, is a long book that hopefully would be an important one. A large New York house could give it the prestige and backing it needs, perhaps more so than the Swallow Press.

Which would be best I don't know. But I think it would be fair if you would look at the Swallow Press with an impartial eye, and give them a chance to make an offer which you could compare with any reactions you get from anyone in New York. I'm certainly in no position to have two publishers bid on a book; I'll feel fortunate in finding one who will do a good job with it. But at the same time, I feel the book deserves—and needs—any break it can get. . . .

Joan Daves replied to Waters on July 14, 1969, that she was reluctant to turn the book over to the Swallow Press and that she was about to send it to several New York firms. On September 19, 1969, she wrote again to Waters, informing him that Holt, Rinehart & Winston and Coward-McCann had seen the manuscript, but had returned it without useful comments or reactions. Waters responded to her letter on September 27, 1969:

. . . The negative reactions of two New York publishers to *Pike's Peak* do not surprise me. After a little soul-searching I believe you should turn it over to Weisman of Swallow Press without submissions elsewhere. He already has five titles of mine, and although his initial sales may be comparatively small, he will keep the book in print with the others for some time. In drawing up the contract with him, I have but few suggestions. I would ask only a nominal advance, whatever he can afford. But in lieu of a larger one, I would ask that he provide a nominal sum for advertising. Also that he take the book as is, without substantial cutting; I have reduced the three volumes as much as I can without losing the original values. The contract should be drawn for this book only, not with options on the *Manby* book and the Mexico-Yucatan book I will do next year under a Rockefeller Foundation grant; but with the tacit understanding he can have these books also if he comes through on this long novel.

This may be against your judgment. But I have found over a long period that small but steady sales over the year offset short successful splurges. In these fast-changing times books on the West, by metropolitan standards, are distinctly old-fashioned. But fully integrated Americana, which cannot be faked by paper research, is coming into its own. David McKay Company and Doubleday both have asked me to do a book—one on prehistoric Indians and one on modern Indians—which I have declined, preferring to land my own, rather stubbornly perhaps, as indicated. I hope you're not too unhappy about this.

The manuscript was sent off to Swallow Press in October of 1969. Shortly thereafter, on November 26, 1969, Durrett Wagner wrote to Waters concerning the original trilogy. While glancing through the latest edition of *Books in Print,* Wagner had noticed that the three original titles were listed as "in print," even though they had not been listed in the previous year's edition. This, of course, raised questions as to the ability of the Swallow Press to contract for the rights to *Pike's Peak.* Waters responded to Wagner on December 2, 1969 [ICIU]:

> Liveright Publishers, N.Y., has been practically defunct for ages; I haven't received a royalty statement for the three Colorado trilogy volumes for twenty years. Copies seem to be collectors' items. A friend of mine last month—a collector and associated with another N.Y. publishing house—paid $100 for a set. So your news that the books are listed is mighty strange. This, however, does not worry me. Several years ago, when Liveright refused to release the rights to me and I was contemplating the present one-volume rewrite, I engaged a lawyer in N.Y. He advised me that if I reissued the books with *revisions in any way,* this would constitute a new book over which Liveright had no control of rights whatever. Hence we have a clear field. . . .

Although Waters' answer seemed to satisfy the Swallow Press, it did not satisfy Joan Daves, who, although she had worked out contract arrangements with Swallow Press, felt it necessary to get clearance from Liveright.

After waiting several months, the Swallow Press finally decided that they would risk any problems which might arise due to Liveright and in order to protect Waters put a clause in the contract absolving him of any culpability should the questions of rights come up later. A contract, incorporating this clause, was drawn up and dated July 15, 1970; the contract outlined an advance of $1,500.00 against royalties of 10% on the first 5,000 copies, 12½% on the next 3,000 copies, and 15% thereafter.

During the process of reading the manuscript, Durrett Wagner queried Waters about the nature of his revision of the original trilogy. Waters explained this to him in a letter on October 1, 1970 [ICIU]:

> . . . Regarding the trilogy. The three volumes were published in 1935, 1937, and 1940, and comprised a total of about 1511 pages, about 476,000 words. They have been reduced in this one-volume narrative to 270,000 words or to the neighborhood of some 800 pages—about 58%.
> The cutting was accomplished by three ways. First, as the novels were published two years apart, each contained recaps to familiarize the reader with what had gone before, so this repetitious material was eliminated. Second, a number of inconsequential minor characters were eliminated in order to build up the characterizations of the principal characters and sharpen the narrative as

an integrated whole. Third, all this necessitated rewriting great portions of the ms. to weld it into a close-knit unity. Hence while the whole story of the trilogy is here, it is virtually rewritten to clarify and dramatize its inherent values while omitting the dead wood in the early, diffuse version. The trilogy has been out of print for years, and has been forgotten by all except a few collectors. This is virtually a new novel based on the early work. . . .

A19   PIKE'S PEAK   [1971]

A19a   First edition, first printing

[open face] PIKE'S PEAK: | a family saga | [open face] Frank Waters | SAGE BOOKS | [publisher's sagebrush device] | [small caps] THE [caps] SWALLOW PRESS [small caps] INC. | CHICAGO

$8^{15}/_{16} \times 5^{7}/_{8}''$. [1-24^{16}]: 384 leaves. Pp. [i-x], [1] 2-9 [10] 11-16 [17] 18-24 [25] 26-31 [32] 33-42 [43] 44-51 [52] 53-63 [64] 65-71 [72] 73-79 [80] 81-85 [86] 87-93 [94] 95-101 [102] 103-109 [110] 111-115 [116] 117-122 [123] 124-128 [129] 130-136 [137] 138-143 [144] 145-150 [151] 152-157 [158] 159-163 [164] 165-169 [170] 171-177 [178] 179-187 [188] 189-193 [194] 195-201 [202] 203-210 [211] 212-219 [220] 221-228 [229] 230-237 [238] [238a-238b] [239] 240-246 [247] 248-254 [255] 256-264 [265] 266-270 [271] 272-278 [279] 280-285 [286] 287-293 [294] 295-299 [300] 301-306 [307] 308-310 [311] 312-315 [316] 317-323 [324] 325-329 [330] 331-338 [339] 340-349 [350] 351-359 [360] 361-367 [368] 369-377 [378] 379-385 [386] 387-393 [394] 395-401 [402] 403-410 [411] 412-422 [423] 424-428 [429] 430-434 [435] 436-444 [445] 446-452 [453] 454-460 [461] 462-466 [467] 468-474 [475] 476-482 [482a-482b] [483] 484-490 [491] 492-501 [502] 503-509 [510] 511-516 [517] 518-523 [524] 525-530 [531] 532-540 [541] 542-548 [549] 550-555 [556] 557-561 [562] 563-568 [569] 570-575 [576] 577-583 [584] 585-594 [595] 596-602 [603] 604-612 [613] 614-621 [622] 623-632 [633] 634-641 [642] 643-646 [647] 648-656 [657] 658-664 [665] 666-672 [673] 674-680 [681] 682-687 [688] 689-695 [696] 697-703 [704] 705-714 [715] 716-724 [725] 726-733 [734] 735-743 [744-754] = 758. Numbers printed in italic in headline at outer margin of type page.

CONTENTS: pp. i-ii, blank; p. iii, half-title: "[open face] Pike's Peak"; p. iv, "*OTHER BOOKS BY FRANK WATERS* | [list of 11 titles]"; p. v, title; p. vi, copyright notice: "Copyright © 1971 by Frank Waters | All rights reserved | Printed in the United States of America | Sage Books are published by | The Swallow Press Incorporated | 1139 South Wabash Avenue | Chicago, Illinois 60605 | [small caps] ISBN [caps] 0-8040-0503-6 | [small caps] LIBRARY OF CONGRESS CATALOG CARD NUMBER [caps] 77-150753"; p. vii, contents; p. viii, blank; p. ix, divisional half-title: "[open face] BOOK ONE | [fancy rule] | [open face] The Wild Earth's Nobility"; p. x, blank; pp. 1-237, text; p. 238, blank; p. 238a, divisional half-title: "[open face] BOOK TWO | [fancy rule] | [open face] Below Grass Roots"; p. 238b, blank; pp. 239-482, text; p. 482a, divisional half-title: "[open face] BOOK THREE | [fancy rule] | [open face] The Dust Within The Rock"; p. 482b, blank; pp. 483-743, text; pp. 744-754, blank.

BINDING: Orange cloth. Publisher's swallow device stamped in blind in lower right corner of front cover. Lettered on spine: "WATERS | PIKE'S | PEAK | SAGE [publisher's swallow device] | SWALLOW". Chocolate-brown endpapers.

DUST JACKET (white paper): Front, spine and rear printed overall with a photograph, in black and orange, of the author against an unfocused background. Lettered on front: "[blue] A NOVEL BY | [white] Frank | [white] Waters | PIKE'S PEAK | [next four lines in blue] *a family saga* | *an epic journey* | *of the* | *American soul*". Spine: "[white] WATERS | [blue] PIKE'S | [blue] PEAK | [following lines in white] SAGE | [publisher's swallow device] | SWALLOW". The front flap carries a blurb for this book, which is carried over onto the rear flap, which also carries a short notice of the author.

Published at $8.95 on June 30, 1971; 4,640 copies were printed. Copyrighted June 30, 1971; deposited February 15, 1972.

REVIEWS: *Chicago Daily News,* July 3-4, 1971 (Panorama section, p. 7); *Chicago Sun-Times Showcase,* July 18, 1971 (p. 18); *Denver Post,* July 18, 1971 (p. 18); *Albuquerque Journal,* July 25, 1971 (p. C-3); *Kirkus Reviews,* November 1, 1971 (p. 465).

COPIES: DLC; NmU (d.j.); TAT (2 copies, d.j.).

NOTE: At least one copy was specially bound in full green imitation leather. This copy was inscribed by Morton Weisman to Waters and is in the personal collection of Frank Waters.

A19b   First edition, second Swallow Press printing   [1972]

Title page identical with A19a.

Size identical with A19a. [1¹⁶ 2¹² 3-24¹⁶]: 380 leaves. Pagination identical with A19a, except that the final four blank leaves are not present in this printing.

CONTENTS: Identical with A19a, except for p. vi which carries the additional lines, inserted above the publisher's name and address: ". . . | First Edition | Second Printing 1971 | This book is printed on 100% recycled paper. | . . .".

Cloth. Published at $8.95 in March, 1972. 1,862 copies were printed.

COPIES: TAT.

A19c   Second edition, only printing   [1972]

PIKE'S PEAK | *A Family Saga* | Frank Waters | BALLANTINE BOOKS   NEW YORK | An [next word in sans-serif type with swash 'x'] Intext Publisher

7$\frac{1}{16}$ × 4$\frac{3}{16}$". Perfectbound: 352 leaves. Pp. [i-vi], [1-2] 3-220 [221-222] 223-449 [450-452] 453-694 [695-698]. Page 695 carries a note about the author; pages 696-697 carry advertisements; and pages vi, 2, 222, 450, 452 and 698 are blank.

COPYRIGHT PAGE: "Copyright © 1971 by Frank Waters | All rights reserved | Library of Congress Catalog Card Number: 77-150753 | SBN 345-02768-X-195 | This edition published by arrangement with The Swallow | Press, Inc. | First Printing: August, 1972 | Printed in the United States of America | Cover art by Bob Schultz | BALLANTINE BOOKS, INC. | 101 Fifth Avenue, New York, N.Y. 10003".

Paperback. Ballantine Book 02678-X-195. Published at $1.95 in August, 1972; 73,065 copies were printed.

COPIES: NmU; FW.

NOTE: According to royalty records in the files of the Swallow Press, 7,980 copies were printed for distribution in Canada. According to the publisher, these copies were identical with those distributed in the United States.

A20 TO POSSESS THE LAND

While writing to Emily Morison Beck, of the Atlantic Monthly Press, on January 11, 1967, Waters briefly mentioned his current work on the life of Arthur Rochford Manby:

... The new book I am working on is laid in ... New Mexico ..., but has for its subject the greatest unsolved murder in the Southwest. Whether it should be handled as a documented biography due to its almost unbelievable facts, or as a novelized treatment to allow for more character development, I am not yet sure. In either case, its final rewrite will be delayed somewhat as I am committed to work this winter with our New Mexico Arts Commission here in Santa Fe.

After sending Joan Daves a draft of the work in the summer of 1968, Waters apparently unearthed more material relating to Manby, and in a letter to Joan Daves on June 2, 1969, asked that she return the manuscript to him for further work.

Shortly after this, Waters briefly mentioned the work in a letter, dated June 17, 1969 [ICIU], to Durrett Wagner at the Swallow Press:

... I've almost completed a novelized biography of a certain Manby, whose strange death remains one of the great unsolved mysteries of the Southwest. It involves the history of a Spanish land grant, a subject now growing in importance ... I'm still trying to keep this under cover, as it is a very touchy subject in New Mexico.

Picking up on this subject some months later, Wagner wrote to Waters on January 6, 1970, saying that if he could assume the Swallow Press could have the Manby book was there any chance that it could be finished by October. He also inquired about the possibility of starting work right away on illustrations for the book.

Waters responded on January 10, 1970 [ICIU]:

... The thinking in your letter is good. This spring I'll finish up the Manby ms. so it will be ready for submission before I leave for Mexico on October 1st. Before then, in case you come here again, we can talk about illustrations. Due to the difficulties I mentioned, I haven't photostated original documents in the Court House or made a search for photographs. It may be, as the book is written as a novelized biography rather than as a documented history, that too much illustrative matter would detract rather than add to the narrative approach. However, I have a fine sample letter in Manby's handwriting with a colored crayon drawing which would reproduce very well. Also I have three official maps of the Antonio Martinez Grant from which a staff artist should make two simple line maps (similar to that in *Midas of the Rockies*) showing: (1) the regional location of the Martinez Grant in relation to the Great Maxwell and Sangre de Cristo grants in northern New Mexico and southern Colorado, and (2) a more detailed map of the Martinez Grant itself, including Taos and nearby villages between the mts. and Rio. Grande. These could be used as end papers. Also I could scrape up some photos of people, locations, and documents if necessary.

This may be an explosive book here in the SW. due to its inherent nature. But my main concern is first the *Pike's Peak* novel you have at hand, which I think we should concentrate on now. This is the meat-and-potatoes that will outlast the Manby melodrama, true as it is.

After having completed most of the preparations for *Pike's Peak,* the Swallow Press again brought up the question of the Manby book in early 1971. Waters replied on January 28, 1971 [ICIU; misdated 1970]:

... The *Manby* book is finished. Very few final touches need to be made. I'll send you the ms. as soon as I get back and would like you both to read it carefully and give me your honest impression. The facts are so preposterous as to seem almost unbelievable. Moreover, it throws into focus the whole subject of Spanish and Mexican land grants stolen from the grantees by English and American entrepreneurs. This is a hot subject nowadays, which might be good for the sale of the book, but it plays into the hands of the current forces, which might not be good. I have not littered the book with footnotes, but can attribute every statement to official sources. To make sure that there are no grounds for a libel suit, I can send the ms. to a lawyer friend in Santa Fe for perusal, or you should have your own lawyer go through it there, whichever you prefer. ...

On July 27, 1971, Morton Weisman of the Swallow Press reported to Waters that he had finished the manuscript and that Swallow Press definitely wanted to publish it, and that as soon as others had read it they would send along their comments. Waters wrote back to Weisman on July 31, 1971: "We can talk about *Manby* when you and Durrett come in October. It has a main fault, and you might have some helpful suggestions about it."

On February 16, 1972, Weisman again wrote Waters about Manby, informing him that he was going to schedule the book for publication in the fall, and would be sending along a contract soon. Waters responded on February 21, 1972 [ICIU]:

. . . I haven't done a thing on the Manby ms. However, I've run into a woman descendent of the Manby family in England with information that doesn't jibe with that I obtained from England. The first time I can get down to Santa Fe, I'll go over the discrepancies with her. Then rewrite parts of the ms. and document all of it, trying to steer it more to the biographical side of the fence—which should please Durrett. Right now its a real bastard, half-fish, half-fowl, I know. To do this I'll need the copy of the ms. you have there, as I have here only one carbon. . . .

On June 1, 1972, Waters wrote to Donna Ippolito at the Swallow Press, telling her that his revisions on Manby were finished, and that as soon as the typing was completed he would send it along. Immediately afterwards he received a long list of questions about the manuscript from Durrett Wagner (mailed 5/13/72) which he answered on June 4, 1972 [ICIU]:

. . . . Upon receiving Mort & Donna's many itemized suggestions for changes I revised the ms.: converting many dialogue sequences into straight narrative, and documenting it in back with footnote material to insure us against any possible libelous charges. Much as I generally dislike footnotes, I think for a book like this they add documentary evidence which gives it a firmer basis. In addition, and as you suggested, I have written the Introduction carefully.

The revisions were sent to be typed before your letter came. I will try to answer all your questions before sending you the complete ms. which should reach you in a couple of weeks. Go through it carefully, and if there are still any bugs in it let me know. We can then get down to questionable details. At the same time I hope to send you illustrative material.

Your one suggestion I don't like is that I mention I live in Arroyo Seco on land that once was part of Manby's grant, and that some time ago a note was slipped under my door warning me to lay off the investigation of the Manby murder. Also I have avoided expressing my personal opinion of who the murderers of Manby were, leaving it to the reader to make up his own mind whether Manby was murdered or disappeared. Don't forget, confidentially, that one of my close neighbors has the same family name of one of the men I personally suspect as being closely associated with the murder. Fortunately he died a few months ago. But nevertheless all these Spanish families are closely related, and have close ties with past injustices. Aside from this personal point of view, the murder of Manby has never been legally proved, so I think a book written objectively, without personal bias, is justified. . . .

On July 5, 1972 [ICIU], Waters wrote to Donna Ippolito:

The revised *Manby* ms. and illustration material is being mailed to you under separate cover.

Almost all of Mort's, Durrett's and your own suggested revisions and questions have been covered. The book has been pretty thoroughly documented and more material is included in the notes. The new Introduction, which I discussed with Durrett in Oklahoma City, has been carefully written. This gives justification to the few fictional and subjective passages which are necessary to give depth and human interest to what would otherwise be a dull recital of documented facts. On the whole, I'm much more pleased with it, and I hope you will be too.

. . . I've written Durrett the reasons why I don't want to express my personal opinion of whether Manby was murdered and by whom, preferring to let the reader form his own opinion. The first is that it has never been legally established that Manby was murdered and by whom. The second is that I live here. . . .

The contract for Manby, dated April 19, 1972, outlined an advance of $1,000.00—half on signing, half on publication, against royalties of 10% of the first 3,999 copies, 12½% over that up to 7,500 copies and 15% thereafter.

A20 TO POSSESS THE LAND [1973, i.e. 1974]

A20 First edition, only printing

To Possess the Land | A Biography of | Arthur Rochford Manby | Frank Waters | SAGE BOOKS | [publisher's sagebrush device] | [small caps] THE [caps] SWALLOW PRESS [small caps] INC. | CHICAGO

$8^{15}/_{16} \times 5^{7}/_{8}''$. [1-2^{16}, 3^{4}, 4-10^{16}]: 148 leaves. Pp. [i-vi] vii-viii, 1-6 [7] 8-19 [20] 21-31 [32] 33-37 [38] 39-41 [42] 43-52 [53] 54-63 [64] 65-73 [74] 75-81 [82-85] 86-113 [114-115] 116-142 [143] 144-177 [178-181] 182-184 [185-188] 189-223 [224] 225-246 [247-251] 252-256 [257] 258-259 [260] 261-273 [274] 275-287 [288]. Numbers printed in italic in headline at outer margin of type page, except for pages 1, 17, 25, 34, 40, 52, 62, 73, 87, 98, 108, 117, 121, 135, 146, 155, 167, 175, 192, 202, 209, 218, 227, 242, 256, 261, 275 and 279 on which the numbers are printed in the center of the foot of the page.

CONTENTS: p. i, half-title: "To Possess the Land | A Biography of | Arthur Rochford Manby"; p. ii, blank; p. iii, title; p. iv, copyright notice: "Copyright© 1973, by Frank Waters | All rights reserved | Printed in the United States of America | First Edition | First Printing | Sage Books are published by | The Swallow Press Incorporated | 1139 South Wabash Avenue | Chicago, Illinois 60605 | This Book is printed on 100% recycled paper | [small caps] ISBN [caps] 0-8040-0647-4 | [small caps] LIBRARY OF CONGRESS CATALOG CARD NUMBER [caps] 73-13210."; p. v, list of contents; p. vi, list of illustrations; pp. vii-viii, Introduction; pp. 1-4, "Epilogue"; pp. 5-259, text; p. 260, blank; pp. 261-273, notes; p. 274, blank; pp. 275-278, sources and acknowledgments; pp. 279-287, index; p. 288, blank.

ILLUSTRATIONS: All illustrations, except for those noted below, are reproductions from photographs, and all are full-page; they appear on pages 7, 20, 32, 42, 53, 64, 74, 82, 83, 84, 85, 114, 115, 143, 247, 248, 249, 250, 251 and 257. A full-page reproduction of an illustration from a magazine appears on page 224. Reproductions of documents referred to in the text appear on pages 178-179, 180-181 and 185-188.

BINDING: Three states of the binding have been noted. The priority listed below is tentative (see note below):

A. Green cloth. Stamped on front with the author's facsimile signature in black in the center, and with the publisher's swallow device (with a wingspan measurement from tip to tip of 23 mm.) in blind in the lower right corner. Stamped on spine in black: "[reading vertically] Waters [small caps] TO POSSESS THE LAND | [horizontally] SAGE | [publisher's swallow device] | SWALLOW". Tan colored endpapers of laid paper with chain lines measuring 20 mm.; printed on the face of the front endpapers with a map of the Lucero Godoi or Antonio Martinez Grant; and printed on the face of the rear endpapers with a map of northern New Mexico with the Martinez Manby Grant shaded in gray.

B. Brown cloth, as above, but with front stamped all in blind, and with spine stamped in silver.

C. Brown cloth. Front stamped as above, all in blind, but with wingspan of swallow device measuring 28 mm. from tip to tip. Spine stamped as above, but all in white. The endpapers found with this binding are of a heavy wove paper and are of a slightly more orangish color than the endpapers found with A and B.

DUST JACKET (white paper): Front, spine and rear printed overall in orange-brown. The front contains an irregular panel in orange, on which appears, in green and black, a portion of the map of the Martinez Grant; Manby on his horse, shaded in orange-brown and black, is riding out of the panel. Lettered on front: "[orange-brown] TO POSSESS | [orange-brown] THE [next two lines printed directly to the right of the preceding word, in black and in a much smaller type-face] a biography of | ARTHUR ROCHFORD MANBY | [orange-brown] LAND | [white] Frank Waters". Spine: [reading vertically] [white] Waters [small caps] [orange] TO POSSESS THE LAND | [horizontally] SAGE | [publisher's swallow device] | SWALLOW". The rear contains a listing, with blurbs, of nine other books by Frank Waters, set within an irregular orange panel; designer credit appears at the extreme left margin of the rear near the top: "[reading vertically] [orange] *Jacket design by Louis Matis*". The front flap contains a blurb for this book, printed in black and orange-brown, and is carried over onto the rear flap, which also contains a photograph of the author by Robert Kostka, and a short biographical notice of the author.

Published at $8.95. Exact date of publication unknown; 5,000 copies were printed. Copyrighted December 28, 1973; deposited June 16, 1974. The work was originally scheduled to be published on November 28, 1973, but the first copies were not received at the Press until December 28, 1973, and the balance of the copies not received until January 24, 1974.

REVIEWS: *Taos News*, February 6, 1974 (p. B1); *Albuquerque Journal*, February 10, 1974 (p. C-3); *Chicago Tribune Book World*, March 3, 1974 (p. 1).

COPIES: DLC (A binding); NmU (A binding, d.j.); TAT (3 copies B binding, d.j.; one copy C binding, d.j.); John D. Gilchriese, Tucson, Arizona (A binding, d.j.).

NOTE: The inventory records of the Swallow Press record that 800 copies were received into inventory on December 28, 1973, and that on January 24, 1974 an additional 1,996 copies were received. An invoice from the printer, Edwards Brothers of Ann Arbor, Michigan, records that 2,000 copies "Casebound" and 3,000 copies in sheets were shipped from Ann Arbor on January 24, 1974. Although somewhat confusing, this information would seem to indicate that copies were bound at different times. The copy which Charles L. Adams of Las Vegas, Nevada, received for review purposes was in the A binding. I personally purchased five copies in the B binding direct from the Swallow Press in 1974. Copies currently being sold by the Press are in the C binding. Thus it would seem that the priority which has been assigned to the binding variants is reasonable.

A21 MEXICO MYSTIQUE

In June of 1969, Waters was approached by the Rockefeller Foundation and asked to apply for a research grant in his field of interest. He did so, and a grant was approved for research in Mexico and Yucatan during the winter of 1970-71, on the Toltec, Aztec and Mayan religions.

While in Mexico, Waters was queried by Morton Weisman of the Swallow Press as to the nature of his research. Waters answered him in a letter dated January 28, 1971 [ICIU; misdated 1970]:

. . . What kind of book will come out of this Mexican jaunt I don't know. I'm covering all the major Mexican and Mayan ruins, and researching the history of the pre-Columbian civilizations—Toltec, Aztec, Zapotec, Maya, and Olmec. Not to find the differences, as do scholarly archeologists, anthropologists, and historians. But to find the basic religious concept that bound them all together, and how this relates to that of our own Indians today in the Southwest, and to that of the Near and Far East. Quite probably it will shape into a loose, readable form, perhaps like *Masked Gods* or *Pumpkin Seed Point*, rather than a scholarly dull tome. A sense of cosmological unity, a constant flowing of ideas from one succeeding civilization to another, something like that. . . .

Finally, on October 1, 1973 [ICIU], Waters wrote to Morton Weisman:

I've decided it's time to stop work on this new book, *Mexico Mystique,* although I could fuss with it much longer and probably to no great benefit. Should I send it to you now, or wait until *Manby* has cleared your deck?

No one has read the entire ms. except Skipper who typed it, and I've worked on it so long I find myself unable to appraise it. That I will leave to you without pages of unnecessary explanation.

These few comments, however, may answer some questions that may arise during your reading. Part One, a brief factual summary of the major cultures, may seem slow and tedious. But I think it is necessary in order to give a firm historical and rational background to Part Two, The Myths. Now as you know, there is so much mythical material one could not record and document it in several volumes. But this book is not a documentary anthology. It is a thematic exploration of the essence of the religious structure of pre-Columbian Mesoamerican civilization. Hence I have selected the two major cultures, Nahuatl and Mayan, as representing its opposite polarities; and have developed at some depth the controlling principles of each—the Nahuatl concern with space and the myth of Quetzalcoatl, and the Mayan mathematical and astrological obscession [sic] with time, as illustrated by their Great Cycle whose beginning they projected to 3113 B.C. and whose end they projected to A.D. 2011. On these two threads are strung of course more material of world scope that seems relevant.

The book undoubtedly will be open to criticism from both orthodox scholars and far-out non-conformists. The last section comprising my own interpretation of the meaning of the Mayan Great Cycle is purely speculative, entering the field of astrology which is certainly circumspect, but based on a mathematical study included as an appendix. Nevertheless it seems to be in tune with the phenomenal flood of popular fantasies which do reflect the insecurity and hopes of our present tragic time.

This book is submitted to you with some misgivings, as I'm unable to judge whether its written content has come out as I intended—like the village trumpet player who blew in sweet only to have it come out sour; nor whether its admittedly odd approach to a most difficult subject will appeal to you at all, to say nothing of whether it might be saleable. Of one thing you may be sure. I will not be disconcerted if you decide it is not for you. I rely on your judgement [sic] as my publisher as well as on your warmth and honesty as a friend. . . .

After hearing from Mort Weisman that the Swallow Press did want to publish the book, Waters wrote again on February 16, 1974 [ICIU]:

. . . *Mexico Mystique* will be expensive to publish I'm afraid, with all those astrological charts. But I'm glad you still want to handle it. But do return the ms. After laying it aside for a couple of months, I have a better perspective of it. It seems in parts too crowded with detailed documentary research; it reveals the working of the machinery of thought processes too noisily for the readers' smooth ride. I'm thinking of condensing Book III in Part One—The In-Flowing Streams—to a few pages; moving the Pyramid chapter into Part Two; and rewriting the Atlantis Myth chapter only from a psychological viewpoint. I'm not too concerned with rendering so much homage to the academic world; only with more clearly delineating my own views of the Aztec-space and Maya-time relationship. Before I do this revision do let me have your appraisal of it as a whole, your questions, suggestions, and comments. Also your thoughts on the problem of attribution—footnotes, chapter notes, etc. . . .

Weisman returned the manuscript as Waters asked, noting only that they would reserve comment until they saw the revised version. On March 6, 1974 [ICIU], Waters acknowledged receipt of the ms.:

. . . I'm starting to work on the revisions. It's amazing what a fresh look comes after shelving it for several months. I've decided to handle the attribution problem by notes at the back, as was done for the Manby book. This will be a job, for as usual I didn't footnote my sources. Durrett will be pleased and it should also save cluttering up the text.

Don't bother submitting it to book clubs etc. where it wouldn't appeal anyway. I'd rather you simply published it without too much ado, not setting an exact date until you're sure paper shortages won't delay it, and making sure review copies will be available shortly before. Also I'd like to work a little more closely with Donna during her preparation of blurb copy—which shouldn't claim this is a culmination of my Indian studies, just a continuation. I hope this doesn't sound picayunish or preseumptious [sic]; it's only that I think this book is a ticklish, off-beat thing difficult to present. I haven't collected photos, believing that the drawings, tables & astrological charts would be enough. However, I do want to add two zodiacs, one for the year, one for the twelve ages or eras. These will be reproduced from those given me by Jung's daughter in Zurich which she uses in her own work, as did Jung. They are in color but can be reproduced in black and white. If you do want photos, maybe I can think how to get some good ones. . . .

After working on the revisions, Waters mailed the revised manuscript to the Swallow Press on April 9, 1974, and followed it with a letter to Mort Weisman on April 10, 1974 [ICIU]:

The ms. was mailed to you yesterday. I'm sorry it's a little late, but I hope you'll be pleased with it. It needed a lot of work. Chapters have been rearranged, dead wood has been cut out, and a lot of it rewritten to point up what I was trying to get at in such a roundabout fashion. I feel it's really finished now, ready for your reaction to it, questions and suggestions. . . The small pencil sketches inserted in the text were done freehand merely to indicate what they were. I have now traced them more accurately from the Borgia Codex, but they probably need to be redrawn in ink for reproduction. . . .

A rough sketch map of Mesoamerica I think is needed, showing the areas of the prime cultures discussed and a few key sites. If you agree, I'll get someone here to draw it unless you'd rather have it done there. One other item appeals to me for inclusion: a full-color reproduction of one of the Borgia paintings in mandala form, as I know my descriptions of them in the chapter on Quetzalcoatl's journey in the Land of the Dead make it hard to visualize their strangeness, gorgeous color, and beauty of design. If you think this is appropriate, I'll have the same photographer in Santa Fe make a reproduction. . . .

A contract for this book was drawn up and dated May 3, 1974; it outlined an advance of $1,000.00 against royalties of 10% on the first 3,999 copies, 12½% up to 7,500 copies, and 15% thereafter.

A21   MEXICO MYSTIQUE   [1975]

A21a   First edition, first printing

[double-page title, with background map of Central America in black and gray] [right-hand page] [four lines set within a white panel] Mexico Mystique | The Coming Sixth | World of Consciousness | Frank Waters | [left-hand page] [all in white] SAGE BOOKS | [publisher's sagebrush device] | [small caps] THE [caps] SWALLOW PRESS [small caps] INC. | CHICAGO

    The double-page map is titled on the left-hand page in hand lettering within single rules: "PRINCIPAL CULTURE | AREAS AND SITES | OF MESOAMERICA". It is signed in the extreme lower right of the right-hand page "ASAY".

$8^{15}\!/_{16} \times 5^{15}\!/_{16}''$. [1-5^{16} 6^{12} 7-11^{16}]: 172 leaves. Pp. [i-vi] vii-x, [1-2] 3-86 [87-88] 89-218 [219] 220-231 [231a-231b] 232-259 [260] 261-266 [267-268] 269 [270] 271-283 [284] 285-326 [327-332] = 334. Numbers printed in italic in headline at outer margin of type page, except for pages vii-x, 3, 10, 19, 23, 27, 30, 38, 48, 55, 61, 67, 73, 79, 89, 97, 104, 112, 116, 122, 129, 143, 150, 152, 161, 168, 176, 187, 194, 203, 208, 218, 226, 230, 238, 249, 256, 265, 272, 280, 285, 305, 313 and 319 on which the numbers are printed in the center at the foot of the page.

CONTENTS: p. i, half-title: "Mexico Mystique"; pp. ii-iii, title; p. iv, copyright notice: "Copyright© 1975 by Frank Waters | All Rights Reserved | Printed in the United States of America | First Edition | *First Printing* | Sage Books are published by | The Swallow Press Incorporated | 1139 South Wabash Avenue | Chicago, Illinois 60605 | This book is printed on recycled paper | [small caps] ISBN [caps] 0-8040-0663-6 | [small caps] LIBRARY OF CONGRESS CATALOG CARD NUMBER: [caps] 74-18579 | map by Chuck Asay"; pp. v-vi, contents; pp. vii-x, Introduction; p. 1, divisional half-title: "Part One | The History"; p. 2, blank; pp. 3-86, text; p. 87, divisional half-title: "Part Two | The Myths"; p. 88, blank; pp. 89-283, text; p. 284, blank; p. 285, divisional half-title: "Appendix | Predicting Planetary Positions | Roberta S. Sklower | [four-line quotation] | *Marcus Aurelius Meditations*"; pp. 286-304, text of appendix; pp. 205-312, Notes; pp. 313-318, bibliography; pp. 319-326, index; pp. 327-332, blank.

226 SECTION A

ILLUSTRATIONS: In addition to the double-page map which serves as the background for the title, there are a number of other illustrations and tables within the text. Full-page tables appear on pages 219, 260, 267, 268 and 270; small tables set within the text appear on pages 84, 234, 239, 241, 245, 250, 292 and 295; full-page illustrations and figures appear on pages 91, 94, 231a, 231b, 261, 262, 266, 278, 291 and 303; small illustrations set within the text appear on pages 119, 120, 179, 180, 182, 220, 227, 230, 243, 249, 289 and 299.

BINDING: White cloth sides and blue cloth spine. Lettered on front with author's facsimile signature in blue, and with publisher's swallow device stamped in blind in lower right corner. Spine stamped in silver: "Waters | [reading vertically] [open face] MEXICO MYSTIQUE | The Coming Sixth World of Consciousness | [horizontally] SAGE BOOKS | [publisher's swallow device] | SWALLOW". White endpapers.

DUST JACKET (white paper): Front, spine and rear printed overall with a solid blue background, and with an illustration of a Columbian mask in orange and blue and green on the front. Lettered on front: "[white] Frank Waters | [white outlined in red] MEXICO | [white outlined in red] MYSTIQUE | [blue] The Coming | [blue] Sixth World | [blue] of Con= sciousness". Spine: "[white] Waters | [reading vertically] [white outlined in red] MEXICO MYSTIQUE | [blue] The Coming Sixth World of Consciousness | [horizontally] [following lines in white] SAGE BOOKS | [publisher's swallow device] | SWALLOW". Rear lettered in white: "Other Books by Frank Waters | [list of eight titles and blurbs] | [reading downward along inner margin] *Jacket Design: Donya Melanson As= sociates* [slash] *Graphics: Dorothy Kegel''*. The front flap is printed in blue and brown with a blurb for this book, which is carried over onto the rear flap, which is printed in blue only, and also contains a photograph of the author and a short notice of his other works.

Published at $10.00 on June 16, 1975; 5,000 copies were printed. Copyrighted May 20, 1975; deposited January 14, 1976.

REVIEWS: *Kirkus Reviews*, February 15, 1975 (p. 230); *Publisher's Weekly*, February 17, 1975 (p. 74); *Library Journal*, June 1, 1975 (p. 1144); *Chicago Tribune Book World*, August 24, 1975 (p. 3); *Choice*, October, 1975 (p. 1041).

COPIES: DLC (2 copies); NmU (d.j.); TAT (2 copies in d.j.).

NOTE: Four copies were specially bound in full blue calf, with the Swallow Press device stamped in blind on the front cover. One copy was given to Frank Waters (inscribed by Morton Weisman and dated June 25, 1975—copy in the possession of Frank Waters) and the others were kept by Morton Weisman, Durrett Wagner and Donna Ippolito, of the Swallow Press.

NOTE: On page 24 the text of line 20 was accidentally dropped and line 21 was repeated in its place. This error is also present in the second printing.

A21b   First edition, second printing   [1975]

Identical with A21a, except that the line *"Second Printing"* appears on the copyright page beneath the line reading "First Edition".

Cloth. Published at $15.00 in July, 1975; 5,000 copies were printed.

COPIES: TAT.

NOTE: The error on page 24 noted above is still present in this printing.

A22   MOUNTAIN DIALOGUES

Waters first mentioned his book of essays, *Mountain Dialogues*, to the Swallow Press, in a letter to Donna Ippolito on June 8, 1979 [ICIU]:

... My book of essays *Mountain Dialogues* is finished. It comprises pieces on such nebulous subjects as Silence, Movement, Spirits as well as some personal experiences. A highly personal and somewhat "esoteric" combination. The draft was sent to Joan Daves in January, but I've never received a word from her about it. . . .

Anxious to see the manuscript, Donna Ippolito finally wrote to Joan Daves, asking to have an opportunity to see the work. After being sent a copy of her letter, Waters wrote to Donna Ippolito in August, 1979 [ICIU; the letter omits the day of the month]:

Your letter to Joan Daves is excellent . . . I haven't heard from her any report on her submission of my book of essays, *Mountain Dialogues*, nor her reaction to your letter.

Hence, I'm taking the bull by the horns and sending you a copy of the mss. to evaluate while waiting for her eventual reply. If you think it acceptable, I'll let you work things out with her.

The book you will find to be a curious assortment of discussions on many diverse and nebulous subjects, approached from both highly personal and objective viewpoints. Still, I hope, they are all connected by one underlying theme. There may be redundant and repetitious parts, and editing of details, which need attention. But appraisal of whole I leave to your own judgment [sic].

Objectively, I think such a book will not be popular and easy to sell. It will undoubtedly appeal to a small minority of readers vitally interested in such subjects. Like my *Mexico Mystique* it may have limited sales, but arouse interest from many curious places in Europe and Asia. Is this enough to justify the expense of publication? If so, I think it will need a better distribution than in the past, which may now be provided by your merger with Ohio University Press.

In any case, look the mss. over and let me know, quite frankly, what you think of it.

Shortly after receiving word that the manuscript had been received in Chicago, Waters wrote again to Donna Ippolito, on September 10, 1979 [ICIU]:

Thanks for your note saying that the mss. arrived safely.
I have mailed today a letter to Joan Daves saying that I have decided she should let you publish it even though the house to which she has submitted it expresses some interest in it. My own belief is that they will reject it as not having the potential for large commercial sales. I feel that my books just aren't suitable for big houses that necessarily depend upon instant popularity and volume distribution, and are better off in a smaller house like Swallow which keeps them in print year after year, with small but steady sales. I hope this doesn't conflict too seriously with Joan Daves' efforts to do the best she can with the mss.
I am of course eager to hear your own reaction to what may appear to be a strange book.

Waters wrote a follow-up letter to Donna Ippolito on October 11, 1979 [ICIU]:

. . . The *Mountain Dialogues* thing should be straightened out soon. As I wrote you some time ago, I asked Joan Daves to turn over the book to you for handling. She wanted to wait until she had heard from Dutton, to whom she had submitted it. Their reaction came in with several suggested changes which I didn't like, so I have again written her to thank Dutton for their interest and to work things out with Mort. Unfortunately she has gone to Europe again for two weeks, so I haven't heard from her. But when she returns, the matter should be settled.
Dutton was favorably impressed with the middle of the book, but thought the first seven personal essays too loosely bound together, and the last ones disconnected from the rest. They suggested revising the book wholly on the theme of Indian concepts of unity, or on the political history of Indians as they have been affected by white influences. All this of course is far from my original plan of the book's form and content.
I'm letting you know Dutton's comments, to compare with your own first reaction which seems more perceptive. I was most pleased that you found the combination of the personal and speculative works out, and that the whole does have a coherence despite its leisurely pace.
Nevertheless, to make it more convincing to others like Dutton, I'm making numerous revisions. For one thing, I'm forthrightly dividing the text into three parts to emphasize its structure: Part I, chapters 1-7 presenting my own little world as it reflects the unity of the macrocosmic universe; Part II, chapters 8-13 containing the abstract principles of universal structure as viewed by previous ancient civilizations; and Part III, the nature and meaning of man as viewed by Eastern metaphysics and modern Western psychology. These Parts loosely correspond to the *I Ching* hexagram, whose first two lines denote Heaven, the last two earth, and the middle two lines man, who stands between them. There are of course transitional passages, additions and revisions in the text to make

230 Section A

all this simple to understand and easy to read. The book then should show a sound structure, rather than appearing to be a haphazard, rambling arrangement. The *Flying Saucers* piece I'm deleting; it really says nothing new that hasn't been said before. Replacing it will be a Postscript summing up my feeling of the eventual death and transformation of present Western Civilization as we now stand on the threshold of the greatest psychological change since the beginning of the Christian era. . . .

The matter was finally worked out with Joan Daves, and a contract for the book was drawn up between Waters and the Swallow Press on November 6, 1979. This contract called for an advance of $2,000.00 against royalties of 10% on the first 4,999 copies, 12½% on the next 5,000 copies, and 15% on all copies thereafter.

A22   MOUNTAIN DIALOGUES [1981]
A22   First edition, only printing

[rule] | MOUNTAIN | DIALOGUES | Frank Waters | SAGE BOOKS | [publisher's sagebrush device] | SWALLOW PRESS | Athens, Ohio [space] Chicago

9 × 6″. Perfectbound: 126 leaves. Pp. [i-x], [1-3] 4-10 [11] 12-24 [25] 26-34 [35] 36-48 [49] 50-55 [56] 57-63 [64] 65-71 [72] 73-79 [80-83] 84-94 [95] 96-107 [108] 109-117 [118] 119-135 [136] 137-148 [149] 150-160 [161-163] 164-193 [194] 195-207 [208] 209-228 [229] 230-237 [238-242]. Numbers printed in italic at outer margin at the foot of the page.

CONTENTS: p. i, half-title: "MOUNTAIN | DIALOGUES"; p. ii, "Books by Frank Waters | Fiction | [list of 10 titles] | Non-fiction | [list of 10 titles]"; p. iii, title; p. iv, copyright notice: "Copyright © 1981 by Frank Waters | All Rights Reserved | Printed in the United States of America | Sage [slash] Swallow Press Books | are published by | Ohio University Press | Athens, Ohio | Library of Congress Cataloging in Publication Data | [5 lines of catalog information]"; p. v, dedication: "[rule] | TO BARBARA"; p. vi, blank; p. vii, contents; p. viii, blank; pp. ix-x, Foreword; p. 1, divisional half-title: "[rule] | PART ONE"; p. 2, blank; pp. 3-79, text; p. 80, blank; p. 81, divisional half-title: "[rule] | PART TWO"; p. 82, blank; pp. 83-160, text; p. 161, divisional half-title: "[rule] | PART THREE"; p. 162, blank; pp. 163-237, text; pp. 238-242, blank.

The essays included in this volume are: "The Living Land"; "El Cuchillo Del Medio"; "The Sacred Mountain"; "Mountain and Plain"; "Silence"; "Water"; "Air"; "Spirits"; "The Sacred Mountains of the World"; "Ley Lines"; "Movement"; "The Hopi Prophecy"; "The Circle of the Law Belt"; "The Four-Fold Structure of Mind and Matter"; "Jung and Maharishi—On the Meaning of Man"; "Sierre Madre Outposts"; "The East is Red"; and "America: A Footnote". All were previously unpublished.

BINDING: Blue cloth, stamped in gilt on spine only: "[reading vertically] Waters: MOUNTAIN DIALOGUES | [horizontally] SAGE | [publisher's swallow device] | SWALLOW". Blue endpapers.

DUST JACKET (white paper): Front and spine printed overall with a photograph of Waters with mountains in the background, colored in orange at the top and shading to dark blue at the bottom. Lettered on front in white: "Frank Waters: | MOUNTAIN | DIALOGUES". Spine: "[reading vertically] Waters: MOUNTAIN DIALOGUES | [horizontally] [all three lines in white] SAGE | [publisher's swallow device] | SWALLOW". Rear contains a twelve line quotation from *Publisher's Weekly,* and a listing of seven other works by Frank Waters. The front flap carries a blurb for this book, which is carried over onto the rear flap, which also contains a short biographical notice of the author.

Published at $16.95 on September 1, 1981. Number of copies printed unknown. At the time of this writing, the copyright office had not formally entered the work for copyright.

REVIEWS: *Publisher's Weekly,* May 15, 1981 (p. 53); *Small Press Review,* October, 1981 (p. 8); *Library Journal,* January 1, 1982 (p. 95); *Choice,* January, 1982 (p. 645); *New Age,* January, 1982 (p. 66); *American West,* May, 1982 (p. 70).

COPIES: FW (d.j.); TAT (2 copies, d.j.).

SECTION AA.

Pamphlets by Frank Waters

AA1　　THE WHITE SANDS　　[1953?]

AA1a　First edition, only printing?

THE WHITE SANDS

Broadsheet, measuring 10 × 12".

Text printed in two columns beneath title as above. The first column reads: "[large 4-line capital 'T' set against small vignette landscape] THE WHITE SANDS NATIONAL MONUMENT, where | [29 lines of text] | tense heat. That indeed may be your first impression—a des= ert of great". Second column: "waves, often fifty feet high, hardened to an alabaster immobility. Yet | [18 lines of text] | America's strangest, whitest sands. | [facsimile signature of Frank Waters] | [caps] FRANK WATERS: [small caps] AUTHOR, NOVELIST AND BIOGRA= PHER: | WHO LIVES IN AND WRITES OF THE SOUTHWEST | [rule] | [small caps with a capital] PHOTOGRAPHIC DATA: Natural color photograph by Chuck Abbott; 5 × 7 Deardorff | View Camera; Goerz Dagor lens; Ektachrome film; exposure 1/10 second at f/14; about | 5 P.M. in June. The photographer endured a three-day wait for the wind to quiet and settle | the fine white dust in the air that at times obscured the sun. | [rule] | STANDARD OIL COMPANY OF TEXAS".

On the reverse of the sheet is a full-color photograph of the White Sands National Monument by Chuck Abbott.

Published as a promotional give-away by the Standard Oil Company of Texas, a division of the Chevron Company. Exact date of publication unknown, but most likely issued sometime around 1953.

236 SECTION AA

The description given above is taken from a xerox of the only located copy in the files of the Chevron Company, San Francisco, California.

NOTE: In a letter to me on October 1, 1979, Eleanor Burton of the Chevron Company reported that the broadsheet was issued in the early 1950's, but that company records contain no specific information as to publication. I have supplied the date of 1953 based on a reference in the text to the area as "until twenty years ago a comparatively unknown desert valley." The White Sands National Monument was created in 1933.

In the same letter, Eleanor Burton informed me that while no record as to the number of copies printed exists, she believed the printing to be in the area of 1,000,000 copies.

AA1b   Second edition, only printing? [1958?]

[all in gray] THE WHITE SANDS . . . | *"A Landscape spectral as the surface of the moon"*

Broadsheet, measuring 10 × 12".

Printed in gray in three columns. The first column reads: "HOW TO COLLECT | A FULL SET OF | Southwestern Scenic Prints | [34 lines of text] | [Chevron Company emblem] | We Take Better Care of Your Car | CHEVRON DEALERS | STANDARD STATIONS, INC. | This series of scenes is available only in New | Mexico and West Texas. We regret mail requests | cannot be filled.". The second and third columns are separated from the first column by a vertical rule, and are printed beneath the title listed above. The second column reads: "[2-line capital 'T'] The White Sands National Monument, | [29 lines of text] | The ripples spread. The dunes inch forward.". The third column reads: "Geologic ages ago this gypsum began washing | [23 lines of text] | shepherd, to America's strangest, whitest sands. | [facsimile signature of Frank Waters] | FRANK WATERS: Author, novelist and biographer | *To visit White Sands National Monument, follow U. S. Highway | 70 south from Alamogordo, N. M. or north from Las Cruces.*".

Reverse identical with AA1a.

Published as a promotional give-away by the Chevron Company, probably around 1958?

COPIES: TAT.

NOTE: The text of this edition has been cut down by editing, and several changes were made within the text to reflect the passage of time. In the first paragraph of the text, the line reading "in what was until twenty years ago a comparatively unknown desert valley," in the first edition, has been changed to "until about 25 years ago" in this edition. Also, the number of yearly visitors to the park is given in the first edition as 200,000; this has been changed in this edition to read "350,000."

Based upon these changes in the text, it would seem that this edition was probably brought out some five years after the first edition—1958. Chevron Company records produced no information regarding this edition; in fact, no copy of this edition could be located by the company. The only located copy is in my own collection.

AA2 CONTINENTAL NUCLEAR TESTS [1953]

[cover title] UNITED STATES | ATOMIC ENERGY COMMIS= SION—DEPARTMENT OF DEFENSE | Test Information Office | 1235 South Main Street | Las Vegas, Nevada | BACKGROUND IN= FORMATION | on | CONTINENTAL NUCLEAR TESTS | NE= VADA PROVING GROUNDS | and | MILITARY INSTALLATIONS | THE SPRING 1953 SERIES

$10^{13}/_{16} \times 8^{7}/_{16}''$. 37 leaves, printed on rectos only. The first two leaves are unnumbered and the balance of the leaves are numbered 1-35.

CONTENTS: First two unnumbered leaves consist of a table of contents; leaf 1, Foreword; leaf 2, map of the site area; leaf 3, Summary of past continental detonations; leaves 4-8, text, headed on leaf 4: "THE CONTINENTAL TEST PROGRAM"; leaves 9-35, text, headed on leaf 9: "THE SPRING 1953 TEST SERIES".

BINDING: Blue paper wrappers with brown cloth-tape spine, side-stapled. Title on front as above.

238   SECTION AA

Published in 1953; number of copies printed unknown.

COPIES: NmU.

NOTE: This brochure is not signed by Frank Waters. It was prepared as background information for newsmen covering the 1953 thermonuclear tests. At the time he wrote this, Waters was Information Director for the Los Alamos Scientific Laboratory, the scientific institution responsible for the tests.

AA3 LOS ALAMOS SCIENTIFIC LABORATORY [1955]

[in white, within a black rectangular panel] LOS ALAMOS | [within single rules] SCIENTIFIC LABORATORY | [in white within a black panel] OF THE | [within a gray panel] UNIVERSITY OF CALIFOR= NIA | [black and white drawing of buildings at Los Alamos] | [at lower left and printed against background of illustration noted above] Los Alamos, New Mexico

A vertical gray rule passes through all the panels noted above and forms the extreme right edge of the third panel from the top.

11 × 8½". [1^{20}]: 20 leaves. Pp. [1-4] 5-7 [8] 9-40.

CONTENTS: p. 1, title; p. 2, facsimile of citation from President Eisenhower, dated July 8, 1954; p. 3, preface [unsigned]; p. 4, illustrations; pp. 5-40, text.

ILLUSTRATIONS: The work is profusely illustrated with black and white photographs; pages 4, 8 and 12 contain only photographs without text.

BINDING: Green paper wrappers, stapled. Front and rear have green and black aerial photograph of the site of Los Alamos. Lettered on front: "[in white within a black rectangular panel] LOS ALAMOS | [within a white rectangular panel] SCIENTIFIC LABORATORY | [in green within a black panel] OF THE | [within a green rectangular panel] UNIVERSITY OF CALIFORNIA | [at lower left and printed in green within a black panel] Los Alamos, New Mexixo". A vertical rule, in white, passes through the panels, as on the title. The inner front wrapper contains a map of the area; the inner rear wrapper contains a map of Los Alamos.

Published in 1955; number of copies printed unknown.

COPIES: NmU; FW.

NOTE: This short history of Los Alamos was written by Frank Waters as background material for a news conference held at Los Alamos on July 16-17, 1955. Waters remembers that several hundred copies were printed, and such copies as were not handed out at the news conference were mailed out to prospective employees and students of the laboratory.

AA4 LOS ALAMOS LABORATORY OPEN HOUSE [1955]

[cover title] [script] Los Alamos Scientific Laboratory | [script] of the | [script] University of California | [script] Open House | JULY 16-17, 1955

8 7/16 × 5 5/8". [1¹⁰]: 10 leaves. Pp. [1] 2-9 [10-11] 12-16 [17-20].

CONTENTS: p. 1, "WELCOME | [6 paragraphs] | N. E. BRADBURY | Director''; pp. 2-9, text; pp. 10-11, double-page map, labelled: "MAP OF TECH AREA ROADS"; pp. 12-15, text; p. 16, blank except for heading at top: "NOTES"; pp. 17-20, blank.

ILLUSTRATIONS: Map as noted above.

BINDING: Stiff white paper wrappers, stapled, with title on front as above. Rear contains an organization chart of the laboratory, headed at top: "ORGANIZATION CHART". Inner wrappers blank.

Issued on July 16, 1955; numbers of copies printed unknown.

240   Section AA

Copies: NmU.

Note: This pamphlet was written by Frank Waters to be used by newsmen attending the news conference.

AA5   THE SKETCHES OF LEON GASPARD   [1962]

[cover title] [detail from a Gaspard painting of three Indian women] | [script] The Sketches of | [script] Leon Gaspard | *By* | FRANK WA゠TERS | *Published by the Southwest Museum,* | *Los Angeles, California.*

9 × 6¹⁄₁₆″. [1⁸]: 8 leaves. Pp. [1-3] 4-16. Numbers spelled out in roman capitals at the bottom of the page at the outer margin of the type page.

Contents: p. 1, cover title; p. 2, "[illustration of a painting of Leon Gaspard] | *Portrait of Leon Gaspard by* | *Daniel MacMorris, 1951.*"; pp. 3-16, text, with copyright notice at the foot of page 3: "[within parentheses] *Copyright 1962 by Southwest Museum*".

Illustrations: All illustrations are in black and white, and unless otherwise noted are of Gaspard's paintings:
   p. 1:   cover illustration
   p. 2:   portrait of Gaspard, noted above
   p. 5:   "Juanita of Taos, 1919"
   p. 7:   "Taos Pueblo, 1919"
   pp. 8-9:   "Santo Domingo Corn Dance, 1917"
   p. 10:   "Santa Domingo, 1919"
   p. 12:   "Cochiti, 1919"
   p. 14:   "Autumn in Taos, 1919"
   p. 16:   photograph of Gaspard by Mildred Talbert

Paper: Glazed paper.

Binding: White glazed paper self-wrappers, with front containing title as described above, and with rear as page 16, described above. Stapled with two staples.

Published at $.25 in 1962; number of copies printed unknown. A search undertaken by the Registrar of Copyrights failed to find any evidence that this work was ever formally copyrighted.

COPIES: NmU, TAT.

NOTE: According to the Southwest Museum, there was only one printing of this pamphlet, copies of which could still be obtained from the Museum (at $.50) in 1980.

NOTE: Waters wrote this short essay for the Museum while he was preparing his biography of Leon Gaspard (see A18).

AA6 MYSTICISM AND WITCHCRAFT [1966]

Third annual writer in residence lecture sponsored by the fine arts series | Mysticism and Witchcraft by Frank Waters | colorado state university, ft. collins, colorado, 1966

9 × 8⅜". [1¹²]: 12 leaves. Pp. [3-7] 8-13 [14] 15-22 [23-26] = 24.

CONTENTS: p. 3, seal of the university printed in black and paper color within a square black panel; p. 4, full-page photograph of the author; p. 5, title; p. 6, copyright notice: "*© copyright by Colorado State Univer= sity 1966 | all rights reserved | annual writer in residence lecture, no. 3 18-1-66 | library of congress catalog number: 65-65320*"; pp. 7-22, text, printed entirely in italic; p. 23, illustration in black; p. 24, 7-line notice of the author, printed in italic, signed "MB", and with a drawing in black at the bottom; p. 25, "*Fine arts series committee 1965-1966* | [18 lines printed in three columns, in italic] | *published by the fine arts series, with the cooperation of the CSU | libraries and the CSU develop= ment fund.*"; p. 26, seal of the university as on p. 3.

PAPER: This pamphlet was printed on three different colors of wove paper. Leaves 1 and 12 are of yellow-gold paper; leaves 2 and 11 are of red-brown paper; and leaves 3 through 10 are of tan paper.

ILLUSTRATIONS: A full-page photograph of the author appears on page 4; a full-page drawing in black appears on page 23; small drawings in black appear within the text on pages 7, 9, 14 and 24.

BINDING: White glazed paper wrappers, stapled with two staples. The front wrapper contains a large and thick swastika in red-brown on which is superimposed a drawing, in black, of a serpent swallowing its tail. Lettered on front: *"Third annual writer in residence lecture spon= sored by the fine arts series | Mysticism and Witchcraft by Frank Wa= ters"*. Rear: "[at bottom left] *Design ▪ John J. Sorbie"*. The inner wrappers are blank and unglazed.

Published at $1.50 in 1966; 1,000 copies were printed. Copyrighted June 16, 1966; deposited July 11, 1966.

COPIES: NmU; TAT.

NOTE: This work reprints the text of a lecture delivered by Waters at Colorado State University on January 18, 1966. It was incorporated into the author's *Pumpkin Seed Point* (see A18), and later published in *South Dakota Review* (see C65).

AA7 THE ARTS IN NEW MEXICO [1966]

THE ARTS IN NEW MEXICO | First Annual Report | New Mexico Arts Commission

11⅛ × 8 9/16″. [1¹⁸]: 18 leaves. Pp. [1-2] 3 [4] 5-6 [7-8] 9-11 [12] 13-14 [15-16] 17-19 [20] 21 [22] 23 [24] 25-26 [27-28] 29 [30] 31 [32-33] 34-35 [36].

CONTENTS: p. 1, title; p. 2, full-page illustration; p. 3, facsimile of a letter of commendation from Governor Jack M. Campbell, dated November 1, 1966, with an inset photograph of the governor; p. 4, full-page illustration; pp. 5-34, text; p. 35, small illustration of a painting by Andrew Dasburg; p. 36, blank.

ILLUSTRATIONS: This booklet contains numerous photographic illustrations, largely depicting works sponsored or supported by the commission. Full-page illustrations appear on pages: 2, 4, 7, 8, 12, 15, 16, 20, 22, 24, 27, 28, 30, 32 and 33. Smaller illustrations appear on pages: 3, 5, 6, 9, 10, 13, 14, 17, 18, 21, 23, 25, 26 and 35.

PAPER: Tan colored wove paper.

BINDING: Tan wrappers, stapled. In the lower right corner of the front cover appears the ensignia of the commission, consisting of a solid orange sun with 16 rays, also in orange, radiating in groups of four in the four principal directions. The interior of the sun contains the monogram "NMAC", around which is printed in circular fashion: "[at the top] [double wavy-rules] the new mexico [double wavy-rules] | [at bottom] arts commission". The rear is blank. The inner front wrapper contains a fancy design based on an Indian motif, printed in orange, and running from the top to the bottom along the inner margin; to the left of this design appear two columns of print, containing a list of the contents and a list of the photographic credits. The inner rear wrapper contains the same design as on the inner front wrapper, printed along the inner margin.

Published in November (?) 1966; number of copies printed unknown.

COPIES: TAT.

NOTE: The entire contents of this report were written by Frank Waters. Waters had been appointed to the commission at the time of its creation by the New Mexico Legislature, on March 15, 1965. He served on the commission for one year in the capacity of its second vice-chairman, and the following year as its director.

AA8   PRELUDE TO CHANGE   [1981]

UNIVERSITY OF NEVADA, LAS VEGAS | EIGHTEENTH AN= NUAL COMMENCEMENT | May 23, 1981 | Commencement Address | PRELUDE TO CHANGE | by | Frank Waters | Distributed by | The College of Arts | and Letters

244 SECTION AA

11 × 8½". 3 leaves. Pp. [i], [1] 2-5.

CONTENTS: p. i, title; pp. 1-5, text.

BINDING: Plain blue paper front wrapper only, stapled at upper left.

Distributed by the University of Nevada, Las Vegas, after the commencement on May 23, 1981; 500 copies were printed.

COPIES: TAT (2 copies).

NOTE: Reprinted in an edited version in *Taos Rio Grande Magazine,* Summer, 1981 (see C69). A version transcribed from a tape recording of the actual address, which differs slightly, was printed in Charles L. Adams' article "Frank Waters' 'Prelude to Change' ", in the *Nevada Historical Society Quarterly,* Fall, 1981 (see E25).

SECTION B.

Contributions by Waters to books by others

NO DUDES,
B1   FEW WOMEN   [1951]

[double-page title] [left hand page] Foreword by [right hand page] Frank Waters | [thick rule, ascending from left to right] | [left hand page] Life with a | NAVAHO RANGE RIDER | [right hand page] NO DUDES | FEW WOMEN | [left hand page] [thick rule, ascending from left to right, with fancy design extending downward from bottom] | BY ELIZA [right hand page] BETH WARD

7¾ × 5⅛". [1-15⁸ 16¹²]: 132 leaves. Pp. [i-vi] vii-xi [xii], 1-251 [252]. Pages vi, xii and 252 are blank.

COPYRIGHT PAGE: "Copyright 1951, by | THE UNIVERSITY OF NEW MEXICO PRESS | ALBUQUERQUE | All Rights Reserved".

BINDING: Red-brown cloth, lettered on spine only: "[reading vertically at a 45 degree angle] WARD | [design] | [reading vertically] NO DUDES | FEW WOMEN | [design] | [reading vertically at a 45 degree angle] The University | of New Mexico | PRESS". White endpapers.

DUST JACKET (white paper): Front, spine and rear printed overall in black. Front and spine have a white panel ascending from left to right, outlined at top and bottom by fancy designs in brown and white. Lettered on front: "[white] Foreword by Frank Waters | [within white panel and ascending from left to right] NO DUDES | FEW WOMEN | BY ELIZABETH WARD | [below panel, at bottom] [white] Life with a | [white] NAVAHO RANGE RIDER". Spine: "[reading vertically] [white] ELIZABETH | [white] WARD | [within the white panel] NO DUDES | FEW WOMEN | [outside panel, near bottom] [white] The

University | [white] of New Mexico | [white] P R E S S". Rear has two parallelogram panels in white, angled slightly upwards toward the spine; both outlined in brown and connected by a fancy design in brown and white. Lettered on rear: "[within upper panel] MASKED GODS | by FRANK WATERS | [six-line quotation from the *Denver Post*, with price] | [within lower panel] HOPI KACHINA DOLLS | by HAROLD COLTON | [six-line quotation by Oliver LaFarge, with price]". Front flap carries blurb for this book; rear flap carries black and white photograph of the author and a biographical notice about her, with publisher's imprint at the bottom.

Published at $4.50 in 1951; 2,500 copies were printed.

A Foreword by Frank Waters appears on pages vii-viii.

COPIES: TAT (d.j.).

NOTE: Although there is no mention in the published book, Frank Waters did extensive editorial work on the manuscript of this work prior to publication. After receiving the manuscript, the University of New Mexico Press sent it to Waters for a reader's report. His report was essentially favorable, but did suggest several areas which would require revision. The Press worked out an arrangement with Waters and Mrs. Ward whereby the manuscript would be accepted for publication, and for a fee of $150.00, paid by the Press, Waters would undertake to edit and revise the work.
On March 12, 1951, Waters wrote to Elizabeth Ward:

> You have got yourself in a fix, agreeing to let me edit your book for publication; and I have got myself in one by agreeing to edit it. I am not wholly jocular, having had ten books edited for me.
> One of them, *The Colorado* in the "Rivers of America Series", I remember well. After working several years on it, I went to New York to go over the editing job on it done by that excellent writer, the late Hervey Allen. Starting in on the first page, he suggested changes in punctuation, wording, content and interpretation, so precise and minute that I left in a great huff for California. At this safe distance, I later went over in detail all the suggested changes. Some of them I did not agree with, but I recognized how improvements could be made in other ways. Revising the MS with some objectiveness, I realized what a pertinent, helpful job he had done for me, and have always had a warm feeling for him since.
> In starting to edit your own book, I want you to feel that I appreciate your own writer's similar reluctance to having your work tampered with. But I also

want you to feel that my job, as your editor, is to clarify and accent your material for the average reader, and to eliminate as far as possible all grounds for criticism from later critics and reviewers. I do not want to alter a single viewpoint you have expressed, nor your own style. I want only to do a "selling" job on it that will make your work more easily and widely read.

I don't know whether Mr. Mann sent you my original report on it, recommending its publication. But from a perusal of the MS I don't believe it will require much revision.

I'll write you as I get into it. Meanwhile I wish you would start thinking of a better title, and send me a half dozen suggestions. *No Dudes, Few Women* is neither arresting, appealing, nor indicative of the subject matter. *My Neighbor, The Navaho* and *My Friend, The Navaho* have been suggested. But I think a better one can be found.

Throughout the book you have used the "j" in Navaho. The Navaho Tribal Council has objected to this spelling on the grounds that so many Whites call the People "Joes". They prefer the "h"—Navaho. Deferring to their wishes I changed the spelling throughout my last book, *Masked Gods—Pueblo and Navaho Ceremonialism.* Do you agree to a change in yours?

Also may I ask what system you adhere to in the spelling of all Navaho words? As *hogahn* vs. *hogan?* Do you have a dictionary or ethnological guide?

With your permission I would also like to eliminate much of your preponderant use of the semi-colon which makes for constant long involved sentences, which in turn slow the reading. This is good for descriptive passages. But for narrative action, short sentences are better. The change in pace in style should be synonymous with the change in pace in the narrative.

I haven't mentioned how much I enjoyed your book, how excellent I think it is. But that should go without saying.

Mrs. Ward wrote back to Waters on March 19, 1951, agreeing to the suggested changes in Navaho spelling and the use of the semi-colons, and agreeing to try to come up with a new title. Waters wrote back to Mrs. Ward on this same date with a two-page list of specific suggestions and questions, adding: "Your book on second reading seems better than ever, and I have great hopes for the warm and wide reception it deserves."

After finally working out all the changes with Mrs. Ward, Waters sent the manuscript on to E. B. Mann at the University of New Mexico Press on April 9, 1951. On the same day he wrote to Mann about the book:

I have finally finished editing the Elizabeth Ward ms. and am returning it to you today.

As you will note by the ms. markings, it has given me a real workout. The constant, long, involved sentences with their repetitious use of semi-colons and dashes was worse than I thought. I have corrected and revised the style freely, after having secured her permission.

The attached copies of letters I sent Mrs. Ward indicate more serious errors of historical reference, ethnology etc. I have also secured her permission to correct all these.

With reference to your own and Jim Threlkeld's excellent suggestions, I shortened the first chapter by eliminating 4 pages, so as to get into the main subject-matter of the narrative as quickly as possible; deleted all but a few references to antecedent material; marked out most of the "dusky" and "dark-faced" references. I left in, however, the short incident of the treatment of drunken Indians in Gallup, on the grounds that 1) it was a specific eye-witness incident germane to the subject-matter of the chapter and 2) it happened nearly 20 years ago, which should remove any onus from present conditions if they have changed. His suggestion of the author's inclusion of the reception by Navahos of gifts of food and clothing was not applicable to the present book, which ends about 1941, whereas the flood of Federal and public gifts did not come until 1946-1947 after the Wards had left the Reservation.

The only two questions remaining are the final selection of a title, and the author's use of phonetic spelling of Navaho words and expressions. After some discussion with her, I have thought it best to adhere to the most ethnologically popular spelling of important Navaho deities, but to permit her use of her own phonetic spelling of short dialogue expressions, which would be difficult, if not impossible, to duplicate in the few existent Navaho dictionaries and grammars. The alternate, if you think best, would be to ask Mrs. Ward to stop by St. Michael's Mission and check with Father Bernard Haile, the best present-day authority. But personally I don't think this necessary; it is a loose, charming, informal book.

Mrs. Ward is now back home in San Bernadino, but writes that she would be glad to come to Albuquerque and go over the final corrections if necessary. I am inclined to believe that, although the ms. seems horribly marked, it does not need retyping.

It reads well; the styling is concise and clear; no changes have been made that the author is not in agreement with; and I will be glad to meet her in Albuquerque if she would like to discuss the ms.

Mann wrote to Waters on April 26, 1951, that work on the manuscript was going well, and that they were waiting for the foreword which Waters promised to supply for the book. On May 10, 1951, Mann wrote to Waters telling him that they had received the foreword, which they thought was excellent. He also told Waters that the Press had just about decided to keep the original title, with a blurb stressing the Navaho angle. Waters responded to this in a letter to Mann, dated May 23, 1951:

I don't mean to be stubborn. Just honest. *No Dudes, Few Women* I don't like yet. In the first place it's a negative approach rather than a positive. In the second, its connotation is that of an Arizona Ranch background instead of the Navaho Reservation.

Navaho Range Rider, Riding Navaho Trails, Turquoise Trail, etc. don't hit the button either. It's a tough one.

As a last suggestion, I'd offer *Horse Leader to the Navahos,* and start right off with sentence No. 1:

"He was really a Range Rider, but the Navahos called him *Kleenk-lohse* which meant "Horse Leader", because a Range Rider was almost always seen riding one horse and leading another. This is his story, and only indirectly mine". . . .

Then pick up paragraph 1 as is. And delete the above sentence or equivalent from the second or third chapter when the narrator enters the reservation.

The advantage is a catchy title phrase that has never been used before; that is an authentic Navaho phrase with an odd flavor; and that is explained in the first sentence in the book, setting the tone of the whole, to carry the reader through the antecedent material—a sound narrative construction.

Roll it around a bit and see how it catches the tongue and ear—and credit me with a last try in any event.

Mann responded on May 31, 1951, saying that although Waters' suggestion was not well received at first, after a while it did seem the best title. However, Mrs. Ward strongly objected to it. And although she promised to come up with another title, Mann expressed his feeling that they would probably end up with the original title, which they did.

B2 THE SPORTSMAN'S HANDBOOK [1964]

[large gray vertical band descending from top of page] | [immediately beneath band: publisher's device of an oval containing a lighthouse against a background of water and sky, in black, gray and white, on top of which is printed in small caps with a capital, and with the capitals heavily shaded in black: "PORTS O CALL"] | THE SPORTSMAN'S HANDBOOK | [another gray vertical band descending towards the bottom of the page] | [to the right of the band] WORLD GUIDE TO THE PLEASURE WORLD | [at bottom and to the right of the band] SPORTSMAN'S HANDBOOK, INC. [slash] NEW YORK AND CAMBRIDGE | Mailing Address: P. O. Box 224, Cambridge, Mass. 02138

$9^{15}/_{16} \times 7^{15}/_{16}''$. [1-14^{18}]: 252 leaves. 504 pp., irregularly paginated on rectos only.

252   SECTION B

COPYRIGHT PAGE: "Copyright © MCMLXIV [balance of line printed in a larger type-face in small caps with capitals] BY SPORTSMAN'S HANDBOOK, INC. | All rights reserved including the right to reproduce this book | or parts thereof in any form | [12 lines of credits for cover and endpaper photographs, printed in roman and italic] | *Designed by Harold Franklin* | FIRST PRINTING | MANUFACTURED IN THE UNITED STATES OF AMERICA".

BINDING: Blue paper over boards in imitation of cloth. Front contains a color photograph of "Big Game Fishing, Bay of Plenty, New Zealand," and is lettered: "[small caps] WORLD GUIDE TO THE PLEASURE WORLD [caps] THE | SPORTSMAN'S | HANDBOOK". Spine: "THE | [reading vertically] SPORTSMAN'S HANDBOOK | [horizontally] WORLD | GUIDE | TO THE | PLEASURE | WORLD | SPORTSMAN'S | HANDBOOK | INCORPORATED". Rear contains three color photographs of golfing, fishing and skiing. Front and rear endpapers of cream-colored paper, with sepai photograph on the face of the front endpapers of grand prix racing at Watkins Glen, New York; and with sepai photograph on the face of the rear endpapers of a flock of birds on the Mississippi Flyway.

No dust jacket was issued.

Published price unknown. Published in 1964; number of copies printed unknown.

"Taos Pueblo Indian Races" by Frank Waters appears on page 180. Curiously, no credit is given to Waters in the table of contributors.

COPIES: FW; Eastern New Mexico University Library.

NOTE: This work is not listed in *Books in Print* for 1963, 1964 or 1965; nor is it recorded in the *Cumulative Book Index* for 1964. The copy in the library of Eastern New Mexico University has the words "Compliments of Hertz" at the top of the front cover, and it may be that this book was issued on a subscription basis of some sort.

NOTE: The book was edited by Houston Branch (see A7 and A11), and it was Branch who asked Waters to supply the article on the Taos races for inclusion in the work.

B3   THE ARAPAHO WAY   [1966]

The Arapaho Way | A [small caps with a capital] MEMOIR | [small caps] OF AN [small caps with a capital] INDIAN BOYHOOD | *by* | *Althea Bass* | Introduction by Frank Waters | Illustrations by Carl Sweezy | [publisher's device of a sea-creature within an oval] | *Clarkson N. Pot= ter, Inc.* [slash] *Publisher* | NEW YORK

$8^{15}/_{16}$ × $5^{7}/_{8}$". [1-6⁸]: 48 leaves; gatherings of 4 leaves of illustrations have been wrapped-around signatures 2 and 4, making a total of 8 leaves of illustrations. Pp. [i-vii] viii-x [xi-xiv] xv-xvi [1] 2-7 [8] 9-16 [17] 18-25 [26] 27-37 [38] 39-48 [49] 50-55 [56] 57-67 [68] 69-76 [77] 78 [79] 80. Page xii is blank.

COPYRIGHT PAGE: *"For my son, John* | [small caps] COPYRIGHT © [caps] 1966, [small caps] BY ALTHEA BASS | [small caps] LIBRARY OF CONGRESS CATALOG CARD NUMBER: [caps] 66-17885 | ALL RIGHTS RESERVED | PRINTED IN THE UNITED STATES OF AMERICA | FIRST EDITION".

BINDING: Light brown cloth, lettered on spine only: "[reading vertically] THE [next two words in slightly larger type] ARAPAHO WAY [space] Althea Bass [space] *Clarkson* | *N. Potter*". White endpapers.

DUST JACKET (white paper): Front and spine printed overall in brown. Lettered on front: "[all within a large white panel] THE | ARAPAHO | WAY | A Memoir of an Indian Boyhood | Althea Bass | [drawing by Sweezy of an Indian on a horse killing a buffalo, in black, red, yellow, brown and gray] | INTRODUCTION BY FRANK WATERS | 22 Il= lustrations in full color by CARL SWEEZY". Spine: "[reading vertically] THE [next two words in slightly larger type face] ARAPAHO WAY [space] Althea Bass [space] *Clarkson N. Potter*". Rear contains grayish panel with an illustration by Sweezy of the Petote ceremony, in red, black, green, blue, yellow and brown. Front flap and rear flap carry a blurb for this book, with a notice of Althea Bass on the bottom of the rear flap.

Published at $5.95 on October 15, 1966; number of copies printed unknown.

An Introduction by Frank Waters appears on pages xiii, xv-xvi.

COPIES: TAT (d.j.).

NOTE: At least one copy was specially bound by the publisher in half brown morocco and marbled boards and inscribed by Clarkson N. Potter to Waters at Christmas, 1966. Presumably there were others so bound, certainly one for Althea Bass. The copy inscribed to Frank Waters is currently in his private collection.

B4 SUPPRESSED MURDER OF WYATT EARP [1967]

Suppressed | Murder of | Wyatt Earp | By | Glenn G. Boyer | [imprint set to the right of publisher's device consisting of three books leaning against a cactus plant] *The Naylor Company* | *Book Publishers of the Southwest* | San Antonio, Texas

$8\frac{3}{16} \times 5\frac{3}{4}$". [$1^{10}$ 2-9^{8} 10^{4}]: 78 leaves; three inserted plates. Pp. [i-vi] vii-ix [x] xi [xii] xiii-xix [xx], 1-11 [12] 13-43 [44] 45-59 [60] 61-67 [68] 69-125 [126] 127-135 [136]. Pages vi, x, xii, xx, 12, 44, 60, 68, 126 and 136 are blank.

COPYRIGHT PAGE: "Copyright ©, 1967 by THE NAYLOR COM= PANY | [4-line notice concerning rights of reproduction] | Library of Congress Catalog Card No. 67-12279 | ALL RIGHTS RESERVED | Printed in the United States of America".

BINDING: Black cloth. Lettered on front in white: "SUPPRESSED | MURDER OF | WYATT EARP". Spine lettered in white: "BOYER | [reading vertically] SUPPRESSED MURDER OF WYATT EARP | [horizontally] NAYLOR". White endpapers.

DUST JACKET (white paper): Front and spine printed overall with an illustration, against a brown and peach-color background, of two portraits in antique frames, with a six-gun and two bullets in the foreground, printed in brown, black, and peach-color; signed in the lower right corner of the front: "[swash capitals] DONALD M. YENA". Lettered on front: "SUPPRESSED | MURDER OF | WYATT EARP | *GLENN G. BOYER*". Spine: "BOYER | [reading vertically] SUP= PRESSED MURDER OF WYATT EARP | [horizontally] NAYLOR".

Rear contains black and white photograph of the author and an eight-line biographical notice of the author. The front and rear flaps contain a blurb for the book.

Published at $3.95 in 1967; number of copies printed unknown.

The author interviewed Frank Waters in the process of writing his book and there are numerous references to Waters throughout the text. On page 105 an excerpt is quoted from a letter Waters wrote Boyer on May 5, 1965; on page 106 Boyer quotes Waters from his interview; and on page 124, an excerpt is quoted from a letter from Waters to Mrs. Charles A. Colyn dated March 10, 1959. A photograph of Waters is included among the illustrations.

COPIES: TAT (d.j.).

B5   MICHIO TAKAYAMA   [1969]

[Cover title] [facsimile autograph] Michio Takayama

7⁵⁄₁₆ × 8½". [1⁴]: 4 leaves. 8 unnumbered pages.

BINDING: Orange paper wrappers, with title as above on front.

Issued in March, 1969, for an exhibition of the works of Michio Takayama, held at the Palm Springs Desert Museum, Palm Springs, California, from March 11, 1969 to March 30, 1969. Number of copies printed unknown.

"Michio Takayama" by Frank Waters appears on page 4, printed in two columns.

COPIES: FW.

NOTE: A reprint of this brochure was produced by Mr. Takayama himself, and consists of 2 leaves only, bound in white glazed paper wrappers, with facsimile autograph of Takayama on front in brown. In this printing, the date of which is unknown, the appreciation by Waters appears on page 2. This reprint measures 7½ × 8½".

B6   OO-OÓNAH ART   [1970]

[double-page title] [right hand page] BY THE TAOS PUEBLO IN= DIAN SCHOOL'S | 7th-8th GRADE PUPILS OF '67-'68 | Edited by CONSTANTINE AIELLO | [across both pages, with the page break coming in the middle of the fourth 'o' just before the accent mark] [calligraphic letters with very large initial 'o'] Oo-oónah Art | [right-hand page] TAOS INDIAN FOR 'CHILD'

8¼ × 11". [1⁸ 2¹² 3⁸]: 28 leaves. Pp. [i-xii], [1] 2-40 [41-44]. Pages iii, viii, xi, 1, 41 and 44 are blank.

COPYRIGHT PAGE: "ALL PROCEEDS FROM THIS BOOK WILL GO INTO THE TAOS PUEBLO INDIAN GOVERNOR'S | OFFICE FUND TO BE USED FOR THE HEALTH AND WELFARE OF THE TRIBE'S CHILDREN. | Copyright © 1970 by the TAOS PUEBLO GOVERNOR'S OFFICE | PUBLISHED BY THE TAOS PUEBLO GOVERNOR'S OFFICE, BOX 258, TAOS, NEW MEX= ICO 87571".

COLOPHON (page 40): *"Color separations by* | WARNER COLOR LABORATORIES | Los Angeles, California | *Paper by* | TREASURE PRODUCTS, INC. | Billings, Montana | *Type setting by* | COMPOSI= TION SERVICE CENTER | Salt Lake City, Utah | *Printing by* | PRESS PUBLISHING COMPANY | Provo, Utah | *Binding by* | MOUNTAIN STATES BINDING | SALT LAKE CITY, UTAH | *Printed in the U. S. A.".*

SPECIAL CONTENTS: p. ii: "Special Collector's Edition | *copy no.* ———— | presented to | ————".

Tipped onto page i is a reproduction of Andrew Dasburg's "Spring Orchard", signed by the artist. Tipped onto the verso of the front free endpaper is a leaf of paper with a quotation from Frank Waters, signed by him at the bottom: *"Life is like the still surface of a deep blue lake into which a stone is cast. Who knows how far, on what | shores the ripples spread? But the stone, having been cast, has done its work. Let it sink, unnoticed and | forgotten, into the blue, troubled depths. Until one day when the turmoil has ceased men may gaze into the | placid face of the water and see there, still bright and shining, the stone lying at the bottom like a gleaming | star......* | [Water's holograph signature]".

BINDING: White cloth. Front printed overall with detail from "Fish Blowing Bubbles" by Robert Concha (p. 32 in the book), in blue, green, orange, brown and black. Lettered on front: "[title in calligraphic letters in white outlined in black] O | o | [white dot outlined in black] | o | ó | n | a | h | Art | [black] INTRODUCTION BY [large calligraphic letters] Frank Waters". Spine: "[reading vertically] OO-OONAH ART [large black dot] Aiello, ed.". Rear: "[black and white photograph of the class] | [immediately beneath photograph] Photo by Regina Tatum Cooke | "They make one say of our innumerable art theories, schools and techniques, | 'What's the use?'"—Andrew Dasburg | Andrew Dasburg (seated) shares a classroom joke with Polly Concha, Luis | Archuleta, Geraldine Concha, Gary Lujan, Joseph Concha, Clifford Lujan, and | their teacher, Stan Aiello.". White endpapers, printed on the face of both the front and rear endpapers with an illustration of two deer, in blue, yellow, green, brown and gray.

Published at $100.00 in 1970; according to an article by Charlotte Trego, in *Empire Magazine,* February 4, 1973, 1,200 copies were printed.

An Introduction by Frank Waters appears on pages ix-x, printed in double column.

COPIES: FW; Peter J. Powell, Chicago, Illinois.

NOTE: It would seem that not all of the copies printed were sold at $100.00. I know of at least two copies of the first printing without the tipped-in quotation from Waters and the Dasburg print, and which are unnumbered. Presumably more exist.

NOTE: A second printing of this book was published in February, 1971; 4,000 copies were printed and sold at $10.00. This second printing is so identified on the copyright page and carries an additional line giving the Library of Congress Catalog number. It contains none of the special contents listed above.

B7 ÁCOMA [1970, i.e. 1971]

[blue] *H. L. JAMES* | [small square drawing from an Ácoma design in black] | [fancy red type outlined in white and shaded in red] ÁCOMA |

Section B

[yellow] The People of the | [yellow] White Rock | [blue] *Introduction by FRANK WATERS* | [swash] The [publisher's device of a circle with nodes at the four principal points of the compass, a sword and a feather, in white, within a solid black oblate vertical rectangular panel, which extends downward into the next line] | [swash] Rio Grande Press, Inc. | GLORIETA, NEW MEXICO · 87535

$10^{15}/_{16}$ × $8^{7}/_{16}$". [1-6⁸]: 48 leaves. Pp. [1-4] 5-12 [13-15] 16-23 [24] 25-54 [55-56] 57-63 [64-65] 66-96. Page 6 is blank.

COPYRIGHT PAGE: "© Copyright 1970 | H. L. James | Albuquerque, N.M. | A short article on this subject, by author | Frank Waters, using several of the photographs | reproduced in this book, was published in | the July [slash] August 1970 issue of | NEW MEXICO MAGAZINE. | A RIO GRANDE PRESS PICTORIAL SPECIAL | LIBRARY OF CONGRESS CARD CATALOG 72-139224 | I.S.B.N. 87380-072-9 | First printing 1970 | [swash] The [publisher's device as on title page, and descending downward into next line] | [swash] Rio Grande Press, Inc. | GLORIETA, NEW MEXICO · 87535".

BINDING: White cloth, with a grain in imitation of morocco. Stamped on front in red: "*H. L. JAMES* | [small drawing as on title] | [fancy type outlined in white and shaded in red] ACOMA | The People of the | White Rock | *Introduction by FRANK WATERS*". Spine stamped in red: "[reading vertically] [fancy type outlined in white and shaded in red] ÁCOMA [space] *JAMES* | [horizontally] [three lines in swash] The | Rio | Grande | [publisher's device as on title in red against white] | [swash] Press". White endpapers.

DUST JACKET (white paper): Front with large color photograph of three Acoma women. Lettered on front: "[black on top, white on the bottom] *H. L. JAMES* | [drawing as on title] | [fancy type] [black outlined in white] Á [white outlined in gray] COMA | [white] The People of the | [black] W [black and white] h [white] ite Rock | [black] *Intro* [white and black] *d* [white] *uction by FRANK WATERS*". Spine: "[reading vertically] [fancy type, in black outlined in white] ÁCOMA [black] *JAMES*". Rear: "[color photograph of Ácoma] | [fancy type, in black outlined in white] ÁCOMA | [three paragraph blurb for the book]". The front flap contains a blurb for the book; the rear flap contains a notice of the author.

Published at $10.00 on January 18, 1971; number of copies printed unknown.

An Introduction by Frank Waters appears on pages 7-12.

COPIES: FW (d.j.); University of Illinois, Urbana, Illinois.

NOTE: Although Waters dated his introduction for this book "November, 1970," it had appeared earlier, in slightly revised form as "Sky City: Venerable and Venerated Acoma Faces the Future", in the July/August, 1970, issue of *New Mexico Magazine* (see C52).

B8 THE LITERATURE OF THE AMERICAN WEST [1971]

[thick-thin rules] | The Literature of the American West | [rule] | *Edited by* | J. GOLDEN TAYLOR | *Colorado State University* | HOUGHTON MIFFLIN COMPANY • BOSTON | *New York* • *Atlanta* • *Geneva, Illinois* • *Dallas* • *Palo Alto* | [thin-thick rules]

9$\frac{7}{32}$ × 5$\frac{21}{32}$". Perfectbound: 304 leaves. Pp. [i-iv] v-ix [x-xvi], 1-77 [78] 79-519 [520] 521-592. Pages ii, x, xvi, 78 and 520 are blank.

COPYRIGHT PAGE: "[thick-thin rules] | Copyright © 1971 by J. Golden Taylor. The | selections reprinted in this book are used by | permission of and special arrangement with the | proprietors of their respective copyrights. All | rights reserved. No part of this work may be | reproduced or transmitted in any form or by | any means, electronic or mechanical, including | photocopying and recording, or by any in- | formation storage or retrieval system, without | permission in writing from the publisher. | Printed in the U.S.A. | Library of Congress Catalog Card Number: | 71-132448 | ISBN: 0-395-05458-3 | [thin-thick rules]".

BINDING: Issued in paperback only. Stiff yellow paper covers with front, spine and rear printed overall in orange. The front contains an illustration of a cactus, in gray-brown, beneath a bright orange sun. Lettered on the front in brown: "The Literature | of the | American |

West | edited by J. Golden Taylor". Spine lettered in brown: "Taylor | [reading vertically] The Literature of the American West | [horizontally] HM Co.". Rear lettered in brown: "[paragraph quotation from the editor's preface] | —from the Editor's Preface | [paragraph notice of the editor] | 3-55305".

Published at $5.95 in 1971; number of copies printed unknown.

This work contains a reprinting of "The Western Novel: A Symposium", which originally appeared in the *South Dakota Review* (see C34). Waters' contribution to the symposium appears here on pages 27-32.

COPIES: Lee Nash, Dundee, Oregon.

B9 [DOROTHY E. BRETT RECEPTION] [1971]

[cover title] MANCHESTER GALLERY | P. O. Box 160 El Prado, New Mexico 87529 | sets aside this day | NOVEMBER 10, 1971 | to honor | Dorothy E. Brett | on the occasion | of her 88th birthday | with a reception, and a showing of her paintings | and drawings not before presented | to the public | [small caps] TIME: [caps] 2:30 to [caps] 5:00 | 4 Miles North of Taos on Arroyo Seco Road

5½ × 4¼". Single sheet, French-folded. 4 unnumbered pages.

Issued as an invitation to the Brett reception in November, 1971. According to Mr. John Manchester, 500 copies were printed.

"A Tribute to Brett" by Frank Waters appears on pages 3-4.

COPIES: TAT.

NOTE: Waters' tribute to Brett was reprinted in an exhibition brochure, "The Brett: Fifty Years of Painting in New Mexico, 1924-1974", published by the Jamison Galleries of Santa Fe, in conjunction with the Manchester Galleries of Taos, for a Brett exhibition which opened on March 31, 1974.

CONVERSATIONS WITH FRANK WATERS

B10

[1971, i.e. 1972]

[first four lines with swash capitals] *Conversations with | Frank Waters | edited by | John R. Milton* | SAGE BOOKS | [publisher's sagebrush device] | [small caps] THE [caps] SWALLOW PRESS [small caps] INC. | CHICAGO

8½ × 5⁷⁄₁₆". [1-3¹⁶]: 48 leaves. Pp. [i-vi], 1-3 [4] 5-17 [18] 19-29 [30] 31-63 [64] 65-75 [76] 77-90. Page ii is blank.

COPYRIGHT PAGE: "Copyright© 1971 by John R. Milton | Printed in the United States of America | All Rights Reserved | First Edition | *First Printing* | Published by | The Swallow Press Incorporated | 1139 South Wabash Avenue | Chicago, Illinois 60605 | [three lines of Library of Congress and ISBN catalog data] | Chapter IV was originally published in *South Dakota Review,* | Spring 1971. | Grateful acknowledgement is made to Bob Kostka for permission to | use his photographs of Frank Waters. All rights reserved.".

BINDING: Issued simultaneously in both cloth and paperbound.

CLOTH: Light green cloth, lettered on spine only: "[reading vertically] CONVERSATIONS WITH FRANK WATERS | [horizontally] SAGE BOOKS | [publisher's swallow device] | SWALLOW". Brown endpapers.

PAPERBACK: Perfectbound in stiff white paper covers, printed overall on front with a black and white photograph of Frank Waters. Lettered on front: "[brown] CONVERSATIONS | [brown] WITH | [white] FRANK WATERS | [white] Edited by John R. Milton | [brown] $2.00". Spine: "[reading vertically] CONVERSATIONS WITH FRANK WATERS | [horizontally] SAGE BOOKS | [publisher's swallow device] | SWALLOW". Rear: "[brown] CONVERSATIONS WITH FRANK WATERS | [text printed in double column, with left hand column, printed in black, containing a blurb for this book; the right hand column contains a biographical notice of John R. Milton, printed in brown, and a black and white photograph of Milton, beneath which appears the credit: '[brown] Photo by Sam Sprague] | [beneath right hand column and printed to the right of the publisher's swallow device] [small caps] THE [caps] SWALLOW PRESS [small caps] INC. | 1139 S. WABASH AVENUE CHICAGO, ILLINOIS 60605 | [along hinge, reading vertically in brown] Photo and Design by Robert Kostka". Inner wrappers blank.

DUST JACKET (white paper): Front and spine printed overall with the black and white photograph of Waters which appears on the front cover of the paperbound copies. Lettered on front as in the paper copies, but with the price deleted. Lettered on spine: "[reading vertically] [white] CONVERSATIONS WITH FRANK WATERS [publisher's swallow device, flying to the left, in brown] [white] SWALLOW". Rear: "Sage Books by Frank Waters | [listing of seven titles printed in black and with quotations from the press printed in brown] | [reading vertically along hinge] [brown] Photo and Design by Robert Kostka". The front flap printed in brown and black with a blurb for this book; the rear flap printed with a biographical notice of Milton, in brown, with a black and white photograph of Milton, as on the rear of the paper copies, and with publisher's imprint at bottom in black.

Published at $4.00 for cloth copies and $2.00 for paper copies in May, 1972; 1,020 copies were issued in cloth and 4,030 copies were issued in paper.

The book comprises the texts of taped interviews of Frank Waters. In the sixth interview, Waters and Milton were joined by Karen Kling; in the seventh they were joined by Frederick Manfred. Full-page photographs of Waters, by Robert Kostka, appear on pages vi, 4, 18, 30, 64, and 76. Pages 87-90 comprise a bibliography of Waters.

COPIES: NmU (cloth, d.j.); TAT (cloth, d.j. and paper).

NOTE: Chapter IV originally appeared in *South Dakota Review*, Spring, 1971 (see E5).

THE TAOS INDIANS AND THEIR
B11   SACRED BLUE LAKE   [1972]

Written and photographed by MARCIA KEEGAN | The Taos Indians | and their | Sacred Blue Lake | JULIAN MESSNER [publisher's device of a superimposed 'J' and 'M' within a circle] NEW YORK

8¾ × 7¼". [1-4⁸]: 32 leaves; side stitched. 64 unnumbered pages.

COPYRIGHT PAGE: "Published by Julian Messner, a Division of Simon & Schuster, Inc. | 1 West 39 Street, New York, N.Y. 10018. All rights reserved. | Copyright© 1972 by Marcia Keegan. | Printed in the United States of America | Design by Marjorie Zaum K. | Library of Congress Cataloging in Publication Data | [10 lines of catalog data]".

BINDING: Issued simultaneously in a trade and library binding:

TRADE BINDING: Blue cloth, lettered on spine only: "[vertically] KEEGAN The Taos Indians and their Sacred Blue Lake Messner". White endpapers.

LIBRARY BINDING: Pictorial paper over boards in imitation of cloth, with full color photograph of an Indian child in ceremonial dress on front, spine and rear. Lettered on front: "[seven lines in blue] The | Taos | Indians | and their | Sacred | Blue | Lake | by | MARCIA KEEGAN". Spine: "[reading vertically] KEEGAN [title in blue] The Taos Indians and their Sacred Blue Lake [black] [initials 'MCE' within single rules] Messner". Rear: "$4.79 | The Taos Indians and Their Sacred Blue Lake | [four paragraph blurb] | About the Author | [three paragraphs biographical notice] | *Cover by Marjorie Zaum* | 08211 | [in lower right corner] [five lines within single rules] JM | [rule] | MESS= NER | CERTIFIED | EDITIONS | [beneath single rules] 671-32536-1". White endpapers.

DUST JACKET (white paper): Issued only with the trade binding. Front, spine and rear have illustration identical to that on the covers of the library binding. Lettered as on library binding, except for rear which is blank. Front flap carries a blurb for the book; and the rear flap carries a biographical notice of the author.

Published at $4.95 for the trade binding and $4.79 for the Messner Certified Editions library binding, on October 16, 1972; number of copies printed unknown.

A Foreword by Frank Waters appears on p. 7.

COPIES: FW (trade binding, d.j.); Skokie Public Library, Skokie, Illinois (Messner Certified Editions library binding).

B12   FRANK WATERS   [1973]

FRANK WATERS | [rule] | By THOMAS J. LYON | *Utah State University* | [within an ellipse] TUSAS [outside of the ellipse] 225 | Twayne Publishers, Inc. :: New York

$7^{15}/_{16} \times 5^{3}/_{8}$". [1-2^{16} 3^4 4-6^{16}]: 84 leaves. Pp. [1-14] 15-155 [156] 157-163 [164] 165-166 [167-168]. Pages 2, 6, 10, 12, 156, 164, 167 and 168 are blank.

COPYRIGHT PAGE: "*Copyright © 1973 by Twayne Publishers, Inc.* | All Rights Reserved | Library of Congress Catalog Card Number: 72-13369 | MANUFACTURED IN THE UNITED STATES OF AMERICA".

BINDING: Blue cloth. Lettered on front in gilt: "FRANK WATERS | Thomas J. Lyon | [publisher's series device of an eagle with a flag, palm branches and a banner]". Lettered on spine in gilt: "[thick rule] | [reading vertically] Thomas J. Lyon [space] FRANK WATERS | [horizontally] Twayne | [thick rule] | [within an ellipse] TUSAS | [beneath ellipse] 225". Blue endpapers.

No dust jacket was issued with the book.

Published at $5.50 in 1973; number of copies printed unknown.

The author incorporated within the text material from both personal interviews with Waters and correspondence with Waters. In the notes, on page 157, he quotes directly from a letter from Waters, dated July 24, 1968.

COPIES: FW; Skokie Public Library, Skokie, Illinois.

B13   MY BLOOD'S COUNTRY   [1973]

MY | BLOOD'S | COUNTRY | STUDIES IN SOUTHWESTERN LITERATURE | by William T. Pilkington | [publisher's series device of a double-outline (thick-thin) oval, with a small vignette in the center of a man walking past a university building, and with lettering following the interior form of the oval: "[dot] TEXAS CHRISTIAN UNIVER= SITY MONOGRAPHS [dot] | IN HISTORY AND CULTURE". To the left of the vignette is printed: *"No. 10"* and to the right is printed: *"1973"*] | THE TEXAS CHRISTIAN UNIVERSITY PRESS

$8^{15}/_{16} \times 5^{15}/_{16}"$. [1-7^{16}]: 112 leaves. Pp. [i-iv] v-viii [ix-x], 1-79 [80] 81-95 [96] 97-107 [108] 109-211 [212-214]. Pages 80, 96, 108, 212 and 214 are blank.

COPYRIGHT PAGE: "FIRST PRINTING | Copyright© 1973 by Texas Christian University Press | All rights reserved | [seal of the university] | Library of Congress Catalogue Card No. 72-95053 | Manufactured in the United States of America".

COLOPHON (p. 212): "THIS BOOK WAS DESIGNED BY | JUDITH M. OELFKE | PRINTED IN TEN-POINT GARAMOND | ON WAR= REN'S OLDE STYLE WOVE | AND PRINTED AND BOUND BY | HALLIDAY LITHOGRAPH CORPORATION".

BINDING: Issued in paperback only. White stiff paper with front, spine and rear printed overall in pea-green. Lettered on front: "[drawing in blue and white of a mountain area, within thin single rules, within thick single rules] | MY | BLOOD'S | COUNTRY | [blue] STUDIES IN SOUTHWESTERN LITERATURE | [blue] by William T. Pilkington". Lettered on spine: "[reading vertically] MY BLOOD'S COUNTRY [blue] William T. Pilkington | [horizontally] TCU | PRESS". Rear: "OTHER BOOKS IN THE SERIES FROM | TEXAS CHRISTIAN UNIVERSITY PRESS | [listing of nine titles] | [series device as on title, but in blue] | THE TEXAS CHRISTIAN UNIVERSITY PRESS". Inner wrappers blank.

Published at $3.50 in 1973; 802 copies were printed.

The author quotes from a letter by Waters, dated July 14, 1966, on page vii, and from a letter by Waters, dated February 3, 1968, on page 110.

COPIES: TAT.

NOTE: The essay on Frank Waters included in this work was originally published as "Character and Landscape: Frank Waters' Colorado Trilogy," in Western American Literature, in 1967 (see H23). The essay as printed in periodical form differs slightly from this version, and does not include the excerpt from Waters' letter.

B14 ANASAZI [1974]

[double-page title] [all lines printed in white] [right-hand page] ANA꞊SAZI | *Ancient People of the Rock* | PHOTOGRAPHS BY DAVID MUENCH TEXT BY DONALD G. PIKE | [left-hand page] [publisher's device ^A_W] | AMERICAN WEST PUBLISHING COMPANY | PALO ALTO-CALIFORNIA

All the above set against a double-page color photograph of Long House ruin interior, Wetherill Mesa, Mesa Verde National Park, Colorado.

11 × 8⁷⁄₁₆". [1-12⁸]: 96 leaves. Pp. [1-10] 11-13 [14] 15-20 [21-23] 24-25 [26-28] 29-30 [31] 32 [33-34] 35-36 [37-39] 40-41 [42] 43-50 [51-52] 53 [54] 55 [56-62] 63-72 [73-75] 76 [77-78] 79 [80-81] 82 [83] 84 [85] 86-87 [88-89] 90 [91-92] 93-95 [96] 97-104 [105] 106 [107-108] 109 [110] 111-123 [124-125] 126 [127] 128 [129-134] 135-148 [149-152] 153-154 [155] 156-157 [158-160] 161-167 [168-171] 172-173 [174] 175-177 [178-179] 180-181 [182-184] 185-191 [192]. Pages 10 and 84 are blank.

COPYRIGHT PAGE: "[6 lines of photograph captions for pages 2-7, printed in italic] | FIRST EDITION | © Copyright 1974, AMERICAN WEST PUBLISHING COMPANY. | Printed in the United States of America. All rights reserved. This book or parts thereof | may not be reproduced in any form without written permission of the publisher. | Library of Congress Card Number 73-90795 | ISBN 0-910118-49-0".

BINDING: Dark brown paper over boards in imitation of cloth. Lettered on spine only in gilt: "[reading vertically] ANASAZI *Ancient People of the Rock* muench & pike | [horizontally] $\substack{A \\ W}$". Light brown endpapers, with map of Arizona and New Mexico printed on the face of both the front and rear endpapers, in brown and gray.

DUST JACKET (white paper): Front, spine and rear printed overall with colored photographic illustration as on title page. Lettered on front in white: "ANASAZI | *Ancient People of the Rock* | [reading downwards along hinge] DAVID MUENCH AND DONALD G. PIKE". Spine lettered in white: "[reading vertically] ANASAZI | [horizontally] DAVID MUENCH | AND | DONALD G. PIKE | [publisher's device $\substack{A \\ W}$]". Front flap contains a three-paragraph blurb for the book; a 6-line quotation from Waters' Foreword, printed in italic; and biographical notices of the authors. The rear flap contains a notice of other books.

Published at $16.95 in 1974; number of copies printed unknown. A notice on the dust jacket states that the price would rise to $18.50 after 12/31/74. The work must have been published prior to September, 1974, because a second printing, published at $18.50, was done in September, 1974.

A Foreword by Frank Waters appears on pages 11-13, printed in double column.

COPIES: FW (d.j.).

B15   THE COX LIBRARY   [1974]

A Microfilm Offering from AMERICANA UNLIMITED | [brown] THE | [brown] COX | [brown] LIBRARY | COUNTY, | STATE | & LOCAL | HISTORIES | Copyright © 1974 by Gordon L. Cox

11 × 8½". Perfectbound: 80 leaves. Pp. [1-7] 8-34 [35] 36-73 [74-75] 76-99 [100] 101-113 [114-115] 116 [117-118] 119 [120] 121-129 [130] 131-134 [135] 136-139 [140] 141-144 [145] 146-150 [151] 152-156 [157-160]. Pages 2, 4 and 160 are blank.

BINDING: Stiff white paper wrappers with front, spine and rear printed overall in brown, and with a photograph of the spines of three books on the front, and a photograph of the spines of six books on the rear cover. Lettered on front: "[orange] THE | [orange] COX | [orange] LIBRARY | [next four lines in white] COUNTY, | STATE | & LOCAL | HIS= TORIES". Spine: "[reading vertically] [orange] THE COX LIBRARY [white] AMERICANA UNLIMITED". Lettered in brown on inside rear wrapper near bottom: "Americana Unlimited | P. O. Box 50447 | 1701 North Eleventh Avenue | Tucson, Arizona 85703 | [near inner margin] (This catalogue compiled and published by Americana Unlim= ited.) [near outer margin directly beneath address] Telephone (602) 792-3453".

Published in 1974; number of copies printed unknown.

"History unlimited" by Frank Waters appears on page 74, printed in brown.

COPIES: TAT.

B16   VOICES FROM THE SOUTHWEST   [1976]

B16a   Trade issue

[red] VOICES | [red] FROM THE | [red] SOUTHWEST | *A Gathering | in Honor | of Lawrence Clark Powell* | [ornament in red] | GATHERED BY | DONALD C. DICKINSON | W. DAVID LAIRD | MARGARET F. MAXWELL | [ornament in red, reversed] | *Northland Press • Flagstaff | Mcmlxxvi*

9½ × 6⅓". [1-11⁸]: 88 leaves. Pp. [i-vi] vii [viii] ix [x] xi-xv [xvi], [1-2] 3-16 [17] 18-62 [63-64] 65-130 [131] 132-159 [160]. Pages vi, viii, x and xvi are blank.

COPYRIGHT PAGE: "*Copyright © 1976 by Northland Press* | All Rights Reserved | FIRST EDITION | ISBN 0-87358-157-1 | Library of Con- gress Catalog Card Number 76-26769 | Composed and Printed in the United States of America".

COLOPHON (p. 160): "[publisher's evergreen device] | VOICES FROM THE SOUTHWEST | WAS DESIGNED BY JOHN ANDERSON, | EDITED BY JIM HOWARD, SET IN | 12-POINT GRANJON, PRINTED ON | CLASSIC LAID TEXT AT PAUL WEAVER'S | NORTHLAND PRESS, AND BOUND BY | MARK AND IRIS ROSWELL IN PHOENIX.".

BINDING: Charcoal gray cloth. Stamped on front in silver with ornament from title page. Spine: "[stamped in silver] [reading vertically] [ornament from title page, pointing toward head of spine] VOICES FROM THE SOUTHWEST [ornament pointed toward heel of spine]". Gray endpapers.

DUST JACKET (gray laid paper): Lettered on front: "VOICES | FROM THE | SOUTHWEST | [double ornaments in red, pointing towards the sides] | *A gathering of poetry, essays, and art* | *in honor of Lawrence Clark Powell*". Spine: lettered in black as on binding, with ornaments in red. Rear: "[black and white photograph of Powell] | *Lawrence Clark Powell*". Front and rear flaps carry a blurb about this book, printed in black and red.

Published at $12.50 in September of 1976; 3,532 copies printed.

"The Fifth World—The Ninth Planet" by Frank Waters appears on pages 55-62.

COPIES: TAT (d.j.).

B16b   Limited issue

Published simultaneously with the trade edition was a limited edition. Collation of the limited edition is identical with the trade edition, with the exception of a printed leaf inserted before the half-title: "A limited edition of seventy-five copies of | Voices from the Southwest | has been especially bound, slipcased | and signed by the contributors. This is copy _____ | [below this appear the twenty signatures]".

This inserted leaf is printed on a slightly heavier stock than the rest of the book.

BINDING: Red cloth sides and black vinyl [in imitation of leather] back, stamped on spine in gilt as on the trade binding. Top edges stained black. The endpapers are a white laid paper stock, marbled on the face.

No dust jacket was issued with the limited edition, which was issued instead in a black cloth slipcase, with title-page ornament in gilt on front.

The limited issue was published at $85.00.

COPIES: TAT.

B17   WINDSINGER   [1976]

[double-page title] [left-hand page] *WIND* [right-hand page] *SINGER* | [small caps with a capital] GARY M. SMITH | [small caps with a capital] SIERRA CLUB BOOKS | [small caps with a capital] SAN FRANCISCO | 1976

All of the above set against a double-page color photograph of Fishhook Creek in Idaho by Gary Smith.

$9\frac{3}{16}$ × $6\frac{1}{2}$". Perfectbound: 90 leaves; 6 plates of photographic illustrations inserted. Pp. [i-iv], [1-9] 10 [11-15] 16-18 [19] 20-24 [25] 26-36 [37-40] 41-44 [45-46] 47-49 [50-51] 52-55 [56-57] 58-61 [62-63] 64-67 [68-69] 70-74 [75-78] 79-88 [89-90] 91-97 [98-99] 100-105 [106] 107-108 [109-110] 111-117 [118] 119 [120] 121-136 [137-138] 139-148 [149-150] 151-153 [154-155] 156-160 [161] 162-175 [176]. Pages 2, 6, 12, 14, 38, 76 and 176 are blank.

COPYRIGHT PAGE: "[series of four small color photographs, in two columns] | [five lines of photograph identification printed below left-hand column; six lines of identification printed below right-hand column] | [copyright information printed in two columns] [left-hand column] Copyright © 1976 by Gary M. Smith. | All rights reserved. | Design by Jon Goodchild | Line drawings by Carol Snow | Production by David Charlsen & | Others | Manufactured in the United States | of America | [right-hand column] Library of Congress Cataloging | in Publication Data | [5 lines of catalog data]".

BINDING: Blue cloth. Front blindstamped: *"WINDSINGER"*. Spine stamped in gilt: "[reading vertically at 45 degree angle] *WINDSINGER* | [horizontally] [rule] | [small caps with a capital] GARY | [small caps with a capital] SMITH | [rule] | [small caps with a capital] SIERRA | [small caps with a capital] CLUB | [small caps with a capital] BOOKS". Light brown endpapers.

DUST JACKET (white paper): Front and spine printed overall with a color photograph of a man on a rock overhang overlooking a river. Lettered on front: "[blue] *WINDSINGER* | [small caps with a capital] GARY SMITH". Spine: "[reading vertically] [blue] *WINDSINGER* | [horizontally] [white] [small caps with a capital] GARY | [white] [small caps with a capital] SMITH | [white] [small caps with a capital] SIERRA | [white] [small caps with a capital] CLUB | [white] [small caps with a capital] BOOKS". Rear: Small photograph in color at top, beneath which is a 17-line excerpt from Waters' introduction. Front flap carries a blurb for the book, printed in blue and black; rear flap carries a photograph of the author, with publisher's imprint and ISBN number at bottom.

Published at $7.95 in October, 1976; 21,414 copies were printed.

A Foreword by Frank Waters appears on page 1.

COPIES: FW (d.j.); Skokie Public Library, Skokie, Illinois (d.j.).

B18   FRED ROSENSTOCK   [1976]

[blue] FRED | [blue] ROSENSTOCK | *A Legend in Books & Art* | [fancy rule, comprising a single rule within a double spiral] | *By* | DONALD E. BOWER | Foreword by Frank Waters | [publisher's evergreen device in blue] | NORTHLAND PRESS

$9\frac{9}{16} \times 6\frac{5}{8}$". [1-13^8 14^4 15^8]: 116 leaves. Pp. [i-vi] vii [viii] ix [x] xi-xvii [xviii], 1-40 [41] 42-52 [53] 54-76 [77] 78-104 [105] 106-108 [109] 110-130 [131] 132-152 [153] 154-160 [161] 162-176 [177] 178-184 [185] 186-188 [189] 190-195 [196] 197-212 [213-214]. Pages vi, viii, x, xviii, 196 and 213 are blank.

COPYRIGHT PAGE: "[small caps] THIS VOLUME is based on research and interviews conducted | by Dr. S. Lyman Tyler, Director, American West Center, | University of Utah | *Copyright* © *1976 by Donald E. Bower* | *All Rights Reserved* | FIRST EDITION | ISBN 0-873580-149-0 | Library of Congress Catalog Card Number 76-10419 | Composed and Printed in the United States of America".

COLOPHON (p. 214): "[publisher's evergreen device] | FRED ROSEN=STOCK: *A Legend in Books and Art* | WAS DESIGNED BY PAUL WEAVER, | SET IN 14-POINT LINOTYPE GRANJON, | AND PRINTED ON MOUNTIE WARM WHITE TEXT. | BOUND BY ROSWELL BOOKBINDING, PHOENIX.".

BINDING: Blue cloth, lettered in silver on spine only: "[reading vertically] DONALD E. | BOWER | [in center] FRED ROSENSTOCK | [at bottom] NORTHLAND | PRESS". Blue [laid paper] endpapers.

DUST JACKET (white paper): Front, spine and rear printed overall in blue. Front lettered: "FRED | ROSENSTOCK | *A Legend in Books & Art* | [color photograph of Fred Rosenstock outlined in white and black] | *BY DONALD E. BOWER* [slash] *FOREWORD BY FRANK WA=TERS*". Spine: "[reading vertically] DONALD E. | BOWER | [in center] FRED ROSENSTOCK | [at bottom] NORTHLAND | PRESS". Rear: "[all within a white panel] *Other fine volumes of interest* | to Western bookmen from Northland Press | [blurbs for three books, set in roman] | *At your bookstore or directly from* | NORTHLAND PRESS · [small caps] P. O. BOX N · FLAGSTAFF, ARIZONA [caps] 86 [small caps] 001". Front flap carries a blurb for this book; rear flap carries a biographical notice of the author, with publisher's imprint and device in blue at the bottom.

Published at $12.50 in October, 1976; 3,093 copies were printed.

A Foreword by Frank Waters appears on pages xi-xiv.

COPIES: TAT (d.j.).

NOTE: There was also a limited signed issue of 250 copies, signed by the author and Fred Rosenstock.

CHOKECHERRY HUNTERS
B19   AND OTHER POEMS   [1976]

[xylographic] CHOKECHERRY HUNTERS | [xylographic] AND OTHER POEMS | [woodcut of a man, woman and child outside a chapel] | FOREWORD BY FRANK WATERS | [xylographic] BY JO= SEPH L. CONCHA | [publisher's device] THE SUNSTONE PRESS | Santa Fe, New Mexico

8½ × 5½". [1¹⁶]: 16 leaves. Pp. [1-2] 3-31 [32]. Page 32 is blank; page 6 is numbered but otherwise blank.

COPYRIGHT PAGE: "Copyright © 1976 by Joseph L. Concha | ALL RIGHTS RESERVED | ISBN 0 - 913270 - 57 - 1 | [next four lines within single rules] *Acknowledgements* | *Special thanks to Ruth Hatcher and Dick Spas, who* | *contributed their talents generously to make this* | *book possible.* | WOODCUTS ON COVER AND PAGE 5 BY ALEX CON= CHA | Manufactured in the United States of America".

BINDING: Gray paper wrappers, stapled. Lettered on front in red: "[xylographic] CHOKECHERRY HUNTERS | [xylographic] AND OTHER POEMS | [woodcut as on title, but printed in red and black] | FOREWORD BY FRANK WATERS | [xylographic] BY JOSEPH L. CONCHA". Rear: "[square black and white photograph of the author, outlined in red and black] | [three paragraphs about the author] | $1.95". Inner wrappers blank.

Published at $1.95 in 1976; 1,000 copies were printed.

A Foreword by Frank Waters appears on pages 3-4.

COPIES: NmU, TAT.

NOTE: Copies have been seen with the price on the rear cover pasted over with a small white label, reading: "Publisher's | $2.25 | Price".

SECTION B

B20 FROM THE HEARTLAND [1976, i.e. 1977]

[first two lines in gold] FROM THE | HEARTLAND | [three leaf ornaments in black] | [next two lines printed in *lettres bâtarde* in gold] Profiles of People and Places | of the Southwest and Beyond | BY LAWRENCE CLARK POWELL | *Illustrations by Bettina Steinke* | NORTHLAND PRESS [slash] FLAGSTAFF

9 × 6". [1-9^8 10^{10} 11^8]: 90 leaves. Pp. [i-vi] vii [viii] ix [x] xi [xii], [1-2] 3-4 [5] 6-48 [49] 50-56 [57] 58-64 [65] 66-70 [71-72] 73-86 [87] 88-100 [101] 102-110 [111] 112-120 [121] 122-132 [133] 134-144 [145] 146-152 [153] 154-162 [163] 164-167 [168]. Pages ii, vi, viii, x, xii, 2 and 72 are blank.

COPYRIGHT PAGE: "Acknowledgment is made to *Westways* and *South= ern | Review,* in which these essays first appeared, and to the | staff of the Northland Press and to my wife Fay for | editorial assistance. | L.C.P. | Copyright © *1976 by Lawrence Clark Powell* | All Rights Re= served | FIRST EDITION | ISBN 0-87358-155-5 | Library of Congress Catalog Card Number 75-43347 | Composed and Printed in the United States of America".

COLOPHON (p. 168): "FROM THE HEARTLAND | WAS DESIGNED BY ROBERT JACOBSON, | SET IN LINOTYPE GRANJON, | AND PRINTED ON CLASSIC TEXT. | BOUND BY ROSWELL BOOK= BINDING, | PHOENIX.".

BINDING: Brown cloth. Lettered on spine only in gilt: "[reading vertically] FROM THE HEARTLAND [leaf ornament] [small caps] LAWRENCE CLARK POWELL". Golden-brown endpapers.

DUST JACKET (golden-brown paper): Lettered on front: "FROM THE | HEARTLAND | [three leaf ornaments in gilt] | [next two lines printed in *lettres batarde* in brown] Profiles of People and Places | of the Southwest and Beyond | [gilt rule] | BY LAWRENCE CLARK POW= ELL | *Illustrations by Bettina Steinke*". Spine: "[reading vertically] FROM THE HEARTLAND [leaf ornament in gilt] [brown] LAW= RENCE CLARK POWELL". Rear: "[all within thin brown rules, within thick brown rules] *Other fine volumes of interest to Western bookmen* | [blurbs for four books] | *At your bookstore or directly from*

NORTHLAND PRESS | P. O. BOX N · FLAGSTAFF, ARIZONA 86002". The front flap carries a blurb for this book printed in black and brown; the rear flap carries a black and white photograph of the author and a short biographical notice.

Published at $14.95 in March, 1977; 3,122 copies were printed.

In the chapter entitled "Down Where the Rockies End" Powell quotes from an interview with Waters, and also quotes from a letter from Waters. This essay originally appeared in *Westways,* under the title "A Writer's Landscape" (see E11).

COPIES: TAT (d.j.).

NOTE: A limited issue of 100 copies, specially bound and signed by the author and the illustrator, was published simultaneously with the trade impression.

B21 RIVERTRIP [1977]

[calligraphic] [purple] Rivertrip | RITA DEANIN ABBEY | [calligraphic] [purple] Rivertrip | FOREWORD BY FRANK WATERS | [calligraphic] [purple] Rivertrip | NORTHLAND PRESS • FLAG=STAFF, ARIZONA

9 × 11⅞". [1-5^8]: 40 leaves. Pp. [i-viii], [1] 2-9 [10-11] 12-17 [18-19] 20-35 [36-37] 38-49 [50-51] 52-57 [58-59] 60-67 [68] 69 [70-72]. Pages ii, vi, 10, 18, 36, 50, 58, 68 and 72 are blank.

COPYRIGHT PAGE: *"Copyright © by Rita Deanin Abbey 1977 | All Rights Reserved | First Edition | ISBN 0-87358-152-0 | Library of Con=gress Catalogue Card Number 76-1404 | Printed in the United States of America".*

COLOPHON (p. 71): *"Rivertrip was designed by John Anderson, | set in the Trump and Salto types | and printed on Karma Dull at Northland Press. | Bound by Roswell Bookbinding, Phoenix."*.

276   SECTION B

BINDING: Gray cloth. Stamped on front in silver: "[calligraphic] Rivertrip". Lettered on spine in silver: "[reading vertically] RIVER=TRIP [short wavy rule] [small caps] NORTHLAND PRESS". Purple endpapers.

DUST JACKET: There are two issues of the dust jacket:
1. (white paper): Front carries an illustration by the author in red, gray, brown, and black, signed in the lower right corner in script "Rita Deanin Abbey". Lettered on front: "RITA DEANIN ABBEY | [calligraphic] [purple] Rivertrip | FOREWORD BY FRANK WATERS". Spine lettered in purple: "[reading vertically] RIVERTRIP [small wavy rule in black] [small caps] NORTHLAND PRESS". Rear: "[publisher's device of an evergreen branch within a double-outline oblate square, all in purple] | NORTHLAND | PRESS". The front flap carries a blurb for this book, printed in purple and black; the rear flap carries a black and white photograph of the author and a short biographical notice. The second line of the text of the blurb on the front flap reads: "beauty of the Grand Canyon and the awe-".

2. Identical with the above, except that the second line of the text of the blurb of the front flap reads: "beauty of Cataract Canyon and the awe-".

Published at $14.95 in April, 1977; 1,500 copies were printed.

A Foreword by Frank Waters appears on pages vii-viii.

COPIES: TAT (both issues of d.j.).

B22   VINTAGE   [1978]

The Bold Survivors! | [rule] | VINTAGE | by Joan Dufault | [publisher's device of a three-masted sailing ship] The Pilgrim Press [space] New York • Philadelphia

$9^{31}/_{32} \times 6^{7}/_{8}''$. [1-8^{16}]: 128 leaves. Pp. [1-5] 6 [7] 8-13 [14] 15-21 [22] 23-29 [30] 31-37 [38] 39-43 [44] 45-47 [48] 49-55 [56] 57-61 [62] 63-71 [72] 73-75 [76] 77-81 [82] 83-85 [86] 87-93 [94] 95-97 [98] 99-103 [104] 105-111 [112] 113-119 [120] 121 [122] 123-125 [126] 127-129 [130] 131-135 [136] 137-139

[140] 141-145 [146] 147-151 [152] 153-159 [160] 161-165 [166] 167-169 [170] 171-175 [176] 177 [178] 179-183 [184] 185-193 [194] 195-199 [200] 201-203 [204] 205-209 [210] 211-219 [220] 221-223 [224] 225-229 [230] 231-245 [246] 247-252 [253] 254-256.

COPYRIGHT PAGE: "COPYRIGHT © 1978 BY JOAN DUFAULT | ALL RIGHTS RESERVED | [four-line notice of reservation of rights] | Cover design by Beehive | Book design and layout by Bill Davenport Studio | The excerpt in the Frank Waters interview is from an article entitled "Lessons from the Indian Soul" | by James Peterson and is reprinted from *Psychology Today Magazine,* copyright © 1973 Ziff-Davis | Publishing Company. Used by permission. | [seven lines of Library of Congress cataloging data] | THE PILGRIM PRESS, 287 PARK AVENUE SOUTH, NEW YORK, NEW YORK 10010".

BINDING: Brick-red cloth, stamped on spine only in white: "Dufault | [reading vertically] VINTAGE | [horizontally] [publisher's device of a three-masted sailing ship] | The | Pilgrim | Press". White paper endpapers, with face of front endpapers printed overall with a sepia photograph of a winter scene; and with the face of the rear endpapers printed overall with a sepia photograph of a man bicycling down a forest path.

DUST JACKET (white paper): Front, spine and rear printed overall in brown in a pattern resembling "V" cloth, and with six black and white snapshot portraits outlined in white. Lettered on front: "[white] The Bold Survivors! | [long white rule] | [light tan] VINTAGE | [light tan] by Joan Dufault". Spine: "[white] Dufault | [reading vertically] [light tan] VINTAGE | [horizontally, and all printed in white] [publisher's device as on spine of binding] | The | Pilgrim | Press". Rear: "[light tan] SURVIVORS! | [seven short quotations taken from the book, printed in light tan, with citations printed in white, and the whole enclosed within large white quotation marks]". Front flap carries blurbs for books by Irving Louis Horowitz and W. H. Whyte, Jr., printed in black and brown; the rear flap contains a biographical notice of the author and the publisher's imprint printed in brown and black.

Published at $11.95 on November 2, 1978; number of copies printed unknown.

"Frank Waters", a transcript of an interview with Waters edited into a first-person narrative, appears on pages 247-252. An excerpt from

James Peterson's interview with Waters, reprinted from *Psychology Today* (see E7), appears on page 252. A full-page photograph of Waters appears on page 246.

COPIES: TAT (d.j.).

B23   IN TIME OF HARVEST   [1979]

John L. Sinclair | In Time of Harvest | *Introduction by Frank Waters* | A Zia Book | UNIVERSITY OF NEW MEXICO PRESS | Albuquerque

7^{15}/$_{16}$ × 5⅜". Perfectbound: 120 leaves. Pp. [i-vi] vii-x, 1-226 [227-230]. Pages ii, vi and 227-230 are blank.

COPYRIGHT PAGE: "[9 lines of Library of Congress Cataloging in Publication Data] | Copyright © 1943, 1971 by John L. Sinclair. All rights reserved. University of New Mexico | Press paperback edition re= printed 1979 by arrangement with the author. Introduction © 1979 | by the University of New Mexico Press. Manufactured in the United States of America. | Library of Congress Catalog Card Number 78-21434. International Standard Book Number | 0-8263-0505-9".

BINDING: Issued in paperback only. Stiff white paper covers printed overall on front, spine and a portion of the rear with an illustration in black and blue of a man plowing a field, with mountains and a windmill in the background. Lettered on front: "A Zia Book | In Time | of Har= vest | John L. Sinclair". Spine: "[reading vertically] [publisher's device of a circle with four lines radiating from each of the four principal points of the compass] Sinclair [space] In Time of Harvest [white] New Mexico". Rear: "$3.95 | In Time of Harvest | John L. Sinclair | Intro= duction by Frank Waters | [7 paragraphs about the book] UNIVER= SITY OF NEW MEXICO PRESS | ISBN 0-8263-0505-9.".

Published at $3.95 in February, 1979; 4,066 copies were printed.

An Introduction by Frank Waters appears on pages vii-x.

COPIES: TAT.

B24 FROM ICE MOUNTAIN [1979, i.e. 1980]

[blue] FROM | [blue] ICE MOUNTAIN | Indian Settlement of the Americas | By DON PERCEVAL | *with an Introduction by Frank Wa=ters* | [illustration of an Indian carrying a spear, in gray, brown, black and orange] | NORTHLAND PRESS [publisher's evergreen device in blue] FLAGSTAFF, ARIZONA

9^{7}⁄$_{16}$ × 6⅞". [1-5^8]: 40 leaves. Pp. [I-II], [i-iv] v-viii, [1] 2-65 [66-70]. Pages I-II, 66 and 68-70 are blank.

COPYRIGHT PAGE: "Copyright © 1979 by Edith Perceval | All Rights Reserved | First Edition | ISBN 0-87358-204-7 | Library of Congress Catalog Card Number 79-53088 | Composed and Printed in the United States of America".

COLOPHON (page 67): "DESIGNED BY MARK SANDERS | AND MICHAEL HOLLAR | COMPOSED IN LINOTYPE ALDUS | WITH DISPLAY LINES | IN HANDSET PALATINO | PRINTED ON WARREN'S OLD STYLE | AT THE PRESS IN THE PINES | [publisher's evergreen device] | NORTHLAND PRESS | BOUND BY ROSWELL BOOKBINDING | PHOENIX".

BINDING: Blue cloth. Front with the outline of a sitting Indian stamped in silver in lower right corner. Lettered on spine in silver: "[reading vertically] PERCEVAL FROM ICE MOUNTAIN NORTHLAND PRESS". Blue [laid paper] endpapers.

DUST JACKET (white paper, watermarked "Warren's Old Style"): Front: "[blue] FROM | [blue] ICE MOUNTAIN | Indian Settlement of the Americas | By DON PERCEVAL | *with an Introduction by Frank Waters* | [illustrations of three Indians carrying spears, printed in brown, black, orange, gray and yellow]". Spine: "[reading vertically] [blue] FROM ICE MOUNTAIN [black] PERCEVAL | [horizontally] [publisher's evergreen device in blue]". Rear contains illustration of three adult Indians and two Indian children, printed in brown, black, orange, gray and yellow. Front flap contains a blurb for this book, carried over onto the rear flap, and printed in black and blue; publisher's device [in blue] and imprint appear at the bottom of the rear flap.

Published at $16.00 in January, 1980; 1,752 copies were printed.

An Introduction by Frank Waters appears on pages v-viii.

COPIES: TAT (d.j.).

NOTE: Don Perceval illustrated the Northland Press edition of Waters' *The Man Who Killed the Deer* (see A8f).

B25   THE TIERRA AMARILLA GRANT [1980, i.e. 1981]

THE | TIERRA AMARILLA | GRANT: | *A History of Chicanery* | [circular vignette of Brazo's Peak and "El Puerto" Mesa] | Malcolm Ebright | The Center for Land Grant Studies | Santa Fe, New Mexico

9⅜ × 6¾". Perfectbound: 40 leaves. Pp. [i-iii] iv-xiv, 1-66.

COPYRIGHT PAGE: "[rule-ornament-rule] | COVER: | The cover is a silk screen print by Rini Templeton showing the Brazos Peak and the mesa known as "El Puerto." These | are the major landmarks one sees from the villages of Tierra | Amarilla towards the east and west respec= tively. | Library of Congress Catalog Card Number: 80-69638 | Interna= tional Standard Book Number: 0-9605202-0-1 | [device of Santa Fe Community Press] | [script] labor donated | © 1980 by the Center for Land Grant Studies | 136 Grant Street | Santa Fe, New Mexico 87501 | all rights reserved | [rule-page number-rule]".

BINDING: Yellow-gold paper wrappers. Lettered on front in a fancy roman face: "The Tierra Amarilla Grant: | [vignette as on title] | A History of Chicanery | Malcolm Ebright". Spine: "[reading vertically] The Tierra Amarilla Grant: A History of Chicanery · Malcolm Ebright". Rear lettered in fancy roman: "De la tierra fui formado, | La tierra me da de comer; | La tierra me ha sostenido, | Y al fin yo tierra he de ser.".

Published at $6.50 in January, 1981; 1,000 copies were printed.

A Foreword by Frank Waters appears on pages ix-xii. The quotation in Spanish on the rear cover was taken from Waters' *People of the Valley*. It appears again, with translation, on page vi.

COPIES: FW; TAT.

B26   DESERT WIFE   [1981]

DESERT WIFE | BY HILDA FAUNCE | INTRODUCTION BY | FRANK WATERS | [small illustration of a man and woman in a buckboard] | WITH ILLUSTRATIONS BY | W. LANGDON KIHN | UNIVERSITY OF NEBRASKA PRESS | LINCOLN AND LON= DON

7$^{31}\!/_{32}$ × 5$^{5}\!/_{16}$". [1-10^{16}]: 160 leaves. Pp. [i-viii] ix-xiv, [1-2] 3-304 [305-306]. Pages viii, 2 and 306 are blank.

COPYRIGHT PAGE: "[publisher's device of a plow beneath which appear the initials 'UNP'] | Copyright 1928, 1934 by Little, Brown, and Com= pany, renewed | 1961 by Hilda Faunce Wetherill | Introduction copy= right © 1981 by the University of Nebraska | Press | ALL RIGHTS RESERVED | MANUFACTURED IN THE UNITED STATES OF AMERICA | First Bison Book printing: 1981 | Most recent printing in= dicated by the first digit below: | 1 2 3 4 5 6 7 8 9 10 | Library of Congress Cataloging in Publication Data | [9 lines of catalog information] | Re= printed by arrangement with Ruth Jocelyn Wattles".

BINDING: Issued simultaneously in both cloth and paperback:

CLOTH: Light gray cloth. Lettered on spine: "[reading vertically] Faunce DESERT WIFE Nebraska". Rear: "[at lower right] 0-8032-1957-1". White endpapers. No dust jacket was issued.

PAPERBACK: Perfectbound in stiff white paper covers with continuous black band at bottom of front, spine and rear. The front cover contains a color photograph of a Navaho hogan with mountains in the back= ground. Lettered on front: "DESERT WIFE | [in white against black band] HILDA FAUNCE Introduction by Frank Waters". Spine: "[publisher's device of a bison, beneath which appear the words: 'A |

BISON | BOOK', the whole within a white oval within a solid black rectangle] | FAUNCE | [reading vertically] DESERT WIFE | [horizontally] [in white against the black band] BB 761''. Rear: "[publisher's device as on spine] $5.95 | [paragraph quotation from Frank Waters' Introduction] | [paragraph of quotations taken from contemporary reviews of the book] | Of related interest: | [2-line listing of Martha Summerhayes' *Vanished Arizona*] | [three lines in white against the black band] Cover design by Jack Brodie | from a photograph by Laura Gilpin | ISBN 0-8032-6853-X". Inner wrappers blank.

Published at $5.95 for paper copies and $17.95 for cloth copies on March 3, 1981; 3,071 copies were published in paper, and 216 copies were published in cloth.

An Introduction by Frank Waters appears on pages ix-xiv.

COPIES: FW (paper); TAT (cloth and paper).

B27 CUCHAMA AND SACRED MOUNTAINS [1981, i.e. 1982]

CUCHAMA | and Sacred Mountains | W. Y. Evans-Wentz | Edited by Frank Waters | and Charles L. Adams | [publisher's swallow device] | SWALLOW PRESS | Chicago

9 × 6''. [1-5^{16} 6^4 7-8^{16}]: 116 leaves. Pp. [i-vii] viii-ix [x] xi-xiv [xv] xvi-xvii [xviii] xix-xxxi [xxxii], [1-4] 5-34 [35-38] 39-83 [84-88] 89-118 [119] 120-153 [154-158] 159-183 [184] 185-196 [197-200]. Pages vi, x, xxxii, 2, 36, 84, 86, 88, 154, 156, 158, 184 and 197-200 are blank.

COPYRIGHT PAGE: "Other Books by W. Y. Evans-Wentz | [list of five titles printed in italic on five lines] | Library of Congress Cataloging in Publication Data | [12 lines of catalog data] | Copyright © 1981 by The Board of Trustees of the Leland Stanford Junior University | All Rights Reserved | Printed in the United States of America | Swallow Press Books | are published by | Ohio University Press | Athens, Ohio".

BINDING: Maroon cloth. Lettered on front in gilt: "Cuchama | and | Sacred | Mountains | W. Y. Evans-Wentz | [large design of four-rayed suns with the Swastika] | Edited by Frank Waters and Charles L. Adams". Spine lettered in gilt: "[reading vertically] Evans-Wentz [space] Cuchama and Sacred Mountains | [horizontally] [design of four-rayed sun above a pyramid] | Swallow". White endpapers.

DUST JACKET (white paper): Front, spine, and right-hand margin of rear printed overall in maroon. Lettered on front in white: "Cuchama | and | Sacred | Mountains | W. Y. Evans-Wentz | [large design as on front of binding, in gilt] | Edited by Frank Waters and Charles L. Adams". Spine lettered in white: "[reading vertically] Evans-Wentz [space] Cuchama and Sacred Mountains | [horizontally] [small design as on spine of binding, in gilt] | Swallow". Rear: "[all but final line printed to the right of a thick vertical maroon rule] [first four lines printed in maroon] CUCHAMA AND SACRED MOUNTAINS | By W. Y. Evans-Wentz | Edited by Frank Waters and Charles L. Adams | Introduction and Afterword by Frank Waters | [biographical paragraph about W. Y. Evans-Wentz] | [biographical paragraph about Frank Waters] | [biographical paragraph about Charles L. Adams] | [two paragraph explanation of designs on binding and dust jacket, all enclosed within single rules which are rounded at the corners] | ISBN 0-8040-0411-0". The front flap contains a blurb for this book, which is carried over onto the rear flap.

Published at $22.95 on March 1, 1982; number of copies printed unknown.

Waters served as co-editor of this volume; his Introduction appears on pages xix-xxviii, and his afterword appears on pages 185-193, and is entitled "The Indian Renaissance".

COPIES: TAT (d.j.).

NOTE: Waters began his friendship with Evans-Wentz in the late 1940's, and had read portions of this book in an early draft. Although the book was completed before the author's death in 1965, the unpublished manuscript was placed, along with other papers, in the Stanford University Library. In the spring of 1976, Professor Charles L. Adams visited Stanford to examine the Evans-Wentz papers for material relating to his studies on Frank Waters. During this visit, Florian J.

Shasky, head of special collections at Stanford, suggested to Adams that he (Adams) and Waters should undertake to edit *Cuchama* for publication. Adams was willing to do so, but Waters, at first, turned down the suggestion. However, after a reading of the full manuscript, Waters wrote to Adams on June 27, 1976 [CLA]:

> It has been many years since I read an early draft of *Cuchama,* and this completed version seems to me a beautiful book that should be published.
>
> The mss. needs editing, and I'll be glad to work with you on it mainly because of several comments written by Dr. Evans-Wentz in a letter to Mr. George Bass in January 1958 after I had given him my reactions to some material to be included in the book. He wrote: "Frank Waters' view is trustworthy. . . . I shall be glad to have you send a typed copy to Frank Waters, to adjust to his own liking, and to add to as much as he wishes, explaining that my free editing is for him tentative . . . I anticipate that Frank Waters will greatly improve the presentation. No one other than himself is better fitted to add to it."
>
> Despite his over-valuation of the small assistance I gave him, I am reluctant to tinker too much with the text of such a devout and world-eminent scholar. Nevertheless, in looking over the mss. objectively as possible, I believe some editorial changes would improve it without distorting in any way its illumined meaning. These suggested changes are outlined below.
>
> *Addition*
>
> An Introductory Foreword or Commentary may be appropriate. It would briefly sketch Dr. Evans-Wentz' life and work, his gift to Stanford of the present mss. and the large property embracing Mt. Cuchama; my correspondence with him between 1947-1963; a trip to the summit of Cuchama he conducted for Mr. George Bass (his illustrator), Mrs. Bass, their nephew, and myself; and my talk in Pacific Grove with Hazel Dreis and Theodor Reich (listed in the Preface, P. viii) concerning his mss. which he had given them to read. This would provide some background to Dr. Evans-Wentz' late interest in American Indian culture and religion after his many years of preoccupation with Tibetan Buddhism.
>
> *Rearrangement of Structure*
>
> Parts I and II of the mss. deal with Cuchama and the sacred mountains of the world; parts III and IV with the history and religion of the Indians of the Americas. However, some of the material on Cuchama itself is presented in Part I and some of it in Part III after the lengthy discussion of a new subject in Part II. This results in the diffusion of data on Cuchama and a break in interest for the reader.
>
> Hence I suggest a minor rearrangement of the structure in order to present all the data on Cuchama in Part I. This can easily be done without violating the text itself, by moving the first three chapters of Part III ("Jim Chalco", "The Name Cuchama", and "History and Philology of Tecate", Pages 67-75) for inclusion in Part I, inserted following Chapter IV, Page 10.
>
> I also suggest that Chapter IX, Part I, Pages 20-22, be moved into Part II, preceding Chapter I, Page 27, to give more compactness.
>
> Part III, Historical and Anthropological Complements, will then begin im-

mediately with the history and martyrdom of the Red Man, and lead into his religion.
Deletion
The story told on P. 19, Footnote 1, bugs me. As you will note in my *Pumpkin Seed Point,* P. 16-17, it was first foisted on me as the Hopi Creation Myth. The Creator, to determine if the figures in the oven were cooked enough, poked his finger in the clay. So of course we all have a hole in our belly ever since. Hence the story is generally known among Indians as the Belly Button Story. Here at Taos Pueblo it is told to inquisitive tourists and anthropology students as the Creation Myth. I regard it as no more than an amusing folk tale, bearing no relation to the great Creation Myth of the Mayas as recorded in the *Popul Vuh,* to that of the Hopis which I recorded in *Book of the Hopi,* and to those of other tribes. Perhaps it has a psychological basis; but told badly, tongue in cheek, as it usually is, the story lacks the depth and dignity of Dr. Evans-Wentz' writing on a higher plane, and I suggest it be deleted.
Annotating and Editing
The Indian situation throughout the Americas is far from being as rosy as Dr. Evans-Wentz viewed it. He was influenced by John Collier's organization of the First Inter-American Indian Conference in Patzcuaro, Mexico, which I attended. The institute set up was a failure, and there is no general movement to ameliorate the desperate plight of Indians throughout Central and South America. Dr. Evans-Wentz saw it psychically, of course, so I would let his text stand. A footnote commentary, however, should present the factual conditions now existing.

His coverage of sacred mountains in Africa, South America, and even in North America is skimpy at best. But his book is not a catalogue; and he amply develops the role of all sacred mountains throughout the world. Hence I would not attempt to interject more of them, save in a few necessary footnotes where needed.

Detailed editing of the text I think should be kept at a minimum to preserve Dr. Evans-Wentz' own style.

I haven't gone through it in detail. These observations come from my first general reading. Let me know your reaction and any comments or suggestions of your own, together with those of Mr. Shasky of Stanford University regarding the approach to be made.

SECTION BB.

Contribution to
Encyclopedia Americana

BB THE ENCYCLOPEDIA AMERICANA [1949]
NOT SEEN

In a letter dated April 1, 1980, Mr. Alan H. Smith, Executive Editor of the Encyclopedia Americana, informed me that Waters was approached by letter on July 26, 1948, and asked to write an article on the Colorado River for the *Encyclopedia Americana*. The publisher received Waters' manuscript on August 10, 1948, and Waters was supplied galleys in November of that same year. This article then appeared in the 1949 edition of the Encyclopedia, and was reprinted in all yearly editions after that. Sometime in the 1950's, minor staff revisions were made in the article.

On May 19, 1967, the publisher requested of Waters that he supply them with a completely revised text. They received the revised manuscript on May 26, 1967 and it appeared in the 1968 edition, and has been reprinted in all yearly editions to date.

SECTION C.

Contributions to periodicals

Contributions to Periodicals

In this section are listed all contributions by Waters to periodicals and newspapers, including periodical reprints of previously published material. The only articles not listed in this section are those which appeared in *El Crepusculo,* which have been listed in Section D, and interviews with Waters, which have been included in Section E. All articles listed below are signed by Waters.

1916

C1   "Hallowe'en." *Columbia Sayings and Doings.* Vol. II, No. 2. (Colorado Springs, October, 1916). Pages 8-9.

    The magazine in which this short fictional piece appeared was the literary magazine of Columbia Grade School in Colorado Springs. The only located copy of this issue, as well as that for the following item, is in the possession of Frank Waters.

1917

C2   "How it was Settled." *Columbia Sayings and Doings.* Vol. II, No. 5. (Colorado Springs, January, 1917). Page 11.

    In addition to this short story by Waters, this issue also contains a number of references to him in various class prophecies. The only located copy of this issue is in the possession of Frank Waters.

1931

C3   "Easy Meat: A Story." *North American Review.* Vol. 231, No. 4. (April, 1931). Pages 300-309.

Apart from the juvenilia listed above, this is the only short story published by Waters. It was originally one of a series which he wrote about life in the border towns. The typescript of one of the others, entitled "The Spot," is at NmU.

1939

C4 "Navajo Yei-Bet-Chai." *Yale Review*. Vol. XXVIII, No. 3. (Spring, 1939). Pages 558-571.

C5 "Four Sketches." *Laughing Horse*. No. 21. (Taos, December, 1939). Pages 3-19.
Excerpted from *The Dust Within the Rock*.

1940

C6 "Calling All Tribes." *San Diego Union Magazine*. (March 31, 1940). Page 1.
Waters wrote this article for the King Features Syndicate on the Indian Congress to be held in Mexico in April, 1940. Although Waters covered the entire congress for the syndicate, his later articles were never published.

1943

C7 "Relationships and the Novel." *The Writer*. Vol. 56, No. 4. (Boston, April, 1943). Pages 105-107.

1946

C8 "At the Root of America." *Christian Science Monitor*. (September 23, 1946). Home Forum Page.
This short article was reprinted from *The Colorado*.

1947

C9 "The Magic that Persists: New Mexico's Heritage." *Southwest Review*. Vol. XXXII, No. 3. (Dallas, Summer, 1947). Pages 231-235.
A ten-line excerpt from this article appears on the front cover of this number.

C10 "Men and Atoms—A New Mexico View." *Santa Fe New Mexican.* (July 29 & July 30, 1947). Page 4 in each issue.
A reprint of C9.

C11 Letter to Willard Hougland. *Santa Fe New Mexican.* (August 1 & August 2, 1947). Page 4 in each issue.
This letter to Hougland, guest editor of the issue of *Southwest Review* in which Waters' article "The Magic that Persists: New Mexico's Heritage" (see C9) appeared, was written in response to letters written by John Gould Fletcher and Edward Teller concerning the article. Fletcher's letter, addressed to Hougland and dated June 23, 1947, was printed in the *New Mexican* on July 31, 1947; Teller's letter, addressed to Waters and dated June 30, 1947, was printed in the *New Mexican* on August 1, 1947. All three letters appeared in the newspaper under the heading "Men and Atoms—A New Mexico View."

A long editorial commentary on Waters' article and the correspondence was printed in the *New Mexican* on August 5, 1947, under the title: "Man and the Atom—An Article of Faith."

1948

C12 "Crucible of Conflict." *New Mexico Quarterly Review.* Vol. XVIII, No. 3. (Albuquerque, Autumn, 1948). Pages 273-281.
Later incorporated into *Masked Gods.*

C13 "Navajo Trading Posts." *New Mexico Quarterly Review.* Vol. XVIII, No. 4. (Albuquerque, Winter, 1948). Pages 395-405.
This article is divided into two sections: I. Two Book Reviews; II. The Traders. The two books reviewed in the first section are Hilda Faunce's *Desert Wife* and Alberta Hannum's *Spin a Silver Dollar.* This article was later incorporated into *Masked Gods,* although in the printed book the review of *Spin a Silver Dollar* was dropped and the portion relating to the traders was shortened somewhat.

1949?

C14 "Taos Pueblo Revolt of '49 Same Old Pattern." Source unknown; date of publication unknown.

A clipping of this article was preserved by Waters and is among his papers at the University of New Mexico. A note in Waters' hand at the top of the clipping identifies it as having been published in the *Santa Fe New Mexican*. However, I have been unable to locate the specific issue in which the article appeared. An inquiry to the *New Mexican* itself uncovered no records regarding publication of this article. A search through all issues of the paper for 1949, undertaken by Mr. Orlando Romero of the New Mexico State Library, failed to discover this article.

Although the clipping gives no clue as to the source, it does carry a running head reading: "Centennial Fiesta Edition".

1950

C15 "Search for Cíbola." *Saturday Review*. Vol. XXXIII, No. 12. (March 25, 1950). Page 18.

A review of *Coronado: Knight of Pueblo and Plain*, by Herbert Bolton. This review was reprinted in *El Crepusculo* on April 13, 1950 (D304).

C16 "The Navajo Missions." *New Mexico Quarterly Review*. Vol. XX, No. 1. (Albuquerque, Spring, 1950). Pages 5-20.

Later incorporated into *Masked Gods*.

C17 "Shangri-Putnam." *Saturday Review*. Vol. XXXIII, No. 31. (August 5, 1950). Pages 21 & 28.

A review of *Up in Our Country*, by George Palmer Putnam. This review was reprinted in *El Crepusculo* on August 24, 1950 (D305).

C18 "One Immortal Year." *Saturday Review*. Vol. XXXIII, No. 43. (October 28, 1950). Pages 23-24.

A review of *Ruxton of the Rockies*, by Clyde and Mae Reed Porter. This review was reprinted in *El Crepusculo* on November 9, 1950 (D306).

1951

C19 "A Linotype's a Greedy Thing." *Saturday Review.* Vol. XXXIV, No. 1. (January 6, 1951). Pages 16 & 23.

> A review of *Once More the Thunderer,* by Henry Beetle Hough. This review was reprinted in *El Crepusculo* on January 18, 1951 (D307).

C20 "Indology." *New Mexico Quarterly Review.* Vol. XXI, No. 1. (Albuquerque, Spring, 1951). Pages 94-107.

> In this article Waters briefly reviewed 14 current books relating to American Indians. The works reviewed were:
> Babington, S. H. *Navajos, Gods and Tom-Toms* (1950).
> Beaudoin, Kenneth Lawrence. *Four Sioux Myths and Two Blackfoot Legends* (1950).
> Beaudoin, Kenneth Lawrence. *The Papago Genesis, and Two Other Legends of Origin* (1950).
> Cleland, Robert Glass. *This Reckless Breed of Men: The Trappers and Fur Traders of the Southwest* (1950).
> Collier, John and Ira Moskowitz. *Patterns and Ceremonials of the Indians of the Southwest* (1949).
> Colton, Harold S. *Hopi Kachina Dolls: With a Key to Their Identification* (1949). Waters also reviewed this book in *El Crepusculo* on December 22, 1949 (D302).
> Dale, Edward Everett. *The Indians of the Southwest* (1949).
> Gillmor, Frances. *Flute of the Smoking Mirror: A Portrait of Nezahualcoyotl, Poet-King of the Aztecs* (1949).
> Goetz, Delia and Sylvanus G. Morley. *Popul Vuh: The Sacred Book of the Ancient Quiche Maya* (1950).
> *The Alfred I. Barton Collection of Southwestern Textiles,* with a text by H. P. Mera (1949).
> O'Kane, Walter Collins. *Sun in the Sky* (1950).
> Reichard, Gladys. *Navaho Religion* (1950).
> Stewart, Dorothy, N. *Indian Ceremonial Dances in the Southwest* (1950).
> Stubbs, Stanley. *Bird's-Eye View of the Pueblos* (1950).

C21 "Indian Influence on Taos Art." *New Mexico Quarterly Review.* Vol. XXI, No. 2. (Albuquerque, Summer, 1951). Pages 173-180.

> This article is included with several others under the heading of

"Taos and Individualism," edited by Mabel Dodge Luhan, Spud Johnson and Frank Waters. This special section is preceded by its own special title page: "[sketch of pueblo] | *TAOS AND INDIVIDUALISM* | *A Brief Resume of an Environment* | [four-line quotation from Laurence Sterne] | EDITED BY | MABEL DODGE LUHAN | ASSISTED BY | FRANK WATERS AND SPUD JOHNSON".

1952

C22 "Nicolai Fechin." *Arizona Highways*. Vol. XXVIII, No. 2. (Phoenix, February, 1952). Pages 14-26.

This article was originally part of a projected biography of Fechin; the full biography was never published.

1954

C23 "The Roaring Colorado." *Holiday*. Vol. XVI, No. 2. (New York, August, 1954). Pages 90-97 & 115-116.

C24 "Glittering Cavalcade." *Saturday Review*. Vol. XXXVII, No. 50. (December 11, 1954). Page 19.

A review of *Glory, God and Gold,* by Paul I. Wellman.

C25 Untitled review of *Beyond the Hundredth Meridian: John Wesley Powell and the Second Opening of the West,* by Wallace Stegner. *Landscape*. Vol. IV, No. 2. (Albuquerque, Winter, 1954-55). Pages 39-40.

1955

C26 "The Mystery of Mesa Verde." *Holiday*. Vol. XVIII. (New York, September, 1955). Pages 44-45, 67 & 69-71.

C27 "Tucson." *Holiday*. Vol. XVIII. (New York, October, 1955). Pages 38-41 & 114-118.

1956

C28 "Collaboration in Yankeeland." *Saturday Review*. Vol. XXXIX, No. 1. (January 7, 1956). Page 60.

A review of *Journey Down a Rainbow,* by J. B. Priestley and Jacquetta Hawkes.

C29 "Life on a Ranch." *Saturday Review.* Vol. XXXIX, No. 9. (March 3, 1956). Pages 12-13.
A review of *Beyond the Mountains,* by Oliver LaFarge.

C30 "The Giants Beyond the Rockies." *Saturday Review.* Vol. XXXIX, No. 41. (October 13, 1956). Page 23.
A review of *Men to Match My Mountains,* by Irving Stone.

1957

C31 "The American Indian: Two New Books Report His Heritage in Picture and Text." *Saturday Review.* Vol. XL, No. 6. (February 9, 1957). Page 21.
A review of *A Pictorial History of the American Indian,* by Oliver LaFarge, and *Indians of the Americas,* by James Oliver LaGorce and Matthew W. Sterling.

1960

C32 "The Canyon." *Arizona Highways.* Vol. XXXVI, No. 6. (Phoenix, June, 1960). Pages 12-27.
Reprinted from *The Colorado.*

1961

C33 "The Passion Play that has No Equal." *San Diego Union.* (April 2, 1961). Page a-31.
Reprinted from *The Colorado.*

1964

C34 "Two Views of Nature: White and Indian." *South Dakota Review.* Vol. 1, No. 2. (Vermillion, May, 1964). Pages 23-32.
Originally delivered as a talk in March, 1963, at the Fourth Annual Arizona Historical Convention, Tucson. Reprinted in *South Dakota Review* in 1969 (see C49) and in revised form as Chapter 6 of *Pumpkin Seed Point* (see A18).

C35 SYMPOSIUM: "The Western Novel: A Symposium." *South Dakota Review*. Vol. 2, No. 1. (Vermillion, Autumn, 1964). Pages 10-16.

In this symposium, Waters and other writers responded to a number of questions concerning the nature of their own writing and western writers in general. The other writers who took part in the symposium were: Frederick Manfred, Walter Van Tilburg Clark, Harvey Fegusson, Vardis Fisher, Paul Horgan, Forrester Blake and Michael Straight. The entire symposium comprises pages 3-36 in the magazine.

The symposium was reprinted in its entirety in *The Literature of the American West*, edited by J. Golden Taylor (Boston, Houghton, Mifflin, 1971) (see B8).

C36 Untitled review of *Pueblo Gods and Myths*, by Hamilton A. Tyler. *Arizona and the West*. Vol. VI, No. 4. (Tucson, Winter, 1964). Pages 327-328.

1966

C37 "Bibliography of the Works of Frank Waters." *South Dakota Review*. Vol. 4, No. 2. (Vermillion, Summer, 1966). Pages 77-78.

This bibliography, prepared by Waters himself, lists an article, "The Colorado is an Outlaw", appearing in the June, 1958, issue of *Arizona Highways*. No such article appears in that issue of the magazine, and I have been unable to trace the article. I believe it to be a ghost.

1967

C38 Untitled review of *Six Faces of Mexico*, edited by Russell C. Ewing. *Western American Literature*. Vol. 1, No. 4. (Fort Collins, Colorado, Winter, 1967). Pages 304-306.

C39 "Notes on Alan Swallow." *Denver Quarterly*. Vol. 2, No. 1. (Spring, 1967). Pages 16-25.

C40 Untitled review of *Two Leggings: The Making of a Crow Warrior*, by Peter Nabokov. *Western American Literature*. Vol. II, No. 1. (Fort Collins, Spring, 1967). Pages 63-65.

1968
C41 "'Red Power': Our Awakening Indians." *Chicago Daily News.* (February 24, 1968). Panorama Section, page 8.
> A review of *The New Indians,* by Stan Steiner.

C42 "Quetzalcoatl versus D. H. Lawrence's *Plumed Serpent.*" *Western American Literature.* Vol. III, No. 2. (Fort Collins, Summer, 1968). Pages 103-113.
> Originally delivered as a paper before the Rocky Mountain American Studies Association, in Taos, April 13, 1968.

C43 Untitled review of *Navaho Folk Tales,* by Franc Johnson Newcomb. *Western American Literature.* Vol. III, No. 2. (Fort Collins, Summer, 1968). Pages 160-161.

C44 "Words." *Western American Literature.* Vol. III, No. 3. (Fort Collins, Autumn, 1968). Pages 227-234.
> Originally delivered as a paper before the Western Literature Association, in Colorado Springs, October, 1968.

C45 "North American Indians: A Sociological View." *Chicago Daily News.* (October 26, 1968). Panorama Section, page 10.
> A review of *Man's Rise to Civilization as Shown by the Indians of North America from Primeval Times to the Coming of the Industrial State,* by Peter Farb. This work was also briefly reviewed again in *Western American Literature* (see C46).

1969
C46 Untitled review of *The Indian Heritage of America,* by Alvin M. Josephy, Jr. and *Man's Rise to Civilization. . . . ,* by Peter Farb. *Western American Literature,* Vol. III, No. 4. (Fort Collins, Winter, 1969). Pages 303-305.
> Farb's book was first reviewed by Waters in the *Chicago Daily News* (see C45).

C47 "Momaday's Pulitzer Prize Novel." *Chicago Daily News.* (May 17, 1969). Panorama Section, page 10.
> A review of *House Made of Dawn,* by N. Scott Momaday.

C48 Untitled review of *Cuna Indian Art,* by Clyde S. Keeler. *Western American Literature.* Vol. IV, No. 2. (Fort Collins, Summer, 1969). Pages 149-150.

C49 "Two Views of Nature: White and Indian." *South Dakota Review.* Vol. 7, No. 2. (Vermillion, Summer, 1969). Pages 9-17.
>Originally published in *South Dakota Review* in 1964 (see C34).

C50 "A Manifesto for the Dispossessed Indian." *Chicago Daily News.* (October 11-12, 1969). Panorama Section, page 7.
>A review of *Custer Died for Your Sins,* by Vine Deloria, Jr.

C51 "The Brutal Breaking of Geronimo." *Chicago Daily News.* (November 1-2, 1969). Panorama Section, page 8.
>A review of *The Geronimo Campaign,* by Odie B. Faulk.

1970

C52 "Sky City: Venerable and Venerated Acoma Faces the Future." *New Mexico Magazine.* Vol. 48, Nos. 7-8. (Albuquerque, July/August, 1970). Pages 4-11.
>Reprinted in *Catholic Digest* (see C53) and as the introduction for H. L. James's *Acoma* (see B7).

1971

C53 "Sky City: Venerable and Venerated Acoma Faces the Future." *Catholic Digest.* Vol. 35, No. 12. (St. Paul, October, 1971). Pages 66-77.
>Originally published in *New Mexico Magazine* (see C52).

C54 "Zuni Pueblo: The Middle Place Between Old and New." *New Mexico Magazine.* Vol. 49, Nos. 11-12. (Albuquerque, November/December, 1971). Pages 12-19 & 59-62.

1972

C55 "*The Man Who Killed the Deer:* 30 Years Later." *New Mexico Magazine.* Vol. 50, Nos. 1-2. (Albuquerque, January/February, 1972). Pages 16-23 & 49-50.

1973

C56 "Colorado Fever." *New York Times.* (January 5, 1973). Op Ed page.

According to information supplied me by Joan Daves, Frank Waters' agent, this article, originally prepared as a new introduction for *The Colorado* (see A9f), was sold to the *New York Times* and appeared on the date listed. However, inspection of the microfilm of the *Times* for that date shows no such printing of the article; neither is it listed in the *Times Index* for either 1973 or 1974. Since both the microfilm and the index are based on each day's final edition, it may be that the article did indeed appear in an early edition and was dropped in later editions?

C57 "Crossroads: Indians and Whites." *South Dakota Review.* Vol. 11, No. 3. (Vermillion, Autumn, 1973). Pages 28-38.

1974

C58 Untitled review of *The Zunis: Self-Portrayals,* by the Zuni People and translated by Alvina Quam. *Western American Literature.* Vol. IX, No. 1. (Logan, Utah, Spring, 1974). Pages 59-60.

C59 "Man and Nature: An Indivisible Unity." *New Mexico Magazine.* Vol. 52, Nos. 5-6. (Albuquerque, May/June, 1974). Pages 16-21.

C60 "Four Hundred Years of 'Civilization'." *Chicago Tribune.* (October 13, 1974). Section 7 (Book World), page 2.

A review of *The Westerner,* by Dee Brown.

1975

C61 SYMPOSIUM: "The Writer's Sense of Place: A Symposium." *South Dakota Review.* Vol. 13, No. 3. (Vermillion, Autumn, 1975). Pages 6-9.

C62 "Rain Song." *Arizona Highways.* Vol. LI, No. 10. (Phoenix, October, 1975). Pages 42-43.

Reprinted from *Book of the Hopi.*

1976

C63 SYMPOSIUM: "Western Points of View." *Persimmon Hill.* Vol. 6, No. 3. (Oklahoma City, Fall, 1976). Page 89.

> Waters responded to the question: "Should the Federal Government continue to purchase and control more western lands?"

1977

C64 "Grand Canyon." *Cafe Solo 10.* (San Luis Obispo, Indian Summer Issue, 1977). Pages 25-26.

> Reprinted from *The Colorado*. Title taken from the table of contents. The entire issue of *Cafe Solo 10* was dedicated to Frank Waters and contains some material about him and his work.

C65 "Mysticism and Witchcraft." *South Dakota Review.* Vol. 15, No. 3. (Vermillion, Autumn, 1977). Pages 59-70.

> Reprint of the pamphlet published by Colorado State University in 1966 (see AA6), but deleting the eight introductory paragraphs. This entire issue of *South Dakota Review* was devoted to articles about Waters.

1981

C66 "Fragments of a Correspondence with Frank Waters." *Polis II.* (Boston, 1981). Pages 26-27.

> The text comprises a letter written by Waters to Craig Hanson, dated September 3, 1975, and a follow-up letter written November 26, 1980.

C67 "A Discussion with Frank Waters." *Puerto del Sol.* Vol. 16. (Las Cruces, New Mexico, Spring, 1981). Pages 82-86.

> Originally delivered as a talk to La Sociedad para los Artes, New Mexico State University, Las Cruces, on October 30, 1980.

C68 "Notes on Los Angeles." *South Dakota Review.* Vol. 19, Nos. 1-2. (Vermillion, Spring/Summer, 1981). Pages 14-23.

C69 "Frank Waters Receives Honorary Doctorate." *Taos' Rio Grande Magazine*. Vol. 3, No. 3. (Taos, Summer, 1981). Pages 36-37.

Originally delivered as "Prelude to Change," the commencement address at the University of Nevada, Las Vegas, May 23, 1981. This version was edited and differs slightly from that distributed by the University (see AA8), and also differs slightly from the version transcribed from a tape recording of the address by Charles L. Adams, published in the *Nevada Historical Society Quarterly* (see E25).

C70 "The Magic of 'Seekers of the Fleece.'" *Four Winds: The International Forum for Native American Art, Literature and History*. Vol. 2, No. 2. (Austin, Summer/Autumn, 1981). Pages 53-55.

An introduction for the second part of Bobby Bridger's ballad "Seekers of the Fleece."

SECTION D.

Contributions to *El Crepusculo*

Contributions to *El Crepusculo*

From the issue of September 8, 1949, until the issue of December 6, 1951, Waters served as the editor-in-chief of the bi-lingual weekly newspaper *El Crepusculo,* published in Taos, New Mexico. In fulfillment of his editorial duties, Waters wrote one or more editorials for most editions of the newspaper; all of his editorials appeared in the editorial section on page 4, and were unsigned. Occasionally, other staff members would contribute editorials or in a few instances prepare the entire editorial section. Such editorials written by persons other than Waters were signed and have, of course, been ignored in this listing. For clarity, I have listed all editions of the paper during this period and identified those editions in which no editorials by Waters appeared.

In addition to his editorial duties, Waters also wrote an occasional book review for the paper. These reviews were usually published under the column title "Book Looks by Frank Waters." In a few instances, reviews were given to other writers. These reviews were all signed by their authors and have been ignored for the present listing.

One other aspect of Waters' duties with *El Crepusculo* involved writing occasional feature articles. As far as I have been able to determine, only four such articles appeared, counting the entire "San Geronimo Historical Supplement" as a single contribution. Only one of these articles was signed by Waters, and it may be that others may have been written by him. However, these articles are the only ones which can definitely be attributed to Waters.

A NOTE ABOUT *EL CREPUSCULO:* The file of *El Crepusculo* which went to the University of New Mexico Library with the Waters papers is unfortunately incomplete, lacking the issues of September 8th, 15th and 22nd, 1949, as well as the issue of July 5, 1951. Also, this file lacks the editorial page for the issue of October 13, 1949. The only complete run of this newspaper which I have been able to locate is in the Harwood Memorial Library, University of New Mexico, Taos, New Mexico.

El Crepusculo Editorials

September 8, 1949:
- D1   What! No Street Cars Yet?
- D2   The Pueblo Controversy

September 15, 1949:
- D3   Notes on the Waning Year
- D4   New Road for Arroy Seco Abajo
- D5   Bridge Playing for Prizes Illegal in New Mexico
- D6   What on Earth's the Matter with Me?
- D7   A Leaf Falls
- D8   Sign of the Times

September 22, 1949:
- D9   The Consolidation of School District in the Southern Part of the County
- D10   Penasco is the Place
- D11   A Butter Tower for Taos?
- D12   Who Will Operate?
- D13   Flag over Taos

September 29, 1949:
- D14   Kit Carson Cemetery Again
- D15   Dr. Rosen Protests
- D16   No School Signs at Canyon

October 6, 1949:
- D17   Ride a Pink Horse
- D18   Night Must Fall
- D19   Save that Tree
- D20   Arroyo Seco Abajo Road Progress
- D21   Nichols States Indian Policy
- D22   Pending Bills Set Indian Policy
- D23   Indians Setting Own Indian Policy
- D24   The State Fair

October 13, 1949:
- D25   National Newspaper Week
- D26   Memorial Exhibition for Victor Higgins

        D27   Who's Throwing What?
        D28   We're Trying Not to Shout, Operator
October 20, 1949:
        D29   Keeping Up With the Joneses
        D30   Gertrude Van Tijn
        D31   Abel Plenn
        D32   The Nick of Time
        D33   Now is the Time
October 27, 1949:
        D34   Pride and Prejudice
        D35   The Proud People
        D36   Good Neighbor Policy
        D37   Where are Our Taos Sign Haters?
        D38   Outside Privies Going Out
November 3, 1949:
        D39   Co-op Members Not Interested?
        D40   How They Ran and Who Backed Them
        D41   World-War vs. World-Revolution
November 10, 1949:
        D42   The Health Co-op Buildings
        D43   Smoke Catcher Needed
        D44   What We Need
        D45   India Speaks
November 17, 1949:
        D46   The True Builders of Taos
        D47   3R's on Ice
        D48   Good News: Chapman Heads Interior
        D49   Ersatz Indianism vs. Indian Culture
November 24, 1949:
        D50   Pueblo Self-Government
        D51   "Our" Forests
        D52   How Much Big Government Do You Want?
        D53   Americanese for Moderns
        D54   Why We Have a New Secretary of the Interior
        D55   The Navaho Hopi Bill
        D56   San Luis Valley Water Bill
December 1, 1949:
        D57   The Wind Bloweth
        D58   Land of Disenchantment
December 8, 1949:
        D59   Justice and the J. P.

312 SECTION D

    D60   Captives of Sound
    D61   More of the Same, Please
December 15, 1949:
    D62   What Taos Needs Most
    D63   Pink Toothbrush
    D64   Our Mysterious Roads
December 22, 1949:
    D65   Time for Staying Still
December 29, 1949:
    D66   Read Yr Doughbelly and Reach for Yr Bible
    D67   Hurray for the Common Cold
    D68   The Governor of Montana Comes Down with a Conscience
January 5, 1950:
    D69   The Atomic Year—1950
    D70   Song of the Turtle
    D71   The 81st Congress
January 12, 1950:
    D72   Taos Twelfth-Day
    D73   Optimism and Realism
    D74   New Mexico Matures
January 19, 1950:
    D75   Science's Rainbow Bridge
    D76   Cash War
    D77   Taos Short-Change Club
January 26, 1950:
    D78   Memorial Chapel
    D79   Justice and the D. A.
    D80   June in January
February 2, 1950:
    D81   Written in Air and Water
    D82   The Curtain Rises
    D83   A Swell Idea
    D84   We're Getting There
February 9, 1950:
    D85   Tombstone Travesty
February 16, 1950:
    D86   Community Cooperation
    D87   Racial Discrimination
    D88   Your Roll
February 23, 1950:
    D89   The End or a New Beginning

El Crepusculo Editorials 313

    D90   Vox Populi
    D91   Section 99-100
March 2, 1950:
    D92   Cool, Cool Water
    D93   Outdoor Advertisers Show Hand. . .
    D94   Navajo-Hopi Bill Again
March 9, 1950:
    D95   Insult After Injury
    D96   Those Billboards
March 16, 1950:
    D97   Beware! Stock Still Loose!
    D98   Good for Fred!
March 23, 1950:
    D99   Enthusiastic Cooperation
    D100   Meat-Eaters of America
    D101   Pike's Peak by Barrow
March 30, 1950:
    D102   Men vs. Semantics
    D103   A Timely Warning
    D104   Last Call
April 6, 1950:
    D105   The Immortal Drama
April 13, 1950:
    D106   If the Truth Be Told
    D107   El Dia de las Americas
    D108   Old Versus New
April 20, 1950:
    D109   Whose Plaza?
    D110   Here it is
    D111   The Last Straw
April 27, 1950:
    D112   Questa Community Workshop
    D113   Will History Repeat Itself?
    D114   Mailbag Humor
May 4, 1950:
    D115   Acknowledgment
    D116   Conservation of Resources
    D117   The American Way
May 11, 1950:
    D118   Blame it on Blossoms
    D119   What's The Rush?

SECTION D

    D120   Grand Larceny
May 18, 1950:
    D121   Inter-Community Cooperation
    D122   All America Stands For
    D123   Green Flash
May 25, 1950:
    D124   Bill of Rights—For Whom?
June 1, 1950:
    D125   Adios, Senor Mistanano! Adios, Senor Sin Nombre!
    D126   Safe City Streets
June 8, 1950:
    D127   A Turgid Wake
    D128   Freedom and Discrimination
June 15, 1950:
    D129   Park Here, Please
June 22, 1950:
    D130   Fusion and Confusion
    D131   Portal with a Future
June 29, 1950:
    D132   Interdependence Day
    D133   Humpty-Dumpty Pueblo
July 6, 1950:
    D134   Racial Discrimination in New Mexico
    D135   Tough Competition
July 13, 1950:
    D136   Gilding the Lily
    D137   Moral Rearmament
    D138   A Village Green
July 20, 1950:
    D139   Fiesta—1950
    D140   As Others See Us
    D141   Slow But Sure
July 27, 1950: Waters had no editorials in this issue
August 3, 1950:
    D142   Why Not Plug Chiflo?
    D143   Who-Done-It?
August 10, 1950:
    D144   Ostriches or Men
    D145   Guerilla Warfare
    D146   No Peep-Sights Necessary

August 17, 1950:
- D147 Mentally Unfit
- D148 A Stinking Shame
- D149 If an "A" Bomb Explodes

August 24, 1950:
- D150 Bottle vs. Text Book
- D151 Alaskan Statehood
- D152 Ready for Long Pants

August 31, 1950:
- D153 A Community Affair

September 7, 1950:
- D154 Community & School Board Cooperation. . . .
- D155 Worlds in Collision

September 14, 1950:
- D156 Just One Roof More
- D157 Devil and Deep Blue Sea

September 21, 1950:
- D158 Costilla Gym Too?
- D159 There's Still Hope

September 28, 1950:
- D160 School Bus Transportation
- D161 Who's Got the Broom?

October 5, 1950:
- D162 Fire Prevention Week
- D163 Same Old Story

October 12, 1950:
- D164 Political Hay
- D165 A Small World

October 19, 1950:
- D166 Penasco Versus Questa and Costilla
- D167 A Little Child Shall Teach Us

October 26, 1950:
- D168 A Political Tail Wag
- D169 Bird Communists

November 2, 1950:
- D170 On Record
- D171 Beclouding the Issue

November 9, 1950:
- D172 Call for Unity
- D173 Peace at any Price

316 SECTION D

    D174 National Education Week
November 16, 1950:
    D175 A Small World
November 23, 1950:
    D176 Broadside Against Billboards
    D177 Compound Interest
November 30, 1950:
    D178 Help for Handicraft
    D179 Who Built the Qutah Minar?
December 7, 1950:
    D180 Dump Rats
    D181 The Time and the Place
December 14, 1950:
    D182 At Long Last
    D183 A White Christmas
    D184 Water Bills in Congress
December 21, 1950:
    D185 Safety Rules for a Merry Christmas
December 28, 1950: All editorials on this date were by Ted Cabot
January 4, 1951: All editorials on this date were by others
January 11, 1951:
    D186 Danger—State Highway
    D187 He Who Gets Slapped
January 18, 1951:
    D188 "Happy Little Hospital"
    D189 Be Careful!
January 25, 1951:
    D190 The Questa Gym
    D191 A War Memorial?
    D192 Forest Revenues Pay
February 1, 1951:
    D193 The Costilla Gym
    D194 Kit Carson Memorial Park
February 8, 1951:
    D195 Independent Versus County School System
    D196 Kit Carson Park
February 15, 1951:
    D197 Schools and Politics
    D198 Savages by Nature
February 22, 1951:
    D199 The New Squeeze

El Crepusculo Editorials **317**

March 1, 1951:
    D200 Deeper in the Mire
    D201 Indian Bureau Rehabilitation
March 8, 1951:
    D202 Riding on Our Reputation
    D203 Granny and Sassafras Tea
March 15, 1951:
    D204 E. Pluribus Unim
    D205 Texas on the Spot
March 22, 1951:
    D206 Statement on Policy Regarding School News
    D207 Tent Caterpillars Again
    D208 Even the Mountains
March 29, 1951:
    D209 Science and Society
April 5, 1951:
    D210 Let's Follow Through
    D211 Slow Boat to China
    D212 Red Rain
April 12, 1951:
    D213 Misrepresented Representation
    D214 Pan-American Day, 1951
April 19, 1951:
    D215 Tightening the Squeeze
    D216 Help for Our Forests
April 26, 1951:
    D217 Tuesday Morning Miracle
    D218 Pleading for the Oppressed
May 3, 1951:
    D219 What Price American
    D220 Schools and Politics
    D221 Thirty-Five Years Ago
May 10, 1951:
    D222 A Tottering Step
    D223 Taos County Roads
May 17, 1951: All editorials on this date by Ted Cabot
May 24, 1951:
    D224 No Liquor Shortage
    D225 Unholy Alliance
    D226 Blood, Sweat and Tears

May 31, 1951:
    D227   Unprecedented Precedent
    D228   Suggestion for Democracy
    D229   The Press and Freedom
June 7, 1951:
    D230   Tulip Time vs. Chile Time
    D231   "Save the Spruce"
    D232   Auto-Minded
June 14, 1951:
    D233   Indians on the Jury
    D234   How Times Change
    D235   Those Billboards
    D236   Indian Local Option
June 21, 1951: Waters had no editorials in this issue
June 28, 1951: Waters had no editorials in this issue
July 5, 1951:
    D237   Safe and Sane Fourth
    D238   A Safe Bet
July 12, 1951:
    D239   Not Welcome
    D240   Another Strike
July 19, 1951:
    D241   Viva la Fiesta!
    D242   Catalysts of Unity
    D243   Tree Farming
July 26, 1951:
    D244   Let John Do It
    D245   The Billboard Peace
August 2, 1951:
    D246   Slow Down
    D247   Quien Sabe?
    D248   Fingers Crossed
August 9, 1951:
    D249   Constitutional Amendments
    D250   Gross Misconception
    D251   Navaho Malnutrition
August 16, 1951:
    D252   The House Wives Revolt
    D253   Tempest in a Teacup
August 23, 1951:
    D254   One a Day

El Crepusculo Editorials **319**

  D255 The King is Dead
  D256 Beetle Blitz Halted
August 30, 1951:
  D257 Winds of Freedom
  D258 Big Time, Bit Town
  D259 The Chokecherries are Ripe
September 6, 1951:
  D260 Our Own, Our Native Land
  D261 Eva on Thin Ice. . . .
  D262 Let the Chips Fall
September 13, 1951:
  D263 Smoky's Burned Feet
  D264 Trial by Jury
  D265 Education is Big Business
  D266 But Vote
September 20, 1951:
  D267 Still In Limbo
  D268 The $64 Question
  D269 Official Announcement
September 27, 1951:
  D270 San Geronimo
  D271 Texas Hospitality
  D272 Help for Vets. & Farmers
October 4, 1951:
  D273 Traffic Jam
  D274 The "Dixon Lease"
  D275 National Newspaper Week
October 11, 1951:
  D276 Thanks, Ladies
  D277 Self-Help for Indians
  D278 Go West Young Man
October 18, 1951:
  D279 Fall Clearance Sale
  D280 What's Going On
  D281 Crew to Mohawk
October 25, 1951:
  D282 Road Markers
  D283 Work, Sex & Society
  D284 Bacon and Beans
November 1, 1951:
  D285 A New Penitentiary

D286   Slow But Sure
D287   Highway Deaths & Billboards
November 8, 1951:
   D288   Those Golden Eggs
   D289   They Do
November 15, 1951:
   D290   A Real Challenge
November 22, 1951:
   D291   An Open Hearing—At Last
November 29, 1951:
   D292   War on Earth Ill Will to Man
   D293   More Expensive Motoring
   D294   Women and Work
December 6, 1951:
   D295   Raw Deal for Veterans
   D296   Let's Pull Together

El Crepusculo Book Reviews

These occasional reviews appeared under the column title: "Book Looks by Frank Waters." Unless otherwise noted all reviews appear on page 4 of the newspaper.

D297   Review of *A Scientist on the Trail: Travel Letters of A. F. Bandelier, 1880–1881*. October 27, 1949.
D298   Review of *Lead, Kindly Light* by Vincent Sheean. November 10, 1949.
D299   Review of *Rio Grande* by Laura Gilpin. November 17, 1949.
D300   Review of *The Awakening Valley* by John Collier and Anibal Burton. December 1, 1949.
D301   Review of *Frontier Justice* by Wayne Gard; and *Jeff Milton: Good Man With a Gun* by J. Evetts Haley. December 8, 1949.
D302   Review of *Hopi Kachina Dolls* by Harold S. Colton. December 22, 1949. This review appears on p. 3. This book was also briefly reviewed by Waters in his article "Indology" (see C20).
D303   Review of *Swiftwater* by Paul Annixter. February 2, 1950.
D304   Review of *Coronado: Knight of the Pueblos* by Herbert E. Bolton. April 13, 1950. This review appears on p. 5. Re-

printed from the Saturday Review of March 25, 1950 (see C15).

D305 Review of *Up in Our Country* by George Palmer Putnam. August 24, 1950. Reprinted from Saturday Review, August 5, 1950 (see C17).

D306 Review of *Ruxton of the Rockies* by Clyde and Mae Reed Porter. November 9, 1950. Reprinted from Saturday Review, October 28, 1950 (see C18).

D307 Review of *Once More the Thunderer* by Henry Beetle Hough. January 18, 1951. Reprinted from Saturday Review, January 6, 1951 (see C19).

D308 Review of *Maria* by John C. Neff. October 11, 1951.

El Crepusculo: Miscellaneous Feature Articles

Only a few feature articles written by Frank Waters appear in the pages of *El Crepusculo*. Of course, there may be others as yet unidentified, but it seems unlikely. Unless otherwise noted the articles listed below are unsigned.

D309 "San Geronimo Historical Supplement." September 29, 1949. This four-page supplement issued with the newspaper on this date was written entirely by Frank Waters. The supplement contains a history of San Geronimo, yesterday and today; a history of *El Crepusculo;* and a biography of the paper's founder, Padre Antonio Martinez.

D310 "New High School Dedicated in Navajo Mission." September 22, 1949. Signed.

D311 "Cimarron Not Birth Place of Wild West Show." October 20, 1949.

D312 "Ascent to Olympus." November 24, 1949.

Section E.

Articles by others containing material by Waters, including interviews

Articles Containing Material by Waters, Including Interviews

In this section are listed all articles published in periodicals which contain previously unpublished material by Waters, such as an author quoting from a letter by Waters, and includes published interviews with Waters. Some of the articles listed were written after the author had interviewed Waters, but do not contain direct quotes. This section is almost certainly not complete.

1965
E1 POWELL, LAWRENCE CLARK. "Down Where the Rockies End." *Mountain-Plains Library Quarterly*. Vol. X, No. 3. (Wichita, Fall, 1965). Pages 3-6 & 8-11.
   Powell quotes from a letter by Waters.

1967
E2 GILCHRIESE, JOHN D. "Territorial Tales." *Arizona Currents*. Vol. 3, No. 3. (Tucson, June, 1967). Pages 8-9.
   Gilchriese quotes from a letter Waters wrote his mother on July 30, 1936.

1968
E3 LYON, THOMAS J. "An Ignored Meaning of the West." *Western American Literature*. Vol. III, No. 1. (Fort Collins, Colorado, Spring, 1968). Pages 51-59.
   Lengthy quote from a letter by Waters dated February 8, 1968.

1970

E4 MANCHESTER, JOHN. "The Frank Waters Story." *Encanto Magazine & New Mexico Cultural News*. Vol. 3, No. 3. (Albuquerque, July/August, 1970). Pages 4-7.

Quotes from biographical notes prepared for the author by Waters. The article's title is taken from the contents listing. Reprinted in *South Dakota Review* in 1977 (see E17).

1971

E5 MILTON, JOHN R. "Conversations with Frank Waters." *South Dakota Review*. Vol. 9, No. 1. (Vermillion, Spring, 1971). Pages 16-27.

Reprinted as Chapter IV of Milton's *Conversations with Frank Waters* (see B9).

E6 INGERSOLL, BRUCE. "America's Indians—Pioneer Psychologists." *Chicago Sun Times*. (July 25, 1971). Page 58.

Based on an interview with Waters.

1973

E7 PETERSON, JAMES. "A Conversation with Frank Waters: Lessons from the Indian Soul." *Psychology Today*. Vol. VI, No. 12. (Del Mar, California, May, 1973). Pages 63-64, 66-68, 71-72 & 99.

E8 DANIELS, BRUCE. "Frank Waters Envisions Land as . . . The Wellspring of Pyschic Strength." *Taos News*. (September 5, 1973). Pages 4-5.

E9 TAYLOR, JAMES. "An Interview with Frank Waters." *The Black Bear Review*. Vol. 1, No. 1. (Taos, Fall? 1973). Pages 1-5.

1974

E10 GUSTAFSON, ROBERT. "A Conversation with Frank Waters on American Indian Religion." *Pembroke Magazine*. No. 5. (Pembroke, North Carolina, 1974). Pages 78-89.

E11 POWELL, LAWRENCE CLARK. "A Writer's Landscape." *Westways*. Vol. 66, No. 1. (Los Angeles, January, 1974). Pages 24-27 & 70-72.
   Reprinted in Powell's *From the Heartland* (see B19) under the title "Down Where the Rockies End." This is not to be confused with E1.

1976

E12 DAVIS, JACK L. "The Whorf Hypothesis and Native American Literature." *South Dakota Review*. Vol. 14, No. 2. (Vermillion, Summer, 1976). Pages 59-72.
   Quotes from a letter by Waters dated November 15, 1972.

1977

E13 TARBET, TOM. "The Hopi Prophecy and the Chinese Dream: An Interview with Frank Waters." *East West Journal*. Vol. 7, No. 5. (Dover, New Jersey, May, 1977). Pages 52-60, 62 & 64.

E14 MANNING, MARY. "'Spirit of Place' Novelist Overturns Subconscious Stones." *Las Vegas Sun People Magazine*. (August 28, 1977). Page 1D.

E15 BAER, BERYL [psued. of Jane Ann Morrison]. "Frank Waters: A Sleepy Man on a Cloudy Day." *Las Vegas Review Journal Nevadan*. (September 4, 1977). Pages 6J & 23J.

E16 DAVIS, JACK L. "Frank Waters' *Mexico Mystique:* The Ontology of the Occult." *South Dakota Review*. Vol. 15, No. 3. (Vermillion, Autumn, 1977). Pages 17-24.
   Davis quotes from letters by Waters dated December 16, 1974 and July 9, 1975.

E17 MANCHESTER, JOHN. "Frank Waters." *South Dakota Review*. Vol. 15, No. 3. (Vermillion, Autumn, 1977). Pages 73-80.
   Edited reprint of E4.

1978

E18 ADAMS, CHARLES L. "The Return of Frank Waters: A Postscript." *Nevada Historical Society Quarterly*. Vol. XXI, No. 2. (Las Vegas, Summer, 1978). Pages 149-151.

Includes the full text of Waters' acceptance speech for his honorary membership in the Honor Society of Phi Kappa Phi, awarded on August 23, 1977.

1979

E19 EVERS, LARRY (editor). "A Conversation with Frank Waters." *Sun Tracks Five*. (Tucson, 1979). Pages 61-68.

The conversation included Waters, David Begay, Larry Evers, Cathy Gallegos, Marie Levy, Steve Nelson, Leslie Marmon Silko and Emory Sekaquaptewa.

E20 GORDON, ROBERT. "The Writer's Page." *The New Mexico Independent*. Vol. 83, No. 36. (Albuquerque, May 11, 1979). Page 8.

The article is a "distillation" of a talk Waters gave at the University of New Mexico Writers at Work Series and an interview granted the writer.

1981

E21 OPPENHEIM, SANDY. "Waters' 'Past as Prologue' Presentation Full to Overflowing." *Colorado Springs Gazette-Telegraph*. (July 5, 1981). Section AA, Page 12.

Based on a telephone interview with Waters.

E22 BIRKHEAD, GENE. "Waters Takes Time to Remember." *Colorado Springs Sun*. (July 11, 1981). Today section, pages 9B & 10B.

E23 WENGLER, DIANE. "Frank Waters Discusses Colorado Springs—Then and Now." *Colorado Springs Gazette-Telegraph*. (July 15, 1981). Pages 1D & 4D.

An account of Waters' presentation in the Penrose Public Library's "Past as Prologue" Series, delivered on July 9, 1981, including quotations from his presentation. The text on page

4D carries the heading "Santa Fe Station Became Like a Second Home."

E24 JENKINS, ROBIN. "Sage of the Southwest." *Las Vegan Magazine*. (August, 1981). Pages 26-30.
Interview with Waters.

E25 ADAMS, CHARLES L. "Frank Waters' 'Prelude to Change.'" *Nevada Historical Society Quarterly*. Vol. XXIV, No. 3. (Las Vegas, Fall, 1981). Pages 250-254.
Includes the text of Waters' commencement address at the University of Nevada, Las Vegas, delivered on May 22, 1981, entitled "Prelude to Change." This version was transcribed by Adams from a tape recording he made of the speech, and differs slightly from the version distributed by the University after the event (see AA8). This version is also slightly different from that published in *Taos Rio Grande Magazine* (see C69).

E26 HURST, TRICIA. "Frank Waters: An Author Looks at His Life." *Import: Albuquerque Journal Magazine*. Vol. 5, No. 7. (December 1, 1981). Pages 12-13.

NOTE: An excerpt from a letter by Waters was used within what appears to be an unsigned article published in *The Stonepile*, Summer, 1981. However, upon closer examination, this seemed to me to be an advertisement rather than an article, and so I have included it in the section listing blurbs: see F6.

Section F.

Blurbs

Blurbs

This section contains a listing of the few blurbs written by Waters. I have included not only blurbs published on dust jackets and books, but also two blurbs which appeared in publishers' printed announcements. Books on which the publisher included a blurb quoting from the foreword or introduction by Waters have not been included in this listing.

F1   WATERS, FRANK. *Below Grass Roots*. (New York, Liveright, 1937).

> On July 10, 1937, Arthur Pell at Liveright Publishing Company requested of Waters that he prepare a 250-word description of his novel *Below Grass Roots* for use as a blurb in their catalogue. Waters provided Pell with this description on June 15, 1937. No copy of the Liveright catalogue has been seen, and it is not known whether or not the blurb was used. However, it would seem that Waters' description was used as the basis for the blurb which appears on the dust jacket of the published book: See A4.

F2   NABOKOV, PETER. *Two Leggings: The Making of a Crow Warrior*. (New York, Crowell, 1967).

> Five-line blurb on rear of dust jacket.

F3   UDE, WAYNE. *Buffalo and Other Stories*. (Amherst, Mass., Lynx House Press, 1975).

> Seven-line blurb on rear cover (paperbound). Only the second "edition" of 1976 has been seen, and it is not known whether or not the blurb appears in the first printing.

F4   ANAYA, RUDOLFO. *Tortuga.* (Berkeley, Editorial Justa Publications, 1979).
17-line blurb on rear cover (paperbound).

F5   SILKO, LESLIE MARMON. *Storyteller.* (New York, Seaver Books, 1981).
Four-line blurb on page 2 of a two-page press release issued by the publisher prior to the book's publication on May 1, 1981.

F6   FOSTER, STEVEN AND MEREDITH LITTLE. *The Book of the Vision Quest.* (Island Press, 1981).
Nine-line blurb appearing within an article-length advertisement for the book, published in *The Stonepile,* Vol. II, No. 1. (Novata, California, Rites of Passage, Summer, 1981); p. 1. The authors of the book edited *The Stonepile.*

F7   PAINTER, CHARLOTTE. *Seeing Things.* (San Francisco, Context Publications, 1981).
16-line blurb included in a press release sent to bookstores. This press release was printed on one side only of an 11 × 8½" sheet of yellow paper, which curiously enough does not give the publisher's name.

NOTE: Although not actually a blurb, a few lines from Waters' *Pumpkin Seed Point* were printed on the back of the record sleeve of Michael Murphy's recording "Blue Sky Night Thunder," published by CBS Records in 1975.

SECTION **G**.

Foreign translations

Foreign Translations

In this section are listed all foreign translations of books by Frank Waters. This section is arranged chronologically by title, with each foreign translation of a given title listed chronologically under that title. No attempt has been made to provide descriptions. All the books listed, with one exception, can be seen in the Waters archive at the University of New Mexico. The exception is the German edition of *Book of the Hopi,* a copy of which I examined in the personal collection of Frank Waters.

THE MAN WHO KILLED THE DEER [1942]

G1   GERMAN: *Martiniano und der Hirsch*. (Hamburg, Christian Wegner, 1960).

G2   FRENCH: *L'Homme qui a tue le Cerf*. (Paris, Albin Michel, 1964).

G3   DUTCH: *De Man die het Hert Doode*. (Baarn, Netherlands, Uitgave en druk, 1974).

DIAMOND HEAD [1948]

G4   FRENCH: *Pointe de Diamonte*. (Paris, Hachette, 1951).

MASKED GODS [1950]

G5   JAPANESE: *Kamen no Kamisama* [in Japanese]. (Tokyo, Kagaku Joho Sha, 1974-1975, 2 vols.). Volume one of this title was published in November, 1974; volume two was issued in April, 1975, at which time volume one was also reprinted.

BOOK OF THE HOPI [1963]

G6   SWEDISH: *En Bok om Hopi-Indianerna*. (Stockholm, Almquist & Wiksell, 1977).

G7   FRENCH: *Le Livre du Hopi*. (Paris, Payot, 1978).

G8   GERMAN: *Das Buch der Hopi*. (Dusseldorf/Koln, Eugen Kiederichs, 1980).

NOTE: The bibliography of Waters which appears in Tom Lyons' *Frank Waters* cites a French edition of *River Lady* published in Paris by Hachette in 1948. However, in a letter to me on January 7, 1982, Marthe Ordody, of Libraire Hachette, informed me that the firm did not publish such a translation. Nor was I able to find any evidence that any French edition of *River Lady* has ever been published.

SECTION H.

Selected list of writings about Waters

Writings about Frank Waters

This section contains a selected listing of writings about Frank Waters, both in periodicals and in books. I have made no effort to be complete, but I have tried to list all of the major critical writings on Waters. Some works listed in Section E have been repeated here because they are important.

H1 ADAMS, CHARLES. "Teaching *Yogi* in Las Vegas." *South Dakota Review*. Vol. 15, No. 3. (Vermillion, Autumn, 1977). Pages 37-42.
    This entire issue of *South Dakota Review* concerns Waters.

H2 ADAMS, RAMON F. *Burs Under the Saddle: A Second Look at Books and Histories of the West*. (Norman, University of Oklahoma Press, 1964). Pages 533-534.
    Adams, a noted authority on western outlaws, assesses *The Earp Brothers of Tombstone*. His laudatory comments were repeated in his *Six Guns and Saddle Leather: A Bibliography of Books on Western Outlaws and Gunmen* (2nd edition; Norman, 1969).

H3 BETTS, GLYNNE ROBINSON. *Writers in Residence: American Authors at Home*. (New York, Viking/Studio Book, 1981). Pages 134-136.
    Includes a photographic essay on Waters' home in Taos.

H4 BUCCO, MARTIN. *Frank Waters*. (Austin, Steck-Vaughn, 1969).
    Southwest Writers Series #22.

H5 DAVIS, JACK L. "The Whorf Hypothesis and Native American Literature." *South Dakota Review.* Vol. 14, No. 2. (Vermillion, Summer, 1976). Pages 59-72.
   Whorfian analysis of *The Man Who Killed the Deer* and N. Scott Momaday's *House Made of Dawn.*

H6 DAVIS, JACK L. "Frank Waters' *Mexico Mystique:* The Ontology of the Occult." *South Dakota Review.* Vol. 15, No. 3. (Vermillion, Autumn, 1977). Pages 17-24.

H7 DAVIS, JACK L. and JUNE H. "Frank Waters and the Native American Consciousness." *Western American Literature.* Vol. 9, No. 1. (Logan, Utah, May, 1974). Pages 33-44.

H8 GRIGG, QUAY. "The Kachina Characters of Frank Waters' Novels." *South Dakota Review.* Vol. 11, No. 1. (Vermillion, Spring, 1973). Pages 6-16.

H9 GRIGG, QUAY. "Frank Waters and the Mountain Spirit." *South Dakota Review.* Vol. 15, No. 3. (Vermillion, Autumn, 1977). Pages 45-49.

H10 HOY, CHRISTOPHER. "The Archetypal Transformations of Martiniano in *The Man Who Killed the Deer.*" *South Dakota Review.* Vol. 13, No. 4. (Vermillion, Winter, 1975-1976). Pages 43-56.

H11 HOY, CHRISTOPHER. "The Conflict in *The Man Who Killed the Deer.*" *South Dakota Review.* Vol. 15, No. 3. (Vermillion, Autumn, 1977). Pages 51-57.

H12 HUNTRESS, DIANA. "The Man Who Resurrected the Deer." *South Dakota Review.* Vol. 6, No. 4. (Vermillion, Winter, 1968-1969). Pages 69-71.
   A short impressionistic account of a visit with Waters.

H13 KOSTKA, ROBERT. "Frank Waters and the Visual Sense." *South Dakota Review.* Vol. 15, No. 3. (Vermillion, Autumn, 1977). Pages 27-30.

This issue also contains a photographic section entitled "Frank Waters' Environment" with photos by Kostka and John Milton; pp. 81-153.

H14 LYON, THOMAS J. "An Ignored Meaning of the West." *Western American Literature*. Vol. III, No. 1. (Fort Collins, Spring, 1968). Pages 51-59.
Discussion of Waters' work from the standpoint of the conflict between Indian and White.

H15 LYON, THOMAS J. *Frank Waters*. (New York, Twayne, 1973).

H16 LYON, THOMAS J. "Frank Waters and the Concept of 'Nothing Special.'" *South Dakota Review*. Vol. 15, No. 3. (Vermillion, Autumn, 1977). Pages 31-35.

H17 MALZEPPI, FRANCES. "A Study of the Female Protagonist in Frank Waters' *People of the Valley* and Rudolfo Anaya's *Bless Me, Ultima*." *South Dakota Review*. Vol. 14, No. 2. (Vermillion, Summer, 1976). Pages 102-110.

H18 MILTON, JOHN R. "The American West: A Challenge to the Literary Imagination." *Western American Literature*. Vol. I, No. 4. (Fort Collins, Winter, 1967). Pages 267-284.
Includes a short discussion of Waters.

H19 MILTON, JOHN R. "The Land as Form in Frank Waters and William Eastlake." *Kansas Quarterly*. Vol. II, No. 2. (Spring, 1970). Pages 104-109.

H20 MILTON, JOHN R. "The Sound of Space." *South Dakota Review*. Vol. 15, No. 3. (Vermillion, Autumn, 1977). Pages 11-15.
Discussion of space as form in Waters. This issue also contains a photographic section entitled "Frank Waters' Environment" with photos by Milton and Robert Kostka; pp. 81-153.

H21 MILTON, JOHN R. *The Novel of the American West*. (Lincoln, University of Nebraska Press, 1980).
Chapter VIII relates to Waters.

SECTION H

H22 MORRILL, CLAIRE. *A Taos Mosaic: Portrait of a New Mexico Village*. (Albuquerque, University of New Mexico Press, 1973).
    Includes short discussion of background of *To Possess the Land* and *Woman at Otowi Crossing*. Also contains a Laura Gilpin photograph of Waters.

H23 PILKINGTON, WILLIAM T. "Character and Landscape: Frank Waters' Colorado Trilogy." *Western American Literature*. Vol. II, No. 3. (Fort Collins, Fall, 1967). Pages 183-193.
    Reprinted in the author's *My Blood's Country: Studies in Southwestern Literature*. (Fort Worth, Texas Christian University Press, 1973), in revised form (see B12).

H24 POWELL, LAWRENCE CLARK. "Down Where the Rockies End." *Mountain-Plains Library Quarterly*. Vol. X, No. 3. (Wichita, Fall, 1965). Pages 3-6 & 8-11.

H25 POWELL, LAWRENCE CLARK. "A Writer's Landscape." *Westways*. Vol. 66, No. 1. (Los Angeles, January, 1974). Pages 24-27 & 70-72.
    Reprinted in the author's *From the Heartland* (Flagstaff, Northland Press, 1976), under the title "Down Where the Rockies End", which is not to be confused with H24.

H26 YOUNG, VERNON. "Frank Waters: Problems of the Regional Imperative." *New Mexico Quarterly Review*. Vol. XIX, No. 3. (Albuquerque, Autumn, 1949). Pages 353-372.
    A largely unfavorable critique of Waters' works.

UNPUBLISHED DISSERTATIONS:

H27 CORSER, CRISTIN DAPPER. "The Indian as Symbol of Transcendent Spirituality in Oliver LaFarge, Frank Waters, and Edwin Corle." (M. A. Thesis, Brigham Young University, 1973).

H28 GRIDER, DARYL ALECK. "Rightness with the Land: Spirit of Place in the Novels of Frank Waters." (Ph.d. dissertation, University of Tennessee, December, 1980).

H29 HOY, CHRISTOPHER EARL. "A Study of *The Man Who Killed the Deer*." (M. A. Thesis, Colorado State University, 1970).

H30 JOHNSON, CHERYL G. "Frank Waters' Interpretation and Application of Indian Values in Three Novels." (M. A. Thesis, Brigham Young University, 1976).

H31 KLING, NANCY KAREN. "The Theme of Man's Relationship to the Land in the Novels of Frank Waters." (M. A. Thesis, University of South Dakota, 1964).

H32 MANTERO, ALBERTO. "Frank Waters e la Letterature de Sud-ouest." (Universita di Genova, 1970).

Index

References to names appearing within the correspondence included before the books in the A section are marked with an asterisk. References to the main entry for Waters' books are listed in italics. Editorials in *El Crepusculo* have not been indexed, but feature articles and book reviews appearing in that newspaper have been indexed. All references are to item numbers.

Abbey, Rita Deanin, B21
Abbot, Mary, A17*
Abbott, Chuck, AA1a, AA1b
Acoma, B7
Adams, Charles L., AA8(note), B27, E18, E25, H1
Adams, Ramon F., H2
Aiello, Constantine, B6
"Air", A22
Albin Michel, G2
The Alfred I. Barton Collection of Southwestern Textiles, C20
Allen, Charles, A12*
Allen, Hervey, A9*, A10*
Almquist & Wiksell, G6
"America: A Footnote", A22
American Book-Stratford Press, A9b, A12b(note)
"The American Indian: Two New Books Report His Heritage in Picture and Text", C31
The American Landscape, A12m

"The American West: A Challenge to the Literary Imagination", H18
American West Publishing Company, B14
Americana Unlimited, B15
"America's Indians—Pioneer Psychologists", E6
Anasazi: Ancient People of the Rock, B14
Anaya, Rudolfo, F3
Andrews, Frank, A12a(note)
Anderson, John, A14a
Annand, George, A9a, A9b, A9c, A9d, A9e, A9f
Annixter, Paul, D303
The Arapaho Way, B3
"The Archetypal Transformation of Martiniano in *The Man Who Killed the Deer*, H10
Arizona and the West, C36
Arizona Currents, E2

346

Arizona Highways, C22, C32, C37(note), C62
Arizona Pioneers Historical Society, A13*
Arrowsmith-Fenn Galleries, A16f
The Arts in New Mexico, AA7
Asay, Chuck, A21a, A21b
"Ascent to Olympus", D312
"At the Root of America", C8
Aurelius, Marcus (quoted), A21a
The Awakening Valley, D300

Babington, S.H., C20
Baer, Beryl, E15
Balcomb, Mary N., A16c, A16d
Ballantine Books, A12g, A12h, A12i, A12j, A15j, A15k, A15l, A15m, A15n, A15o, A15p, A15q, A15r, A15s, A15t, A15u, A19c
Bandelier, A.F., D297
Barbosa, A7c
"Barby", A10*
Baroja, A11a
Bass, Althea, B3
Beaudoin, Kenneth Lawrence, C20
Beck, Emily Morison, A20*
Below Grass Roots, A4, A19, F1
Benét, Stephen Vincent, A6*, A8*, A8a
Berkeley Publishing Company, A1b
Betts, Glynne Robinson, H3
Beyond the Hundredth Meridian, C25
Beyond the Mountains, C29
"Bibliography of the Works of Frank Waters", C37
Bird's Eye View of the Pueblos, C20
Birkhead, Gene, E22
Black Bear Review, E9
Em Bok om Hopi-Indianerna, G6
Bolton, Herbert, C15, D304
Book Craftsmen Associates, Inc., A13a
Book Find Club, A15b
"Book Looks by Frank Waters", D297-D308
Book of the Hopi, A15, A16*, G6, G7, G8

Book of the Vision Quest, F6
Bower, Donald E., B18
"Bowl of Gold", A3*
Boyer, Glenn G., B4
Braille, editions in, A6c(note), A8c(note), A17a(note)
Bramall House, A13e, A13f
Branch, Houston, A7*, A7, A10*, A11*, *A11,* B2
Brett, Dorothy, B9
Brinig, Myron, A6*, A7b(note)
Brodie, Jack, B26
Brown, Dee, C60
Browne, Syd, A6a
"The Brutal Breaking of Geronimo", C51
Bucco, Martin, A19*, H4
Das Buch der Hopi, G8
Buffalo and Other Stories, F3
Burs Under the Saddle, H2
Burton, Anibal, D300

Cafe Solo 10, C64
"Calling All Tribes", C6
"The Canyon", C32
Cassell and Company Ltd., A7c
Catholic Digest, C53
Center for Land Grant Studies, B25
"Character and Landscape: Frank Waters' Colorado Trilogy", H23
Charles Ulrick and Josephine Bay Foundation, A15*
Cherry, Richard L., A12l, A12m
Chevron Company, AA1a, AA1b
Chicago Daily News, C41, C45, C47, C50, C51
Chicago Sun Times, E6
Chicago Tribune Book World, C60
Chokecherry Hunters, B19
Christian Science Monitor, C8
Christian Wegner, G1
"Cimarron Not the Birth Place of Wild West Show", D311
"The Circle of the Law Belt", A22
Clarkson N. Potter, Inc., A13*, A13a, A13e, A13f, B3
Cleland, Robert Glass, C20
"Collaboration in Yankeeland", C28

348 INDEX

Collier, John, Sr., A15*, C20, D300
The Colorado, A3b(note), *A9*, A10*, A12*, A13*, C8, C32, C33, C56, C64
Colorado: A Literary Chronicle, A9i
"Colorado Fever", A9e(note), C56
"The Colorado is an Outlaw", C37(note)
Colorado Springs Gazette, A3a(note)
Colorado Springs Gazette-Telegraph, *E21, E23*
Colorado Springs Independent, A3a(note)
Colorado Springs Sun, E22
Colorado State University, AA6
Colton, Harold S., C20, D302
Columbia Sayings and Doings, C1, C2
Colyn, Mrs. Charles A., B4(note)
Concha, Joseph L., B19
"The Conflict in The Man Who Killed the Deer", H11
Conley, Robert L., A12l, A12m
Conron, Jack, A12m
Context Publications, F6
"A Conversation with Frank Waters", E19
"A Conversation with Frank Waters: Lessons from the Indian Soul", E7
"A Conversation with Frank Waters on Native American Indian Religion", E10
"Conversations with Frank Waters", E5
Conversations with Frank Waters, B10
Corgi Books, A13d
Coronado: Knight of Pueblo and Plain, C15, D304
Corser, Cristin Dapper, H27
Covici-Friede, A3*, A3a, A3b(note)
The Cox Library, B15
Crawford, Jean, A9a(note)
"Crossroads: Indians and Whites", C57
Crowell, F2
Crown Publishing Company, A3a(note), A3b(note)

"Crucible of Conflict", A12*, C12
Cuchama and Sacred Mountains, B27
Cuna Indian Art, C48
Curtis Brown Ltd., A2*
Cushman, John A. S., A17*
Custer Died for Your Sins, C50

D. R. Hillman & Sons Ltd., A13b
Dale, Edward Everett, C20
"Dam in the Mountains", A6*
Daniels, Bruce, E8
Daves, Joan, A8c(note), A13*, A17*, A19*, A20*, A22*
Davis, Jack L., E12, E16, H5, H6, H7
Davis, June L., H7
Dell Publishing Company, A11d
Deloria, Vine, Jr., C50
DeMille, Cecile B., A11*
Dentzel, Carl, A15*
Desert Wife, B26, C13(note)
Diamond, David, A7*, A11*, A11b(note), A12*
Diamond Head, A10*, *A11*, G4
Dickey, Roland, A12b(note)
Dickinson, Donald G., B16
"A Discussion with Frank Waters", C67
Donya Melanson Associates, A21a
Douglass, Ralph, A12a, A12c, A12d
"Down Where the Rockies End" (1965), E1, H24
"Down Where the Rockies End" (1976), B20
Dreifus, Louise, A11*
Driver, Jim, A12f
Dufault, Joan, B22
The Dust Within the Rock, A5, A19, G5

E. P. Dutton, A22*
Earp, Mrs. Virgil, A13
The Earp Brothers of Tombstone, *A13*
"The East is Red", A22
East West Journal, E13
"Easy Meat: A Story", C3

Ebright, Malcolm, B25
Editions for the Armed Services, A9c
Editorial Justa Publications, F3
Edwards Brothers, A8d(note)
El Crepusculo, section D
"El Cuchillo Del Medio", A22
Ellingson, H. K., A3a
Encanto Magazine and New Mexico Cultural News, E4
Encyclopaedia Britannica Press, A14
Encyclopedia Americana, BB
The Essay: Structure and Purpose, A12n
Eugen Kiederichs, G8
Evans-Wentz, W. Y., B27
Everitt, C. R., A2*
Evers, Larry, E19
Ewing, Russell C., C38

Farb, Peter, C45, C46
Farrar, John, A6*, A7*, A7b, A9*, A10*, A11*, A13*, A17*
Farrar & Rinehart, A6*, A6a, A7*, A7a, A7b, A8*, A8a, A10*
Farrar & Straus, A11*, A11a, A11b(note), A11c(note), A11d(note), A12*, A13*
Faulk, Odie B., C51
Faunce, Hilda, B26, C13(note)
Faure, Elie (quoted), A12
Fechin, Nicholai, A9*, A9a, A9b, A9d, A9e, A9f, A10*, C22
Fenn Galleries, A16c, A16d
Fenn, Forrest, A16d(note)
Ferris Printing Company, A8a
Fever Pitch, A1
"The Fifth World—The Ninth Planet", B16
Fiore, Kyle, A6i
Fles, Barthold, A15*, A17*
Fletcher, John Gould, C11(note)
Flute of the Smoking Mirror, C20
Foster, Stephen, F5
"Four Corners Country", A12*
"The Four-Fold Structure of Mind and Matter", A22
"Four Hundred Years of 'Civilization'", C60

"Four Sketches," C5
Four Sioux Myths and Two Blackfoot Legends, C20
Four Winds, C70
"Fragments of a Correspondence with Frank Waters", C66
Franklin, Harold, B2
Frank Waters (Bucco), H4
Frank Waters (Lyon) B12, H15
"Frank Waters" (Dufault), B22
"Frank Waters" (Manchester), E17
"Frank Waters: A Sleepy Man on a Cloudy Day", E15
"Frank Waters: An Author Looks at His Life", E26
"Frank Waters and Native American Consciousness", H7
"Frank Waters and the Visual Sense", H13
"Frank Waters Discusses Colorado Springs—Then and Now", E23
"Frank Waters e le Letterature del Sud-ouest", H32
"Frank Waters Envisions Land . . . as the Wellspring of Psychic Strength", E8
"Frank Waters' Interpretation and Application of Indian Values in Three Novels", H30
"Frank Waters' *Mexico Mystique:* The Ontology of the Occult", E16, H6
"Frank Waters' 'Prelude to Change'", E25
"Frank Waters: Problems of the Regional Imperative", H26
"Frank Waters Receives Honorary Doctorate", C69
"The Frank Waters Story", E4
Fredericks, Oswald: see White Bear
Fred Rosenstock, B18
From Ice Mountain, B24
From the Heartland, B20
Frontier Justice, D30l

Gard, Wayne, D30l
Gallegos, Cathy, E19
Garland, George, A11d
Gaspard, Dora, A16d(note)

Gaspard, Leon, A16, AA5
The Geronimo Campaign, C51
"The Giants Beyond the Rockies", C30
Gilchriese, John D., A16*, E2
Gilpin, Laura, D299, H22(note)
Gillmor, Frances, C20
Gilruth, Robert, A14
Giroux, James A., A8x
Giroux, Livia A., A8x
"Glittering Cavalcade", C24
Glory, God and Gold, C24
Goodchild, Jon, B17
Gordon, Robert, E20
"Grand Canyon", C64
Grand Canyon of the Living Colorado, A9j
Grider, Daryl, H28
Grigg, Quay, H8, H9
Gustafson, Robert, E10

H. Wolff, A11a
Hachette, G4
Haemer, Alan, A10a
Haley, J. Evetts, D301
Halliday Lithographing Company, B13
"Hallowe'en", C1
Hampton, David, A2*, A3*, A4*
Hannum, Alberta, C13(note)
Hanson, Craig, C66
Harcourt, Brace, A17*
Harris, Anne, A17*
Harvey, Fred E., A12*
Hawkes, Jacquetta, C28
Helene Wurlitzer Foundation, A15*
Hirsch, Bernard A., A12l, A12m
"History Unlimited", B15
Holiday, C23, C26, C27
Hollen Street Press, A11b
Hollar, Michael, B24
Holt, Rinehart & Winston, A9f
L'Homme qui a tue le Cerf, G2
Hopi Kachina Dolls, C20, D302
"The Hopi Prophecy", A22
"The Hopi Prophecy and the Chinese Dream: An Interview with Frank Waters", E13

Hopkins, Tom, A13*
Hough, Henry Beetle, C19, D307
Houghton Mifflin, B8
Hougland, Willard, C11
House Made of Dawn, C47
Howard, Jim, A16d(note), B16
Howell, Frederick, H., A15*
"How it Was Settled", C2
Hoy, Christopher, H10, H11, H29
Hugo, Victor (quoted), A15a
Hunt, Barnard & Co., Ltd., A13d
Huntress, Diana, H12
Hurst, Tricia, E26

"An Ignored Meaning of the West", E3, H14
Import: Albuquerque Journal Magazine, E26
"The Indian as Symbol of Transcendent Spirituality in Oliver LaFarge, Frank Waters, and Edwin Corle", H27
Indian Ceremonial Dances in the Southwest, C20
The Indian Heritage of America, C46
"Indian Influence on Taos Art", C21
Indians of the Americas, C31
The Indians of the Southwest, C20
"Indology", C20
Ingersoll, Bruce, E6
"An Interview with Frank Waters", E9
In Time of Harvest, B23
Ippolito, Donna, A20*, A21a(note)
Island Press, F6

J. J. Little & Ives Co., A6a, A7a, A7b, A9a, A10a
Jacobsen, Robert, B20
James, H. L., B7
Jeff Milton, D301
Jenkin, John, A19*
Jenkins, Robin, E24
Johnson, Cheryl G., H30
Johnson, Spud, C21
Jones, Peggy, A11*
Joesphy, Alvin M., Jr., C46
Journey Down a Rainbow, C28

INDEX 351

Julian Messner, B11
"Jung and Maharshi—On the Meaning of Man", A22

"The Kachina Characters of Frank Waters' Novels", H8
Kagaka Joho Sha, G5
Kamen no Kamisama, G5
Kansas Quarterly, H19
Keegan, Marcia, B11
Keeler, Clyde S., C48
Kegel, Dorothy, A21a
Kihn, W. Langdon, B26
Kling, Nancy Karen, B10(note), H31
Kluckhohn, Clyde, A12*, A12a, A12g, A15*
Knights, Tom, A16c
Kostka, Robert, A19, B10, H13

LaFarge, Oliver, A12a(note), C29, C31
LaGorce, Oliver, C31
Lake, Stuart N., A13*
Laird, W. David, B16
"The Land as Form in Frank Waters and William Eastlake", H19
Landscape, C25
Las Vegan Magazine, E24
Las Vegas Review Journal Nevadan, E15
Las Vegas Sun People Magazine, E14
Laughing Horse, C5
Lead, Kindly Light, D298
Lee, W. Storrs, A9i
Leon Gaspard, A16
Leon Gaspard (exhibit catalogue), A16f
Leon Gaspard 1882-1964 (exhibit catalogue), A16e
Levy, Marie, E19
Leydet, Francois, A9h
"Ley Lines", A22
"Life on a Ranch", C29
"A Linotype's a Greedy Thing", C19
The Literature of the American West, B8, C35(note)

Little, Meredith, F5
The Lively Rhetoric, A8x
Liveright, Horace, A1*, A2*, A19*
Liveright Publishing Company, A1*, A1a, A2*, A2, A4*, A4, A5*, A5, A6*, A10*, F1
"The Living Land", A22
Livre du Hopi, G7
"Lizard Woman", A1*
Lloyd, Frank, A7*
Los Alamos Scientific Laboratory, AA2, AA3, AA4
Luhan, Mabel Dodge, A8*, A8a, C21
Luhan, Tony, A6*, A8a
Lyman, Mildred, A3b(note)
Lynx House Press, F3
Lyon, Thomas, A19*, B12, E3, H14, H15, H16

McIntosh & Otis, A3b(note), A17*
"The Magic of 'Seekers of the Fleece'", C70
"The Magic that Persists: New Mexico's Heritage", C9, C10, C11
Malzeppi, Frances, H17
"Man and Nature: An Indivisible Unity", C59
Manby, Arthur Rochford, A20
Manchester, John, E4, E17
Manchester Gallery, B9
De Man die het Hert Doode, G3
Manfred, Frederick, B10(note)
"A Manifesto for the Dispossessed Indian Indian", C50
"Manitou", A2*
Mann, E. B., A12*, A12a(note), B1(note)
Manning, Mary, E14
Mantero, Alfred, H32
Man's Rise to Civilization. . . . , C45, C46
The Man Who Killed the Deer, A3b(note), A8, A10*, A12*, A15*, G1, G2, G3
"*The Man Who Killed the Deer:* 30 Years After", C55

"The Man Who Resurrected the Deer", H12
Maria, D308
Martiniano und der Hirsch, G1
Masked Gods, A12, A15*, C12, C13, C16, C62, G5
Matis, L., A18
Maxwell, Margaret F., B16
Maxwell Galleries, A14e
Melville, Herman (quoted), A4
"Men and Atoms—A New Mexico View", C10, C11(note)
Men to Match My Mountains, C30
Messner Certified Editions, B11
Mexico Mystique, A21
"Michio Takayama", B5
Michio Takayama, B5
Midas of the Rockies, A3
Miller, L., A18
Milton, John R., A22*, B8, B10, E5, H18, H19, H20, H21
Momaday, N. Scott, C47
"Momaday's Pulitzer Prize Novel", C47
Morrill, Claire, H22
Morrison, Jane Ann, E15
Morrow, William, A3b(note)
Moskowitz, Ira, C20
"Mountain and Plain", A22
Mountain Dialogues, A22
Mountain-Plains Library Quarterly, E1, H24
"Movement", A22
Muench, David, B14
Musick, A., A3a
My Blood's Country, B13, H23(note)
"Mystery of Mesa Verde", C26
Mysticism and Witchcraft, A18a(note), AA6, C65

Nabokov, Peter, F2
Nash, Roderick, A9j
National Travel Club, A9*, A9b
Navaho Folk Tales, C43
Navaho Religion, C20
"Navajo Missions", A12*, C16
"Navajo Trading Posts", A12*, C13
"Navajo Yei-Bet-Chai", C4

Navajos, Gods and Tom-Toms, C20
Naylor Co., B4
Neff, John C., D308
Nevada Historical Society Quarterly, AA8(note), E18, E25
Neville Spearman Ltd., A8a, A13b, A13c
Newcomb, Franc Johnson, C43
"New High School Dedicated in Navajo Mission", D310
The New Indians, C41
New Mexico Arts Commission, AA7
New Mexico Independent, E20
New Mexico Magazine, C52, C54, C55, C59
New Mexico Quarterly Review, A12*, C12, C13, C16, C21, H26
New York Times, A9f(note), C56
"Nicolai Fechin", C22
Nicolai Fechin, A9a, A9b, A9d, A9e, A9f
No Dudes, Few Women, B1
"North American Indians: A Sociological View", C45
North American Review, C3
Northland Press, A8f, A16*, A16a, A16b, A16c, A16d, B16, B17, B19, B20, B23
"Notes on Alan Swallow", C39
"Notes on Los Angeles", C68
The Novel of the American West, H21

Office of the Coordinator of Inter-American Affairs, A9*
Oelfke, Judith M., B13
Ohio University Press, A3e, A17d, A18d, A22, B27
O'Kane, Walter Collins, C20
Once More the Thunderer, C19, D307
"One Immortal Year", C18
Oo-Oonah Art, B6
Oppenheim, Sandy, E21
Ortega, Joaquin, A12*

Painter, Charlotte, F7
Palm Springs Desert Museum, B5

INDEX 353

The Papago Genesis, and Two Other Legends of Origin, C20
Paramount Pictures, A11*
"The Passion Play that Has No Equal", C33
Patterns and Ceremonials of the Indians of the Southwest, C20
Payot, G7
Pell, Arthur, A4*, A5*, A6*
Pembroke Magazine, E10
Penguin Books, A15n, A15o, A15p
People of the Valley, A6, A7*, A8*, A10*
Perceval, Don, A8f, B24
Persimmon Hill, C63
Peter Davies Ltd., A10*
Peterson, James, E7
Pictorial History of the American Indian, C31
Pike, Donald A., B14
Pike's Peak, A19, A20*
Pilgrim Press, B22
Pilkington, William T., A19*, B13, H23
The Place No One Knew: Glen Canyon, A9g
Pocket Books, A8m, A8n, A8o, A8p, A8q, A8r, A8s, A8t
Pointe de Diamonte, G4
Polis II, C66
Popul Vuh, C20
Porter, Clyde, C18, D306
Porter, Eliot, A9g
Porter, Mae Reed, C18, D306
Potter, Clarkson N., A13*, A13a
Powell, Lawrence Clark, A8f, B16, B20, E1, E11, H25
Prelude to Change, AA8, C69, E25
Press Publishing Company, B6
Priestley, J. B., C28
Psychology Today, E7
Pueblo Gods and Myths, C36
Puerto del Sol, C67
Pumpkin Seed Point, A18, A19*, AA8(note), C34, C65
Putnam, George Palmer, C17, D305

Quam, Alvina, C58
"Quetzalcoatl versus D. H. Lawrence's *Plumed Serpent*", C42

"Rain Song", C62
Random House, A12j; A15s, A15t, A15u
Ranking, John, A15*
Readers Choice Series, A11c
"'Red Power': Our Awakening Indians", C41
Reed, Martha, A16d(note)
Reichard, Gladys, C20
"Relationships and the Novel", C7
Republic Pictures, A11*
"The Return of Frank Waters: A Postscript", E18
"Rightness with the Land: Spirit of Place in the Novels of Frank Waters", H28
Rinehart, Stanley, A3b(note), A6*, A9*, A10*, A17*
Rinehart & Company, A9*, A9a, A9b(note), A9d, A10*, A10a, A12*
Rio Grande, D299
Rio Grande Press, B7
River Lady, A7, A8*, A10*, A11*
Rivers of America Series, A9*, A9a, A9d, A9e, A9f
Rivertrip, B21
"The Roaring Colorado", C23
Robert Gilruth, A14
Rockefeller Foundation, A21*
Rodell, Marie, A13*
Roswell, Bindery, A16a, A16b, A16c, B16, B18, B20, B21, B24
Ruxton of the Rockies, C18, D306

"The Sacred Mountain", A22
"The Sacred Mountains of the World", A22
Sage Books (Alan Swallow, Denver), A3b, A6b, A8c, A8f, A12b, A12c

Sage Books (Swallow Press, Chicago), A3d, A6c, A6d, A6e, A6f, A6g, A6h, A8h, A8i, A8j, A8k, A8l, A8u, A8v, A10b, A10c, A12d, A12e, A12f, A17c, A17d, A18a, A18b, A18c, A18d, A19a, A19b, A20, A21a, A21b, A22, B10
"Sage of the Southwest", E24
St. John Publishing Co., A11c
Salter, Stefan, A11a
Sanders, Mark, B24
San Diego Union, C33
San Diego Union Magazine, C6
"San Geronimo Historical Supplement", D309
Santa Fe & Taos: The Writer's Era 1916-1946, A6i
Santa Fe New Mexican, A12*, C10, C11, C14
Satenstein, Harvey, A13a, A13e
Saturday Review of Literature, C17, C18, C19, C24, C28, C29, C30, C31
Satz, Joel, A3*, A3a(note)
Schaeffer, Samuel Bernard, A2
Scharbach, Alexander, A8w
Schartle, Patricia, A17*
A Scientist on the Trail, D297
"Search for Cibola", C15
Seaver Books, F4
Secret Affair, A11c
Seeing Things, F6
Selby, John, A10*
Seper, V., A18
The Shadow Within, A12l
"Shangri-Putnam", C17
Sheean, Vincent, D298
Sherer, Adelaide A., A9b(note), A10*
Sierra Club Books, A9g, A9h, A9j, B17
"Sierra Madre Outposts", A22
"Silence", A22
Silko, Leslie Marmon, F4
Simon, Christopher, A13a
Simon & Schuster, A8m, A8n, A8o, A8p, A8q, A8r, A8s, A8t, B11

Sinclair, John L., B23
Singleton, Ralph A., A8w
Sington, A11b
Six Faces of Mexico, C38
Six Guns and Saddle Leather, H2(note)
Sketches of Leon Gaspard, AA5
Sklower, Roberta S., A21a
"Sky City: Venerable and Venerated Acoma Faces the Future", B7, C52, C53
Sloane, T. O'Conor, A5*
Smith, Gary M., B17
Smith, Pam, A16c
Smith, T. R., A2*, A4*, A5*
Snoaden, A8e
Snow, Carol, B17
Sonnichsen, C. L., A12k
Sorbie, John J., AA6
"The Sound of Space", H20
South Dakota Review, B8, C34, C35, C37, C49, C57, C61, C65, C68, E5, E12, E16, E17, H1, H5, H6, H8, H9, H10, H11, H12, H13, H16, H17, H20
The Southwest in Life and Literature, A12k
Southwest Museum, A15*, AA5
Southwestern Review, A12*, C9, C10(note), C11(note)
Spargo, Edward, A8x
Spin a Silver Dollar, C13
"'Spirit of Place' Novelist Overturns Subconscious Stones", E14
"Spirits", A22
The Sportsman's Handbook, B2
Standard Oil Company of Texas, AA1a, AA1b
Steck-Vaughn, H4
Stegner, Wallace, C25
Steiner, Stan, C41
Steinke, Bettina, B20
Stewart, Dorothy N., C20
Stewart, Rosalie, A7*
Stone, Irving, C30
The Stonepile, F5
Storyteller, F4

Stratton, Winfield Scott, A3*, A3
Strauss, Harold, A4*, A5*
Strickler, David P., A3b(note)
Stubbs, Stanley, C20
"A Study of the Female Protagonist in Frank Waters' *People of the Valley* and Rudolfo Anaya's *Bless Me, Ultima*", H17
"A Study of *The Man Who Killed the Deer*", H29
Sun in the Sky, C20
Sunstone Press, B19
Sun Tracks Five, E19
Suppressed Murder of Wyatt Earp, B4
Swallow, Alan, A3b(note), A3c, A6b, A6c(note), A8b(note), A8c, A8d, A8f, A12b, A12c, A17*, A17a, A18*, A19*
Swallow Press, Inc., A3d, A3e, A6d, A6e, A6f, A6g, A6h, A8g, A8h, A8i, A8j, A8k, A8l, A8u, A8v, A10b, A10c, A12c(note), A12d, A12e, A12f, A17a(note), A17b, A17c, A17d, A18a, A18b, A18c, A18d, A19*, A19a, A19b, A20*, A20, A21*, A21a, A21b, A22*, A22, B10, B27
Sweezy, Carl, B3
Swiftwater, D303

T. V. Boardman & Co., Ltd., A11b
Takayama, Michio, B5
Taos Indians and Their Sacred Blue Lake, B11
A Taos Mosaic, H22
Taos News, E8
Taos Pueblo Governor's Office, B6
"Taos Pueblo Indian Races", B2
Taos Pueblo Indian School, B6
"Taos Pueblo Revolt of '49 Same Old Pattern", C14
Taos Rio Grande Magazine, AA8(note), C69, E22(note)
Tarbet, Tom, E13
Taylor, J. Golden, B8, C35(note)
Taylor, James, E9
Taylor, S. Lyman, B18
"Teaching *Yogi* in Las Vegas", H1

Teller, Edward, C11(note)
"Territorial Tales", E2
Texas Christian University Press, B13
"The Theme of Man's Relationship to the Land in the Novels of Frank Waters", H31
Tierra Amarilla Grant, B25
This Reckless Breed of Men, C20
Time and the River Flowing: Grand Canyon, A9h
"Tombstone Travesty", A14*
To Possess the Land, A23
Tortuga, F3
Toward Composition, A18e
Transworld Publishers, A13d
Travel Magazine, A9*, A9b(note)
"A Tribute to Brett", B9
"Tucson", C27
Twayne Publishers, B12, H15
Two Leggings: The Making of a Crow Warrior, C40, F2
"Two Views of Nature: White and Indian", C34, C49
Tyler, Hamilton A., C36

Ude, Wayne, F3
Uitgave en druk, G3
University of Denver Press, A3a(note), A3b, A8b, A8c(note)
University of Nebraska Press, A13g, A13h, B26, H21
University of Nevada, Las Vegas, AA8
University of New Mexico Press, A12*, A12a, A12b, A12c, B1. B23, H22
Up in Our Country, C17, D305

Vessels, Phil, A14
Viking/Compass Books, A15g, A15h, A15i
Viking Press, A15*, A15a, A15b, A15c, A15d, A15e, A15f, A15g, A15h, A15i, H3
Vintage: The Bold Survivors, B22
Voice from the Bottom, A8x
Voices from the Southwest, B16

Wagner, Durrett, A8g, A19*, A20*, A21a
Walter, Dr. Paul, A12*
Ward, Elizabeth, B1
Warner Color Laboratories, B6
Washington Square Press, A8n
Waters, Frank (interviewed), B10, B20, E5, E6, E7, E8, E9, E10, E13, E15, E19, E20, E21, E22, E23, E24, E26
Waters, Frank (quoted), B4, B12, B13, B20, B22, E1, E2, E3, E11, E12, E16, E17, E18, E25
Waters, Frank (reviews by), C13, C15, C17, C18, C19, C20, C21, C24, C25, C28, C29, C30, C31, C36, C38, C40, C41, C43, C45, C46, C47, C48, C50, C51, C58, C60, D297-D308
"Waters' 'Past as Prologue' Presentation Full to Overflowing", E21
"Waters Takes Time to Remember", E22
Wayne, John, A11*
Weaver, Paul, A8f, A16*, A16a, A16d(note), B16, B18
Weigle, Marta, A6i
Weisman, Morton, A20*, A21*, A21a(note), A22*
Wellman, Paul I., C24
Wenck, Paul, A1a
Wengler, Diane, E23
Western American Literature, C38, C40, C42, C43, C44, C46, C48, C58, E3, H7, H14, H18, H23
"The Western Novel: A Symposium", B8, C35
"Western Points of View", C63
Western Printing & Lithographing Co., A11d
Western Printing Services Ltd., A7c
The Westerner, C60
Westways, E11, H25
White Bear, A15*, A15
The White Sands, AA1a, AA1b
"The Whorf Hypothesis and Native American Literature", E12, H5
The Wild Earth's Nobility, A2, A4*, A19*
Windsinger, B17
Woman at Otowi Crossing, A13*, A17
"Words", C44
The Writer, C7
Writer's Digest, A11*
"A Writer's Landscape", H25
"The Writer's Page", E20
Writer's in Residence, H3
"The Writer's Sense of Place: A Symposium", C61

Yale Review, A12*, C4
Yena, Donald M., B4
The Yogi of Cockroach Court, A4*, A10
Young, Alfred, A18a
Young, Vernon, H26

Zaum, Marjorie, B11
"Zuni Pueblo: The Middle Place Between Old and New", C54
The Zunis: Self-Portrayals, C58